SET UP RUNNING

Oscar P. Orr, in 1936 at age 53, about to depart home for an EC6 run from Southport to Enola, is dressed right down to the last item he put on, the highly shined shoes that completed his attire.

SET UP
RUNNING

THE   LIFE   OF   A

PENNSYLVANIA
RAILROAD
ENGINEMAN

1 9 0 4 - 1 9 4 9

JOHN W. ORR with an introduction

BY   JAMES   D.   PORTERFIELD

A   KEYSTONE   BOOK

A KEYSTONE BOOK is so designated to distinguish it from the typical scholarly monograph that a university press publishes. It is a book intended to serve the citizens of Pennsylvania by educating them and others, in an entertaining way, about aspects of the history, culture, society, and environment of the state as part of the Middle Atlantic Region.

Library of Congress Cataloging-in-Publication Data

Orr, John W., 1924–
    Set up running : the life of a Pennsylvania railroad
        engineman, 1904–1949. / by John W. Orr.
        p.   cm.
    Includes bibliographical references and index.
    ISBN 0-271-02056-3 (cloth : alk. paper)
    1. Orr, Oscar Perry, 1883–1954. 2. Pennsylvania Rail-
road—History. 3. Locomotive engineers—United States—
Biography. I. Title.

TF140.O77 O77 2001
625.2'7'092—dc21
[B]
                                            00–028818

Second printing, 2002

Printed in the United States of America
Published by The Pennsylvania State University Press,
University Park, PA 16802-1003

It is the policy of The Pennsylvania State University Press
to use acid-free paper for the first printing of all cloth-
bound books. Publications on uncoated stock satisfy the
minimum requirements of American National Standard
for Information Sciences—Permanence of Paper for
Printed Library Materials, ANSI Z39.48–1992.

CONTENTS

LIST OF ILLUSTRATIONS

In memory of

MY FATHER AND MOTHER

Oscar and Amelia Orr

My father always told me I had a favorite expression. It was "Why?" A small word of seemingly little significance, it nonetheless became the major factor in my being able to write this book.

Early in life I developed a profound curiosity and interest in railroads and the complex background that ensured the safe, efficient movement of trains over the rails. I grew up in a small town comprised mainly of men associated with the Pennsylvania Railroad in its many different jobs. My father was among them, working throughout Central Pennsylvania during his career as an engineman. Over those years I saw firsthand the contributions these men—and their families—made to the running of a railroad.

When I graduated from college I assumed the responsibilities associated with adulthood: marriage, family, and career. My father, meanwhile, retired. These turns resulted in my interest in railroading being banked, but not extinguished.

Later, upon my own retirement, time to renew my interest in railroading was at hand. I subscribed to magazines, read books, and explored steam-operated tourist lines throughout the United States. Unfortunately for me, most of the books and magazines emphasized historical, pictorial, and/or technical content. Again that question "Why?" began coming up, but now it was addressed to me. As I thought of all the railroad workers I'd had the good fortune to become acquainted with, and of the countless numbers of their kind elsewhere throughout the United States, all of whom had interesting stories, I wondered why nothing had been written about their experiences and lives.

Reading at that time an article in *Trains,* a magazine about railroading, written by then-editor David P. Morgan, brought to mind an experience of my father's that he had once related to me. I wrote Mr. Morgan, thinking that such a well-known railroading person, and editor of a prestigious magazine, would give my excerpts little of his valuable time. To my great surprise, however, I received a reply a few days later. It opened with "Great!" and he invited me to submit for his personal attention any stories I wanted to. This new development caused me to immediately start recalling the many things my father had told me over the years, now long past.

Which tales or events would be suitable for publication? To me, they were all interesting. With no deadline to meet, I decided the logical approach was to start when my father took his first job with the Pennsylvania Railroad. As I started compiling the stories, I was reminded that my vivid recall of the details was the result of my profound interest in anything connected with railroading, especially the fascinating steam locomotives in use when I was in my formative years. When my father was home between runs, I was constantly asking "Why?" Fortunately, he was always able to give me an understandable answer. To enhance my knowledge, he provided books on the subject. He also used the technique of explaining something by citing an incident from his personal experience. He was a well-qualified teacher. Fortunately, radio reception in our narrow mountain valley left much to be desired, television was not yet perfected, and telephone service was installed in our home only briefly (as you will see, there is even a railroad connection to that fact). Without such distractions, my father and I spent long periods in conversation, much of it about railroading.

I tried to record events in their proper sequence, never hurrying, thoroughly recalling things in advance that I wanted to transcribe. I did not delve into technical details any more than was necessary to describe what I wanted to tell my readers. The manuscript was written in longhand, mostly at night when I was alone. In the afternoon or early evening I would type. Continuing to write and type in this manner for more than two years, I produced a manuscript the final length of which amazed me. Now, rather than harboring the fear something important wasn't included, I found myself wondering if I'd written too much. I carefully reread the manuscript with the thought that some of the text could be shortened or eliminated. In doing so I arrived at the conclusion that eliminating content would distort the theme of the work.

Before my finished work could be presented to David Morgan, I learned that he had passed away. At this, I let the work lie dormant. Then my youngest son, William, visiting on vacation, inquired about the book, and after scanning its contents he asked if he could take my copy to read. Shortly thereafter, he called to inform me that a person in the company he worked for—a Hollywood studio—was willing to edit the manuscript. William also took a postcard-size black-and-white photograph of my father and his fireman standing on the running board of a Pennsylvania Railroad class H6b locomotive, circa 1914, and had a studio enlarge it to 40 by 32 inches, then airbrush it in color. The photo refinisher placed the print in his studio window and reported that a number of people offered favorable comments on it, a few even inquiring about when the motion picture the still was taken from would be released. This picture is found on the cover of the book.

With an edited manuscript, and encouraged by the interest shown in the colorized photograph, I began sending inquiries to publishers of railroad books. But their responses indicated an interest only in pictorial, historical, or technical works. One publisher was interested in reviewing the manuscript but wondered if I had color photographs to illustrate what I had written. I had to tell him that color photographs of the era my book covered—from 1904 through 1949—were rare and that my collection of black-and-white photographs of my father had been destroyed in a fire that consumed my home. Without color photographs, he wasn't interested.

At this introduction to railroad publishing, I did nothing further with the manuscript. From time to time my wife and son William inquired what I intended to do with my work, and I would procrastinate, avowing that sooner or later I would make further inquiries, even perhaps submit short stories. Then, once again, an article appeared in a railroading magazine, *Vintage Rails,* with a byline and a query. It stated that James D. Porterfield, an adjunct professor at the Pennsylvania State University and himself a published author, was looking for fictional accounts of railroading that could be used in that publication. I contacted Jim by mail, explaining that the material I could submit was factual, not fictional. A prompt reply indicated his interest in seeing my work. Included in his instructions was a telephone number, which I took to be an invitation to call him. Doing so, I at one point explained that I was retired and lived but eighty-five miles from his home in State College. If he would designate a date and time, I could present the manuscript personally. An appointment was made, but Mr. Porterfield expressed concern that I might find it difficult to locate his home. I assured him that this was not a problem. I had spent a considerable amount of time in the State College area, first graduating from Penn State in January 1949, then spending more than twenty-two years in that area as a sales representative for an electrical wholesaler. In fact, I had worked with the project developer and the electrical contractor involved in the building of the James Porterfield home.

Our meeting went well, and some time later Jim called to inform me he was impressed by the work and would like to recommend it for publication to The Pennsylvania State University Press. Penn State Press requires both the favorable critical comments of at least two recognized authorities and approval from its editorial board before it can accept a work for publication. Armed with Jim's critical review, and that of noted railroad historian H. Roger Grant, and backed further by favorable verbal endorsements from other noted rail authorities, Peter Potter, presently editor in chief of Penn State Press, agreed to have the press publish the book. A contract was offered, a word count and schedule was established, and an agreement was drawn up and signed. You are holding the results of that process.

Said book would not have been possible without the help of numerous others not already acknowledged. Primary among them were Harold K. Vollrath, Bill Caloroso, Herb Trice, and Jeff Pontius, who kindly granted permission to use photographs from their collection. Cummins McNitt, Curator at the Railroaders Memorial Museum in Altoona, Pennsylvania, and Kurt Bell, Archivist at the Railroad Museum of Pennsylvania in Strasburg, Pennsylvania, were courteous and helpful during my visits to gather pictures of the key locomotives my father ran during his career. My son William Orr, and others at the studio where he works, were instrumental in preparing the maps. Finally, Jim Porterfield, who wrote the introduction and contributed in so many other ways, and Peter Potter, history editor, and Peggy Hoover, copy editor, at The Pennsylvania State University Press, were supportive throughout. And for encouragement and help in various ways that made this book possible, I thank my wife, Mary Louise; my sons, John, David, and William; and my daughter, Kathleen.

I wrote this book to fill a gap that many of those who write about railroading seem to forget exists. The focus of this book is on the daily lives and work of the many workers who endeavored to operate the nation's railroads efficiently and safely. It is my sincere desire that this book will provide insight and enjoyment through the story of the life of one such railroad worker, my father, Oscar P. Orr, a Pennsylvania Railroad engineman. I have made every effort to remain truthful and accurate in my reporting. Any errors made are unintentional and are entirely my responsibility.

INTRODUCTION BY JAMES D. PORTERFIELD

In July 1904, at the age of twenty-one, Oscar P. Orr stepped into the world of American railroading as an employee of the mighty Pennsylvania Railroad. It was a time when railroad employees numbered in the millions, more than any other industry in the nation, and when railroading spanned the continent. The national scope of railroading, combined with the challenging, varied, unique, and alluring nature of the work, and the mystique associated with the railroads in general, made railroading jobs much sought after. Among them, the locomotive engineer was the most admired working man in America—rivaled in story perhaps only by the cowboy. "Don't forget," wrote A. W. Somerville, former trainman turned author, in the *Saturday Evening Post* in 1928, "there is not a boy in [America] who does not look up to [the locomotive engineer] with awe and admiration."

Nevertheless, and despite the many accounts of virtually all the more than one hundred major railroads that once made up America's rail network, firsthand accounts by those who worked for the railroads—that is, from the worker's point of view—have been conspicuously absent. The story of Oscar P. Orr, whose experiences span the first half of the twentieth century in America—the "Golden Age of Railroading"—fills that gap. It is our good fortune that out of that era emerged a valuable combination—a father and his son, a worker and an absorbed onlooker, a storyteller and an astute listener—that produced the work you are about to read.

Oscar P. Orr was both typical and unique as a railroader. His story has significance as cultural history and as industrial history. It provides insights into the work of trainmen everywhere during this half-century, and into the thinking and behavior of an outstanding practitioner of the industry's most respected labor: running a steam locomotive. The father, rising quickly to a position as locomotive engineer, took a thoughtful and learned interest in all aspects of his work and industry. The son, inquisitive, loyal, fascinated by everything around him—which happily for him and us was a busy but isolated railroad town in the mountains of North Central Pennsylvania—has an iron memory for the details his father related to him in many hours of talking about railroading and his work, and the energy and determination to write it all down.

The result is an account of one man's life and work while employed by the largest railroad of its day when railroading was at its zenith, and captured at the pinnacle of the romance and mythology of steam-powered trains. It puts a human face on the massive corporate body that was the Pennsylvania Railroad and on the rigors of being an engineman, and it bears witness to the changes that the railroads and their workers experienced during that period. This book, then, provides a complete and comprehensive picture of railroading work and life in this era.

Here we ride with O.P. on his first run, which turned into a whopping seventy-two-hour shift. Over the years, work rules are imposed to whittle shifts down, first to sixteen hours and eventually to twelve. In the process, we learn the consequences of being "outlawed," or reaching the maximum number of hours an engineman can work without rest.

We hear how he once customized the coal bunker of a locomotive's tender in an early attempt to correct one of his common complaints—that the Pennsylvania Railroad's tenders were not large enough for the runs assigned. We then learn his secret for replenishing the coal in the tender in an unorthodox manner, and then confounding his co-workers as his trains passed theirs at an intermediate coaling facility, giving him the coveted edge for the next assigned run.

We spend nights with him in the engine house as he polishes his locomotive to meet his high standards, we are with him in boardinghouses and eateries far from home when he has to lay over on a long run, and we learn how he could frequently make it home in a day when passenger train runs were frequent and extensive.

We despair with him at the scene of a suicide on the tracks, or as he prepares to give a statement after striking an automobile with passengers that lost a race with his train to a crossing, or as he passes a locomotive destroyed by a boiler explosion while one of his friends was at the controls.

We laugh with him at the whimsy of some of his co-workers—railroad men being among history's finest practitioners of the prank—and side with him as he has to discipline rowdy crew members and put loudmouthed workers from other divisions or railroads in their place.

More than that, we gain insights into his family life and what it was like to raise a family in small-town America—a railroad town—in the first half of the twentieth century. We learn how the family coped with the physical injury of their son (the author) and with O.P. himself once being declared physically unfit for mainline running for a time.

We share the tricks of his trade. How *do* you stop a train of tank cars loaded with sloshing oil directly under a water spout? How do you uncouple a helper engine on the fly? What happens when a moving steam engine hits livestock? What does it look and feel like to plow ahead through a blinding snowstorm? What are the pros, cons, and peculiarities of running those famous Pennsylvania Railroad steam locomotives every day?

He details matter-of-factly even the things that fans of railroading today might consider romantic or legendary, such as bank firing a K4 locomotive to maintain speed over distance without incapacitating the fireman; pounding up a 3 percent mountain grade with the assistance of double-headed pushers; and racing the clock with a symbol freight of perishables on a run that averages a mile a minute.

In every detail of his story, Orr demonstrates skill, intelligence, and common sense. He advanced by his determination, acquisition of knowledge, and heads-up savvy. He was a "company man," taking pride in his profession, defending his locomotives against critics but critiquing them for his superiors, refusing to speak harshly of his fellow enginemen to outsiders but letting his feelings be known one-on-one.

On the job, his responsibilities were to his crew, his train, his employer, and others who worked out on the line and in the shops. He had to check and sign for his locomotive and his train, operate his train in obedience to the rules, the latest orders, and signals, and be responsible for the safety of the crew and his train.

He had to be certified to operate on his routes and know all the official details—for instance, run-specific rules and the timetable—and the unofficial features of the route, such as any unique and telling aspects of certain segments of the track and run, as well as the priorities assigned to trains he would encounter. He had to be aware of the strengths, weaknesses, and peculiarities of the people he worked with, including those in the cab with him and those in the caboose, in the yard, in the signal towers and stations he passed, and in the cabs of trains running with and against him.

How typical or representative is the story of Engineman Oscar P. Orr? On the one hand, his experiences were similar to those of men working in the cab of a locomotive anywhere in America. Yet Orr himself and his career were not typical. During his half-century career with one of America's most recognized and often-modeled corporations, he had the opportunity to move virtually every kind of train the Company had: passenger trains, coal drags, symbol and fast freights, specials, work trains, and yard freights. And he was never laid off or forced by the layoff of others to go back to being a fireman. Furthermore, he was respected enough to be regularly entrusted with the responsibility for evaluating locomotives for the Mechanical Engineering Department in the Company's all-important Altoona shops, and with testing locomotives that had been shopped in Renovo. His reputation for completing his runs swiftly, and even moves within those runs, accorded him and his trains rights out on the line usually reserved for passenger trains. And Oscar P. Orr never sat back or held out on his employer. The Pennsylvania Railroad got its money's worth from this worker.

The respect and confidence that the Company and his co-workers had in Orr can be attributed to his skill and integrity as an engineman, which made him stand out among the other rugged, dedicated co-workers, and can be seen in any number of episodes from his life's story.

The story of Oscar Orr also demonstrates characteristics that are essential for those who operated trains. First, there is the absolute faith they had, in the system, the rules, and their orders as they ran their trains, in a day when train movements were guided by co-workers without benefit of computers, satellite guidance systems, and telecommunications devices. Second, there is the alertness of mind that enabled them to comprehend instructions and situations that would boggle the minds of other mortals. Orr describes, for example, occasions when he would have to make decisions that would affect the revenue, capital investment, and customer relations of the Pennsylvania Railroad. That kind of responsibility left little room for the indecisive. And Oscar Orr was a man who left little doubt who was in charge of the train.

Oscar P. Orr's detailed and compelling story gives us a picture of how pervasive the railroad was during its "Golden Age" and why people, especially young boys, came to love the trains that were all around them—at school, sled-riding, fishing, hunting, attending a wedding. Large, noisy, powerful, seemingly alive, yet mastered by one man sitting high above—as if on a throne. More than anything, this is the story of one man's life and love of railroading.

Welcome aboard!

Oscar Perry Orr was born July 20, 1883, on a large farm located in the Little Nittany Valley, eight miles northeast of Bellefonte, Pennsylvania. He was to be the oldest of six children—three boys and three girls. The rail line nearest the Orr farm was some five miles away at Howard, on the Bald Eagle Branch of the Pennsylvania Railroad. According to Oscar's father, the boy never expressed much interest in the steam locomotives working that line, but from early childhood he was fascinated by the steam traction engine that came to the farm each year towing a threshing machine to thrash the oat and wheat crops. On the day this machine and equipment was due to visit the farm, young Orr would walk miles just to ride it. When he grew older, he appointed himself as the person in charge of the steam engine rather than help with the thrashing chores.

After finishing eight grades of schooling, the number required of him at that time, Oscar remained at home working on the farm until the spring of 1902. Then, just before his nineteenth birthday, he decided that farming was not what he wanted to do for the rest of his life. But he did not travel too far from the farm to find employment. He had little trouble landing a position firing the stationary boilers of the Central Steam Heating Plant in Bellefonte, which supplied steam heat to a number of the city's businesses, commercial buildings, and residences. The Company also utilized its large boilers to manufacture gas for use in residential cooking and illumination.

In warm weather the boilers operated at reduced generating capacity, curtailing the need for constant firing. In these off-peak periods, Oscar and the other workmen were sent out into the community to repair and make adjustments to the existing steam and gas lines. While working outside, Oscar made many acquaintances—one especially, a veteran passenger locomotive engineer for the Pennsylvania Railroad, who offered him some advice.

Suggesting that it would be to his advantage to hire out as an engineman on the railroad, he said he would sponsor Oscar by signing his application for such a job. The young man accepted this advice and, in 1904, as soon as he turned twenty-one, traveled to Sunbury, headquarters of the Williamsport Division of the Pennsylvania Railroad. It was the practice at that time to submit the application to the division road foreman of engines.

By the turn of the twentieth century the Pennsylvania Railroad had established qualifications for all applicants desiring to enter engine service. The main requirements were that the applicant had reached his twenty-first birthday, had enough education to fill out the application, could pass a simple reading test, and was in excellent physical condition. The "rule" that was not included in published requirements concerned the applicant's genealogy—or rather the spelling of his last name. Preference was given to those of Irish or English origin. The signature of a promoted engineman presently employed by the Company on the application further facilitated hiring.

After meeting all these requirements for the road foreman of engines and submitting to a short interview, Oscar P. Orr was hired immediately in July 1904. That was the beginning of a job and a career—engineman for the Pennsylvania Railroad—that gave Orr fulfillment throughout his forty-five years with the Company. It was also where his nickname—O.P.—came from, for it was customary for the railroad to refer to its employees by their initials.

Oscar started his career as a fireman on the Williamsport Division (formerly the Philadelphia & Erie Railroad) working out of Sunbury. Before being assigned to a crew, he had to complete a series of trial trips working with and being trained by experienced crews on various locomotives and over various routes. On his first trip he learned the vast difference between firing a stationary boiler and firing one traveling at speed down a railroad track, where, for one thing, the surface he stood on was in motion. In addition to having to maintain his balance, he also had to hit a moving target—the firebox door—with shovelfuls of coal thrown to just the right spots. He easily met these challenges, though, and passed his trial trips with satisfactory recommendations from every crew with which he worked.

He was assigned to a crew that ran on a first-in, first-out basis. Such crews were assigned new runs based on the order in which they brought in their trains from the previous assigned run. Pay was set based on the length of each trip and the number of trips made each month. Sunbury did not generate large volumes of freight, because it was a crew and engine exchange terminal. Runs were made to the western end of the division at Renovo, with side runs made to Mount Carmel to the east, and to Enola east on the main line. Oscar quickly found that the only directions Pennsylvania Railroad trains ran were

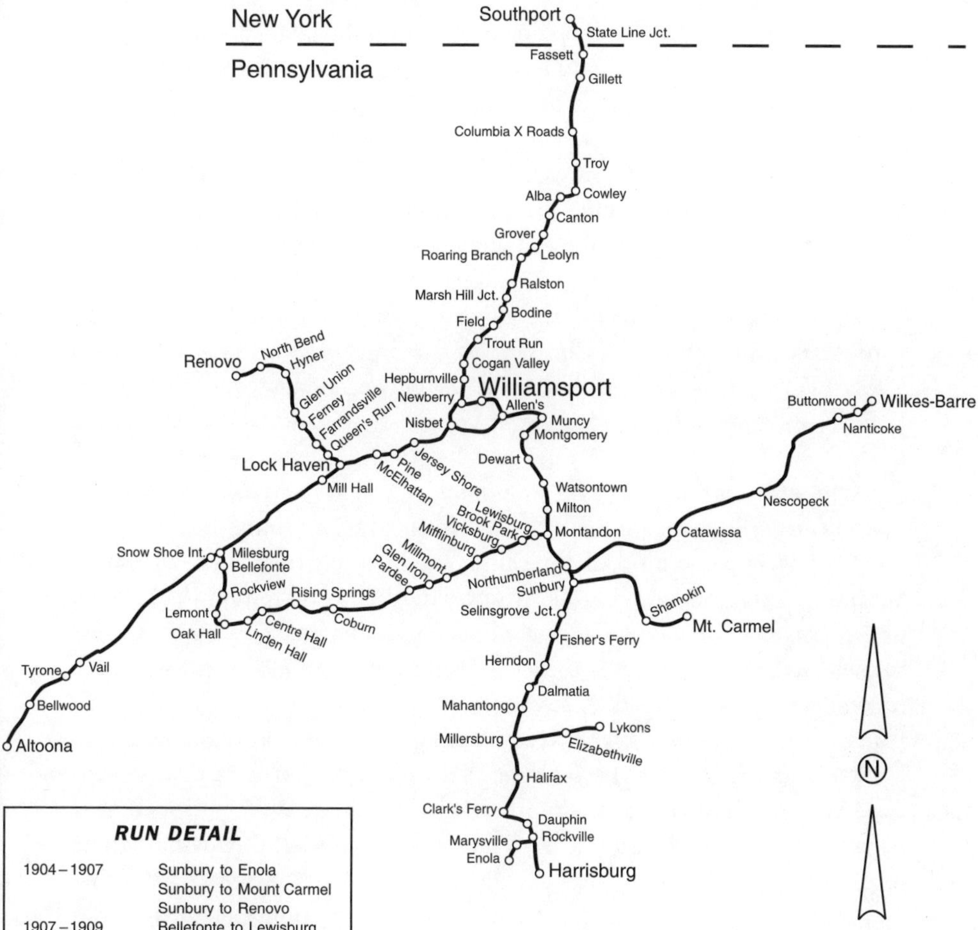
New York
Pennsylvania
Southport
State Line Jct.
Fassett
Gillett
Columbia X Roads
Troy
Alba
Cowley
Canton
Grover
Roaring Branch
Leolyn
Ralston
Marsh Hill Jct.
Bodine
Field
Trout Run
Cogan Valley
Hepburnville
Williamsport
Newberry
Allen's
Nisbet
Muncy
Montgomery
Renovo
North Bend
Hyner
Glen Union
Ferney
Farrandsville
Queen's Run
Lock Haven
Mill Hall
Jersey Shore
Pine
McElhattan
Dewart
Watsontown
Milton
Lewisburg
Brook Park
Vicksburg
Mifflinburg
Montandon
Millmont
Glen Iron
Pardee
Northumberland
Sunbury
Snow Shoe Int.
Milesburg
Bellefonte
Rockview
Rising Springs
Coburn
Centre Hall
Linden Hall
Lemont
Oak Hall
Tyrone
Vail
Bellwood
Altoona
Selinsgrove Jct.
Fisher's Ferry
Herndon
Dalmatia
Mahantongo
Millersburg
Lykons
Elizabethville
Halifax
Clark's Ferry
Dauphin
Rockville
Marysville
Enola
Harrisburg
Buttonwood
Wilkes-Barre
Nanticoke
Nescopeck
Catawissa
Shamokin
Mt. Carmel
N

RUN DETAIL

1904–1907	Sunbury to Enola
	Sunbury to Mount Carmel
	Sunbury to Renovo
1907–1909	Bellefonte to Lewisburg
1909–1910	Williamsport Yards
1910–1930	Ralston to Tyrone
1930–1931	Southport to Altoona
1931–1933	Altoona to Wilkes-Barre
1933–1934	Altoona to Harrisburg
1935–1936	Lykons to Millersburg
1936–1937	Southport to Enola
1937–1947	Williamsport Yards
1947–1949	Williamsport to Renovo

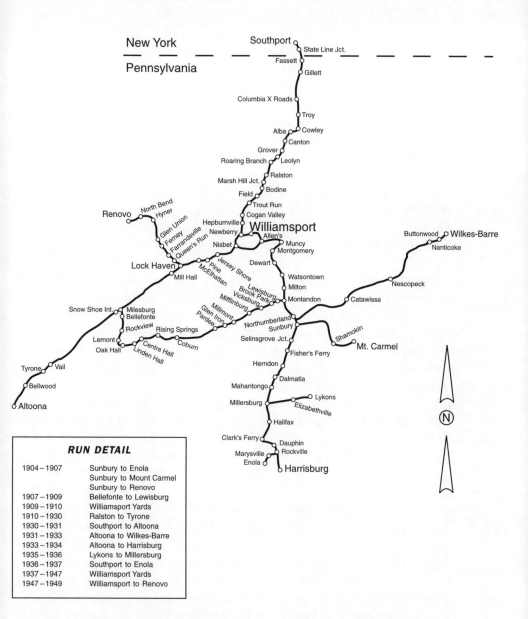

Map 1. O.P. Orr's Runs: The Williamsport Division, Elmira Branch (to Southport, N.Y.), and surrounding railroad locales over which O.P. Orr worked throughout his career with the Pennsylvania Railroad. The Run Detail (inset) documents the periods during which he ran trains between the terminal cities listed.

east and west. Whatever the map direction within this system—north, south, east, or west—southbound and eastbound trains ran *east*, and northbound and westbound trains ran *west*. This was true until the Pennsylvania Railroad ceased to exist some sixty years later.

Payday was once every month, and as a fireman Oscar averaged nearly $75 a month—a small fortune to a young man who was enjoying his work. Eight to twelve hours on duty completed most runs. The locomotives then in use were the Class R (H3) type Consolidations, with a 2-8-0 wheel arrangement. The new and larger H6a Consolidations were just making their appearance, and some could be seen at the engine house in Enola or on Enola-Renovo through-runs. The main line between Harrisburg (Enola) and Renovo was double track; the Mount Carmel runs took place over a single track.

One early trip proved to be memorable. The crew was called for a westbound trip to Renovo, and before it was finished Oscar found himself wishing there were some kind of time limit in the work rules. Not far out of Sunbury, as the train approached Muncy, the right side rod on the Class R broke, disabling the train on the main line. Fortunately, a following train came to their aid and its crew pushed the disabled train into a nearby siding before it could tie up the railroad. A few hours later two machinists from the Williamsport engine house arrived on an eastbound train with a replacement rod.

Once the repairs had been made, they were again on their way to Renovo. As they were nearing Allens Tower and the South Williamsport freight cutoff, where trains bound for the Williamsport yards left the main line, the locomotive's right cylinder head packing started to leak so badly that another breakdown was inevitable if they tried to continue. Stopping at Allens Tower and reporting the situation, the crew got orders to take the train into the Williamsport yard, set it off, and proceed to the roundhouse for repairs. In a later day, they would have been given another engine to finish the trip, but in 1904 each engineer and crew had their own engine and were therefore compelled to wait until repairs were made. When they left the yard, everything was working fine, and they were given a clear block all the way to Lock Haven. The remainder of the trip could now be made in less than four hours.

After drifting down the Jersey Shore hill, the engineer engaged the engine again, O.P. opened the fire door to start firing—and quickly discovered that trouble was aboard again. A flue had ruptured and was leaking so badly that the front portion of the fire in the firebox was nearly dead. Reaching the tower at McElhattan, they advised the dispatcher of their plight and were instructed to take the siding and wait until an engine could be sent from Lock Haven to tow them to the engine house there for necessary repairs. Again a long time passed before help arrived. Hunger pangs set in, and even the crew in the cabin (the Pennsylvania Railroad's name for a caboose) ran out of supplies. Finally, after the flue was fixed in Lock Haven, the fire was rebuilt and again they were steaming on the main, arriving at Renovo after being on duty more than seventy hours since the Sunbury departure. They had covered less than 100 miles.

At this point in his career, another helpful locomotive engineer passed on to Oscar words of wisdom about the promotion examinations the railroad gave to all firemen after their first, second, and third years of engine service. If a fireman successfully passed his exams, he was promoted to engineer and was eligible to be "set up running." The engineer advised Orr to enroll in a course offered by the International Correspondence School in Scranton that would prepare him for the exams. O.P. took that advice and received books that covered all the technical aspects of the steam engine, the mechanics and use of the air-brake system, and even the little-used acetylene gas system for lighting passenger trains. His monthly worksheets were completed and sent in for evaluation by the school. At the end of the prescribed course of study, he got a diploma stating that he had met all the standards required to complete the course. This course work and diploma were not recognized by the Company, but they were of definite assistance when he took the promotion examinations.

Early in the twentieth century, hard, or anthracite, coal was a major item on the Pennsylvania Railroad's revenue shipping list. A large portion of the product hauled by the Company originated around the Mount Carmel mining area and was transported eastbound by Sunbury crews. In the latter part of each summer and early fall, when the demand for coal on the East Coast was at its peak, crews were permitted to make as many trips as they wanted without a layover rest period. Because their pay was based on the number of trips made in a month, O.P.'s crew elected to haul coal nonstop, making one trip after another. The idea was that the resulting increased income could serve as a reserve for the ensuing winter months, when freight movements were slack.

Starting this duty on a Monday morning, they ran "light" to the Mount Carmel yards, picked up a loaded train of some thirty cars, and were on their way to their destination: the Enola yards. The conductor, flagman, and head brakeman all agreed that after the train was under way they would help O.P. with firing chores, giving him time to eat in the cabin and take rest breaks. They would do the same when they were forced to lay over in a siding. All went as planned for a little more than three days: loaded cars to Enola, empties on the return to Mount Carmel. But after the third day the work detail started to deteriorate. Food was not always available, and not much effort was exerted to help with the firing when they were under way. When a siding stop was made, everyone, including the engineer, decided they should sleep, leaving O.P. to keep the engine hot, watch the boiler water level, and arouse the crew when the train was clear to occupy the main track. Perhaps it was fortunate in one respect: he was unable to sleep deeply while sitting up, maybe take a snooze but not a sound sleep. On the fifth day of this marathon of trips, O.P. declared himself, stating that when they got to Enola he was "marking off," or removing his name from the available fireman's list. In effect, he was going to take time off. The crew became agitated at that announcement, and all the crew members, even the engineer, promised that if he would stay with them for a few more trips they would give him all the help he needed.

The next few trips went fine, but soon things began to fall apart again. At every stop the entire crew took the opportunity to nap. On the seventh day, while traveling down the main to Enola, O.P. began to feel odd. Although he was wide awake, he couldn't coordinate his body's motions. It took desperate concentration for him to push a shovelful of coal through the fire door. When the train was spotted on the assigned track in the Enola yard and the engine was placed on the pit track, O.P. removed his traveling bag from the bulkhead and announced to the engineer that all the trips were over. He was marking off.

The crew again tried to persuade him to stay and make just one more trip, but, hardly hearing their pleas, Oscar headed for the bunkhouse, telling them to request an extra fireman. Completely exhausted, he notified the crew clerk at the yard office that he wouldn't take any calls, and he told the bunkhouse attendant not to disturb him. Nearly twenty-four hours elapsed before he awoke, and at first he had trouble trying to recollect what had actually transpired over the past few days. After a much-needed shower, a shave, and donning clean clothing, he discovered he was very hungry.

As he entered a nearby restaurant, the first people he saw were his entire crew seated in the lounge area. After he marked off, they explained, they too had decided to enjoy the comforts of the bunkhouse rather than wait until an extra fireman was called. But before O.P. had finished his meal the crew was already planning another marathon of trips. Still feeling the effects of the seven-day stint, he told them that if this was to be the work schedule he would fire back as far as Sunbury, remove his name from the board, and bid in with a crew that worked normal trips. After some debate, everyone agreed to take the allotted eight hours of rest upon finishing a round-trip, so to keep peace with his fellow workers, O.P. stayed on.

O.P. never had any fear of the steam engine, or of the speeds it attained on the rails, but he had a fear of having an accident. It was not the possibility of physical injury that concerned him, but rather the prospect of being cooked alive by ruptured high-pressure steam lines, an event that could befall someone pinned in a locomotive's wreckage. Fortunately that never happened.

The only wreck he was ever involved in occurred on a trip from Sunbury to Enola. His regular engineer had marked off and an extra man was filling in, a man who had been "set up running" only recently. O.P. noted that this extra engineer was quite moody: at times he conversed freely, on other occasions he completely ignored any attempts at conversation. Knowing that this man was only an extra, O.P. didn't press the issue. On this particular trip, the eastbound was running as an extra, so, as usual, orders were received at a passing tower to take a siding for a scheduled passenger train, and to occupy the main again after the passenger train passed. When the movement passed, the engineer told O.P. to go to the call box and inform the operator that they were entering onto the main. Just as O.P. hung up the telephone, he heard the Class R engine take steam and saw that the engineer was getting the train started in a hurry. Realizing there wasn't enough time to unlock and throw the switch to allow the train to enter the main, he ran toward the moving locomotive, waving the stop signal, but that was to no avail. The engine still was blasting out. For some reason the engineer was not going to stop. The only alternative O.P. had was to retreat out into the brush. When the engine hit the derailing device placed on the track at the end of the siding to prevent a train from entering the main unless the switch is open, it upset on its side, and the tender and three following cars derailed in a zigzag fashion, tearing up and blocking the eastbound main. Running to the engine, which was shrouded in a cloud of steam and smoke, and expecting to find the scalded bodies of the engineer and head brakeman, O.P. was relieved to see them crawling out of the wreckage, apparently unharmed.

After the commotion abated and the wreck was reported, the crew received orders to board a westbound passenger and return to Sunbury. On their way back, O.P. finally asked the engineer why he didn't stop, but he got no answer. Once back at the yard office, Oscar and the engineer filled out the necessary reports on the incident, but then they were informed that both of them had been taken out of service. A formal hearing would be held by the division superintendent and the road foreman of engines, and they could expect written instructions on when and where to appear.

The hearing was held three days later in the superintendent's office. The idea of being called on the carpet for such a disaster, and the uncertainty about whose word would be accepted, caused O.P. some anxious moments.

He was called first, and after his report was read he was questioned in detail by the road foreman of engines to verify his statements, including the fact that neither the locomotive whistle nor the bell signal had been given before the train began to move, as the work rules required.

Next the engineer's report was reviewed, and O.P. couldn't believe what he heard. The engineer stated that Orr had given him a "highball" signal knowing that the switch was in the closed position, that O.P. had deliberately tried to cause a wreck. The superintendent and the road foreman retired to private chambers to review their findings while O.P. and the engineer waited in tense silence for what seemed an eternity.

Upon returning, the officials presented their conclusions. They said that in Orr's nearly three years of service he had compiled an exemplary record, passed promotion examinations with high scores, knew the work rules and procedures, and had received praise for his constant concern for the well-being of the Company from the crews he worked with. The engineer's record, however, showed that the engineer had a difficult time passing the promotion examinations, had occasionally been negligent in his duties as a fireman, and was considered moody by the crews he had worked with. The final question posed to the engineer was "What position was the switch target in when Orr gave you the highball?" After a brief pause and then some stammering, he replied that he couldn't remember. The superintendent concluded the hearing by stating: "Orr, the yard office will be instructed to place your name back on the board. You will report for duty when called." The engineer was told that he would get a written transcript of the findings, and he received notice that his service as an engineman for the Pennsylvania Railroad was terminated. O.P. felt that the proceedings had been conducted in a just fashion and took comfort in knowing that the Company had a complete record of the manner in which he had been conducting himself on the job.

When not working as an engineman, O.P. pursued interests not related to railroading—primarily outdoors activities. He was an avid hunter, and Sunbury offered many avenues for enjoying that sport. He discovered, for example, that the Susquehanna River had an abundant variety of wild waterfowl, and after he observed concentrations of ducks during his almost daily working trips along this waterway, he purchased a collapsible canvas boat that he transported in the baggage car of a westbound passenger to nearby Northumberland, where he placed it in the river and went shooting ducks as he floated leisurely back to Sunbury. He also used this boat for transportation to various river islands that were teeming with rabbits. In the fall of each year, he would "mark off" for a few vacation days, return to his home in Centre

County to hunt wild turkeys, and consistently bag one of these elusive birds. Also, a group of train-crew men invited him to join them at a hunting cabin located near Hyner, in the upper reaches of Pennsylvania's Clinton County on the old Coudersport Pike, where they all hunted deer and bear.

Another sport he enjoyed—as observer, not participant—was baseball. Attending a game one Sunday afternoon, he met a friend who had recently been promoted to engineer and was working the extra board—and who apparently, other than enjoying the game in progress, had also been imbibing in some sort of strong beverage and was slightly inebriated. As it would happen, a call boy appeared to inform this fellow that he had been called and was to report for duty in one hour. Knowing the man was in no condition to go to work, O.P. attempted to persuade him to refuse the call and mark off, but his friend said he had time to sober up and didn't want to refuse the call because it would be a black mark on his record, which he couldn't afford now that he had only just been "set up running."

Before the end of the game, O.P. too was called for a run to Enola. Midway in the run, an operator handed up an order advising the crew that they were to be switched to the westbound main and should proceed with caution to the next block station, where they would be switched back to the eastbound main. The assumption that a breakdown of some sort had occurred appeared to be correct when they spotted a train sitting on the eastbound track. When they reached the head end of the train, what they saw was difficult to believe. The stalled train's locomotive's boiler had exploded. The tender, engine frame with pony (leading) truck, cylinders, and driving wheels were sitting on the rails, while the boiler and cab lay in a nearby field. When they arrived at Enola, O.P. learned that it was his intoxicated friend's crew that had the mishap and that all three men on board had been killed. What caused the explosion was never determined, but O.P. was of the opinion that his friend had allowed the water level to become too low in the boiler. Under such circumstances, the firebox crown sheet, which is normally covered with water, is exposed, and without water to moderate its temperature the crown sheet becomes red hot. When the injector was opened and cold water from the tender rushed into the boiler and struck the overheated crown, the Class R exploded.

Life for O.P. was not all railroading. Young men are attracted to young women, and O.P. was no exception. A local young lady he had been courting invited him to accompany her on a picnic excursion conducted by her church, scheduled to be held at the then popular summer resort at Eagles Mere, Pennsylvania. Departing Sunbury early on a Sunday morning aboard a Reading Railroad passenger train, the two traveled with the group to Halls

Station, where they transferred to the Williamsport & North Branch Railroad and traveled on this line to Sonestown, where another transfer was necessary, this time to the Eagles Mere Railroad. That narrow-gauge railroad employed a geared locomotive whose small wheels were driven by gears, not rods, to enable it to ascend the heavy grades encountered on the 12-mile run to Eagles Mere. The scheduled running time for this distance was one hour.

Two enclosed coaches and an open flatcar with benches made up the consist that the little three-foot-gauge "stem winder" took up the mountain. O.P. and his girl were seated in the rear car as the trip began, and the rapid exhaust of this engine sounded like a regular locomotive running 50 miles an hour or faster. O.P. had read about geared engines that were widely used by the logging industry, but he had never seen one in operation. About halfway into the journey, he couldn't sit still any longer and announced he was going forward to the open car to watch the engine performing its chores. Somewhere along this stretch, the rear car became disengaged at a sag in the track and was not discovered missing until the train arrived at the station. This was an awkward situation: O.P. was at the destination and his girl was in the stranded car. The engine was immediately cut off and sent back down the mountain to retrieve the errant car.

While waiting for the return of the car, and his girl, he spied a fellow fireman from Sunbury who had also been talked into coming to this outing. This fellow had by chance brought a flask of spirits with him, so while his friend's girl set up things for the picnic, and they all awaited the arrival of the lost car, the two men indulged in a few snorts. When the car finally arrived, O.P.'s girl was not at all happy about being left behind, but she was really upset when she found out O.P. had been drinking an alcoholic beverage. She politely informed him that she no longer wanted him to accompany her to the picnic, or any other place for that matter. Thus ended a budding romance. O.P. poked around Eagles Mere alone for the rest of the day and rode by himself on the return trip to Sunbury.

In 1907, after passing his third year and last promotion exam, O.P. began watching the bid board in hopes of finding a firing job other than in freight service. Such a job was finally posted: firing on the pay-car train that covered the entire division once every month. The railroad paid its workers in cash, but only at a designated point and specified time, and that was accomplished by dispatching a locomotive and a single car, the pay car. The Williamsport Division pay car left Harrisburg the first of the month and proceeded to each designated pay point, took the assigned siding, then stopped. Those to be paid would present themselves at the pay car at an appointed time, when the paymaster would then pay in cash every section crew member, tower operator, shop worker, engine-house and office personnel, and anyone else on the pay-roll at that location. Despite the protests issued by fellow crew members that this was perhaps the most boring job on the entire railroad—lots of waiting and not much running—O.P. placed his bid and in the allotted time was awarded this position.

Orr's friends might have been right about its being boring duty, but the engineer on this job was an older man who knew how to pass the waiting time. He spent it by maintaining and polishing the old "D"- class American 4-4-0 assigned to him. He invited O.P. to help with these chores, all the while showing him some of the finer points of a steam engine. A variety of paints and polishing materials were stored in the bulkhead on the tender: brass polish for the bell, gauges, valves, and fittings; special paint for the smoke box, stack, and smoke-box front; polish for boiler jacket, tender, rods, and wheels; red paint for the cab roof. Bon Ami in cake form was used to clean the cab windows, the headlight lens, and reflector and marker lights. After a few pay stops, they had the American shining like a jewel, and only occasional wiping was needed to keep it in that condition. In fact, O.P. found, firing on such a splendid-looking locomotive a pleasing experience.

Security measures were a requirement when working on the pay-car run. Each crew member was issued a .45 caliber revolver with holster and ammunition belt, with instructions to wear it at all times on duty, but O.P. found this heavy weapon burdensome while firing the locomotive, and it rubbed his right hip raw. So, he reasoned, the best place to wear it was in his seat box, not on his hip. On one occasion, spotted near the roundhouses at Williamsport while the shop men were receiving their monthly wages, two rather well-dressed men approached the engine and requested to come aboard. Their request was at first denied, but when they produced badges identifying them as federal agents and stated that they were checking security procedures, they were of course invited aboard. Their first question concerned the firearm that was supposed to be on the fireman's hip. O.P.'s explanation—that it was awkward to fire while wearing such a weapon—did not arouse the agents' sympathy, and they ordered him to strap it on and keep it on. In parting, they gave O.P. a big *if*: If they did another inspection and he wasn't wearing his sidearm, his firing days on the Pennsylvania Railroad would end.

After only a few trips with the pay car, the job became routine, but there were always exceptions. The pay schedule allowed an hour for lunch, so the paymaster promptly closed the pay-car door at noon. Normally the conductor and the paymaster lunched together in the pay car, while the engineer and fireman went to the nearest restaurant, leaving the brakeman to guard the engine. One day, a brakeman at Lock Haven was confronted with a small problem. A train operated by a yard crew came up behind the pay car with a freight car they had to set off, only to find the switch blocked by the pay train. One of the crew approached the engine and asked the brakeman if it would be possible to move a few feet so the switch would be clear for their movement. Assuring the yard crew member that this matter would be adjusted immediately, and that he knew how to run the engine, the brakeman believed nothing would be disrupted, especially for such a short move. Inside the restaurant, O.P. and the engineer heard the American roar to life, followed by a wide open spin. Leaving the restaurant in a dash toward the engine, the engineer hollered, "My God, Oscar, someone is trying to steal the pay car."

Crawling aboard just as the spin stopped, they found the visibly shaken brakeman at the controls. He explained that after releasing the brakes and dropping the Johnson Bar (reversing lever) full forward, he had pulled out the throttle, but couldn't shut it off quickly enough. Observing that nothing had been damaged, O.P. and the engineer found this amusing and were having a good laugh, until the conductor came aboard to try to calm them down but instead adding more mirth to the incident.

According to the conductor's version, when the American took steam it gave a mighty lunge before it began spinning, and this sudden jerk threw both the conductor and the paymaster to the floor, plus the lunch dishes in a pan and the dishwater and tableware. To top everything off, the money trays were dislodged, scattering their contents all over the car's interior. The paymaster was never overly friendly with the crew, and this fiasco downgraded their status with him to absolutely nothing. He was, to say the least, furious. Soon after, the Company issued a general work rule instructing that an engineman must be on board the locomotive at all times when the pay car is in service.

CHAPTER TWO
FIRING AND SETTING UP RUNNING, 1907–1909

Oscar Orr found that an old adage, "When you are doing something you like, time passes quickly," could be applied to his first three years spent rail-roading. From the beginning, firing a Class R was a gratifying experience, but seeing more modern locomotives at the engine house in Enola, and passing them in service while crossing the Rockville Bridge over the Susquehanna River north of Harrisburg, made him want to move on to better things. The big H6a Consolidations and the F3c Moguls (2-6-0) certainly outclassed the R in every detail. Discussing the merits of these new engines with crews using them, and listening to those men talk about how they hauled trains much more easily at higher speeds, increased his desire to work on one of those monsters. However, one new class of locomotive, which hauled the named limited passenger trains, was the thing to behold. O.P. knew just from look-ing at it that the high-drivered E2 series Atlantic (4-4-2) had to be superior to the American 4-4-0 class. The trainmen frequently wondered when an E2 would be sent to the Williamsport Division.

Seeing these passenger trains started O.P. thinking. The time he had spent on the pay car made him realize that he enjoyed rolling along at high speeds more than poking along on a freight train, and he decided to bid on any passenger job listed. Passenger runs originated out of Sunbury, Williams-port, Renovo, and Tyrone, and on branch lines serving the hard-coal region. There was one exception. On the L&T (Lewisburg & Tyrone Railroad) Branch running through Penns Valley, one train originated and terminated in Bellefonte. The other train originated and terminated at Lewisburg.

O.P. had placed his name on the bid list every time a passenger job was posted but he had never been awarded the position. Passenger jobs were always taken by men who held numbers at the top of the roster, the men who had had more seniority. Finally, however, a job did open up for the run originating out of the Bellefonte terminal. As usual, O.P. put his name on the bid list, but he wasn't too optimistic, sure that someone else would probably get the job.

But he was pleasantly surprised. Perhaps one reason he got the job was that the remote location of the terminal didn't appeal to most engine crews, but for O.P. it was nearly home. Not wasting any time, he packed his belongings, had his name removed from the order board in Sunbury, and was on his way to start firing on a passenger locomotive. He traveled as a passenger on the train he was to work on, to acquaint himself with the crew and to renew an old friendship with the engineer who had signed his employment application. After marking up on the order board and finding a rooming house near the Bellefonte yards, O.P. went to the Orr homestead to announce his good fortune to the family.

Reporting for duty on a midsummer morning in 1907, he prepared the American locomotive for the 8:30 A.M. departure. This locomotive, a Class D-11 originally known as the "P" model, rode on eighty-inch drivers and was called an "Apperson Jackrabbit" by the crews. From outward appearances, it didn't qualify as the typical engine that head-ended the Pennsylvania Railroad's passenger trains. It was covered with a generous coating of light-gray dust, which was typical of everything in the Bellefonte area—even the houses and tree leaves had the same cover, generated by the residue from numerous limestone quarries and lime-processing plants there. O.P. discovered it was even impossible to keep his shoes shined.

The first 5 miles of the eastbound segment of this 65-mile trip included a heavy grade, tight curves, and three station stops. The high-drivered American, with a postal car, a baggage car, and two wooden coaches in tow, handled the task with ease; its drivers didn't even slip on the rail when making fast starts on the upgrade. Best of all, it steamed freely. From the third station stop on, the run was an up-and-down affair—no long gradients, but the line twisted through the farming country of Central Pennsylvania until it entered Penns Valley. There the trackage straightened out somewhat and, of all things, passed through a short tunnel at Coburn. Numerous station stops reduced fast running conditions—except the last few miles, where the 4-4-0 could attain speeds of 50 miles an hour, still a slow pace for a former "high iron" racehorse.

The run O.P. bid on successfully was the Bellefonte to Lewisburg train, but the name didn't correctly apply to this run. Passing Lewisburg, it continued across the Susquehanna River to Montandon, and at the station on the Williamsport Division main it discharged passengers, mail, and baggage to be picked up by connecting trains. After this exchange, it wyed the consist and returned to Lewisburg, laying over there for more than two hours before starting the return trip to Bellefonte. The only chores to occupy a portion of this time were taking water, cleaning the fire, and sweeping the deck. It would have been a waste of time to polish the engine—the Bellefonte dust couldn't be avoided. Other than that, about the only thing O.P. could keep shining were the cab windows and gauges.

It didn't take O.P. long to determine that his engineer, nicknamed "Cherry," was somewhat of a legend on the L&T line. He was always ready to offer anyone assistance, and he began looking after O.P. in a fatherly manner. On the seat box of the Apperson Jackrabbit he displayed an unusual trait every time he started the engine. Making good use of the generous chew of tobacco ever present in his mouth, and as soon as the locomotive took steam, Cherry started chewing, synchronizing a chew with each exhaust. This chewing would match the exhausts until the engine was set up at running speed, jaw ratcheting rapidly—and then stopped with the expectoration of a large volume of tobacco juice out the cab window. Trying to duplicate this feat with his own chew, O.P. couldn't accomplish it to running speed without stopping to spit.

On the afternoon return trip, a station stop of ten minutes was made in Mifflinburg, the largest town on the line between Bellefonte and Lewisburg. Most of the industry here was small and related in lumber manufacturing. The largest plant was a whiskey distillery. Other than bulk shipment in boxcars, the distillery shipped a portion of its products via express, mostly bottled case lots and small kegs. Loading these products into the baggage car was the reason for the lengthy stop at this point. When the stop was made, Cherry would drop off the engine, go back to the baggage car, and remain there until almost departure time. This daily routine aroused O.P.'s curiosity, and after a few trips he decided to see for himself what attraction there was in that car. He too dropped off, but on the opposite side. Walking back to the baggage car, he peeked in through a partially opened door and saw the baggage master and Cherry each holding a round-bottom Pennsy-issue tin drinking cup.

About the time O.P. spotted the pair, they saw him. Cherry hollered, "What took you so long, Oscar? We've been expecting you for some time." At this O.P. was invited into the car and presented with a tin cup, which the baggage master proceeded to fill from the contents of a small keg. "Drink that, Oscar," said Cherry. "It's good stuff. It will clear the cinders out of your throat."

On subsequent trips, O.P. learned how the whiskey was removed and how detection that the liquid had been withdrawn was avoided. The baggage master had used a hand-operated drill with a fine bit to produce a tiny hole where the staves in the keg were joined. After the tin cups were filled, he took a wooden match, whittled it to fit into the drill hole, and cut it off smooth with his knife. Then he put a small amount of dirt on a wetted finger and smeared it over the hole, thus making the patch nearly invisible. O.P. enjoyed his "tea" with the culprits every day he was on this run. How long this practice had been going on, or how long it continued after he left, he never knew.

Cherry was willing to share the engineer duties with O.P., and in doing so he provided invaluable instruction. He started out by allowing O.P., when in Bellefonte after each run, to wye the American and the train, take the cars to the station siding, and then take the engine back to the pit at the engine house. After a few days of this, Cherry told him to take over the right seat box at a station stop so he could learn how to make a passenger start, telling him to place the Johnson Bar full forward, open the throttle until the engine takes steam, shut off, then start to notch out slowly until the throttle is nearly wide open. Once speed is gained, the Johnson Bar is slowly notched back toward the center position at running speed. The throttle is closed until this speed is maintained. Mastering this maneuver without jerks, and applying the right amount of sand, would prevent slipping.

Cherry realized he had an eager student who could handle an engine and follow his instructions. Once, blasting out of a station with the 4-4-0 set at running speed, O.P., as was his custom, started to relinquish his position on the right side to assume his firing duties. But Cherry told him to remain on the seat box. It was now time to learn how to make a fast, smooth passenger-train stop. Cherry stressed that this move was as essential as starting the train but entailed more coordination. Approaching the next station, Cherry told O.P. how to shut the engine off and make the first air reduction with the automatic brake valve, how to determine how much the air pressure should be reduced and held, and finally, how to make the last application of brakes until the train came to a smooth halt. Judging the distance to complete this move and spotting the train at the correct position at the station without losing time were the most important criteria.

After Cherry was confident that O.P. could capably run the train, he allowed him to run on various stretches of the trip while he, Cherry, took over the firing chores. O.P. considered himself fortunate to be working with an engineer who gave him such opportunities. He applied the valuable lessons he learned for the rest of his career.

The closest rail connection for students at the then Pennsylvania State College, "Penn State" (now The Pennsylvania State University), for eastern points was some three miles from State College at the little town of Lemont.

This was the third station stop for the eastbound L&T passenger out of Belle-fonte, and the influx of students boarding the train on holidays or at the end of the school year disrupted the normally leisurely scheduled run. On holidays, two or three extra coaches were added. At the end of the school year, when everyone was leaving, four or five coaches plus another baggage car were attached. The heavier trains, the longer loading time, and the twist-ing pattern of the tracks in the area made it next to impossible to make up any time, so on those occasions they always ran late. Another feature O.P. observed when stopping at Lemont was the parade of horse-drawn vehicles used to transport the students to Lemont: buggies, jitneys, and an assortment of wagons lined the street leading to the depot.

One bleak winter morning when the train pulled into Lemont, the weather did not at all reflect the approaching Christmas holiday—instead of snow, a cold, misty rain was falling and fog filled the valley. But the condi-tions did not seem to bother the students who thronged the station platform. All seemed eager to occupy the extra cars in tow. After spotting the train, Cherry dropped off the engine and went back to the operator's quarters in the station to report that he'd be late leaving this stop. As he was preparing the engine for departure, O.P. heard someone calling him. Standing next to the steps at the right gangway was a young male student, who wasted no time saying he wanted to come aboard the locomotive. O.P. explained that it was against the rules, that only the engineer could grant permission for anyone other than employees to be aboard his engine.

The ensuing discussion revealed that the student had very little money but that if he could get to Northumberland he would have enough for a ticket home to Philadelphia. He added that he had experience firing steam loco-motives and would fire to pay for his ride. Although he sounded sincere, O.P. explained to the young man that he still had to speak to the engineer. When Cherry returned he was told the same story, and the young man was allowed to board the engine. Cherry told O.P. that it was so close to Christmas, and the weather was so inclement, that it was unlikely any officials would be around checking things. Besides, Cherry said, "If this young fellow can fire, I'll let you run. Just riding on your seat box will be like having a half-day off for me."

From Lemont there was a downgrade for about three miles, to the next stop at Oak Hall, where a slight uphill grade started and held most of the distance to the next stop at Centre Hall. Leaving Oak Hall, the engine was working hard and it was time to start firing, so O.P. told their passenger it was time for him to start earning his ride. The first shovel was well placed, the sec-ond was also made like a professional. Maybe he did know how to fire. While making the third pass, though, the unexpected happened: the 4-4-0 lurched sharply sideways, which was characteristic of this class because there was no trailing truck. This, combined with a wet deck, caused the student to slip. Unable to right himself quickly enough, he landed rather ingloriously flat on his back, spilling coal all over the cab deck. O.P. helped a grimy and much embarrassed erstwhile fireman to his feet, and after finding no injuries told him to stay on the seat box for the remainder of the trip. It would be safer.

As time passed, O.P. found this job with regular work hours more and more to his liking. The Bellefonte area had many excellent trout streams that provided the enjoyable relaxation of fishing during the spring and summer months. In the fall he enjoyed small-game hunting, especially turkey hunting near his homestead. Deer hunting still was pursued with the group of railroaders from Sunbury at the cabin in the upper reaches of Clinton County. Bellefonte offered a host of other social events, and, through an invitation extended by Cherry, he joined and became a member of the Blue Lodge, a Masonic order. Most of his weekends were spent with his family on the farm some eight miles from Bellefonte.

At home he had the privilege of using the driving horse and buggy to attend events, if any, in the hamlet of Jacksonville. While there he became reacquainted with a neighboring farm girl and began squiring her about. In due time, to show that his intentions were honorable, he presented her with a diamond engagement ring, and she accepted. Perhaps the highlight of his engagement was an invitation proffered by an uncle living in Washington, D.C., to any members of the family to visit him and witness the forthcoming Presidential inauguration. O.P., his betrothed, his mother, and his sister accepted the offer, traveled to Washington, and saw all the pomp and pageantry associated with the swearing-in ceremonies for President-Elect William Howard Taft on March 4, 1909.

In the nearly two years he had spent on the L&T, Oscar had advanced in seniority from the middle of the Fireman's Roster to within a few numbers from the top. When he would reach the top and be "set up running" as an engineer couldn't be determined, but the inevitable was not too far in the future. One day, upon entering the yard office to turn in his time slip after an afternoon run from Lewisburg, the crew clerk handed him an official-looking Company envelope, which turned out to be from the road foreman of engines in Williamsport, announcing that he had been set up to the status of an engineer. His position on the Engineer's Roster, though, was at the exact bottom. Reading further, he noted that the road foreman had the authority to assign the youngest engineer on the roster to a crew that was not bid in. That had just occurred at the Williamsport terminal, and since O.P.'s name was at the bottom he was assigned as the regular engineer on a yard crew.

He had seven days from the date of the notice to register his name on the order board at the Williamsport yard office. Finishing out the rest of the week on the L&T, he bade farewell to Cherry and the rest of the crew members, all expressing their good wishes and stating they could see he had the makings of a good engineer.

He spent the weekend with his family, who were pleased that he had been promoted, because they knew he was pursuing a career he liked. However, it turned out to be a different matter when he informed his bride-to-be of his promotion. She was pleased that he was now an engineer, but she refused to get married and accompany him to Williamsport. She wanted to stay at home on the farm and wait until he got a job in Bellefonte again. O.P. tried to explain that he wouldn't be able to return to the area for quite a while, but his attempt was futile. It almost seemed, he thought, that she was giving him a choice: Either take me or go to Williamsport as an engineer.

O.P. left Bellefonte on a midsummer Monday morning in 1909 aboard an eastbound train traveling the Bald Eagle Branch en route to Williamsport. Upon arrival, and according to orders from the road foreman, he reported to the yard office, announcing to the crew clerk that he was O.P. Orr, the designated engineer assigned to an open yard crew. The clerk was aware of all the details and informed him that his name would be placed on the board and that he was to report for duty the following day at 6:00 P.M, and that the hours his crew worked were from 6:00 P.M. to 6:00 A.M., seven days a week. With a schedule like this, it didn't take long to realize why this job wasn't bid in. The clerk also helped O.P. find a rooming house that catered to railroaders, one that was located within easy walking distance to all the railroad facilities.

Reporting for duty at the scheduled time, O.P. signed in and was introduced to his crew members. As he and his fireman made their way to the roundhouse, the array of different types of locomotives was impressive. On the many tracks sat Americans, the new and larger Atlantics, "B"-class switchers (0-6-0) known as "swallow-tailed dinkies," the big H6a Consolidations, plus the very familiar Class R H3's. The sight of these engines stirred his imagination. Other than starting out as a promoted engineer with a regular yard crew job, he had envisioned that his elevation to this status would be to the "extra board," which would have placed him at any one of the division's terminals and handling an assortment of assignments: passenger, freight, and last of all the yard crews. Presenting his engine number to the roundhouse foreman, he discovered that he was back with the motive power he had started with—not firing, but now in command of a Class R.

After completing the routine inspection and accepting the engine for service, he climbed aboard to begin his new duties. Leaving the roundhouse on the inlet track, he backed to the yard office for the train crew, crossed over the mains to the entrance track into the west end of the freight house, and began his first twelve-hour "trick" (the length of a work day in yard service). The work of the yard crew involved pulling out empty cars, cutting loaded cars to the various tracks, and spotting cars for the next day's loading and unloading. Pleased as he was to be running a locomotive, he was also somewhat dejected, but he reasoned that he wouldn't be in the yard forever.

By six o'clock the next morning, O.P. realized they had been busy all night, and it had been no picnic switching with a freight engine equipped with a Johnson Bar. Every night proved to be much the same. The Company always had plenty of cars to be switched. In the course of this routine duty, O.P. became acquainted with the crew members, all of whom were native to the Williamsport area. His fireman had less than a year's service, and this was the only regular job he could hold down. The two brakemen and the conductor were committed yard men who aspired to a daylight trick. All were single, except the conductor.

Nearly two months passed before O.P. marked off and returned home—not because he was homesick but because he had to check on the status of his love life. His fiancée was still saying she didn't want to get married until he got a job working out of Bellefonte. It wouldn't be proper, she said, to start a marriage with the kind of hours he was presently working, especially seven days a week. Realizing there was nothing he could do to change that, he boarded the Sunday afternoon passenger train for Williamsport to continue his duties.

The work hours were not conducive to engaging in any social activities in Williamsport either, but the crew could indulge in breakfast at the City Hotel, which at the time was one of the best places to eat in the city. After finishing their night trick, cleaning up, and donning their finest attire, the crew would meet there once or twice each week.

During these early morning breakfasts they became well acquainted with the proprietor, who seemed to enjoy their company, and after a leisurely breakfast the group would retire to the bar for a round of drinks. One morning, the proprietor said he had a surprise for them—that he wanted to treat them to a new brand of ale at the bar. What was unusual was the way the drink was dispensed: by means of a rinky-dinky chain arrangement with a pulley and a crank that allowed the bartender to affix a mug, drop it attached to the chain through an opening in the floor into a keg in the basement, then winding up a full mug.

The owner was so proud of his new discovery that the first mug was on the house. The ale didn't taste too bad, so the crew figured they would stick to that drink. But after finishing off the fifth mug, O.P. began to feel the effects of the elixir and announced he was going back to his room. How he got back to the rooming house he couldn't recall. In fact, his first recollection was early the next morning when he awoke to find the sun shining into his room. Gathering his senses, the first thing he thought of was that he'd missed a call—his first since hiring out.

That evening when reporting for duty, the yardmaster demanded to know what was going on with the crew. The conductor's wife had marked her husband off, but the other members had not marked off, but had not showed up either. While O.P. was explaining the whole episode to the boss, the conductor arrived and told the same story. No other crew members showed up.

The following evening, the fireman and one of the brakemen finally made it to work. A friend—O.P. and the others learned—had found the fireman on the street and taken him home to sleep it off until the next day. There, his parents couldn't revive him to go to work. The brakeman had made it out of the hotel to a shoe repair shop, where he spent the day. How he got home he didn't know, but, still under the effects of the ale, he missed the second day's work. On the third day the other brakeman, who had spent two days in bed at the hotel and a day in bed at home, showed up still feeling like an express train had hit him—each of the cars striking his head.

Every evening it was part of an engineman's routine to light the locomotive's oil-burning marker lamps and the front and rear headlights while in the yard. Performing these chores as usual one night, O.P. was cleaning the lens of the front headlight before lighting it when the Class R "puked"—that is, emitted excess water that was at or over boiler temperature of 212°F, accompanied by dirt and cinders from the smokestack. This was characteristic of a steam engine whose boiler was full of water, pops valves "singing" to indicate steam pressure was at the maximum, valves in just the right position. But this discharge was unpredictable.

On this particular night, O.P. managed to escape its full force, but a small amount landed on his cap, scalding his scalp. Although he experienced some discomfort during the rest of the shift, it didn't seem serious enough to fill out an accident report. But his scalp became blistered, and when it healed it produced the effects of a bad case of dandruff. The next symptom to show up was more devastating. Every time he combed his hair large tufts came loose, and finally only a few scraggly hairs remained; he was bald before reaching twenty-seven years of age.

Correspondence and an occasional trip back home kept O.P.'s hopes for eventual marriage alive, at least for a few months, but one day the inevitable letter came: his fiancée told him that a local man had taken over O.P.'s position in her life, but that she would keep the engagement ring as a remembrance of his devotion.

Williamsport did provide an advantage for O.P. It was the home of the consistory that held the jurisdiction of the Blue Lodge in Bellefonte. Joining this order, he attended monthly meetings. Furthermore, this gave him a day off in preparation to become a Mason. He received his thirty-second degree in 1913.

When he began the yard job, O.P. was convinced that it would be for only a short time, that before long he'd have a job on the "head end" hauling trains between the many points on the division. But nearly a year passed and he was still switching—and with a 2-8-0 locomotive originally designed for freight service but now only used for back-and-forth movements. It was also more than evident that no more senior engineer would ever bump him from this crew. So, using the only power that would get him out of the yard, he began bidding on any job advertised. For weeks this seemed to be in vain, until the unexpected appeared on the bid board: O.P. had placed a bid on a Ralston-to-Tyrone crew, but the advertised date had expired and no one had been posted as the successful bidder. He assumed, however, that there had merely been a posting oversight, that for some reason his bid had not been honored.

During the night as the usual tasks were being accomplished, O.P. kept thinking about the Ralston job and why it had not been awarded. The answer had to lie, he figured, with the road foreman of engines. Rather than wrack his brain further, he determined that when the shift was over he would ask the boss personally. He was at the office in his best attire when the road foreman arrived to assume his duties for the day. With no hesitation, O.P. stated the reason for his presence: "Why wasn't the Ralston-Tyrone job awarded?"

Remaining silent for a moment, the road foreman then came forth with his answer: "Orr, other officials, the yardmaster, and even myself find that you've done an exceptionally fine job handling your yard crew, and we'd like to see you remain in this position. Lately I've noticed you've been bidding on quite a few jobs, and I'll give you my personal assurance that someday you'll get one of these good jobs, but the Ralston run is one of the worst on the entire division. It's a pool crew arrangement, with first in, first out, and no regular working hours. You're on call twenty-four hours a day. Besides, these crews handle mostly heavy coal trains. The Elmira Division segment from Newberry Junction is single track with an upgrade all the way to Ralston, plus the engineers say they use half their boiler's steam capacity whistling for the unusual number of grade crossings. On the Bald Eagle from Lock Haven to Tyrone, in addition to being single track, grades are found going in either direction. Then too, on these single-track segments more time is spent in sidings than spent running. The only good portion of this run is the double track from Newberry Junction to Lock Haven. There's nothing in Ralston, either. It's a small town between a couple of mountains. Really, it's the end of the world."

Having listened intently, O.P. responded without hesitation: "I appreciate your compliments on how I've handled my assignment in the yard, but even if this Ralston-Tyrone run is straight up and straight down, I still want this job." Then, having been somewhat taken aback by the explanation of the road foreman, who was not strictly following procedures, O.P. asked: "Since I have some seniority, why don't you use your authority as you did in my case before and assign the youngest man on the roster to the yard job?" Then, assuring the road foreman he had no intention of withdrawing his bid, and adding that if this was the way the Company ran the railroad he wanted no part of it, he said: "I'll finish my trick tonight. In the morning my name will be removed from the board and I won't be an employee of the Pennsylvania Railroad any longer." On his way out of the office, he added: "You won't have to worry either. I'm not going to file a grievance with the Brotherhood. I've had enough."

That evening, signing up for what he reasoned would be his last night, O.P. was handed an envelope from the road foreman's office by the crew clerk. The contents stated: "O.P. Orr, Engineman, Williamsport Division, has been awarded the Ralston-Tyrone job, reporting time, 6:00 P.M. July 4, 1910." Perhaps another small amount of authority was displayed with this notification: it allowed him only twelve hours to finish his present trick, and another twelve hours to be marked up for call in Ralston. A check of the Elmira Division timetable showed that four passenger trains were scheduled in each direction daily: the westbound best suited left Williamsport at 2:45 P.M., arriving in Ralston at 3:29 P.M. Managing to get a few hours of sleep, O.P. then packed his work clothes and a few necessities in his traveling bag before departing in mid-afternoon.

At the station, O.P. found the train was already made up, consisting of five cars and, on the head end, an American-class 4-4-0 locomotive. Boarding, he chose the designated smoking car, three cars to the rear of the engine, and seated himself on the right side of the coach. Raising his window provided some comfort on this warm summer day, but that wasn't his primary concern. O.P. mostly wanted to hear how the engine was handled.

Leaving the station, the train ran a short distance on the Williamsport Division and then was switched right to a single track. Crossing the bridge over Lycoming Creek, the engineer opened the 4-4-0 up and had it snapping all the time—not easing off until making a station stop, indicating the line was on a steady upgrade. Even though the valley the train was traveling narrowed, the whistle was still sounded repeatedly, almost continuously. The paralleling highway seemed to zigzag across the tracks. Reaching Milepost 24, the conductor announced the next stop was Ralston. The trip had taken almost forty minutes.

Alighting, O.P. quickly surveyed the surroundings. He saw a town that was home to approximately 2,000 people. It was founded in 1837 and named for Matthew C. Ralston, a Philadelphia entrepreneur. In that year it also became the terminus for the Williamsport & Elmira Railroad, chartered in 1831. At its peak, between 1900 and 1910, upward of four hundred Ralston residents were employed by the Pennsylvania Railroad. They either worked in Ralston or commuted to nearby Company facilities.

Ralston was located in a narrow valley with steep mountains on either side. A block-long, wide street that was the main part of town led to the highway. What was presumably the engine house was located a few hundred feet north of the station. The road foreman had been correct so far: Ralston certainly didn't seem very impressive. Perhaps that was because it was the end of the line, or maybe like the end of the world. Nevertheless, this was where O.P.'s job was now, and he'd have to take things in stride.

Entering the block operator's office at the front of the station, O.P. announced that he had bid on a crew working from this terminal and would appreciate being directed to the yard office. The operator responded courteously, instructing him to walk up the tracks past the engine house. The yard office was a two-story building at the upper end of the wye near the bridge. On the way, O.P. spotted a large water tower, a section crew shanty, a bunkhouse, and a large icehouse to his left. The engine house was a large rectangular building on the right side with a coal dock and loading facilities. Later, he learned that the local term for the entire structure was not engine house, but "coal hoist." Because no passenger trains originated from this terminal, the only locomotives lined up were freight engines, mostly the big H6a class with a scattering of the older Class R's, and a single B8 yard class. As he walked past the line of engines, he couldn't help thinking that, the way his luck was running, his assigned engine would probably be a Class R.

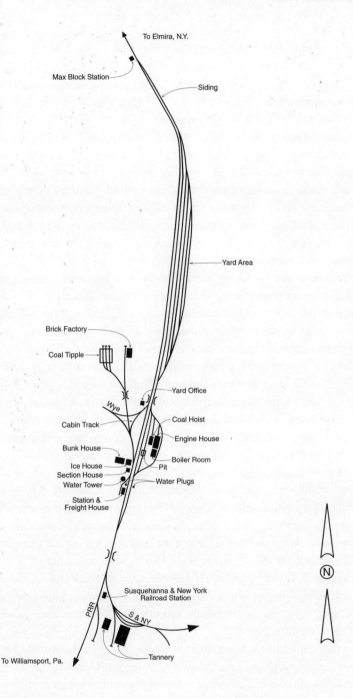

To Elmira, N.Y.

Max Block Station

Siding

Yard Area

Brick Factory

Coal Tipple

Yard Office

Wye

Coal Hoist

Cabin Track

Engine House

Bunk House

Boiler Room

Ice House

Pit

Section House

Water Tower

Water Plugs

Station &
Freight House

Susquehanna & New York
Railroad Station

PRR

S & NY

N

Tannery

To Williamsport, Pa.

Map 2. Ralston Area Detail, 1910: The layout of railroad facilities in Ralston, Pennsylvania, at their peak, between 1900 and 1930.

At the yard office he presented the letter announcing that he had been awarded the bid on a Ralston-Tyrone crew and that his name should be placed on the board—that he was available for call. He also told the clerk he was going to take a temporary room at the hotel across the street from the station and would wait there to be called. After registering and taking a room, O.P. decided he'd join the people celebrating the July 4 holiday at the bar. A cold drink surely would be in order. After all, he figured he had plenty of time for a few cold beers, dinner, and some much-needed rest. His crew stood at four times out.

His interlude and plans were soon interrupted when a call boy entered the bar announcing he was looking for O.P. Orr. Oscar presented himself and signed the call sheet, which indicated he was to report for duty at 6:30 P.M. With this change of events, he ate a quick dinner, had a lunch packed, and changed into his work clothing.

Reporting to the yard office before the specified time and marking up, he received his orders, which informed him that he had been assigned an engine but was not going out on the head end with a pilot. Instead, he was to attach his engine, running in reverse, to the cabin of an eastbound extra, proceed to Newberry Junction, and uncouple. At that point, he was to remain in the siding until a westbound extra arrived, then push this train to Ralston, uncouple, and place the engine on the pit track. Further orders would then be issued. The yardmaster explained that the Elmira Division used this method to qualify enginemen on this section—instead of the normal procedure, which was to have a qualified pilot accompany the engineer over foreign sections.

Accepting these unexpected orders, O.P. headed for the coal hoist, wondering again about being denied the privilege of handling a train. It seemed he would probably be assigned a Class R. Engine numbers were random, pertaining to no one particular class, so the number he had been provided with did nothing to ease his anxiety. At the coal hoist he presented his orders to the engine-house foreman, who in turn told him his engine was ready for inspection on the pit track. "Lo and behold," he said, using one of his favorite expressions as his eyes beheld a big H6a. Except that the engine was grimy, which was typical for a freight locomotive, his inspection found everything to be in working order mechanically. Signing the foreman's sheet, O.P. now had his own locomotive.

His move off the pit track and up through the yard with the big H6a 2-8-0, to the awaiting eastbound train was enough to indicate that this engine really outclassed the older R's. Riding out of Ralston attached to the rear end of the eastbound (south), O.P.'s fireman, a native of the area who had spent all his railroading time on this line, obligingly pointed out the blocks and sidings as they passed by. The first was Mile Siding, controlled by the Ralston operator. The next, some three miles out, was Bergen, controlled by a tower operator. On this evening they occupied the Trout Run siding while waiting for a westbound. Proceeding after their "meet," they passed Cogan Station (Cogan Valley on the railroad), 18 miles from Ralston, the last siding and operator before reaching Newberry Junction. The fireman explained that instead of crossing the Lycoming Creek bridge as the Elmira Division main did, they would run over a cutoff known as the "dike" to Newberry Junction. The Company didn't own this cutoff, the fireman explained, but merely had trackage rights. It belonged to the Susquehanna & New York Railroad (S&NY), which had only been in operation for a short while and had expanded with trackage rights over the Pennsylvania Railroad from Marsh Hill Junction to its new yards in Newberry. In order to reach its yard, the S&NY, in an agreement with the City of Williamsport, laid its roadbed from the Elmira Division main along Lycoming Creek to the Williamsport Division main in Newberry—a distance of less than a mile. This spur provided a levee as flood protection for the west end of the city by restraining the creek's water. It also eliminated entering the Williamsport yards, switching the cabin, and turning the engine for a westbound move, previously a time-consuming move for the Pennsylvania's trains and crews. The only expense the Company incurred was for establishing a tower on the main to control movements on and off the Elmira Division. That point was named Newberry Junction, and that cutoff, once in operation, came to be classified by the crews as the "dike," and the trains using it were dubbed "dikers."

When they reached the Williamsport Division main, O.P.'s engine was uncoupled according to the Ralston order. The operator at Newberry Junction issued orders for him to cross over the main and occupy the adjacent siding to await the Tyrone extra. Once this move was complete and they were waiting, the fireman offered additional advice: On the map, the Elmira Division was almost directly north and south, but Company policy was that when running north you were westbound, and that running south you were eastbound. So, coming off or entering the dike track, directions on orders were reversed. If close attention wasn't given, orders could become confusing at this point.

The maximum tonnage allowed an H6a over this route was 1,500 tons, which usually came out of Ralston in a mixture of freight and empty hoppers. An average of forty cars made up a train. Out of the Tyrone terminal, with mostly loaded coal cars, around thirty-five loads could be expected; the hoppers held 40 tons each.

The first in, first out rule was worked at Ralston. Cabins were placed on

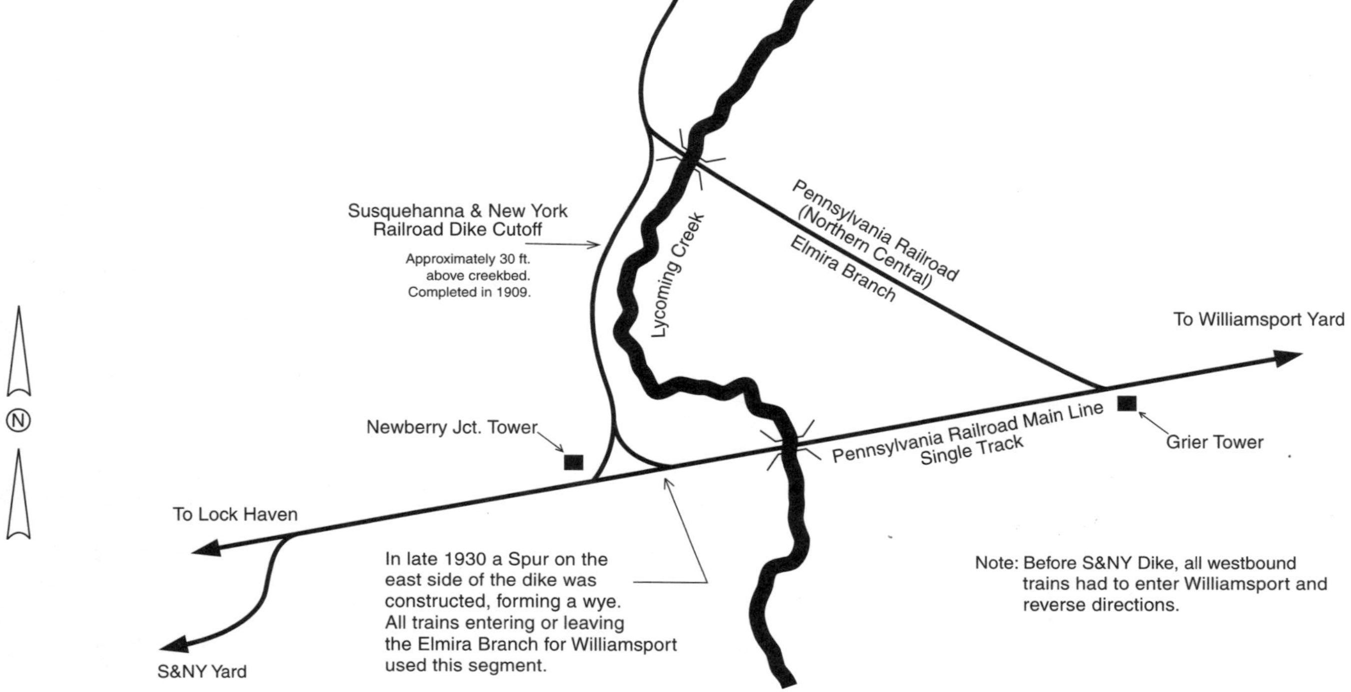

Map 3. Williamsport Dike Detail, 1910: Throughout his earlier career (1910–1937), O.P. Orr ran through this track work configuration. The S&NY "Dike Cutoff" gave birth to the nickname given to the trains loaded with coal from the west that ran over it: "Dikers."

To Ralston

Pennsylvania Railroad
(Northern Central)
Elmira Branch

Lycoming Creek

Susquehanna & New York
Railroad Dike Cutoff

Approximately 30 ft.
above creekbed.
Completed in 1909.

Newberry Jct. Tower

To Lock Haven

S&NY Yard

In late 1930 a Spur on the
east side of the dike was
constructed, forming a wye.
All trains entering or leaving
the Elmira Branch for Williamsport
used this segment.

Pennsylvania Railroad Main Line
Single Track

To Williamsport Yard

Grier Tower

Note: Before S&NY Dike, all westbound
trains had to enter Williamsport and
reverse directions.

N

the "cabin track," each advancing when another coming in was placed behind it. Crews could tell how many "times out" they were by checking the position of their cabin. Only one symbol freight ran out of Ralston, with an opposite out of Tyrone: RA13 and RA14 (Ralston-Altoona). Fast freights and locals would set off preference merchandise cars from upper New York State destined for western points. The same applied in Tyrone; cars for northern points were assembled for movement to New York State points on the RA14. The RA out of Ralston was also the only scheduled train with crews called for 11:00 P.M. seven days a week. The crew that was first out in the diker pool got that run.

Ralston, although it was squeezed in between two mountains, did not have the credentials to be one of the worst places in the universe. With this thought, O.P. realized that the fireman had been reading his mind. Highlighting the makeup of the town, the fireman revealed that it had two churches, a bank, stores that could fulfill any need, four hotels, and, other than the bunkhouse, many rooming houses available for the railroaders. On both of the surrounding mountains, coal-mining operations were being conducted. The mines on the west side provided the Company with a substantial amount of coal for its passenger locomotives. At the south end of the town a large sole-leather tannery, reputed to be one of the largest in the nation, was in operation.

Other than the Pennsylvania Railroad, the S&NY had four passenger trains in and out of the station, plus its bridge line freight connection. A third railroad operated by the Central Pennsylvania Lumber Company ran out of South Ralston. It used Shay-geared locomotives to haul logs and bark from the valley to the east, and to service lumber camps located along Rock Run Creek to its headquarters. Here, the fireman gave O.P. a bit of a warning relating to lumbering personnel. Spending a month in a lumber camp out in the wilderness, these men, known as "wood hicks," would come to town on payday to spend their earnings, most of it in the hotels for booze. Other than getting drunk and spending their money, they enjoyed brawling. Who they fought with didn't matter. If an unsuspecting victim wasn't available, they would fight among themselves. A favorite practice was to get a person on the ground, then kick the victim with their hobnailed boots, tearing clothing, bruising, and inflicting shallow lacerations. The numerous cuts resulted in profuse bleeding, and after such fracases their victims appeared to have been tangling with a buzz saw. In the winter, around the hotels it looked as if there had been a massacre, for the snow accentuated every drop of blood spilled. It was a good idea to steer clear of these men when they were in town relieving pent-up emotions.

When the Tyrone extra passed and entered the dike, the operator posted a clear signal. O.P. crossed over, also moving up this track, and coupled onto the cabin. After the air was cut in, the fireman offered more advice: when the head end whistled off, the air gauge would fluctuate, indicating that the brakes had been released and that it was time to start pushing in the slack. Proceeding according to these instructions after the five long whistle blasts from the head end were sounded, and when the air gauge fluttered, O.P. dropped the Johnson Bar to full forward. Opening the throttle to give the big H6a steam, he then shut off, opened the sand valve, and began notching out on the throttle.

Working almost wide open with a well-sanded rail, the H6a didn't slip a wheel. A smooth, quick start was accomplished. As running speed was reached, O.P. cut back the locomotive's valve motion toward a center position from full forward, admitting less steam to the cylinders in order to adjust to the train's momentum, though still pushing hard. This was enough to indicate to him that his locomotive could handle this chore well. The results of this test were clearly shown on the gauges: steam pressure hadn't decreased, there was no trouble keeping the water glass full, and, better still, the fireman wasn't even working hard.

Running conditions only lasted for about six miles before speed was reduced and they were placed in the Cogan Valley siding. From there the train ran through the next block at Trout Run, but orders were handed up to the conductor. The fireman explained that this was a good indication they were to meet another train at Grays Run or Bergen (Marsh Hill). Pusher crews never got copies of orders; they were just along for the ride.

After Grays Run, they continued on, slowing as they passed through Bodines and stopping at the east end of Bergen to spend some time in this siding awaiting an eastbound passenger and an eastbound empty diker. Eventually proceeding from this siding, they finally reached Ralston. This first trip had taken nearly eight hours, and after the train was put on the designated track in the yard, the engine cut off and moved down to the pit track. From there O.P. reported to the yard office, ready to mark off and thinking he was now qualified. But the crew clerk handed him a set of orders that dispelled that thought; he was still considered to be in the process of qualifying, and as soon as his engine received the proper servicing, he would again be attached to an eastbound and cut off at Newberry Junction to push the next westbound into Ralston. While the engine was on the pit being serviced, O.P. had enough time for a meal and to get a lunch prepared to take along.

This routine remained in effect for two and a half days. Nearly sixty hours had elapsed since he had been called for the first push, and he couldn't remember how many times he had gone back and forth, for as time wore on he grew weary and stopped counting. When the crew clerk notified him that he had qualified, he also received a crew assignment number and was informed that the crew was presently in Tyrone and that he should be available for call after twenty-four hours.

With this grace period, O.P. returned to his room at the hotel to clean up and get some much-needed rest, but he was startled awake by a train that seemed about to come through the room. He soon realized that the hotel's proximity to the tracks was not conducive to good sleeping. Even with these adverse conditions, however, he managed to get the rest he needed. After arising and assembling his thoughts, he followed his fireman's advice and procured a room farther away from the railroad. He still had plenty of time within the twenty-four-hour off-period—enough to catch the early evening passenger to Williamsport, pack his belongings, and return to Ralston by 9:00 P.M. Now he was an official resident of Ralston, ready to start out as a head-end engineer.

After more than twenty-four hours, O.P. was well rested when the call boy came to tell him to report for duty in one hour. At the yard office, he and his fireman met their train crew members, who all seemed amiable in accepting them as in charge of the forthcoming trip. Orders issued read that their made-up train was to be moved from the yard track down the siding to the station, at which point they would get written running orders controlling their movement once they were cleared to occupy the main.

The orders from the block operator indicated they would run clear to Newberry Junction. This first trip hauling a train with a clear block for this distance on the Elmira Division was like giving O.P. a gift. Wasting no time once the clear signal was dropped, he got the 2-8-0 in motion and set up properly for running. He found that it handled the train easily, and at a speed faster than the American he had run on the L&T had been allowed. Pleased with everything, he decided he was happy to be an engineer on the Pennsylvania Railroad.

Coming off the dike, there was a stop signal posted at Newberry Junction Tower. Orders read that the wait was for a westbound passenger. Once the passenger train passed, O.P. was cleared to run the single-track main to Linden, where orders controlling his movement on the double track to Lock Haven would be issued. A clear block was posted at Linden, and another one when he approached the Antes Fort (Jersey Shore) block. There, however, the operator handed up orders to be prepared to stop when the train reached McElhattan Tower.

At McElhattan a stop signal was displayed, and, after stopping, O.P. went forward to the tower, where the operator told him why he was being held: a New York Central train off the Beech Creek–Clearfield Branch had permission to cross over the Pennsylvania main on its way to the Central's yard in Avis. After this movement cleared, written orders allowed O.P. to run to the yard office in Lock Haven, take water, pick up the pilot for the run over the Bald Eagle line, then proceed to the switch-over point, where they would leave the double-track main.

The pilot boarded while they were taking water, and gave permission for O.P. to continue to handle the engine; the pilot would just ride along and explain details as they went. Leaving Lock Haven, which was about the midpoint on the Ralston-Tyrone trip, there was a green signal at the controlling tower that permitted entry to the Bald Eagle main. From there it was all single track for the remaining 53 miles. Orders gave them clearance to the next block, Howard, where orders would be issued covering movement on to Milesburg. Two sidings existed between Lock Haven and Howard, one at Mill Hall and the other at Blanchard-Eagleville. Approaching Howard they had a clear signal. Orders read that they were to take the siding when they reached Milesburg.

Just past the station in Howard, the pilot offered more instructions: the engine should be opened up more, because a grade of more than one percent would be encountered for a couple of miles before the downgrade to Milesburg began. The H6 took this hill in stride, with little loss of running speed. Entering the small yard area at Milesburg, the pilot stressed that this was the busiest block on the branch. It not only controlled the eastbounds and westbounds, but also was responsible for the movements in and out of Bellefonte on the L&T Branch. It was 21 miles from Lock Haven and 32 miles before Tyrone. A clear board seldom showed on the signal at Milesburg, but even if it did it was always prudent to stop and take water—the next 28 miles westbound was all upgrade.

Clearing out of Milesburg, orders advanced them over opposing movements past the blocks at Julian and Port Matilda, both of which were controlled sidings. Orders handed on at Port Matilda indicated that they would be placed in the siding at Vail, the last block out of Tyrone. A short way past Port Matilda, the pilot again advised O.P. to open the H6 up a little more as the grade from there to Vail gradually increased. Following instructions, they crested this grade with speed to spare as they approached the siding they would enter.

Even waiting in a siding could be a learning experience, depending on whether or not a person really wanted to know how a particular block handled its duties in the operation of the railroad. The tower at Vail was at the crest that divided the Logan and Bald Eagle valleys. Vail, the first tower out of Tyrone, regulated through trains and controlled movements of the pushers used on all eastbound tonnage freight trains. When the eastbound extra blasted past, the pilot saw that it was a diker bound for Ralston and told O.P. to watch the procedure used to uncouple the pusher. As the cabin went by, the conductor lifted the coupling rod to pull the pin, and at the same time closed the air valve. Once the air was shut off, the pusher came to a quick, grinding halt. This maneuver, the pilot explained, required some quick moves by the pusher's engineer. He had to shut off the engine, and then compensate with the air release to prevent the locomotive from sliding. There was no hesitation. The pusher reversed, the operator presented the engineer with a clear block and handed on orders, and he was on his way back down the grade.

With this move completed, the operator gave O.P. permission to occupy the main to their destination in the Tyrone yards. As they were pulling out of the siding, the pilot advised O.P. not to open up too hard, because a 35-mile-per-hour speed restriction was in effect all the way down this heavy grade until they reached the yard limits, necessitating constant braking. They didn't encounter any difficulty on the way down, and as they were rolling into the designated yard track the pilot commented that it had been a fine trip, and especially good for someone that had never been over this branch.

Once the train was set in the proper siding, the only remaining duty was to place the 2-8-0 on the pit and mark off. In the yard office O.P. was met by the conductor and flagman, who complimented him on making a good run, noting that they had been on duty for only just over eight hours since marking up in Ralston. Also, the conductor offered a compliment of sorts: "You made good time when you had an open railroad. I'll ride behind you no matter how fast you can get things running on the head end." On this initial run, the comments of the pilot, and now the train crew, were enough to give O.P. confidence in his ability to handle a train out on the road.

Receiving the call to report for duty for the return trip to Ralston, after the layover in Tyrone, O.P. met his pilot in the yard office for the trip over the Bald Eagle segment. Standing before him was a character wearing overclothes that apparently hadn't been laundered since they were new, and whose face was adorned with a flowing, unkempt full beard. At the roundhouse they accepted the H6 from the foreman, acknowledging that it was suitable for road service, and once aboard the engine the pilot took command of the controls. He assured O.P. that he would demonstrate how the heavy train should be handled on this line.

Out of Tyrone, with the pusher behind, the pilot had the engine working hard but not wide open—at least the fireman didn't have any trouble keeping steam up. Cresting the grade at Vail a clear block was on the board, and the orders gave clearance all the way to Milesburg. Shutting off as they started the descent down the Bald Eagle Valley, O.P. watched the air gauge, and when he saw just a flutter he knew the pusher had been cut off. If he had not already witnessed this operation on the trip in, he wouldn't have known about the move that had just taken place, because the pilot offered no explanations. As they proceeded down the valley, everything seemed to be under control. Although some of the brake applications were not the smoothest, it was no cause to be alarmed. O.P. did find one thing about the pilot's action rather amusing. Every time he put his head out the cab window, the beard would blow back around his ears, creating an unusual sight.

In the siding at Milesburg for an opposing movement, O.P. took another good look at the pilot. His beard was now full of cinders and truly matched the rest of his appearance, for he was completely covered with dirt. Under way after their meet had passed, the pilot eased the 2-8-0 out onto the main, and after the siding was cleared he abruptly changed things. Instead of gradually opening up, he dropped the Johnson Bar full forward and opened the throttle out to the last notch. After blasting this way for a short distance, O.P. asked why he didn't cut back to pick up some running speed. The pilot replied, "We have a heavy train. I've got to have the engine opened up to get over the Howard hill."

While retreating to the opposite side, O.P. kept thinking that this did not seem to be the accepted way to hit a grade, but he rationalized that maybe he didn't know everything about the operation of a locomotive. The only thing he could do was sit back and watch. Not even near hitting the grade, the pilot had his injector wide open. Even so, with the way he was hammering the H6, the water glass just continued to drop, indicating that not enough water was getting into the boiler. To compensate, the fireman was instructed to open his water pump. The next indication that things weren't progressing right was that the steam pressure started to drop. At this point the fireman hollered, "Oscar, I can't keep up the way he's working this engine. Everything I'm putting in the firebox he's blowing out the stack." The only way O.P. knew to correct this situation was to go immediately to the right side. "You'd better get off the seat box," he said to the pilot. "I'm taking over. Apparently you don't know the first thing about running an engine. This is my first trip, and I'm not going to have a steam failure shown on my records." The pilot relinquished his position without any argument.

At the controls, O.P. cut back on the reverse lever and shut off the throttle, maintaining just enough momentum to keep going. If he stopped, it would be impossible to start again. Working the engine in this manner, the fireman managed to bring up the steam pressure, and, with the boiler full of water, Orr was able to open up to get the train over the hill. What could have resulted in a major tie-up on the main turned out all right, and showed him what the big 2-8-0 could do in a tight situation. At Lock Haven the pilot disembarked without a word, and that was the last O.P. ever saw of him. The remainder of the trip was a prototype of the many runs that followed, and once on the pit in Ralston, O.P. was confident he was capable of handling the head end.

Now that the first round-trip had been successfully completed and he was fully qualified, O.P. had other objectives in mind. If the Company trusted him to be in charge of one of their locomotives, he would show his appreciation: his engine would reflect how much this honor meant to him. From the stores at the Ralston coal hoist or the Tyrone engine house, he gathered tools—wrenches of various sizes, pins, a variety of nuts and bolts, plus a machinist's hammer—that were essential for making minor repairs out on the road. He also laid in a supply of all types of polishes and paints that were available from the Company's stock or even from hardware establishments, to use as he had done previously to keep the pay car's engine shining. All this would be required to prepare the H6. Special polish was used on the smoke-box front, the stack, the smoke-box door and ash pan, the boiler jacket, the domes, the cylinders, the cab exterior, the tender, and the drivers and rods. There was also a special preparation for the boiler backhead; red lead paint on the cab roof; green paint for the seat boxes and wood cab interior portions; black paint for the deck and steps; brass polish for the bell, cab gauges, and brake valve levers; and last but not least, a cake of Bon Ami for cab windows, headlight lens, and reflectors. Another item for his stock of supplies was a bottle of camphor, which when mixed into the kerosene produced a flame of greater brilliance. He then affixed a "bachelor's button" (a button on a pin that could be pushed through cloth and held in place with a cap when a regular button was lost) to the middle of the wick to spread the flame. That way he could be sure the headlight was in order for night running.

When all the paraphernalia had been carefully stashed in the left tender bulkhead, O.P. waited until a daylight layover at Ralston gave him an opportunity to give the H6 a bath. The coal hoist foreman cooperated and granted permission to have his engine cut out of the ready line, where it was placed at the rear of the shops near the high-pressure steam/water line. Using this cleaning method to the fullest advantage, all accumulated dirt, grime, and grease was removed from the engine, including the tender. Once this chore was completed, his 2-8-0 was perhaps the cleanest engine in the line, but it still didn't shine. The Company did permit an engineer to shine an engine or even apply paint; the only rules were that the scheme of things could not be changed and that no one could add any adornments of his own.

Using idle time while in sidings on daylight trips, O.P. began polishing. Of course, he enlisted the aid of the fireman, who seemed to enjoy this diversion from normal tasks. At either terminal, and if layover time permitted, extra time was also spent on this project. It didn't take too many trips until the engine looked as good, or better, than it had when it was brand-new out of the erecting shop. This well-groomed Consolidation didn't go unnoticed. Some of the crews complimented O.P. on its fine appearance, while others, out of envy or jealousy, chided that he was only hauling coal trains, not the Company's premier passenger train, the Pennsylvania Limited.

But what others thought was of no concern to him because the cleaning and polishing also allowed him to make a close inspection of everything that made the machine function. Accumulated dirt and grease could hide the presence of loose fittings, worn parts, and cracks, but if discovered early such things could be repaired promptly with only a minor adjustment. Unattended, such minor matters could cause major breakdowns out on the road—and that was what he wanted to prevent. (In the ensuing years, all Orr's assigned H6 engines were always polished to perfection, both "a" and "b" models. One of these engines would last about a year before it was shopped, but one "b" model made every trip the cabin did for more than fourteen months.)

O.P.'s big Consolidation in its shiny attire soon became an object of attention of other employees along the entire route. One group especially—the machinists—watched in curious interest how this young engineer spent his free time grooming an engine and keeping it in proper running order. Years later one machinist said: "It didn't take long for us to learn that what Oscar put on the engine report needed to be fixed. There was no reason to recheck his findings either. And before taking his engine out he made a thorough inspection, and if the repairs needed that were listed on his report had not been made, he simply refused to accept the engine as ready for road duty. That then came to the foreman's attention, and that's when all hell broke loose."

On every trip made, O.P. categorized all aspects of the route between Ralston and Tyrone, principally to find the areas best suited to making time with either a string of empties or a loaded train. His H6 proved to be capable of handling trains at speeds allowed the high-drivered American and Atlantic classes, especially on the Elmira Division. Running on a clear block, his small eight driving wheels could easily exceed freight speeds anywhere along the line. Each trip, whether leaving from Tyrone or Ralston, presented a challenge: how to get his train over the rails in the shortest possible time. He concentrated on trying to get to his destinations faster.

The personnel controlling train movements also were watching his efforts with keen interest. Operators manning the blocks discovered that the engineer with the shining engine knew how to carry out their orders, and the dispatchers noticed that O.P. always had his train where it should for scheduled meets, with time to spare. Furthermore, he never seemed to have the railroad tied up due to mechanical failures. As he gained the confidence of this group, he received the privilege many times to go an extra block before taking a siding for a meet—a seemingly small favor, but it placed him a block closer to his destination.

After a time, the dispatchers started to leave him out on the main ahead of passenger trains. Perhaps this was just a way to test his running ability. Very few engineers were ever allowed ahead of a passenger train, but once O.P. proved he could do such a thing—and after a few times they could tell he wasn't just doing this kind of running for plaudits—they realized that this was just his method of getting trains over the road. The trust they put in him was an honor that he guarded with respect during his entire career as an engineman.

In the background there was another group, a nonessential group not even associated with the railroad, who also watched the movement of trains and the men sitting on the right side of the cab: small boys from the younger generation. In communities throughout the country where the railroad played an important role in everyday life, many young boys viewed the man in the cab of an engine as an object of admiration. They imagined that at some time in the future they too might be able to run one of these steam monsters over the rails. Ralston, a terminal town, was no exception. O.P. never ignored this youth faction. As he moved in or out of the yards, he would offer a friendly wave or a few soft toots on the whistle, but he never paid them too much attention either.

One misgiving the road foreman had about working out of Ralston was collecting the monthly pay. The Elmira Division's pay car visited this terminal, but that didn't help O.P., because he was a Williamsport Division man and his pay point to collect monthly wages remained at Williamsport. During his first two months on the Ralston crew, a layover in Ralston allowed him to go to Williamsport to collect his wages. When the third payday arrived, he was on his run back from Tyrone and could in no way meet the Williamsport schedule. Rolling into Linden for the normal coal and water stop, the first thing he spotted was the pay car placed in a siding to pay the workers tending this facility. Without a doubt that was a stroke of good luck. A pay period wouldn't be missed after all.

Cutting the engine off and spotting it under the coal chute, he alighted and made his way to where his wages were being held. Passing the American locomotive on the head end was almost like seeing an old friend, and a cursory inspection revealed that it was still well attended. No other employees were present when he went into the pay car, just the paymaster sitting in his cage reading a newspaper. Greeting the man that held the purse strings, O.P. announced his intentions, explaining he had been out on the road and was unable to be in Williamsport on payday.

Not bothering to put his paper aside, and in a gruff tone becoming his position, the paymaster stated, "Orr, you can draw your pay in Williamsport, and according to rules, that's the only place." Taken aback by this rude treatment, O.P. offered no pleas or argument. He just bid farewell and left. But from previous experience he knew that all the paymaster had to do was open the Williamsport drawer, present the money, and have him sign the record book.

Frustrated about the inflexibility of the rules, O.P. reasoned that he too worked by rules. When he was called, he accepted the call, payday or no payday. If he had a layover in Ralston, he'd go to Williamsport and collect his pay. If not, the paymaster could keep it. In the more than six years that he was in the Company's employment, he had worked regularly and had a substantial amount of money in the bank to tide him over.

The next two monthly pay periods were also missed, because he was out on the road in hauling trains, but as it neared time for the next pay car monthly visit, he received a letter from the division superintendent instructing him to be in Williamsport, without fail, to collect the wages due him. The General Accounting Office in Philadelphia was having problems balancing the books because of this open payroll account, and the paymaster was also running into difficulties trying to keep his records in order with this accumulation of wages. O.P. complied, and on succeeding paydays he "laid off" for half a round-trip just to be present at the appointed time. Fortunately, soon after this the Company abolished the pay-car method of paying wages and adopted the check system. The check could be picked up anytime at a yard office the employee designated. Working as a Williamsport Division engineman, O.P. picked up his check at Williamsport.

There were always challenges along the 115-mile run between Ralston and Tyrone, and O.P. and his Consolidation routinely conquered them all. He had the pattern of every mile of track cataloged, he knew exactly what his H6 was capable of, and above all he knew the design features that made the engine inadequate to handle this particular assignment. Mechanically it was a fine locomotive; it steamed freely, rode well, could handle a train of nearly forty cars (loaded or empty) with ease—and it was fast. The tender, however, was too small to store an adequate amount of coal and water.

Running both eastbound from Ralston and westbound from Newberry Junction with a string of empties, the Consolidation could carry enough coal to complete the trip, and only water stops had to be made. The return trip presented a different picture. A heavy train of loaded cars required a time-consuming stop at Linden to replenish the coal supply, an inconvenience that frustrated O.P. The coaling station both serviced a steady flow of dikers and handled the Williamsport Division westbounds out of Enola and Sunbury and the eastbounds out of Renovo, trains that bypassed Williamsport on the tracks located on the south side of the Susquehanna River. Only seldom was the Linden coaling station without engines being coaled or taking water, meaning long waits for the passing crews. O.P.'s determination to find a way to eliminate this stop grew.

One solution to the Linden coal stop problem would be to find methods to conserve coal—enough coal that the final 27 miles from Linden to Ralston could be traveled without taking on a full tender of fuel. To that end, coming out of Tyrone, O.P. allowed the pusher engine to bear the brunt of the work on the grade to Vail, which put a little more coal in reserve but also slowed his running time. Another strategy—slower starts at the necessary stops along the line—further reduced consumption. However, working up the grade on the Howard hill offset some of these gains, and this plan fell through when it came to ascending the grade of the Jersey Shore hill, by which time his coal supply was so low that he was forced to stop at Linden.

Once, this plan did seem to work, when O.P. had clear blocks on the Bald Eagle to Lock Haven run and then was also given the green signal as far as Linden. At Antes Fort there evidently were no pressing passenger movements against him, as a whistle signal to the operator for the passenger cutoff resulted in his being switched to this track. This route usually took passenger trains around the Jersey Shore hill at a level grade instead of having them climb over the hill, as freight trains did. Eliminating the climb saved a valuable amount of coal. Approaching Linden, O.P. decided to take a gamble and bypass the coaling stop. Here too by means of a whistle signal he notified the operator that he wasn't stopping. The switch to occupy the main into Williamsport was thrown, clearing the way to Newberry Junction.

On the dike, things changed, and not for the better. A lengthy wait before he could occupy the Elmira Division main did not help, neither did his running orders: a siding stop had to be made at Cogan Valley, plus an opposing meet at Trout Run. Leaving the siding at Cogan Valley, he still felt comfortable with the amount of coal remaining, but a red block at Trout Run made him uneasy. While waiting for the meet to clear, the fireman and head brakeman actually scraped bottom, placing what little coal remained forward in the tender so it was within the fireman's reach. Getting under motion again made a serious dent in this small pile. The remaining 11 miles to Ralston seemed to take forever, but they made it. On the pit track O.P. determined that this method was a little too risky—less than half a dozen shovelfuls remained.

Although this attempt was not an unqualified success, it wasn't a failure either. For one determined to find a way to bypass Linden, it proved one thing: an additional three or four tons of coal was all that was needed to make the run through. It would cover anything that might occur and still be safe. Now that the quantity of coal needed to eliminate the spot at Linden was known, O.P. calculated that if eight-inch planks were affixed around the coal compartment of the tender his problem would be solved.

Convinced that this idea had merit and would be easy to implement, O.P. approached the lead foreman at the Tyrone engine house with these findings. Agreeing that his idea was practical, and that in the long run it would probably save the Company many dollars, the elderly foreman politely told him nonetheless that such an addition was not permitted, that the Motive Power Department in Altoona did not tolerate any modifications to locomotives other than those from prints authorized by the Engineering Department.

He added that over the years other enginemen had made the same complaint—and especially just a short time ago by the men on the Class R's: the tenders, they had reported, did not have the capacity to allow the engine to perform effectively on long hauls out of Tyrone. But the answer the Mechanical Engineering Department would give the foreman was always the same: tenders were designed to handle the locomotive's capabilities.

Both the foreman and O.P. concluded that although the design people were technically correct in adhering to this premise, it only worked under the optimal conditions that existed on the Middle Division or the main lines. On these multiple-track systems an engine could be operating at sustained running speeds, perhaps without stopping between terminals, scooping water from track pans conveniently spaced, or, if coaling was necessary, encountering no long waits to get under a single chute, as there were on single-track lines. But the Engineering Department had failed to consider the needs of the engines on the many secondary lines.

The engine-house foreman's advice about how to get permission to add more sides on the tender had enlightened O.P.'s view of his employer. It would probably be easier to get an act through Congress than to have a simple modification requested by one individual on this vast railroad accepted, even one that would involve substantial savings for the Company. Undaunted, however, O.P. came up with another solution. While sitting in the siding at Milesburg as an eastbound passed on the main, he noticed that the passing hopper cars were higher than the H6's tender, and that if his train wasn't moving, and if his crew would cooperate, a few minutes of shoveling could transfer all the coal he needed to run by the Linden bottleneck.

Completing the run and marking off, the crew assembled in one of Tyrone's convenient bars to wash the cinders from their throats, and it was there that O.P. presented his plan, explaining in detail how they could help themselves by running all the way to Ralston and eliminating the stop at Linden. Extra scoop shovels were essential. Selecting a car of good coal would be the brakeman's responsibility while he inspected the train; he would make a chalkmark on the chosen hopper. Furthermore, while they were being held in a siding—any of the ones beyond Milesburg—a ruse, such as a supposed bad car that should be checked, would be concocted to get the dispatcher to allow them to occupy the main to check on a supposed bad car. O.P. would then back to the chosen hopper car, where three or four tons of coal could be loaded onto the tender. Everyone agreed that the plan had merit and that they would do their part to make it successful.

Any new idea must be tested to determine its worth. O.P.'s new theory, as practical as it seemed, depended entirely on the crew's willingness to shovel.

Rumors he had heard—and he'd also heard his own conductor bragging, "I wouldn't get out of my cabin to help any engineer in trouble no matter where we were on the railroad"—made him unsure about whether he could rely on his conductor to support the plan. On previous trips, when minor problems were experienced, the conductor, contrary to his boasts, had always been willing to replace a broken air hose or arrange the switching movements to set out a disabled car, and he'd never complained about riding on the rear of the train when speeds over the allowable limits were exceeded. Only time would tell what his reaction would be to shoveling.

On the first trip out of Tyrone after O.P. had outlined the plan, O.P. received orders at Milesburg to run a clear block to Howard. He had a clear block at Howard too, but orders handed on here told him to take the siding at Mill Hall. After the westbound passenger had passed, however, the Lock Haven operator didn't grant permission to occupy the main; a westbound diker was in a siding that was urgently needed for another westbound movement and therefore had preference to occupy the Bald Eagle main. O.P.'s eastbound extra would remain in the siding until the westbound passed.

When it was determined that this opposing train would be held for an eastbound movement on the Williamsport Division's main before crossing over to the Bald Eagle Branch, probably fifteen to twenty minutes, time was in O.P.'s favor. He immediately called the dispatcher and requested permission to occupy the main to run back along his train to check for a suspected brake problem on a car. Permission was granted to make the check, providing he was back in the siding within fifteen minutes. Leaving the call box, O.P. opened the switch and hurried back to the engine, instructing the brakeman to uncouple—they were going out on the main.

Wasting no time, the brakeman on the rear footboard closed the switch and the backup move began. Nearing the rear end of the train, O.P. whistle-signaled, and, lo and behold, both the flagman and the conductor came out on the platform of the cabin with their shovels. With the entire crew aboard, a run was made forward to the marked car to begin the chore of replenishing the fuel supply. The five men shoveled in unison, and in a little more than five minutes the tender was filled with enough coal to allow them to bypass Linden. With his locomotive back in the siding well within the time allotted, O.P. notified the dispatcher that the problem had been adjusted and that they had cleared the main.

Off the Bald Eagle and on the Williamsport main, O.P. stopped in Lock Haven to top off his water supply. Ralston was less than 60 miles away, so he could cover those miles without stopping for coal, but even if odds were not in his favor, water was available on the Elmira Division at Trout Run. Whistling to the operator at Linden that he was running through, the board came up clear and he was on his way to Newberry Junction. Being able to run by the waiting line gave him a feeling of satisfaction. (Meanwhile, however, crews getting "scooped" [run by] while in operation have historically experienced feelings substantially short of satisfaction over the event.) Furthermore, O.P. scooped a fellow diker crew waiting to take on coal, putting his crew one slot ahead for another trip according to the first in, first out operating schedule. When the 2-8-0 was on the pit track in Ralston, there was still some coal left in the tender. Without a doubt, the experiment had accomplished its purpose.

How long this method of borrowing coal from hopper cars would be practical was unknown. The maneuver couldn't be used on every trip, but O.P. used it whenever there was an appropriate opportunity. His major concern was that if other crews learned about it they would adopt the technique for their own advantage, and if that happened officials surely would be alerted, making it trying for all parties involved. Other crews (including many that had been scooped) did indeed ask how he managed to run by Linden when they were always forced to stop for coal, and O.P. answered, "I've got a couple of hidden coaling stations along the Bald Eagle Branch."

This unorthodox method of getting better running time, and thus saving the Company money, was always in danger of coming to light, especially when there were changes in crew members. Firemen, brakemen, and flagmen were constantly being bumped, promoted, or bidding off on other jobs, and if they were to reveal what was going on, other crews might follow suit. Why this never happened was a bit puzzling to O.P. Perhaps they didn't tell because it involved extra work, or maybe they did tell and no one would believe them. The dispatchers and operators never bothered to question him, either. Perhaps because he was getting his trains over the road with no trouble, and continuing to do so, it didn't matter to them how he accomplished that.

The only other crew member who might divulge O.P.'s manner of procuring extra coal would be the conductor. But that fear was dispelled when that conductor continued to make the same boast in the bars: "I wouldn't get out of my cabin to help the best engineer on the railroad." At least the people in his audience believed him, but O.P., knowing what was actually going on, was rather tickled.

A strong friendship developed between O.P. and his conductor. The two even established something of a ritual. After each run into Ralston they made their last stop one of the convenient hotels, where in this pre-Prohibition era they would purchase a quart of whiskey. Setting the bottle on the bar, each would take drink for drink until the bottle was empty, and then go on their respective ways—O.P. to his rooming house, the conductor back to the cabin.

Why the conductor spent his layover time in the cabin was a bit of a mystery, but because he regarded that as a personal matter, O.P. never asked any questions. The conductor was a married man, had a family, and owned a house in Ralston, and he had all his meals and laundry taken care of at home, but he still stayed in the cabin. He and his wife seemed amicable, though, and even attended various social events together.

Working out of Ralston wasn't anything like the road foreman had described, nor did it turn out to be the end of the world—which was what O.P. thought when he first arrived. More and more O.P. had to agree with his first fireman. A friendly atmosphere prevailed among employees working at this terminal, and even though there was some competition among the over-the-road crews operating on the first in, first out basis, they too would lend a helping hand when needed. The townspeople as well accepted his presence, and that alone made living in the community enjoyable.

The proximity of Williamsport, and its accessibility, provided attractions for Oscar too, such as Masonic programs and sporting events. The foothills and mountains surrounding Ralston provided excellent hunting and fishing. It was even possible to find a stream containing native trout. Every morning at 7:00 A.M., six days a week, a Central Pennsylvania Lumber Company log train departed from the S&NY's yard in South Ralston with twenty-two log cars and a car that hauled the steam-powered log loader. Ahead of this consist was a Shay-geared locomotive. When it began ascending the steep grades into the Rock Run Valley to the east, its exhaust sounded like a rod engine running 50 miles an hour or better. That was misleading, however, because a person running at a slow trot could easily keep up with the pace at which it was moving the train. It always left on schedule, but returning was a different story. It made its way back only when its twenty-two cars were loaded with logs—whether that was 10:00 in the morning or 10:00 at night. Using this conveyance on various occasions, O.P. didn't know which was more interesting: the fishing, or observing this logging operation. When all factors were taken into consideration, O.P. had no problem deciding that it would be nearly impossible to find a terminal better suited than Ralston to satisfy his immediate needs.

At the start of the second decade of the new century, advances in forms of transportation were becoming ever more evident—principally the airplane and the horseless carriage, or automobile. On rare occasions during daylight runs an airplane could be spotted. The automobile, on the other hand, was to be seen more and more often around urban areas anytime after 1910. By 1912, especially during the summer months, these mechanical contraptions were even traveling on the rural highways, most of which bordered and frequently crossed the railroad.

Chugging along at relatively slow speeds on dirt roads, automobiles were no match for O.P. and his train powered by the big H6, which easily overtook and passed them, with a friendly wave or a soft whistle salute, of course. Most of the cars were rather boxy; the enclosed versions were called sedans, the open models, with collapsible tops and side curtains, were classified as touring cars. A third version, the roadster, was more sporty, with sleek lines and only a windshield and single seat. That was the model that made a lasting impression on O.P. It was an oddity that an automobile would cause a railroad engineer any consternation, but this particular type of car did.

On a routine westbound trip on the Bald Eagle one Sunday afternoon in the summer of 1912, and after the usual water stop at Milesburg, O.P. was running on clear blocks to Vail. By the time the first block at Julian neared, the 2-8-0 had been set up at running speed, around 45 miles an hour. The track for the next five miles to Martha Furnace was straight as a die and paralleled by a dirt highway, either on the same level or slightly below the grade.

Not far beyond Julian, a large cloud of dust was forming—presumably by a motorist out for a Sunday drive. When O.P. overtook and passed this vehicle, it turned out to be a roadster operated by someone clad in the uniform of the day: cap, goggles, and duster. Obviously irritated at being passed by a freight train, the driver sped up and managed to position himself just short of the engine's gangway, but evidently at the maximum speed the car could generate. O.P. too was in the same predicament. He had the H6 stretched out to the maximum speed it would produce on this slight upgrade. The fireman and brakeman joined in watching this unusual race, urging O.P. to open up a little more, at least enough to run away from the newfangled automobile. Neither won the race. The car hung on until the roads separated near Martha Furnace.

This first encounter with a racing machine on the straight segment of the Bald Eagle, amusing as it seemed, was just a prelude of the challenges that were to come. The sleek roadster that was able to run neck-and-neck while attempting to outrun O.P.'s Consolidation was spotted again on a later trip, but this time moving in the opposite direction. Later, toward the end of the summer season on a weekend trip, a dust cloud was seen west of Julian, this time it was produced by not one but three roadsters, led by the original challenger. As the train passed, the drivers sped up and managed to overtake the engine without difficulty and passed with ease—except for the third car, which barely got by the locomotive's pilot, where it hung on, neither gaining nor losing ground.

Prevailing winds lifted the dust these cars were generating toward the H6, which was soon enveloped in dust, making it necessary to close the front cab doors, the window, and the back of the cab. Running under conditions that obscured all vision gave O.P. an eerie feeling, and he and the crew were having difficulty breathing as well. Fortunately, these conditions lasted for less than five minutes. Once the dust had cleared, an examination revealed that the interior of the cab was covered with a heavy film of dust, but there was more. Arriving at Tyrone, the once shiny black engine was now the color of the dirt on the highway—and not a spot was spared, from the pilot to the footboards on the tender. Dismayed at what he saw, O.P. couldn't help wondering when another confrontation of this sort would happen.

The roadster never descended on him again, but according to the ever-active railroad grapevine of information, other crews were experiencing the same racing bouts and resultant dustings. As the automobile gained in popularity, an increasing number of these vehicles were traveling on rural roads during the summer months—and not just on weekends, but any day of the week.

The straight section between Julian and Martha Furnace began to entice drivers of sedans and touring cars, who also pitted their flivvers against the passing trains. O.P. began to dread a daylight run over those five miles in dry, hot weather. Whether eastbound or westbound, his engine always ended up covered with dust churned up by these vehicles.

Motorists were exposing themselves to an element of danger when they ran alongside a fast-moving train. If something were to break loose or an object were to fall off one of the railroad cars, the results could be disastrous. Motorists, however, never seemed to take this into consideration while they were amusing themselves, but their antics always worried O.P.

During this early period of the twentieth century, the Company was developing and building steam locomotives that dwarfed the classes already in use. These engines turned out by the erecting shops usually first saw service on the main lines, and O.P. deduced that, after they were well worn, the secondary lines got the chance to squeeze out the usefulness that remained. Newspaper articles announcing new creations and published operating instructions made it easy to keep abreast of all new classes. Passenger classes were the most admired. The K2, with the 4-6-2 wheel arrangement, was dubbed a Pacific; it could haul a string of passenger cars that previously needed a pair of the E2 Atlantic 4-4-2's for such a chore. The newer E6 Atlantic, because it was powered by the same boiler that the new freight-class H8 2-8-0 Consolidation used, was indeed a powerful passenger locomotive.

The H8 was regularly hauling fifty or more freight cars at speed over the entire system. Associated with Middle Division crews in Tyrone, O.P. was able to garner more information on a firsthand basis from the men who had either run or fired on these new classes of locomotives, either H8's on freight trains or E6's on passenger runs. All seemed to agree that the piston valve and the outside-mounted Walscheart reverse gear were far superior to slide valves with the inside-mounted reversing gear arrangement. Another device being installed on the engines equipped with piston valves was something the manuals classified as a superheater, which removed the water from the steam. Middle Division men attested that a superheater really added to the performance of these piston-valve engines, referring to the differences it made, particularly on the K2 passenger class. The ones using saturated steam were sluggish compared with the ones using dry steam.

Even though Tyrone, where O.P. terminated, was on the Middle Division's main line, the yard area was far enough removed that he was unable to observe this new power in actual use while laying over at this terminal; there was little time for just train-watching. The only alternative was patience. Sooner or later these new engines would come to the Williamsport Division.

Early in 1913 the first opportunity to inspect a piston-valve engine presented itself. It wasn't a new locomotive, but rather a familiar H6 that had been converted to use this mechanism. The builder's plate classified this engine as an H6b. The Company was evidently satisfied with this method of transferring steam to the cylinders on its engines. More and more H6b's were coming into Tyrone off the Middle Division. They also were being used to handle the symbol freights on the Williamsport Division's main line. Furthermore, some Atlantic E2's and their subclasses on the passenger runs were also re-equipped with piston valves coupled with the outside reverse gear.

When O.P.'s H6a was shopped in 1914, the assigned replacement he received was of the converted "b" class. All the controls on the replacement were exactly the same as the former slide-valve "a" model; it still had the Johnson Bar to regulate the new valve motion, so coordinating the throttle was the only thing that had to be done to move a train over the rails with this engine. The correct amount of steam used to turn the drivers basically could not be changed. Initially, O.P. noted that the "b" had a sharper *bark* as the exhaust left the stack. It did not seem to have more power, but it could start a train more easily and could get under way more quickly.

Once a set-up-running speed was attained, the H6b responded better in handling a train, plus it used less coal and water. This saving was not an important factor, however. The small tender still required "borrowing" coal from the hoppers or from the inconvenient fuel stop at Linden. After a few trips, the performance of the piston-valve-equipped H6b proved that it was a better engine than the H6a in most categories except one: O.P. couldn't crowd any more speed out of its eight drivers.

Normally, over-the-road crews were made up of men who accepted calls on a regular basis and completed their runs as a working unit, moving trains over the designated portion of the railroad. When a member marked off, the crew would receive a replacement from the extra board. O.P. had made runs with extra firemen, and although they did not handle the firing chores as ably as the regulars, he managed to get the trains over the road with no hardships.

Marking up for one evening run to Tyrone, he found the regular fireman had marked off and an extra man would be filling in. Before they got permission to occupy the main, this fireman went about his duties in an orderly manner, and when the clear block was presented they left Ralston with a full head of steam. After making the start and setting up at running speed, however, the fireman was still sitting on his seat box. Finding this strange, O.P. hollered across the cab that it was about time to pick up the scoop shovel and start firing, or soon they would run out of steam. The fireman remained seated. O.P., supposing the fireman hadn't heard him over the noise of the engine, crossed the dimly lit cab, again telling the extra man it was time to commence firing. Not even looking around, the fireman just stared straight ahead and blurted: "I'm not going to get up. I've never gone this fast before in my life. If I get up and try to fire, I'll fall off in the dark for sure."

This unexpected situation on a main line with a train running at full speed without the assistance of a fireman needed to be addressed immediately. Realizing what was transpiring, the brakeman said, "Oscar, I've been on this run for quite a while and fire quite a bit. Maybe I could take over until you get something worked out." This of course met with O.P.'s approval, and when everything was in order again he called the brakeman over to the right side. "If I stopped now and requested a replacement out of Williamsport, we'd probably be tied up in Newberry half the night. When we get the next stop order, I'll call the dispatcher and tell him the fireman is sick and we have to have another man in Lock Haven." But no stop signals came up all the way down the Elmira Division, and at Newberry Junction the board was clear for the Williamsport Division main. Orders handed on noted that they took precedence over other movements to McElhattan. On this section, O.P. gave the brakeman some assistance firing while the brakeman rode O.P.'s seat box as a lookout. With this method they got the train over the road in fine shape.

During the stop at McElhattan, the fireman got off his seat box and began taking care of the fire as if nothing had happened. This raised hope that perhaps he'd get over whatever was ailing him and take care of his duties for the rest of the trip. Not sure of what would transpire, O.P. and the brakeman concluded that they were too close to Lock Haven to call for a replacement. If they chose that solution, they would again be tied up for hours. Since they had gotten this far, it would be easy enough to continue sharing the firing chores until they reached Tyrone.

The fireman's display of taking care of his chores did not last. As soon as they started moving at McElhattan, he again affixed himself to the left seat box, and that was the pattern he followed after every stop until they put the engine on the pit in Tyrone. Before marking off, O.P. took the brakeman aside and thanked him for taking over, explaining that without his help they would still be tied up somewhere out on the railroad. This brought on a response that was enlightening. "I like to fire, and you know, Oscar, I especially liked sitting on your seat box ringing the bell and whistling for the crossings." With this information at hand, O.P. felt he could now say what he was thinking: "If I go into the yard office and file my report stating that the fireman refused to fire the engine," he told the brakeman, "the man will lose his job, but if we could work the same way on the way back we could get him back to Ralston without causing any problems."

The brakeman figured that was a good idea, and added that the young man had told him he'd only been firing for less than a month and all his work was out of Ralston on pushers to the north. This was his first time out on the head end. In fact, he hadn't worked long enough to collect a paycheck. Perhaps if this fireman could have worked during a daylight run he would have gotten over his fright of falling off, but the return trip was also a nighttime one.

Working up the hill out of Tyrone, the extra-board fireman fired like a professional. After passing Vail, however, when the train began picking up speed on the descent into the Bald Eagle Valley, it was back to the seat box. O.P. and the brakeman made the trip with no difficulties and deposited the fireman in Ralston as if nothing had happened. Sometime later, curious about what had become of this fireman, O.P. asked the crew clerk at the yard office and was informed that he had bid in a yard crew in Southport (Elmira), New York. Reasoning that was probably the best place for a man with such fears, at least he was still working for the Company. This incident left O.P. with a lasting phobia, though, and just marking up for a trip that indicated an extra fireman was enough to cause him to shudder.

An engineer who was for many years one of Orr's hunting, fishing, and social companions recalled meeting O.P. for the first time. Accepting a late call on short notice as an extra fireman, he found that he had been called for the RA13 crew, with O.P. Orr as the engineer. Acquainted with the name only through stories told among other railroaders, he'd heard as a Ralston native that Orr was one of the best engineers working out of Ralston—and this was a good chance to find out for himself.

As he tells it, when he left the yard office the shiny H6 was already moving out of the coal hoist, forcing him to get aboard on the fly. Once in the cab, he explained that he'd gotten a short notice on this extra call and apologized for not getting around sooner. O.P. greeted him gruffly: "That's all right. All I hope is that you know how to fire this engine."

During the air test after they had coupled to their train, O.P. asked him pointedly, "How long have you been firing?"

As he set the lubricator and did the chores that were necessary before leaving on a run, the fireman replied: "I've been on the railroad for over a year. I had a regular crew for quite a while, but I was just bumped and I couldn't get on another crew out of Ralston, so I put my name on the extra board, allowing me to continue living at home with my parents. I also had some other firing experience. I worked for the CPL Company for over two years as the log loader fireman."

O.P. offered no comment on the qualifications presented, and the only other conversation came after the station operator issued the orders: "You better get your fire in order. As soon as the eastbound midnight passenger train passes, we're leaving. We are running on their orders with a clear block all the way to the dike."

The engineer continued with his story: "After the passenger passed, it was only a few minutes until we got the clear block, and O.P. wasn't fooling when he said we were leaving. We blasted out of Ralston just like the second section of the passenger that had just cleared, and it wasn't too long before we were running at passenger speed. I had made enough trips aboard an H6, but I never realized a small-drivered 2-8-0 would run as fast as we were going. My first thought was that if this pace was continued I'd really earn my pay before we reached Tyrone, but it wasn't long until I found it was easier to keep steam up running fast than it was when you were poking along.

"All the way down to the dike it didn't take much shoveling to keep a full head of steam. We only slowed going around the restricted Powys Curve, and again before we got on the dike cutoff. How O.P. had the engine set up, it didn't bother the fire. It burned even, and the pops were singing all the time. At Newberry Junction we had a clear block for the Williamsport main, and orders handed on read that we could run on clear blocks to Lock Haven.

From this point on we really were running, but only a few scoops now and then were needed to keep the H6 hot, plus the brakeman even took over firing for a while, allowing me to ride the seat box.

"The brakeman volunteering to help with the firing was another thing that I had never experienced. After a water stop in Lock Haven and on the Bald Eagle, we were slowed down by meets, but when O.P. had a clear block he ran just as hard as ever. Arriving in Tyrone, I determined this had to be the easiest and fastest trip I ever had firing an engine. One of the best parts came as we left the yard office after marking off. O.P. stated: 'You did a good job coming over. Most generally I have a couple of beers to wash the cinders out of my throat before eating, and you're welcome to join me—I'm buying.' A compliment of that nature coming from O.P. Orr really raised my ego, and with no hesitation I accepted his offer.

"The return trip with a loaded train proved to be much the same as running empty. When we had the proper conditions, we ran at top speeds, and the firing was just as easy. By the time we were back in Ralston, I made up my mind that somehow I would get on this crew as a regular fireman, but it never happened; someone with more seniority always was there ahead of me. I made only one other trip with O.P., and that was as an extra man."

I asked, "Do you know why O.P. was brusque in his initial greeting when you boarded his engine?"

The fireman answered in the negative, remembering that his late arrival on the short call probably caused some aggravation, but that didn't bother him. The only thing he had to do was keep steam up, not keep the engineer happy. When I explained that O.P. had a phobia concerning extra firemen, he was surprised. He replied, "Oscar and the brakeman held on to their secret pretty close," he said, "or at least it never got out in the railroad grapevine."

Soon after the beginning of World War I in Europe in 1914, the long shadows of this catastrophe were falling on America. Industries expanded to meet the growing need for war materials by increasing production, and additional supplies of coal became a priority. The railroads were forced to meet this demand by adding more trains to transport this vital commodity, and more trains required more crews. The terminal at Ralston was not spared while this transition was taking place. Operating personnel were promoted to handle newly assigned crews, and the shuffling required the hiring of additional people.

These changes did not bypass O.P. His regular fireman was "set up running," and a young, inexperienced man on the extra board bid on the fireman's job. At their first introduction it was apparent that the new man was physically capable of handling the firing chores. He stood six feet five inches in a big raw-boned frame. Not too far on the initial run with this recruit, O.P. saw that the young man also made well-coordinated body movements while placing coal into the firebox. He could plant himself on the deck, reach half-way back into the tender with the scoop shovel, and hit the fire door without spilling an ounce of coal. This made it easy for him to keep the H6 hot. In fact, he had a tendency to overfire, which resulted in having the safety pop valves raised more often than necessary. The steam going out the pop valves wasn't turning the wheels, so it was wasted; it amounted to added water and coal consumption—something O.P. wasn't about to condone.

His solution was to start coaching the young man. Careful not to offend him regarding the method he was using to fire the locomotive, O.P. nonetheless began suggesting when to ease up a bit or when to add a little extra coal. An adept pupil, the man adjusted quickly to over-the-road firing, and after he had a few trips to his credit O.P. came to consider him one of the better firemen that ever rode with him on one of his engines.

Other than being a good fireman, this young man was good-natured and got along well with the other crew members. And as they soon learned, he was also a prankster. They never knew what to expect next, for he was constantly involving them in one kind of trick or another. Even O.P. was on the receiving end of some of this fireman's amusements. Notably, he wasn't overly fond of assisting when it came to polishing the engine, and when a certain type of polish required heating by placing it on the scoop shovel and inserting it into the front of the firebox, he conveniently allowed it to slip off, to his amusement. The first time this happened was sort of amusing, but after a repeat performance O.P. didn't see anything funny about it. Besides, it was the kind of polish he was required to purchase.

Another playful action on the part of the fireman was to knuckle-punch O.P.'s left arm muscle while he rested it on the throttle. That hurt, and left the muscle sore and the arm bruised. A counterpunch could be expected without prior notification, O.P. warned the fireman. But the warning went unheeded, and O.P. was apt to get a thump at any time, especially while concentrating on train movements. One day, as they were pulling into a siding for a meet, the fireman positioned himself in the gangway on the right side, supposedly watching the movement—or possibly getting ready to sneak in another punch. Sure enough, that was the objective, but as he raised his arm to strike, O.P. arose from the seat box and, as he said he would, and delivered a blow to the chin that flattened his fun-loving fireman.

"Oscar, you hurt me," said the fireman, lying flat on his back and shaking his head with blinking eyes.

"I wouldn't have hit you if I didn't want to hurt you," O.P. replied, "and if you keep punching my arm, next time I won't be so gentle." Fortunately it only took one lesson to cure the fireman of that habit.

But it was just an idle thought to think that the fun-loving fireman would reform. His next caper occurred on the dike while the pusher was being coupled up and they awaited clearance to occupy the Elmira Division main. A trolley car was his selected victim this time. Watching one of these trolleys as it came up the grade to cross over the dike tracks, he bet the brakeman that he could stop the car before it reached the crossover point. The brakeman foolishly accepted the bet, and soon was aware that he was about to lose.

Arming himself with a broom and the kerosene can, the fireman applied a generous amount of oil, sweeping down one side of the trolley's rail, and an equal amount coming back up. Before the unsuspecting trolley appeared, a light rain started to fall, further disguising his efforts. When the car did arrive, it started up toward the crossover at its normal speed, but then a little more than halfway up the grade it came to a slipping halt. It didn't make a backing movement, but rather a sliding move to the bottom of the grade, much to the fireman's enjoyment. The fireman had won the bet that he could stop the trolley. The motorman almost made it on the second try, but he again failed to crest the hill. On the third try, under sand and with lots of juice, it made it over the top. On a later date the fireman tried the same stunt, but this time he lost the bet. Evidently the motorman, seeing a train on the dike, knew what to expect and just increased his speed and applied the sand, crossing over with speed to spare.

Pulling onto the dike late one summer day, the fireman spotted something else that could provide some entertainment: a circus was set up in the fields across the creek adjacent to their stopping point. Before making a complete stop, he had talked the brakeman into going across the bridge to the amusement area. They could tour the grounds while the pusher was being attached and would be back to the engine by departure time. O.P. cautioned them not to get too involved in the activities, because when a clear block to occupy the Elmira Division main was presented he was leaving. About the time the pusher had been coupled on and the air test had been performed, the block dropped clear.

Whistling off, to notify the pusher engine he was starting, O.P. still didn't see any of the missing crew members, and a moment or two later he made the same call, but still no one appeared. He had no alternative to accepting the clear block, so he started the train without his crew. As he was picking up speed, they came running and grabbed onto a car about halfway back in the train. Somehow they made their way over the loaded hoppers of coal to a boxcar three lengths back of the engine. When they reached the front of the car, they sat down and waved, obviously glad to be aboard. O.P. returned the gesture with a thumb to the nose salute. In addition to running the engine, he had to get off the seat box and fire occasionally, which he did until they neared Trout Run. Coming forward to the engine, they complimented O.P. on the fine job he was doing by himself. The compliment wasn't very well taken, though, and O.P. assured them that if he had been able to get off dike faster they would have had a circus of their own explaining to officials why they had been left in Williamsport.

The climax of the pranks came one day in the west end of the Trout Run siding while waiting for an eastbound meet. O.P. and the fireman, as usual, were outside polishing the H6 on this summer afternoon. When the meet approached on the main, they gave up the outside chores and made their way back to the cab to prepare for running the 11 remaining miles to Ralston. Inside the cab they were greeted by not only the brakeman but also the flagman, who had come forward intending to handle the switching as they left the siding.

Actually, the true purpose of the flagman's presence was soon to be revealed. Somehow it had been learned that the fireman was deathly afraid of snakes, so during his absence from the cab they had placed a large but harmless black snake in his seat box. On some pretext they asked the fireman for something he always kept in the seat box, and obligingly he lifted the lid to get it for them. But as he lifted the seat, out popped the snake's head, and whoever had clued the crew members in about the fireman's fear of snakes was correct. At the sight of the emerging reptile, he let out a shriek that could have been heard in Ralston, and in a blur of motion, jumped off the engine, landing in a water-filled ditch full of brush and weeds.

As he crawled out of the ditch, O.P. and the other members of the crew saw that he wasn't hurt, but he was wet and covered with mud. The obscenities he shouted, plus his muddy appearance, gave the crew reason to be convulsed with laughter. Collecting his senses, the fireman, realizing he had been the pawn of this frightening experience, began to shout dire threats along with his curses. The situation needed to be addressed immediately, to squelch any unfortunate repercussions from the incident. O.P., now ired by the threats, commanded that the snake be thrown into the firebox, then ordered the fireman to get back on board the engine.

Confronting a now sullen crew, O.P. explained they were adults with responsible jobs, not schoolboys with nothing better to do than have fun, and that if such shenanigans continued somebody would wind up hurt, perhaps seriously. What had just occurred would be a fine example to consider. If they had been running when the fireman jumped off, he would undoubtedly have been seriously injured and someone would be held responsible. O.P. added that if the pranks persisted the only other way to bring these activities to a halt would be to file a report outlining everything that was transpiring contrary to established work rules. He never had to take that step.

The year 1916 brought many changes that affected O.P. for the rest of his railroading career and throughout his personal life. Notably, the federal Railroad Retirement Act would provide a pension for his retirement, as well as what was known as "Railroad Relief," accident and health benefits paid to railroad workers in case of sickness or injury. Work rules also were changed by the sixteen-hour-on-duty law. No longer could the Company compel an employee to remain on duty with a train until the trip was completed. A new term was coined for crews that exceeded this time limit: they were considered "outlawed," and in such a situation the Company had to provide a relief crew, or the engine crew would have to stop, even if they were occupying a main line, and dump the fire. The Company was careful not to get into such a bind, and if a crew neared the outlaw time they were tucked away in the first convenient siding.

Other work rules went into effect too. A run of more than 100 miles was put on a mileage basis; runs of less were on an hourly rate, as were yard crews. Any work time over eight hours was paid at time-and-a-half. All pay rates were scaled to the amount of weight an engine placed on its drivers. These long-overdue changes were welcomed by railroaders and enhanced their position among the other working classes. In essence, it was legislation that other workers would strive to attain—the Social Security Act being the outcome of their efforts.

Even though work rules changed, the work itself did not, and the escalation of the war in Europe broadened the demands on railroads. O.P. was experiencing shorter layovers and more time hauling trains. He also couldn't help wondering why the Company did not assign the newer and more powerful locomotives to this vital line in order to increase the tonnage on the trains. The H8 2-8-0 classes were more and more common at the Tyrone engine house, as Middle Division crews were using those engines on many runs. The H6 was slowly being supplanted. The reason behind this shift of power was all-out production of the L1s, or Mikado-class locomotive, a 2-8-2 that was taking over the freight hauling on the main lines. O.P.'s particular run was now two classes of motive power behind the times. They still used the now small H6 class.

Still, during this busy period, O.P. found time to enjoy the social life in the Williamsport complex. When he did frequent this city he almost always paid a visit to his friend from yard-service days, the proprietor of the City Hotel, and on one such occasion this friend introduced him to a young woman who was the cook at this establishment. After the introduction, and during the ensuing conversation, he learned that her home was in Ralston and that, much like himself, she'd had a love affair with an unhappy ending. This young woman had been married and divorced and was the mother of a young daughter. O.P. and this woman went to social events together, in Williamsport and Ralston, and after nearly two years of courtship, they were married in July 1917 at the Pine Street Methodist Church in Williamsport. O.P. was thirty-five years old and his bride was thirty-four. Their first home in Ralston was on the main street less than a block from the coal hoist and the yard office. O.P. still spent his layover time grooming his H6 though. This polishing chore brought about some chiding from other crews about whether he thought more of the H6 or his new bride, but that secret remained his own.

The year 1917 saw other major events, one of the greatest being when the United States declared war on Germany. The conflict in Europe was now referred to as World War I, and in anticipation of this the Company's Engineering Department had designed and was now out-shopping a super freight hauler that had a 2-10-0 wheel arrangement intended to alleviate increasing tonnage generated by the war. This huge locomotive was classified as an I1s and reportedly could haul any size train it could start. In comparison, the H6a that O.P. began with in 1910, a large engine at the time, had in seven years been relegated to the smallest-class freight locomotive in general use. Yet he was still using one of these H6's almost daily. Meanwhile, the Company had developed three types of more powerful locomotives, although none had shown up on the Bald Eagle and Elmira divisions.

In early fall 1917, the Company's people in charge of transportation decided that coal could be moved more efficiently to the northern New York and New England areas if the diker's trip was shortened. According to plans, the Middle Division crews would run through Tyrone with loaded trains and continue down the Bald Eagle to Lock Haven, where they would turn their engine, pick up empty cars, and return to the point of origin on the same time card. Ralston crews would follow the same procedure, except in reverse, bringing empties to Lock Haven and returning to Ralston with loaded trains.

For a few trips, everything operated as the planners had intended, but the synchronization of these movements began to lag. Ralston crews delivering empties found no loaded cars to be picked up in Lock Haven, requiring marking off with a layover. At Ralston, meanwhile, another situation developed. There were no empty cars returned from Southport to that point, and the loaded trains bound for Ralston and Southport were laying in Lock Haven. To compensate for this unbalance in the movement of loads and empties, crews were run light—with just the locomotive and the cabin. O.P. liked this kind of move (either Lock Haven at this time, and both earlier and later to Tyrone and Altoona), saying, "Running light, I can go so fast you can't see my coattail for dust." Following this principle, but with a string of empties in tow, O.P. later found out that yet another faction was watching the way he ran his trains.

Called out late one subsequent morning, after taking the train out of the yard down to the station operator's position, his orders informed him that he was being held for the passenger train due to pass this point at noon. As soon as that train cleared, orders read that he would run on the passenger's orders with a clear block over all other movements to Newberry Junction. Once the passenger cleared Ralston, O.P., with a wide open railroad, lost no time covering the 24 miles on the Elmira Division. At Newberry he received a clear block, and orders that he was clear to Antes Fort, where he again had a clear block; further orders gave him a clear block to the Lock Haven yards, unless he would get held by McElhattan Tower due to a crossover movement by the Central. Running in anticipation of a stop signal, he began slowing when McElhattan came into view. Of all things, a clear signal was displayed.

They set off their train in the Lock Haven yard after this nonstop trip from Ralston, ran back along the train, got the cabin, and placed it on the cabin track. Then, following the usual routine, the H6 was taken to the engine house for normal servicing, and from there the engine crew went to the yard office for return trip orders. The crew clerk presented their standing: they were five times out and no movement was in sight at Tyrone. It would be at least twenty-four hours before a call could be expected.

Checking the time, the crew, except for the conductor, decided that rather than laying over at least twenty-four hours they would go home and return the following day. Just enough time remained to get to the station to catch the eastbound Buffalo Flyer to Williamsport, where it made connections with the afternoon train to Ralston. The passenger trains were on time, and O.P. and his crew alighted in Ralston at 3:30 P.M. Less than three and a half hours had passed since their departure for this 60-mile run, on a supposedly slow-moving freight train.

The first person to react to their presence back in Ralston was the station operator, who couldn't imagine how this crew had made the trip to Lock Haven and have already returned. As one of the major "ears" of the local grapevine, the operator soon was spreading the news of this amazing feat. Even Company officials heard about it.

It didn't take the officials long to react. On the return trip from Lock Haven nearly two days later, O.P., when marking off at the yard office, was handed a message from none other than the trainmaster, instructing him to report to his office at his earliest convenience. When he reported, the trainmaster laid a copy sheet from the train dispatcher's office on the desk and explained that it was a record of the time of all movements on the Elmira Division the day of the fast run. He also pointed out that it clearly indicated the extra engine number, the Ralston departure time of 12:03 P.M., and the time it passed the tower controlling Elmira Division trains. According to that document, he had covered this distance two minutes faster than the passenger train schedule. The extra movement they were detailing gained two minutes on the 50-mile-per-hour passenger schedule in the 24 miles between those points.

Time wasn't all the trainmaster submitted for review. The next item was a copy of the extra's train orders. O.P. knew something was amiss when the well-rehearsed official said, "Oscar, your orders permitted you to run clear on the same blocks as the preceding passenger to Newberry Junction, but nowhere did these orders give you permission to run a freight train at passenger speeds." Ending his presentation, the trainmaster produced a letter from the Elmira Division superintendent that stated: "Effective on the date that this notice is received, Engineman O.P. Orr is hereby suspended from active service for a period of fifteen days. Such action is necessary due in regards to his flagrant disregard of established freight train speeds from Ralston to Newberry Junction."

As O.P. was leaving the trainmaster's office, the official pointed out: "You can protest this action if you present a letter requesting a formal hearing at the superintendent's office in Elmira." O.P. responded that he would reserve his decision and that if he chose to file a letter of protest the trainmaster would be notified.

Next O.P. had to notify the road foreman of engines on the Williamsport Division about the suspension, and rather than do that by telephone he elected to go directly to the office and handle it personally. The road foreman wasn't exactly proud of the reason for the suspension, but he thought the length of the suspension was unjust. Five days was normal for this offense, he said, and suggested that the suspension be protested. The Brotherhood representative would be notified, he added, and he would also personally attend a hearing if this route was pursued.

Mulling the situation over, O.P. informed the road foreman that he wasn't going to protest the suspension, reasoning that it would cause a great deal of inconvenience and that if he succeeded in having the time shortened it would give the officials cause to watch every move he made. Also, if any infractions of the rules did occur, it left the door open for a more severe penalty. Another reason was that hunting season was at hand and he had planned to mark off for a few trips to enjoy this sport. The suspension was made to order. The time the reprimand allowed was like an overdue vacation, and being able to hunt at leisure made it more relaxing.

One evening, when more than a week had passed since O.P. began the suspension, his fireman arrived to deliver a newspaper that was published weekly by the Williamsport Division to keep employees informed of changes, events, and other things the Company deemed necessary for a well-balanced work force. "Oscar, we made the front page!" he announced. The article, titled "Engineman Makes Outstanding Run," listed all the crew members, the extra engine number, the time of departure, and the arrival time at the tower controlling the east end of the Lock Haven yard, all of which made it clear that the person who wrote it had gotten his information from the dispatcher's office. Running time too was mentioned, citing the fact that Engineer Orr had made this trip of nearly 60 miles nonstop in exactly one hour and eleven minutes. The last paragraph of the article carried comments by the division superintendent praising the crew and Engineer Orr for their excellent performance. It also noted that the superintendent had personally reviewed Engineman Orr's records, found that O.P. had a perfect safety record, and, after consulting with colleagues, that this was just an example of how he normally handled his trains. "If other engineers would take note of this fine run and follow suit," the superintendent declared, "it would greatly expedite the transportation of vital wartime materials." No reference was made to the different ideas the Elmira Division official had about how the railroad should be operated. Although O.P. lost a half-month's pay, he considered the whole incident a moral victory.

In mid-December 1917, the government, supposedly to facilitate the movement of urgently needed wartime supplies, took over railroad operations under the U.S. Railroad Administration (USRA). Initially, there was little change in the ways railroads were run; trips were the same, engines were the same, and even management personnel was the same. One aspect of the new operation that met with workers' approval was the wage increases, but then also, soon after the USRA assumed control, the practice of assigning a specific engine to an individual engineer was abolished. That did not meet with O.P.'s approval. Now, instead of leaving on a run with a locomotive he knew was personally cared for and capable of making the trip, he could get any engine on the ready track suited for his immediate requirement.

The selection of the engine required a bit of coordination between the engine-house foreman and yard office personnel and caused him no small amount of consternation, especially at the Lock Haven terminal. Middle Division crews were bringing in decrepit H6b's and the even older H6a's, and engines under this exchange program eventually ended up assigned to the Ralston terminal. O.P. found that these 2-8-0's were in poor mechanical condition and showed other indications of neglect: gauges were encrusted with dirt, making it difficult to read their indications; windows were so dirty they obstructed the view; even headlight reflectors were dull, emitting less than adequate light. Until the USRA took control, it seemed that even though the Company was taxed in meeting wartime movements, they were keeping things rolling on a fairly even keel. Under the new regime, however, the employees seemed to be displaying a certain amount of laxity now that they had a big crutch to lean on: if things weren't working properly, or if repairs lagged, it was all the government's fault.

Someone in the higher echelons must have noted that coal shipments were falling behind the demand, and to correct this situation newer, bigger H8 2-8-0 power started coming on the scene in the spring of 1918. Some screening must have occurred, for the locomotives assigned to this classified secondary division were of the H8a class, saturated steam-powered engines that had not received superheater treatment and that still had oil-type head-lights. But it was a far better engine than the H6b. Instead of hauling a train of thirty-five or so cars, this bigger Consolidation could handle fifty or more cars with ease.

O.P. liked these engines from the first one that he got in exchange. His previous concern, that this large 2-8-0 with a big boiler and higher driving wheels would be slippery, proved unfounded. A few tests showed that it would dig in under most conditions without a slip and that it rode well, steamed freely (easily enough that the fireman wasn't overworked), and ran fast. Even though it was equipped with 62-inch drivers, these larger wheels wouldn't generate any more speed than the smaller H6b's 56-inch wheels.

Perhaps the one feature incorporated on the H8's that appealed most to O.P. was the screw reverse mechanism, which allowed the engine to be set up under running conditions so the optimal amount of steam was transferred to the cylinders and on to the drivers. With the older Johnson Bar, one notch on the lever admitted too little steam in many cases, and two notches admit-ted too much. The newer engines eliminated another disadvantage of the Johnson Bar, which when used to control reverse motion, especially when parts became worn, was treacherous. Unlatching this lever when the engine was working hard could, without warning, cause the lever to lurch forward with such force that the unsuspecting engineer felt as if he was about to be hurled through the forward cab door.

The introduction of the H8a, with its power to haul trains with more cars and greater tonnage, eased coal deliveries to some extent, but it also created an unexpected problem. According to management's plan, loaded cars would not be held over. But trains of fifty or fifty-five loaded hoppers arriving off the Bald Eagle to be set off in the Lock Haven yards ready for the next phase of the journey to Ralston led to the discovery that the only power to move this train farther was an H6 class. Because that locomotive's hauling capacity was limited to about thirty-five cars, an extra switching move was needed, and fifteen or twenty cars needed to be held in the yard to be moved later. This imbalance could have been adjusted by double-heading H6's east, but they too were in short supply, as were extra crews to man them.

The only way officials operating this region could address this bottleneck and move the trains faster was to call crews out after the mandatory eight-hour rest period. They were also using engines to haul more tonnage than they were designed to haul, and the resulting slower movements and mechanical failures further complicated their problems. As conditions continued to worsen, the Lock Haven yards were becoming congested with loaded hoppers, and empties were far short of their delivery destinations. Using the discretion at their command, the USRA solved this problem by confiscating a number of new 2-8-0 Consolidations being built by Baldwin Locomotive Works for the Atchison, Topeka & Santa Fe Railway. The coming of these Santa Fe locomotives, much the same in many respects as the Pennsylvania Railroad's H8, balanced the power differential. The now smaller H6's slowly disappeared.

An addendum to operating rules instructed engine crews on the finer points of these foreign Consolidations, and one warning read: "Levels on indicating water bottles should not be permitted to go lower than the three-quarters full mark." The Baldwin-built Santa Fe locomotives had round-top conical boilers with rounded crown sheet, making water levels critical—a factor not as prevalent on the Pennsylvania's Belpaire boilers with a flatter crown sheet. O.P. wasn't concerned about this warning. He had found it impractical to sacrifice water and to run on lower water levels to make steam.

Under actual operating and train-handling conditions, the Santa Fe 2-8-0's proved to be less efficient than the well-worn H8's also being used, but the new engines had more-modern features that made them a pleasure to run. The superheater equipment made for a snappy response in train handling. Electric cab lights enhanced nighttime running. The electric headlight, which came on with just a flick of a switch, was a big improvement over ascending to the top of the smoke box to light an oil-type headlight. And O.P. liked the whistle, which emitted a passenger tone rather than the shrill, screeching sound that identified all the Company's freight locomotives.

Another feature incorporated in the Santa Fe locomotive's design proved to be extremely dangerous when it was activated at locations not acceptable for its operation. For example, a diker engineer was assigned one of these foreign engines at Lock Haven for the return trip to Ralston—his first trip aboard one of these strangers—and after pulling to the yard office to await his train crew's arrival, he began out of curiosity to examine the many different things within the cab.

Valve placement, he noticed, was different than on an H8, so to learn their function he began opening and closing the valves. When he tested one that was larger than the others, there was a tremendous roar and immediately the right side of the engine was enveloped in a cloud of steam. Looking out the cab window as the steam was clearing, he saw that what had been the glass-enclosed front of the yard office was now a gaping hole. All the window-panes were missing, as was most of the sash. Alighting and entering the building, he found that no one had sustained any injuries but that the office was in shambles. Papers, books, and other desk items were just piles of debris, and everything was wet. When the commotion calmed down, shop personnel determined that the engineer had opened a valve that was needed on loco-motives for western divisions of the Santa Fe to discharge alkali deposits found in desert water that fouled boiler interiors. The effect was much the same as blowing down a boiler under pressure. Not long after this incident came orders that under no circumstance was this particular valve to be oper-ated. Since no one was hurt, other crews regarded this untimely discharge as amusing, and the hapless diker engineer was the subject of their joshing.

The war in Europe raged on, and with a conscription law in effect a draft was made in mid-September 1918 for able-bodied men ages thirty-five to forty-six. O.P. fell into this category and presented himself at the designated time and place in Williamsport for the preinduction physical examination. He received the results of this exam in the mail, with a card that classified him as 1-A and instructions advising that when the call for his age-group came he should be prepared to leave. Adhering to Company rules, he notified the trainmaster at Ralston that he had been drafted and that when the next call was made he would be leaving with this contingent of men.

The trainmaster voiced his disapproval: "Oscar, you can forget about the 1-A card. As an engineer, the Company has it arranged with the draft boards to exempt you from military duty. I'll handle this with the local board." Without hesitation, O.P. rejected the offer, explaining that he had firsthand knowledge of the problems employees who had taken advantage of the exemption clause had: they always seemed to end up in conflict with draft boards due to such things as late filings or incorrect or not enough information. Also, other employees openly regarded those who received draft exemptions as slackers or draft dodgers.

The trainmaster countered this reasoning, though, still trying to persuade him to accept an exemption: "You'll find army life no bed of roses, and just like other engineers that have been drafted, you'll wind up in a railroad battalion running trains in France."

Again, O.P. did not accept this advice. "I know a little bit about army life," he said. "When I worked in Bellefonte before hiring on the railroad, I was in the National Guard for more than two years. I spent two summer encampments at Gettysburg, and during the hard-coal strike conducted by anthracite miners in 1902 I slept in a tent near Wilkes-Barre for three months while on active duty. If they need me to run trains in France, that's where I'm going." When the war ended in November 1918, though, O.P. was still waiting for his call. He never got to France.

In early fall 1918 the USRA hierarchy ruled that the Lock Haven turn-around by the dikers and Middle Division crews wasn't fulfilling its intended purpose, so once again these Ralston crews were run to and from the Tyrone terminal. Whether this move would mean that coal shipments would get to their destinations more efficiently was never determined. The war in Europe ended too soon after the change.

The end of World War I did not have an immediate effect on shipments, but by the end of 1918, and into 1919, a gradual slowdown took place as the economy returned to peacetime status. The demand for coal did not slack off. The diker crews continued to be called out after their eight-hour layover, but the easing off in transportation of other commodities began showing up in the condition of the engines they received. Middle Division crews were coming into Tyrone with renovated H8's that were then transferred to the Ralston runs. Most of these engines were equipped with superheaters and electric generators, indicating that they were being shifted from main-line use to make way for the L1 and I1 classes. Even the AT&SF (Atchison, Topeka & Santa Fe) Baldwin 2-8-0's, well-worn after their wartime service on the Pennsylvania, disappeared as they made their way back to their original destination on the AT&SF. The newer counterpart of the H8—the H9 class—would also on rare occasions be assigned to the diker crews. The H9, being a later-model Consolidation, had a larger, 25-inch bore cylinder that gave it more power, but it had an identical boiler.

In this postwar period, the H8's met the coal-hauling requirements of the Company. Performance-wise, O.P. found the H8 locomotives quite capable on this long haul. A fifty-car or better train could be moved with the same ease the H6's displayed with thirty-five cars. In comparison, however, both the H6 and the H8 classes had a common feature that restricted their efficiency: their tenders. The H8, because of its size, was hauling a larger, flat-sided tender than the H6, and it could carry enough coal to run the distance to Ralston without stopping to refuel at Linden or "borrowing" coal from a hopper car in the train. It was the water capacity of this tender that was in-adequate to supply this bigger-boiler engine. Out of necessity, water stops had to be made more often, resulting in slower running time. A series of clear blocks on the single-track mains of the Bald Eagle and Elmira divisions eased the problem, but these signals weren't presented often. Water stops were always present. Again, O.P. realized that if this was the way the Company chose to run the railroad, he, as an engineman, could do nothing but comply and run the engines assigned at the best of his ability.

Marking up for duty one day at the yard office in Tyrone in the later part of 1919, O.P. learned that he had been selected for an assignment that was different from his usual duties of just hauling trains. The crew clerk, upon handing over the orders, commented: "You must be something special, Oscar. The shops at Altoona checked on your calling time, and just a short time ago they sent an engine down for you to take out on the run to Ralston." At the engine house, sitting on the ready track, was a shiny H8 whose engine number matched the engine number on his orders. While the fireman checked out the cab, O.P. inspected the engine and found that everything appeared to be brand-new. The engine was even as clean as the H6's that were once his own assigned locomotives.

Completing the inspection and signing the engine-house report to indi-cate that he accepted the engine for road service, he climbed aboard. In the cab he was greeted by a gentleman clad in clean coveralls who introduced himself as a mechanical engineer from the Altoona test shop, accompanied by another man introduced as one of the lead machinists from this same shop. The engineer enlightened O.P. on the purpose of this engine and why he and his colleague were aboard. The consensus of the Motive Power Department, he explained, was that the H8 class of 2-8-0's could be revamped into an engine that was more powerful and more efficient, and that his department had been assigned to put this theory into practical usage. After studying var-ious improvements that could be made without completely rebuilding the existing engine, the department had concluded that modifying the valve motion and adjusting the controlling linkage would achieve that goal.

Before starting on this project, the 2-8-0 had been shopped for class repairs, to be refurbished to as near new as possible. The modifications had been made, and the engine tests on the stationary plant had proved that the locomotive could produce additional horsepower. Now the only test remaining was to actually place it in service with a tonnage train. After some discussion, the nearby segment of track from Tyrone to Ralston, with its diversified conditions, was ideally suited for this final test. Furthermore, the engineer added, they needed not only a qualified locomotive engineer but one also who was adept at handling an engine with a tonnage train. They had consulted the Williamsport Division's road foreman of engines, who had recommended Engineman O. P. Orr for this test run.

All that remained was to get the engine to Tyrone so that it would be available for service when the crew was called. The machinist would also accompany them on the run in case any mechanical adjustment was required along the way. As they backed from the ready track to the awaiting train, the engineer explained that normally he never made road trips but that in this case, given the amount of time already devoted to the project, he felt he should be present to personally observe his accomplishments. While waiting for a clear signal allowing them to depart, the engineer positioned himself on the seat box behind O.P. and, in an amiable bit of conversation, asked him if, other than running this engine on the test run, he could be approached to do another favor. At this he displayed a large manila folder and pulled out a sheet of paper that had printed on it "engine number, engine class, time of departure, stops made and for what purpose, approximate amount of coal used, approximate amount of water consumed, and mark-off time." At the bottom of the page was a blank space for comments. Almost apologetically he suggested that such actual data would help the department in future research projects. Keeping this log was voluntary though, and no compensation in wages would be provided. O.P. responded that he would consider it an honor to be allowed to assist in any phase of locomotive development.

Under motion, and starting to hit the grade out of Tyrone, O.P. had the H8 working hard, but not completely wide open. It seemed to respond with ample power at this setting and was issuing a sharp sound as the exhaust left the stack. About this time the engineer said: "I forgot to tell you that I want you to handle this engine the same way you would any other engine off the ready track. I'm not even going to offer any suggestions as to how this engine should be run. In fact, just forget I'm riding with you."

That still did not make O.P. comfortable with the unexpected assignment, but he followed instructions and showed no mercy on the 2-8-0 as they moved up the grade to Vail. Approaching the summit, he reasoned that, out of courtesy, the important passenger should be briefed on what was taking place. He pointed out that not too much regarding an engine's handling abilities could be determined from this initial leg of the trip because the pusher's effort compensated for any lack of power, but that this grade always gave him an idea how an engine steamed, and this H8 was steaming exceptionally well; the fireman didn't even work hard. From Vail, the next few miles to Milesburg, they would have a continuous downgrade, so nothing of any consequence performance-wise would be shown.

Reaching Milesburg, they had a siding stop and, once cleared, the first opportunity to find out what this souped-up Consolidation had to offer presented itself. Running at creek level, the train was picked up in a hurry, and for a short distance it was possible to set up to 50 miles an hour. When the Howard hill grade was encountered, O.P. began compensating by gradually screwing the reverse gear forward and opening the throttle wider until almost maximum power was being used. It pleased him to find the abundance of power this engine was producing. Nearing the top of the grade, he turned to the engineer and told him that this probably was about the best test this run could offer, adding, "This is one of the best H8's I've ever had. Usually coming up this hill you drop back to around 20 miles an hour, but right now we're making better than 30 miles an hour."

Just after offering this compliment, they entered a slight "S" curve, and all hell broke loose. The engine seemed to be seized by a violent convulsion, shuddering and banging, and everything under the boiler hammering. Fire was belching out the stack, and smoke and soot were being forced out the fire door. Before the engine could be shut off, the reverse segment of the curve was rounded, and as suddenly as things went awry everything settled down. Even the engine resumed its normal exhaust.

They made an emergency stop, and the first examination found that not much of a fire remained in the firebox. Dropping off, the machinist, the engineer, and O.P. made a thorough check of the running gear. Nothing was loose, and nothing in the assembly was broken or out of shape. Discussing what had happened, they all decided that the engine, working under nearly full throttle and reverse gear almost fully forward, had gone out of square when the curve was entered, causing the cylinders to work in opposition to each other, and that the shift of the boiler as the curve was reversed corrected what had gone amiss in the linkage controlling the valves.

Since there was no damage other than to the fire, they resolved to continue the trip based on their analysis. The downgrade through Howard would allow the fireman ample time to get the fire back in shape, and they would be closer to Lock Haven if they needed help. Beyond Howard, the line was mostly level and straight—an easy piece of track. Furthermore, they concluded, if they had had a breakdown at the crest of this grade the railroad would have been tied up.

Resuming the trip, they drifted through Howard and found the H8 to be running like a precision watch the rest of the run to Lock Haven. As they were coming off the Bald Eagle, the tower presented a clear signal to enter the Williamsport Division's main. Occupying the main, the first order of business was to take water, but foremost in the mechanical engineer's mind was the need to decide whether to continue or ask for a replacement engine from the Lock Haven engine house. The engineer did not make the decision. Instead, he posed this question to Orr: "If I wasn't along, would you take this engine the rest of the way to Ralston?" O.P. assured him that he wouldn't have any doubts about using this locomotive, and that evidently was the answer the engineer wanted. He granted permission to proceed.

On the double-track river-level main, with ample distance between blocks, a fair test was made of the ability of the H8 to handle a heavy train at sustained running speeds. Approaching nearly 50 miles an hour, the 2-8-0 was set up to maintain this output. Keeping the engineer posted on what was taking place, O.P. further advised him that although more speed could be developed he wasn't going to go any faster, because of the previous mishap. That would be pressing their luck. To substantiate his remarks, he showed the engineer that there were still several notches remaining on the throttle to provide more steam to the drivers, and that the screw reverse was backed off toward center. He also noted that the engine's pop valves were singing under a full head of steam, remarking: "This engine could easily be set up to run at 60 miles an hour, plus the way it's handling with all the tonnage a regular H8 could haul, ten more cars could be added and there wouldn't be any problem moving this increased load." They covered the double-track section to Linden in fine shape. The 2-8-0 wasn't shut down until the single-track section leading to Newberry Junction was crossed and they entered the dike. The last leg of the run to Ralston with a pusher wasn't a test for the H8, but it continued to do its intended chore better than any engine O.P. had ever operated.

Reaching Ralston and setting off the train, the H8 was placed on the pit track. All that was left to complete this test run was to fill in the mark-off time on the log sheet. Attending to this last entry, O.P. was advised by the engineer that it wouldn't be necessary to file any comments. He had witnessed how the locomotive was handled, and he appreciated all the explanations that allowed him to know exactly what the conditions were as the trip progressed. The engineer parted, saying, "This engine performed better than I had expected, but because a flaw exists somewhere in the valve linkage, I'm going to arrange to have it towed back to the shops. We'll make more adjustments and conduct another test run. You can be sure you will be given this assignment." Naturally O.P. was proud to have been selected to handle the test run of this modified super H8, and offered that he was always willing to assist in any future developments.

One thing about this incident bothered O.P. It didn't make good common sense for the Company to be spending time and money on an engine class that was already outmoded. The vast fleet of the L1s class of locomotives had been built and was in daily use over much of the railroad's entire system. Also, a large number of huge 2-10-0 class I1's were in use, and plans for constructing hundreds more of this type had been announced. As the weeks went by, O.P. carefully read bulletins and other news reports, seeking some indication that work was being conducted to modify the H8 class into a more efficient and powerful locomotive. But there were no reports of modifications, nor did an H8 with that particular number ever show up for additional testing. In fact, O.P. never saw an engine carrying that number anywhere along the line. This led him to reason that some of the officials in the Motive Power Department came up with the same logic, and the project was shelved. Although this engine was definitely a superior H8, it probably met the same fate as many of its sisters in this class: having a new set of cylinders attached, and being renumbered and classified as an H9 or the later-still model H10 class.

O.P. considered being chosen to run an experimental engine only part of his duty, and something that any Company qualified engineman could be asked to do. But the manila folder the crew clerk at Tyrone handed him contained instructions to complete the enclosed log sheet and also to provide his own evaluation of the performance of the assigned H8, both with a loaded train to Ralston and on the return trip to Tyrone with empties. The Engineering Department would appreciate these comments, the memo said.

The 2-8-0 that O.P. received turned out to be just an ordinary, well-worn engine that had been in service for some time. Nothing unusual transpired on the round-trip, and he dutifully filled out the sheet with data relating to the run and turned in his comments. It was an opportunity finally to address someone with authority about something that had bothered him for years: the tender was inadequate to accommodate the locomotive's boiler requirements, and not enough water could be stored in the small tank, which necessitated frequent, costly, and time-consuming water stops.

The Engineering Department was apparently collecting an entire file on the H8 class, because from time to time O.P. would be presented with the now-familiar manila folder. On one occasion he was even assigned an H9 to evaluate. However, he was concerned that he never got any special instructions with these requests for his evaluation, and he never learned what happened to the reports after they reached the Engineering Department. Regardless of their final disposition, though, his evaluations tended to present a positive picture of an engine's performance in handling trains over that section of the railroad. As O.P. studied the sheets, he was amazed at how clearly they established things that he had been aware of but had never actually taken the time to prove.

One factor that stood out, though: the efficiency of a locomotive was affected by starts and stops. Taking a siding was not just a one-stop movement. Instead, it required one or two stops—and, of necessity, two starts. To enter a siding, a stop would be made while the brakeman threw the switch, unless at a tower where the operator controlled the switch. To continue onto the siding track the train again had to be started. At the opposite end of the siding another stop was necessary. Once cleared to occupy the main again, another start had to be made. The more stops made, the more coal and water the locomotive consumed. A review of his log also revealed that water especially was depleted rapidly, requiring yet additional stops to replenish that necessity. This stopping in turn increased the amount of coal consumed.

Filling out these log sheets nonetheless provided O.P. with insights into how the many and varied conditions that arose on a trip affected not only an engine's performance but also the time picture. On most runs, more time was spent in sidings or awaiting meets than in moving the train to its destination. In every respect, keeping these records was worthwhile and a learning experience.

CHAPTER FOUR | CHANGES DURING THE ROARING TWENTIES

At the start of the Roaring Twenties, the postwar demand for coal remained high. Diker crews were busily engaged hauling this important form of fuel. Short layovers were the pattern at both Ralston and Tyrone. In effect, they were making money, plus they continued to help fill the Company's coffer. In 1921, after the USRA relinquished control of the railroads and economic conditions slowed, a shift in motive power became apparent. More and more of the L1s-class engines were coming into Tyrone off the Middle Division. Nothing was out of the ordinary when O.P. marked up at the Tyrone yard office, and the crew clerk handed him a manila folder, but the comments that accompanied it were different: "Oscar, I believe you have something on the Engineering Department. They sent down an engine with orders to assign it to your crew. It's a dandy too. Looks like it just came out of the shop. I'm sure you're going to be pleased with this one."

On the ready track at the engine house sat the described locomotive, and it *was* pleasing to behold. An L1s 2-8-2 always looked good, and better yet when polished. After the preliminaries were conducted, O.P. climbed aboard and entered a cab much smaller than the ones carried by the previous H classes. It only had single cab windows, but one of the most noticeable differences was the absence of the elevated platforms for the seat boxes. On this engine, the seat boxes were flush-mounted on the deck. Accustomed to roomy cabs, O.P. thought this cab crammed too much into a small space, but once he was seated and under motion, the smaller space seemed to be more convenient, at least in relation to the placement of the controls.

When the clear block to leave the yards was presented, there was no trouble starting a heavy train of more than seventy cars. The heavy train picked up easily as they left Tyrone on this bright summer morning, gaining enough speed that the big 2-8-2 could be set back, on reverse gear and throttle, allowing the pusher to assume its intended role. As the grade increased, O.P. proceeded to again open the engine up, and with the valve motion nearly full forward in the "company notch," it was still providing an unbelievable amount of power.

It soon became apparent that this locomotive was capable of burning coal at a rapid rate. Before reaching the summit at Vail, the fireman was struggling to get a sufficient amount of coal into the large firebox with his scoop shovel, and the steam gauge began to show that. Steam was being used faster than it could be generated, so O.P. cut back on his settings and still had plenty of power to crest the grade faster than it was possible to do with an H8. He recalled something he had picked up soon after hiring on the railroad: if an engineer failed to set up an engine properly under running conditions, it could in the long run be very difficult for the fireman. O.P. always tried to avoid abusing his fireman, but this L1 was demonstrating that there might now be situations that would be difficult to control: it used steam faster than hand-firing could produce it.

Dropping down the grade from Vail to Milesburg revealed that this engine had riding qualities like a seat in a passenger coach. While being held at Milesburg as usual, O.P. informed his fireman that another test of the 2-8-2 was in order once they hit the Howard grade. Blasting out of Milesburg with a full head of steam, the heavy train was soon moving at a rate of speed that allowed setting back on the amount of steam used, making firing easier and providing time to bring the pop valves up and singing. As they approached the grade, the throttle was set to give the locomotive more steam, and the screw reverse gear was moved farther forward to compensate for the need for more power. And as they continued up the grade, final valve adjustments were made to full forward, allowing the engine to produce the amount of power it was designed to exert. Again it became apparent that it was physically impossible for a fireman to satisfy the needs of the large firebox with a scoop shovel. But even though that made it necessary to cut back on the settings, the L1 continued to haul the train up and over the crest of the grade with ease.

While awaiting a clear block to enter the Williamsport Division main at Lock Haven, O.P. checked the water and found that he had used more than half a tank coming down this 21-mile section of the Bald Eagle. The L1's were equipped with the same size tenders that the H8's and H9's hauled, except for small raised sides on the coal bunker, and it was not hard to determine that they were inadequate to supply the needs of this big-boilered locomotive. On the main heading for Williamsport, the 2-8-2 picked up the heavy train, and in a short time it was accelerated to more than 50 miles an hour. It easily maintained this speed with a setting on the valve motion well back toward center, plus it continued to steam freely in this cut-back position. This running condition did not reduce its ability to burn coal to any great degree, and the fireman was busy shoveling to keep steam up, not spending much time on the seat box admiring the scenery as it rolled by. However, on this leg of the journey the brakeman relieved the fireman, giving him a well-earned breather. While on his break, the fireman pulled the slides in the tender, which held the coal in a full tender so all of it wouldn't fall forward, to allow coal to come within the range of his shovel. Enough coal remained to complete the trip to Ralston, but rather than deplete the supply to the point where double work would be required—shoveling it forward to within the fireman's reach, then shoveling it into the firebox—they made a refueling stop at Linden.

Under motion after leaving the dike and on the Elmira Division main, O.P. relinquished his seat, allowing the fireman to handle the engine while he gained firsthand knowledge of what was entailed in firing an L1. The last stop before reaching their destination was made at Marsh Hill's Bergen Tower, to await a late meet to enter the siding. From this point, O.P. took over the controls and, as required, gave his whistle signal when he approached the south end of Ralston to notify the operator he was ready to enter the yards.

Crossing the bridge over Lycoming Creek that served as the entrance to Ralston, the fireman suddenly shouted across the cab, "Oscar, I wonder what's going on. It looks like all the people in town are out." Unable to look until he was in the siding, O.P. crossed the deck for a quick glimpse to see what the fireman was hollering about. A throng of people lined the street parallel to the tracks, and a large crowd was gathered at the station. All that was missing was a brass band. His only thought was that perhaps on this summer afternoon the townspeople had assembled to greet a circus train.

But that wasn't the reason all the people were gathered, and when he marked off at the yard office he learned why. After he had left the dike, and as each block was passed on the way up the Elmira Division, the operator relayed the message to the operator farther on that Oscar Orr was heading up the valley with a brand-new engine, one of the largest the Company used in freight service, and it really was something to behold. When the station operator at Ralston got this message, he inadvertently passed on the information, and by word of mouth it circulated rapidly throughout the town. Curiosity, and the fact that the town was centered on railroad activities, drew the large crowd. The arrival also provided a different kind of excitement on an otherwise normal Saturday afternoon. It was not every day that a new locomotive came to this terminal.

On the return trip to Tyrone, O.P. could perform more tests on the L1 with a string of empties than he could coming into Ralston with a loaded train. He found that it would steam easily no matter what the valve settings were. It could reach a speed of 60 miles an hour, possibly even more, and if forced to slow down it could pick up the train with rapid acceleration to resume running speed. However, even with this train of much less tonnage, the valve and throttle settings had to be made carefully, to allow the fireman to keep the firebox satisfied.

After the big 2-8-2 was put to rest on the pit track in Tyrone, O.P. finished filling out the log sheets, and for his own information he carefully reviewed his notes relating to this round-trip. Fifteen tons of coal (approximately) were used going to Ralston, and on the return trip approximately 12 tons were burned. This, he determined, was quite an amount of coal for one man to put into the firebox with a scoop shovel. Compared with an H8, he had made an extra stop for water each way, and a refueling stop had been required at Linden.

Under the section reserved for comments, O.P. described his personal findings pertaining to the L1's performance, noting without reservation that it was an excellent steam engine. The tonnage train eastbound had been handled without any complications; it steamed freely, it could easily run at allowable freight-train speeds, and it rode even better than he had ever experienced on a locomotive. He also mentioned the shortcomings of the L1: the size of the firebox made it physically impossible to hand-fire this locomotive and use it to its full potential; only brief periods of full throttle and wide-open valve gear could be used; and coal could not be fed rapidly enough with a scoop shovel to keep steam up. To compensate, it was necessary to reduce settings, resulting in a sacrifice of power and hampering the engine's efficiency. As always, he pointed out that the size of the tender was inadequate, necessitating frequent water stops and a coal stop. These stops compounded the use of coal and water, increasing operational costs and adding to the time it took to reach the designated terminal.

O.P.'s report was submitted, but as in the case of all other reports turned in, he never received a reply. Whether or not the Engineering and Motive Power Departments reviewed O.P.'s findings, the H8's and H9's were shifted to other assignments soon after this trial run. L1's coming in to Tyrone off the Middle Division were transferred to the diker crews and before long became the engines hauling the coal trains. The reign of the H8 and H9 lasted only three years, and during that period the sister class H10's never made an appearance on these Central Pennsylvania runs.

The big 2-8-2's readily met with the approval of the engine crews, but a comment O.P. made in his report began to be echoed by the firemen. Their initial trips on the L1's with the heavy-tonnage trains had given them an example of what to expect, now that this class of engine was designated as the prime hauler for diker runs. They were finding that when the engineer or brakeman shared the firing chores it was possible to cope with the demands for steam this engine could make, but that was not always possible. Engineers did what their title authorized: ran the engine; firing had been their job only before they became engineers. Brakemen too did not always lend a helping hand; some didn't have firing experience, others flatly refused to assist with the firing.

Other than the lack of assistance on these long runs, if an engineer had no compassion for the woes of a fireman and abused the L1's with improper throttle and valve settings, conditions would make it impossible for the fireman to endure. Frequent near steam failures became commonplace, and occasionally full steam failures occurred. A steam failure occurs when the firebox cannot burn hot enough over a period of time to produce the steam the locomotive is using to keep itself moving. When steam drops to a certain boiler pressure, the air pumps stop, forcing the locomotive to stop. Many factors can cause this failure, such as poor-quality coal, overfiring and plugging the firebox arch, and using more steam than the boiler can produce through improper throttle and valve settings.

The many adverse conditions under which firemen did their firing on this big locomotive over the undulating rails between Ralston and Tyrone soon brought out bitter complaints. Some firemen even threatened to refuse a call if the assigned engine was an L1. In order to relieve the plight of their members, the Brotherhood of Locomotive Engineers and Firemen, joined by their counterpart, the Brotherhood of Locomotive Engineers, entered the picture. These powerful unions gave the Company an ultimatum. If the L1 locomotive was not equipped with a stoker when used on the Ralston and Tyrone run, their members would refuse to use this class of engine; in other words, they would initiate a local strike.

The Company listened to the Brotherhoods' demand but flatly refused to install mechanical stokers, stating that a practical mechanical device of this nature, and one applicable to the L1, was not available. The Company did acknowledge that a problem existed on the particular run when the 2-8-2 was used, and to appease the Brotherhoods the Company agreed to assign two firemen to handle the firing chores. But there was little logic in that agreement. Two firemen would ease the burden of firing the locomotive, but O.P. still contended that the L1 could not operate at full efficiency when coal had to be placed in the large firebox by means of the scoop-shovel method. It also was difficult to understand the reasoning of officials in the Motive Power and Engineering Departments when they continued to limit the fine L1's capabilities. They had designed an outstanding engine, and without a doubt someone on their staff possessed sufficient knowledge to design a workable mechanical stoker. It seemed to Orr that the consensus, especially in that day and age, was that the stoker was nothing but a troublesome gadget.

The use of two firemen on the Ralston-Tyrone round-trips worked to everyone's satisfaction; perhaps the engineers became better acquainted with the L1, or maybe the firemen developed more endurance. This practice lasted for only a relatively short period, though. In less than a year, the Company came up with another plan to present to the Brotherhoods: they would shorten the trains and reduce the tonnage on this run, reverting to the single fireman on the engine crews. To the dismay of the firemen, the Brotherhoods agreed to this arrangement. Reduced tonnage improved running conditions, but the Company was not about to relinquish the hauling capabilities of this engine. As time went on, additional cars were added, and soon trains were being made up to consist of the maximum tonnage an L1 could haul on this route.

The Company came up with another change in 1921: they merged the Elmira Division into the Williamsport Division and reclassified it as the Elmira Branch. When this merger proposal was announced, the Brotherhoods were not caught off guard; the Elmira Division crew members were protected by an important clause that gave all Elmira crew members hired before the effective date of this merger seniority over Williamsport Division crews on the Elmira Branch segment. At first O.P. didn't regard this as a significant move, but years later he learned that the seniority clause affected job selections.

Entering 1922, diker crews were still kept busy hauling coal until the summer months rolled around, at which time the demand for coal dropped and the crews began experiencing longer layovers at both terminals. Even the Engineering Department slacked off. O.P. hadn't received a manila folder in the past few months and was beginning to think that they no longer were interested in his contributions.

Idle time as the result of longer layovers prompted another bit of activity in the Orr family. O.P. and his wife decided that instead of renting they wanted to purchase a home of their own. In no great hurry to make a selection, they examined several properties before making a decision. The house that met their approval was a large, thirteen-room, three-story structure that had been built and occupied by a former mine superintendent and a state representative. It was located on an acre of land on the westside hill overlooking the town and railroad facilities. One of its best features was a spring-fed water supply that provided for indoor plumbing, something few other houses in town had to offer.

Before moving in, another improvement was added: the house was wired to accommodate electrical power supplied by the town's new power plant. Further enhancing the purchase was that no encumbrance was necessary; the Orrs had accumulated enough in savings during the recently concluded war and the boom period that followed to make a cash settlement. As a property owner, O.P. now was a permanent resident of Ralston, a status he regarded with pride.

In the early months of 1923, Middle Division crews began to bring their trains into Tyrone headed by the enormous 2-10-0 I1s-class locomotive. Not all the crews were using this class of engine, nor was it assigned to any of the diker crews. The coming of the 2-10-0 class engine coincided with the Pennsylvania Railroad's previous public announcement that a large order for this type of locomotive had been placed with the Baldwin Locomotive Works, and that it was to become the Company's prime freight hauler. When the opportunity presented itself, O.P., in informal discussions, queried Middle Division engine crews about the characteristics of the I1. All agreed that it was a superpowerful engine but not a particularly good steamer. In fact, all engines seemed to differ where steaming qualities were concerned and were sluggish getting a train over the road due to their slow speed. All the men he talked to had one common complaint, that the I1 rode rougher than a lumber wagon without springs.

Late one spring afternoon, after receiving a call, O.P. was marking up as usual for a return trip to Ralston. This time, however, in addition to receiving orders from the crew clerk, he was given a familiar manila folder, the clerk commenting, "You're getting a brand-new big one today, Oscar. They sent an I1 in with orders that it be assigned to your crew for a round-trip." After taking care of the routine preliminaries at the engine house, O.P. climbed aboard that monstrous-looking piece of machinery. He noticed that although it had the same size cab as the L1, it was more cramped. The large duplex stoker barrel and the brake valves pedestal made it necessary to squeeze to get to the seat box. Another noticeable difference in the cab was the absence of the screw reverse gear wheel, which had been replaced with a reversing lever mounted on a quadrant—in retrospect, a Johnson Bar in miniature. Air-activated, this method of controlling valve motion was simple in principle. In fact, O.P. often described it as a throwback to the earlier valve motions, when one notch was not enough and two notches were too much. If the Engineering Department could design this assistance to provide reversing, why couldn't they devise a mechanism and apply it to the screw principle?

Before leaving the yard, O.P.'s conductor came forward and exclaimed, "Oscar, we have over ninety cars in the train you're coupled to. Is it possible this engine can handle that much tonnage?" O.P. could provide no assurances, but he knew it would be an interesting challenge hauling as many cars in one train as it would have taken three H6's to haul only six years ago.

What concerned him most about this locomotive was the stoker firing mechanism. Neither he nor his fireman had ever been on an engine so equipped. According to the manuals and word of mouth by the men who had fired with a stoker, it was advisable for the fireman to place his heels (that is, a built-up amount of coal), one along each side of the firebox and one to the rear with the scoop shovel. When the engine was being worked, the fire in the middle of the firebox should be maintained with as light a mass of coal as possible to support combustion, the explosive effect that took place when fine coal was sprayed into this chamber. Most of the coal was burned before it dropped onto the fire if the stoker was properly set, and the residue went out the stack in the form of cinders.

The fireman was following these instructions, and the locomotive's steam gauge was holding at nearly 250 pounds as they started up the grade out of Tyrone. One thing O.P. noted was that it continually belched nothing but black smoke from the stack. Hand-fired engines would do this when starting, but once under motion they would begin emitting gray smoke. This unusual smoke worried O.P., so he kept a watch on the fire through the sight hole. Appearances to the contrary, everything seemed to be in fine shape. Even as hard as he was crowding the I1 the entire way up the grade, it did not cause any fluctuations on the steam gauge.

Just as they neared the crest, and the tower at Vail came into view, the steam pressure started to drop. Alarmed at this abrupt change in pressure, O.P. reflected on some advice a Middle Division fireman once gave him: if the stoker motor was operated too fast and the air jets were set too high, these factors, combined with the exceptionally strong draft the I1 produced when worked hard, caused an excessive amount of coal to be placed in the front section of the firebox. As a result, the arch would become plugged with unburned green coal and cause a steam failure.

O.P. immediately got off the seat box and opened the fire door for a closer inspection. Sure enough, the arch was nearly plugged, but not to the point that it was completely sealed off. It was still allowing a portion of the draft to pass by. Rectifying this unexpected dilemma, and still facing getting the train over the summit without stalling, allowed no time for an incorrect decision. Instructing the fireman to shut off the stoker, open the blower wide, and start shoveling coal to the center and sides of the firebox, he reasoned that, if they were lucky, steam could be maintained to get them over the top. This was the correct method. The steam gauge even rose a trifle before they started the downhill run to Milesburg. But the fireman still had to contend with the mass of unburned coal blocking the front of the combustion chamber. The blower helped burn off a small amount of this constriction, but he was left with no alternative but to use the long two-pronged hook to rake or break it into pieces.

Assisting the fireman, the brakeman manned the grate shaker bar, dropping the residue and clinkers into the ash pan. The rake could only be used for a short time, though, as the inferno in the firebox acted as a forge, heating the long rod to the point of melting. After a session of raking and pounding, the fireman, while the instrument was cooling, expressed his distaste for the chore: "Oscar, that coal up front is harder than concrete. I'm having a helluva time busting it up. I haven't worked this hard in a long time, and if this is what a stoker does for you, I'm sure I'm not going to like it."

Satisfied that the problem of producing steam had been resolved, O.P. began concentrating on learning what other characteristics this locomotive was demonstrating on the drift down the Bald Eagle. One of the most noticeable features was the noise the rods that connected the ten driving wheels made when no force was being applied to them from the cylinder and main rod. It gave the impression they were about to break loose at any moment. The quality of the ride confirmed the testimony of the Middle Division men: the big 2-10-0 not only bounced up and down, but also exhibited a pronounced lateral motion. To the men riding in the small cab at the extreme end of this huge boiler, these sideways movements were sudden, and the shifting added nothing but more misery to the rough ride the I1 was demonstrating.

After stopping at Milesburg as usual to take water, it was evident that water consumption was another attribute. More than half a tank had been consumed since leaving Tyrone. While waiting for the clear block permission to leave, O.P. and the fireman discussed using the stoker on the next leg of the run to Lock Haven and decided to use it more sparingly. Furthermore, they planned to keep an eye on what was going on in the firebox by opening the fire door more often for closer inspections.

Starting the heavy train seemed easy enough, and some speed was gained before they entered the grade on the Howard hill. Once into this grade, O.P. began putting the I1 to test, and found the power it was exerting was amazing. It wasn't pounding up hill as fast as the L1 class, but he was dragging nearly one-third more tonnage than the 2-8-2 could handle. No problem was encountered with the stoker either. In fact, before they reached the top, and under wide-open working conditions, the pop came up, proving that the locomotive was capable of producing steam.

Over the hill and descending into Howard, the I1, as expected, continued to issue pounding rod noise while drifting. Riding conditions were still exceptionally rough. Approaching Howard, the semaphore showed clear, but orders handed on prevented releasing the brakes for a running start to test what this engine could do handling a train on level track; another eastbound movement occupied the same block, and a proceed with caution to Lock Haven order ruled out this speed test. Cleared coming off the Bald Eagle at Lock Haven, and occupying the Williamsport main, O.P. made another water stop. More than a half a tank had been used on the leg from Milesburg, a good indication that the I1 had an appetite for water.

Orders received at Lock Haven allowed him to run clear to Linden, and, except for the Jersey Shore hill, level track would permit enough miles for the speed test. As O.P. started his train after taking water, the 2-10-0 again showed that it had been designed to produce power. Valve motion was set full forward, and with the throttle almost wide open he easily gained speed enough to start throttling back as the I1 picked up its tonnage. It blasted along almost to perfection until it reached approximately 25 miles an hour, at which speed it suddenly became sluggish. Running at cut-back settings, the steam gauge started to drop, requiring adjustment to a more forward valve setting to produce more drafting. Opening the throttle wider, O.P. was finally able to get rolling a little faster. No matter what the settings, however, he was unable to coax this engine much above 30 miles an hour. It seemed that it was controlled by a "governor" (a device that limits how fast an engine can operate), and this was the top speed.

Between Lock Haven and Linden, the slides on the tender were pulled, making a coal stop mandatory. While the fuel was being replenished, it was determined that on this leg of about 25 miles another half-tank of water had gone through the boiler. From this point, the trip to Ralston was routine. But even with the pusher attached on the Elmira Branch portion, the I1 failed to show any signs of being able to run at more than 30 miles an hour.

After the trip was over and the I1 was on the pit track, O.P. made one more inspection of the water level in the tender and found that he had used almost three-quarters of a tank on the last leg of the run from Linden. Reviewing his records, he calculated that on this 115-mile trip his locomotive had used 27,000 gallons of water and 18 tons of coal, and that the time required to haul this train of more than 4,500 tons was just over thirteen hours. About the only good thing about bringing this monster 2-10-0 into Ralston was that O.P. arrived in the early morning hours, so throngs of townspeople were not gathered to see the arrival of what he now was considering a poorly designed example of a steam locomotive. Not a proud arrival, as it had been with the L1.

On the return trip to Tyrone, O.P. reasoned as he left Ralston that the heavy tonnage might have been what kept the I1 from developing speed. Downgrade all the way to Newberry Junction, and on the level tracks to Lock Haven, he jockeyed valve and throttle positions, attempting to build up speed with a string of empties. If he moved the reverse gear back toward center, the steam gauge would decline, just as it did hauling the tonnage train. The only speed that could be crowded out and still allow the engine to steam was almost full forward on the reverse lever and just under half throttle. Opening the throttle, even to the last notch, proved futile. The valves would only accept so much additional steam.

O.P. timed his progress as mileposts were passed, and the top speed was 34 miles an hour. As he finished recording the results of this return run to Tyrone, he noted that approximately 24,000 gallons of water had gone out the stack, and nearly 15 tons of coal were burned, plus the trip took more than twelve hours. In the comments space, O.P. cited that almost wide-open valve settings were needed to create draft to keep the engine steaming, whether with a loaded train or pulling empties. The engine would not take any steam beyond the halfway point on the quadrant when running and attempting to build up speed. This resulted in using an excessive amount of coal and water. The inability to operate at allowable freight speed made the I1 too sluggish for this particularly long run. And as usual, he added, the tender was grossly inadequate for the size of the engine it was attached to.

Elaborating further, O.P. explained that the I1 was able to move a train with the tonnage the huge locomotive was designed to haul from a start, and on all grades encountered it could lug down but still exert sufficient power, causing no problems in this category. Above the speed of 20 miles an hour, though, the engine became sluggish, and 34 miles an hour was the maximum speed it could develop on level track—and that was hauling empty cars of light tonnage. In order to generate steam for power, and what little speed it could attain, valve motion had to be set almost full forward. Running under this condition, which allowed no cutback, resulted in excessive consumption of water and fuel.

Turning the folder over to the crew clerk, O.P. was apprehensive that, as in the case of his test run of the L1's, regardless of his report, a shift would be made to the I1s class. This run had raised many questions. Foremost, and perhaps most basic, was why a railroad the size of the Pennsylvania, with the best engineering staff in the world, would design such a useless monstrosity. The Company, in previous locomotive designs, as they evolved, had placed an emphasis on power as well as on speed, even for locomotives to be used in freight service. Now, however, they were building a large number of engines with unlimited power, supposedly engines that could handle all the tonnage they could start—but after they got the train started they could only run at slow speeds. Another observation O.P. made about the I1s class he kept to himself: "The only good thing the Company really had going for itself when it constructed this engine was that the I1s was built when iron was cheap."

No I1's were transferred to the diker crews as O.P. had expected they would be, even though they continued to be used by the Middle Division crews, making their presence commonplace at the Tyrone terminal. Their eastern migration to this central region would not come until sometime in the future.

With everything back to normal after the test run, and with the L1's still in command of the coal-hauling assignments, O.P. again settled down to a routine. He was especially proud of, and enjoying, his new status as a property owner. Then, on May 20, 1923, his pride increased when he and his wife became the parents of a baby girl. To help celebrate the birth of his daughter, the speakeasies in town were opened to his fellow railroaders and townspeople alike.

The remainder of the year passed without any more memorable incidents. Through the winter months and into the spring of 1924, coal shipments were at normal levels, but as summer approached, demand for this product again dropped off. As a result, trips for the dikers slackened, and layovers of forty-eight hours or more were being spent at both Ralston and Tyrone terminals.

O.P. began scanning the bid sheets—the first time he'd had to since coming to Ralston in 1910. One job on the list involved different responsibilities: it was for someone to road-test and do break-in runs of engines that had undergone class repairs in the rebuilding shops located at Renovo. For many years the facility at Renovo had been used for rebuilding locomotives used by the Philadelphia & Erie segment of the railroad, covering the central regions and the numerous branch lines. Engines shopped there came from the Buffalo, Erie, Southport, and Williamsport areas. In conjunction with this service, Renovo also maintained a large car-rebuilding shop.

O.P. was the successful bidder and was awarded the job. The road test of these rebuilt locomotives directly out of the shop was a 58-mile round-trip to Lock Haven. Freight engines were scheduled to be operated at 45 miles an hour, passenger classes at 60 miles an hour. On every trip a machinist would be on board to adjust or fix any minor problems that might occur. O.P. discovered that the machinist came well equipped for this work, carrying a variety of tools, grease, and oil, plus a generous amount of "waste." A few test runs told O.P. the shop men did their jobs to perfection. It was rare to find a loose connection leaking, or bearings and journals heating. One thing he learned was that the shop men must have had an affinity for grease, for everything was covered with a generous amount of that substance—handrails, controls, seat box, windows, even the deck. It was impossible to avoid, and after a trip O.P.'s overclothes and gloves reflected that.

Testing wasn't done on a daily basis, but rather when two or three engines were out-shopped. O.P. would be given a twenty-four-hour notice when his services would be needed, with a time span of two or three days elapsing between calls. Once testing was completed, he returned to Ralston, so he had no layovers in Renovo. Every class of locomotive used went through this shop—except for the I1's, which were stabled at Altoona. Freight engines from the H6, H8, H9, L1, and even the odd F3c 2-6-0 classes were tested. The F3c class had escaped O.P.'s command up until this point. He often observed this engine type at Enola when he was firing out of Sunbury, but it was never used to any extent on the Williamsport Division, and now it was relegated to local freight work on branch lines. Running a light engine was not a true indication of how the engine would perform handling a train, but it did provide a feel for what its capabilities were under that condition.

In the twenty years he'd worked for the railroad, O.P. had been able to admire passenger engines as they passed, but the only passenger engines he'd worked aboard were the old D class on the pay-car train and the odd D11 Class P type used on the L&T Branch when he was firing. He had envisioned that, when set up as an engineer, he would be able to draw an occasional passenger run as an extra man, but assignment to the Williamsport yards, and the following placement to a diker crew in Ralston, had squelched that thought. Now, however, he was in a position to actually test all the passenger classes the Company had to offer. He experienced more than a small amount of satisfaction when a D16 American was on the line, and even more so when the E2 and subclasses E3 and E7 were present. These engines had once pulled limited trains as they crossed the Rockville Bridge, and their prestige was no less in O.P.'s mind, even though they had been relegated to lesser assignments. The larger Atlantic class E6 had a feature he had never found in any other locomotive he had handled. With the reverse gear screwed back almost to center, and with only a very few notches on the throttle, this engine could attain speeds that indicated it could really fly if it was opened up. Running with this cut-back setting, it produced steam, and did it with apparent ease.

Pacific classes too came out of the shops to be tested: K2's; the pride of the railroad, K4's; and the smaller-drivered modified K2 and K3. After having had the opportunity to operate almost all the classes of locomotives the Company had in use on over-the-road service, with the exception of a few odd models, test running, in a relatively short time, became just another routine job.

On the morning of October 7, 1924, while my father, O.P., was running a test engine, I made my arrival in Ralston, and on time. It wasn't until he detrained from the 8:00 P.M. passenger train that he received the news from my older sister that I had been born. The news that he had a son was reason enough to celebrate, but he had to proceed with caution. Twenty hours earlier he had left Ralston on the 12:01 A.M. passenger. He had tested two engines and was nearly exhausted. Stopping briefly at the hotel adjacent to the station, and treating the patrons on his good fortune, O.P. then proceeded up the hill home to be with his wife and new heir.

The Renovo job did not last too much longer. An engineer with more seniority who decided that he wanted to test engines bumped O.P. Reviewing the bid lists and other jobs available, O.P. decided that because the dikers were entering the winter season, a bump back on his old crew would be the most advantageous move at this time.

Winter quickly evolved into spring 1925, and before long the Company inaugurated a change. A low-grade freight line had been constructed, following the Bald Eagle Creek to bypass the Howard hill and the town of Howard. With this obstacle eliminated, and given the fine performance of the L1's on this run, it was decided to eliminate the Tyrone terminal. Dikers would now run through to East Altoona. When this new ruling went into effect, the engine crews expected a protest from the Brotherhoods, but there was none. There would still only be one fireman on this 125-mile trip.

On his first trip into the new territory, O.P. had a pilot guiding him over the four-track Middle Division main line into the complex of the East Altoona yards. Movements on the main were controlled in a more sophisticated manner. In addition to train orders being handed on by the operator at Tyrone, semaphores, overhead distant signals, and an array of pot signals at the entry to the yard were used to ensure that trains arrived at the correct destination. The pilot had to keep alert for the signals and, above all, when occupying the main line, run as fast as possible. The train dispatchers frowned on slow movements. O.P. always kept alert for signals, but it wasn't necessary to remind him to run fast; poking along was also something he frowned on. Although he had only 11 miles of main-line trackage to cover, that was a privilege he had always looked forward to, and in a sense he considered it an honor.

About the only thing Orr found undesirable about running in to Altoona was the bunkhouse, which served not only the Middle Division crews but also crews off the Pittsburgh and Williamsport Divisions. He complained to his conductor that, because of the overcrowding and the hubbub in the bunkhouse it was difficult for him to get enough rest, and that he might get a room in a private residence instead. The conductor came up with an unexpected solution. If it met with O.P.'s approval, he could use one of the bunks in the cabin, and also eat with him if he wanted, providing he contributed to supplying the food. This turned out to be a satisfactory arrangement: showers and restrooms were near where the cabin was stored; it was close to the shops; and it afforded a view of locomotives of every description, some that O.P. knew existed but had never actually seen.

One looked like a fine engine: the relatively new M1 class 4-8-2. Another stranger, the N1 and N2 class 2-10-2, looked at first glance somewhat like an I1 equipped with a trailing truck. Other odd features of the 2-10-2 N1's were the inverted, sloping-sided tenders and the words PENNSYLVANIA LINES painted on their sides instead of just PENNSYLVANIA. O.P. learned from local enginemen that a few N2-class engines would periodically be shopped to convert their fireboxes from the USRA-designed round-top type to the Company's standard Belpaire. The tenders had the same water capacity as the ones used on the L1 class on Lines West. The only difference was the built-up inverted coal bunker arrangement that increased the amount of fuel they could carry. The name used to describe this modification fit the area where they were used, the Midwest, and they had been dubbed "Prairie Schooners." The only road experience the crewmen could describe was west of Altoona, where on the hill to Gallitzin they were used as either snappers or pushers. The consensus was that they steamed well, were decent to ride on, and seemed to be powerful.

O.P.'s inquisitiveness almost led to trouble not long after he began running to this terminal at Altoona. Arriving late one night, he retired to the cabin without paying much attention to the types of locomotives that surrounded the shops. Upon arising, and after a leisurely breakfast with the conductor, he stepped out on the cabin's platform to survey the situation. An L1 under steam was setting close by, and an unusual attachment caught his eye. Mounted on the steam dome where the normal whistle would normally be affixed was a manifold pipe that contained not only one whistle but eight, all lined up in a row. Taking a closer look, he could see that no whistle cords were fastened to the whistle arms, and wanting to know how these whistles were activated, he decided to conduct an inspection.

Wandering over to the L1, he climbed aboard, and once in the cab he spotted a board mounted on the boiler backhead. On this board, push-button stations were attached, but no description of what they controlled was visible, other than "ON-OFF" markings on the buttons. That answered his question: the whistles were operated by an electrical solenoid. Not at all acquainted with this electrical system, but as long as "ON-OFF" could be determined to mean "either-or," O.P. decided to try one of the whistles to find out what kind of sound it would make. Selecting a button, he pushed it to "ON." After a momentary wait, not a sound came forth. Somewhat perplexed by the failure to produce a sound, he tried other buttons, and still nothing happened. Pondering his inability to activate the system, he reasoned that a manual valve on the line from the steam dome must be shut off, so he was about to leave well enough alone. He noticed, however, that one of the push buttons in an offset location still hadn't been tested, so without any more thought he pressed the "ON" side.

This simple gesture erupted into a deafening din that scared him out of his wits, and not knowing how he got things started, he didn't know how to stop the whistles from blowing. The immediate solution was to depart post-haste without attempting to correct the situation. He more or less vaulted off the L1, and just as he reached the sanctuary of the cabin's platform, shop men, engineers clad in coveralls, and officials clad in their symbolic well-worn suits and slouch hats came scurrying out of the shop from every direction. Someone in the crowd who knew how to operate the controlling mechanism shut off the whistles. Quiet once again prevailed.

As the people were reentering the shops, an official-looking person strode over to the cabin and said to O.P., "Did you see anyone monkeying around that engine?" Not about to incriminate himself, he answered in the negative: "I was in the cabin reading when all the noise started. I just came out to see what was going on." The official responded, "If we find out who pulled off this trick, he's going to be in big trouble."

Since the change of terminals, enough time had elapsed to convince O.P. that the Engineering Department had lost track of his whereabouts, even though he was running right out of their backyard. That assumption proved wrong, however, when he was presented with a manila folder at the yard office with instructions to evaluate the L1's performance on this extended run that passed Tyrone and went on into Altoona. The report after completing a round-trip indicated that the additional 11 miles resulted in a negligible additional amount of coal and water being consumed and that an additional hour of time was required. Most of the time was spent coming off the Middle Division main into Tyrone, where the tank was refilled, the pusher was attached, an air test was conducted, and a wait was required for a clear signal to leave this point. Apparently, one report failed to satisfy this department, so another report was requested on the same subject: time spent, amount of coal and water consumed, and so on. The results for this second trip were almost identical to the findings for the previous round-trip.

The folders kept arriving, and running records were compiled on foreign western 2-10-2 class N1's and N2's. Both those engines had slight differences in design but produced almost identical performance characteristics. On the round-trips to Ralston, each was assigned the same tonnage in a consist of eighty to eighty-five cars that carried approximately 4,000 tons. Abundant power could be exerted when starting the trains, but once under motion they were unable to attain sufficient speed for fast over-the-road movements. Attempting to run at a maximum speed of just over 30 miles an hour reduced their efficiency and resulted in consumption of an excessive amount of coal and water. On the positive side, the engines were good steamers and rode easily. In some comparisons they were similar to the I1's, sluggish handling their assignments.

The fact was that the Company now had more than 700 engines in the I1, N1, and N2 classes that were supposed to be modern freight locomotives. That bothered O.P., who wondered why so many had been built when in use they were just massive, worthless hunks of iron in use. Fortunately, none of the N1's or N2's was assigned to the diker crews. Some N2's did make it to the Williamsport roundhouse, where they served mostly on the Elmira Branch as pusher engines. O.P. still contended that the Company would have been further ahead if they had equipped the efficient L1's with stokers and larger tenders.

In 1926, O.P. succumbed to the use of the automobile as a means of conveyance. Before that he had little interest in this increasingly popular mode of transportation. His lack of interest, or perhaps some skepticism about driving a car, was due to an embarrassing happening on the family farm in 1915. Spending a brief vacation at home, he'd decided to take his father's new Model T for a drive while the family was attending a nearby social function.

He had been shown how to operate the new car, but he couldn't remember all the intricate details. Still, he knew how to get the motor started, so he put the vehicle in reverse and backed out of the barn onto the lane leading to the main highway. At this point, the Ford's pedal arrangement stymied him. Try as he might, no forward progress could be made; he could only go in reverse. In utter frustration, he shut the motor off, leaving the car in the middle of the lane. When the family returned, he had to explain his plight. Then his fifteen-year-old younger brother went out, started the motor, and, like an expert, drove the Model T to the barn. Good-natured chiding from the brother followed: an accomplished locomotive engineer surely should be able to drive a simple car, he stated.

Remembering this incident, O.P. shied away from buying a Ford controlled by foot pedals and bought a Dodge with a clutch-operated transmission. It was an enclosed sedan, robin's-egg blue with yellow wooden-spoked wheels. With operating instructions provided by the salesman and a little practice, he became adept at driving this new automobile. Seasons and road conditions restricted its use, though, because the highways into and out of Ralston were dirt, so from late fall until early spring the Dodge remained in the garage jacked up on blocks, with the battery in the cellar for safekeeping.

During 1926 and into 1927, O.P.'s Altoona-Ralston runs were routine, but occasional incidents broke the monotony. In the siding at the east end of the Bald Eagle Branch, before entering the Williamsport Division main at Lock Haven, O.P., while in the tower, spotted a man dressed in a suit climbing aboard his L1. The fireman and brakeman were on the engine, so he gave little thought to why this gentleman would be monkeying around. When the meet cleared, the operator gave Orr running orders to proceed to the main and O.P. said to the visitor, "I think you've seen enough by now. As soon as the signal shows clear, I'm leaving, so you'd better get off." This direct order didn't seem to bother the visitor. Instead, he presented his credentials and stated, "I'm the federal boiler inspector. You're not going to go until I tell you it's all right to leave." The clear block signal came up, but O.P. had to return to the tower and inform the operator that his orders should be nullified, that he couldn't leave until the government man had finished his inspection.

When O.P. returned to the cab, the inspector had just finished checking the water bottle. A thorough firebox inspection came next, and then the inspector removed some wrenches and a small machinist's hammer from a satchel much like one a physician would carry. The most important instrument was the hammer, and the inspector used it to gently tap every steam pipe in the cab, much to O.P.'s dismay. That accomplished, he dropped off and tapped his way completely around the engine, underneath the boiler, the smoke-box front, and what he could reach from both of the running boards.

Back in the cab, the inspector still had not uttered a word. He was evidently finished with his work, though, as he sat down on the fireman's seat and leisurely filled out a report sheet. The form completed, he gave a copy to O.P. with the instructions to present it to the engine-house foreman upon arrival at his terminal, not even bothering to ask where that might be located. As the inspector departed, a time check revealed the inspection had resulted in a time loss of more than an hour and a half. Then an additional half-hour was spent before clearance was obtained to occupy the main. This time loss was a direct result of O.P.'s usual practice of getting rolling as quickly as possible, and of a hasty and gruff command to the wrong individual to get off his engine.

Across innumerable miles, including numerous round-trips between Ralston and Tyrone, and now to Altoona, O.P. had never experienced a major breakdown en route other than minor problems that could easily be adjusted. That record held true not only with the L1's now in use to handle the dikers, but also for all the previous classes of locomotive he had used. The inevitable happened on an eastbound trip from Altoona to Ralston.

Running time for that trip was exceptionally good. There were no delays coming out of Altoona on the Middle Division, and in Tyrone the pusher was coupled on faster than usual. Then a clear block order was issued covering O.P.'s movement to Milesburg. At Milesburg another clear block was posted, and he was given clearance for the remaining distance on the Bald Eagle to Lock Haven. Near the end of the Howard freight low line, smoke began appearing from the right side pilot (pony) truck frame. Easing off, O.P. ran the short distance to the block tower, and even though a clear block was in position an inspection stop was made. Examination confirmed O.P.'s suspicions: the journal was running hot. Less than 10 miles separated him from Lock Haven, and if he could reach that point he could exchange this engine. As close as Lock Haven, and salvation, was, it was presently a million miles away as far as O.P. was concerned. The last thing he wanted was to pull into the available siding and waste time waiting for a replacement engine to rescue him. Mulling over his predicament, O.P. came up with a plan, and if the brakeman would cooperate he could take the L1, train included, into Lock Haven.

Nothing about his plan was complicated. The brakeman was to lie in a prone position on the pilot and occasionally pour oil on the ailing journal to keep it cool, and the brakeman agreed to do that. O.P. went to the tower to explain why he had stopped when a clear block was showing. When he told the operator that because of the hot journal they would have to proceed at a restricted speed to Lock Haven, he was told that he had sufficient time to reach this intersection, that no eastbound or westbound movements were in sight for at least two hours. While in the tower, he contacted the train dispatcher and asked that a replacement engine be available in Lock Haven so that he could continue the run without a lengthy delay. The locomotive he was presently using could not be expected to go any farther than that point or major mechanical damage would occur.

After making all these arrangements, O.P. once more got under way, running at about 20 miles an hour, and his plan seemed to be working well: the small amount of lubricant was doing its job. Near the halfway mark, however, about seventy car lengths past the Blanchard siding, things abruptly changed. He ran over a torpedo, a warning device that consisted of an explosive cap the size of a can of snuff tobacco fastened on the top of a rail with a lead strap, to explode when a rolling wheel passes over it. The torpedo exploded with a roar equal to the discharge of a small cannon. In seemingly one movement, the brakeman rose about a foot in the air, hurled the spouted oil can into the brush, and, seemingly in one movement, was on his feet. When a second torpedo exploded, he was starting up the step to the running board and, wasting no time, making his way forward to the cab. All of a sudden the cab was filled with unprintable utterances, ending with: "Oscar, if you want oil on that blankety-blank journal, you go out and put it on yourself." O.P. tried hard to keep from laughing at the man who had clearly been so frightened.

Although they had been running at a relatively slow speed, it would have been a mistake to stop to attempt to retrieve the lost oil can, and it soon became clear that the oil had succeeded in keeping the journal cool, for smoke was again appearing. As the train approached the west end of the siding at Mill Hall, enough smoke was pouring from the hot bearing to compel O.P. to instruct the brakeman to open the switch so an entry could be made when they stopped. To continue, knowing that such a condition existed, might cause a breakdown that would tie up this single-track main, or possibly a derailment.

Safely in the siding, they notified the operator at Lock Haven that they were unable to proceed and also called the dispatcher to let him know they'd been forced to stop short of the destination. The reply wasn't encouraging: "Oscar, I'll have to have an engine sent out, either from Renovo or Williamsport. The biggest-class engine Lock Haven has on hand is an H9." O.P. did some quick figuring: if an L1 was dispatched from either of the two locations, it would involve a wait of at least four hours. Opting against this wait, O.P. notified the dispatcher that he would take the H9 if that was permissible. After discussing whether that engine could handle the tonnage the train was carrying, it was resolved that an attempt should be made, with the H9. The dispatcher cautioned, "If you have problems with this locomotive, take the nearest siding and wait until an L1 can be sent out." Accepting the order, O.P. made one further request, that the operator at Antes Fort give him the passenger low-line because the only obstacle in his way was the Jersey Shore hill. The dispatcher agreed.

An hour and a half passed before the replacement engine arrived at Mill Hall, where the engine exchange took place, allowing the trip to the Ralston terminal to resume. Cleared to occupy the main, the H9 dug in, a smooth start was accomplished, and the train was hauled out of the siding, though perhaps not as easily as by an L1. Once off the Bald Eagle and on the Williamsport Division main, there was no shortage of power. Perhaps the Company's engineers had underrated the H9. That engine was handling more than 500 tons above its rated maximum capacity with ease.

Screwing back on the valve motion and opening the throttle wider, O.P. was able to coax more than 45 miles an hour out of this locomotive. Reaching Newberry Junction and heading onto the dike, he received orders from the tower operator for the last leg of the trip up the Elmira Branch. While at the tower, O.P. took the opportunity to advise the dispatcher that the H9 was performing almost up to L1 standards and that he would use that engine the rest of the way. The dispatcher agreed and said, "You brought that train through faster than we thought possible with an H9." That acknowledgment pleased O.P. With the pusher on the rear end, there were no problems hauling the train on the up-grade on the Elmira Branch, and the train was placed safely in the Ralston yard with some time before the sixteen-hour law would have taken effect.

Compiling data and filling out reports regarding performance of different classes of engines had become part of the routine when a manila folder from the Engineering Department showed up. One folder O.P. received from the crew clerk in East Altoona contained instructions of a different nature: the test was to be made on a device called a booster attached to the locomotive, not on the locomotive itself. The folder contained details explaining the operation of this auxiliary unit, which was mounted on the trailing truck axle of the 2-8-2. Essentially it was a small steam engine that increased the amount of tractive effort that could be produced. The booster was to be cut in when the locomotive started the train, used until a speed of 10 to 12 miles an hour was reached, and then shut off. It was also to be used on grades when lugging conditions forced speeds to drop below 10 miles an hour.

O.P. read the instructions carefully, and as he left the yard he opened the booster to find out what this addition was capable of doing when starting a train. Initially, everything the device was designed to do was being accomplished. Just the small thrust being exerted gave the train an increase in speed during this start. When O.P. opened the throttle wider as he entered the main line something alarming occurred when the engine attained a speed of five or six miles an hour: the steam gauge at first started to drop slowly, then dropped suddenly as if a lead weight had been affixed. Shutting off the booster and throttling back steadied the gauge, though, and steam pressure began to rise. Not dismayed by this sudden drop in steam pressure, O.P. resolved to make a more conclusive test when he started out of Tyrone with a pusher. Then, perhaps, he thought, this device would prove beneficial.

Using the booster going out of Tyrone produced the same circumstances: steam pressure disappeared as if by magic. During the round-trip to Ralston and back, the booster was used in a variety of circumstances, but it always had a disastrous effect on the steam pressure. Reporting in the comments space, O.P. noted that, although the booster was a practical device, the L1 could not generate sufficient steam when the booster was used to make a normal start with a train. Either a slower start using the booster could be made with reduced throttle settings, or a normal start could be accomplished with a wide-open throttle—but in combination the booster caused too much steam to be sacrificed, forcing a situation in which both the booster and the engine had to be shut off in order to build up enough steam to continue. What it amounted to was that the booster was a hindrance rather than the help it was intended to be.

During the summer of 1927, a young man bumped on O.P.'s crew as the head brakeman. From the onset, when he first climbed into the cab, this new crew member gave assurances that he would cooperate to the best of his abilities in getting the trains over the rails. Living up to his commitment, he willingly shared the firing chores, attended to coupling up, and always dropped off to open and close switches when necessary, all without wasting time or being told.

The way this young man worded things sometimes amused O.P. For instance, when pulling into a siding or stopping near a water plug, he would ask, "Oscar, are you going to 'load' water?" instead of "Are you going to *take* water." But this brakeman never seemed to have lengthy conversations with other members of the crew, preferring, it seemed, to daydream and live in his own world. That never affected the way he did his job, though.

Summer passed and autumn was at hand when, one day, they left Altoona on an eastbound run to Ralston. The trip progressed as it should on a fall day in Central Pennsylvania, when the brilliance of the changing leaves is pleasing to the eye and makes running an engine a special pleasure. Coming off the Bald Eagle with a clear block onto the Williamsport main, they got orders handed on to run to McElhattan, where their "extra movement" would take the siding until the Buffalo Flyer passed. In the siding, O.P.

climbed down to oil around and check the running gear. The brakeman followed, saying he was going forward to the call box to contact the operator for permission to occupy the main after the passenger passed. Agreeing to that, O.P. continued his own routine and then climbed back aboard.

Idling away time in the cab talking, O.P. and the fireman were startled to hear the Flyer's whistle sound just before it reached their engine. The passenger's K4 made a brake application just as it went by, accompanied by the shrieking of brake shoes against the wheels of the passenger cars as the passenger's K4 applied its brakes. Rushing to the gangway on the left side, O.P. watched as the train ground to a halt approximately seven car lengths beyond the call box. Still unable to determine the reason for this sudden stop, neither he nor the fireman could see anything wrong with the train. But when the Flyer's engineer and his fireman dropped off and started running back along the cars, it was clear that something was amiss. Rather than just stand by watching what was going on, Orr and his fireman climbed down and began hurrying toward the stopped passenger train. A short distance past the call box, O.P.'s fireman, in the lead, hollered, "Holy Jesus, Oscar, they just killed our brakeman!"

Arriving on the spot, O.P. saw what looked like a discarded large rag doll lying a few feet to the side of the roadbed. By the time the passenger's crew reached the young man's body, it had been determined beyond a doubt that he was dead. The engineer, an old acquaintance, blurted out: "I saw this fella standing with his arms behind his back in the middle of the tracks, and I tied the whistle down, but he never moved, and when I saw I was going to hit him I threw the train into emergency. Believe me, that's all I could do."

The dispatcher, notified of this unfortunate incident, issued verbal orders that both trains remain exactly where they were until the Clinton County coroner arrived to examine the body. Normally that took a while to complete, but in this case, because of the remote location, an engine crew in Lock Haven was called to transport the coroner to McElhattan aboard a light engine.

After examining the body, the coroner interviewed both engine crews about what had transpired. O.P. noted especially the victim's habit of daydreaming. The passenger engineer told of his attempts to warn the person standing in the middle of the tracks and stated that he'd been unable to stop because he was running at more than 60 miles an hour. Ruling the death accidental, the coroner advised placing the body in the baggage car and transporting it to Williamsport. Both trains could now continue their runs. The Flyer and O.P.'s freight had been detained nearly four hours by the unexplained behavior of the brakeman that resulted in his death.

This was the first time anyone on the many crews O.P. had worked with had been injured. Something like that, even if not as tragic, he reasoned, was bound to happen sooner or later.

Pushers—as essential as they were on the Elmira Branch when meets took place, and for entering and leaving the many sidings that required a stop and a start—did not always synchronize their movements with the head end. Westbound up this branch one exceptionally cold winter night, orders handed on at Trout Run instructed that O.P.'s extra take the siding at Bergen (Marsh Hill) to clear the main for a passenger that was also westbound. In the siding after the passenger was by, the block operator at Bergen gave a clear signal to occupy the main. Whistling off, O.P. allowed the L1 to take steam, then started opening the throttle wider for his start, applying sand liberally. The cold journals, however, slowed his movement and, reaching the end of the train's slack, he stalled. He waited a moment, expecting the pusher to shove in the slack, but that did not happen.

Reversing the 2-8-2, he backed up, pushing the slack back to the pusher with enough force to jiggle up the engine crew even if they'd been asleep. Whistling off again, and with the rails well sanded, he made another start, only to stop at the end of the slack again, in a violent spin. Concerned that his second attempt had failed to get the train under motion, and at the same point of forward progress as before, O.P. wondered whether the engineer on the rear end was inexperienced. In fact, it felt as if the independent brake might be set on the pusher, causing the sudden stops. Nothing like this had ever happened, which caused him some consternation.

For the third attempt, O.P. reversed and slammed the slack back with all the power the L1 could muster. He whistled off and, under motion, opened the throttle to the last notch, but he was stopped by an emergency brake application at the same spot as before. The only thing that could cause this was a parted air line, which in turn would be caused by a pulled drawhead. Thoroughly irritated, O.P. envisioned spending the rest of the night dragging a portion of the train to the Ralston yards, switching out the crippled car somewhere, then returning for the remainder of his train, plus the cabin. That loss of time would be extremely aggravating, but he could also expect a five-day suspension for pulling a drawhead.

Going forward to the tower, he notified the operator about the problem and suggested that if he could get moving quickly enough he might be able to get a portion of the train to Ralston on the clear block. Returning to the engine, he found that the conductor had come forward and was in the cab. "Do you know what you just did, Oscar?" he asked.

O.P. responded, "I just pulled a drawhead. Now what do we do?"

Laughing, the conductor assured him there wasn't much of a problem. "All we need," he said, "is to get a helper engine out of Ralston. You pulled the drawhead right out of the pilot of the pusher."

With that bit of good news, O.P. again went to the tower and told the operator he would need an engine to help get the train the remaining three miles to Ralston, and that he would contact the dispatcher to arrange for a helper engine. The dispatcher of course asked what was wrong with the assigned pusher. Revealing that the engine had been disabled because the drawbar normally affixed to the pilot had been pulled out, O.P. explained that the coupler had been pulled loose in an attempt to start the train. Registering disbelief, as he had never heard of something like that happening, the dispatcher arranged to have an engine dispatched from Ralston immediately.

Word soon came that the pusher crew on duty in Ralston would proceed immediately to Bergen, arriving in less than half an hour. Rather than take the role of a pusher, however, they coupled to the head end, double-heading the train to the Ralston yards.

A short time later, almost the same situation arose, this time involving a certain Elmira Branch engineer who had worked out of the terminal at Ralston, handling runs westbound (north), to the terminal at Southport, or in pusher service. In every respect he was adept at running a locomotive, and he wasn't ashamed to let anyone who would listen know about the feats he could perform. Most of this boasting took place in the bars, where he was likely to have a good audience. More than a few times O.P. had listened to his bragging, and somehow this engineer never passed up an opportunity to say he could show the Williamsport Division men a few things about running an engine. Whether this was directed at O.P. or not, O.P. never acknowledged these jibes, for that would only start an argument and put himself on the same level as the person attempting to exalt himself.

The unpredictable happened every day in railroading, and so it was on another cold winter night, when O.P. was the victim. Running westbound up the Elmira Branch, orders at Trout Run placed him in the siding at Bergen— almost a duplicate of the situation of less than a month ago when problems with the pusher were experienced. This night, however, he was nearing the sixteen-hours-on-duty provision and had only enough time remaining to clear the siding and get into the Ralston yards before he "outlawed."

Orders issued at the Bergen Tower gave permission to occupy the main after the eastbound extra cleared. When his meet passed and the block showed clear, Orr figured on taking less than forty-five minutes to get to his destination. This meant that the extra should clear the main at Ralston before 11:50 P.M. and not detain an eastbound movement. Whistling off, O.P. got under motion, but he stalled reaching the end of the slack between the cars. He repeated by reversing, pushing in the slack, and trying to get started. Three more times this move was repeated: when he came to the end of the slack he stalled. Finally he gave up in disgust. On none of the four tries did he feel even a slight nudge from the pusher—obviously the engineer never opened up his engine. The only thought O.P. had was that maybe the same engineer who had earlier lost the drawhead on the rear end was on the rear end of this train again, and that because of the razing he and the other pusher crewmen had received for that loss, perhaps he was now trying to show O.P. Orr that pusher crews too could offer a little hardship.

It was now impossible to reach Ralston in the time allotted, so Orr went to the tower and notified the operator that he couldn't get started and that his orders should be annulled. Checking what was scheduled after the eastbound passenger left Ralston at midnight, he learned that an extra would follow on the same orders. That movement would not clear at Bergen until around 12:30 A.M., so there wouldn't be enough time to reach the terminal before he outlawed at 1:15 A.M. O.P. therefore placed a call to the dispatcher, requesting that a relief crew be sent out to relieve him; his sixteen hours would be up before he could get out of Bergen.

The dispatcher asked, "What the hell is going on, Oscar? You should have been in Ralston almost an hour ago."

Explaining that because once again the pusher didn't help, and because he therefore couldn't get the train started, O.P. apologized to the dispatcher. That was the first time since the sixteen-hour law had been enacted that he was forced to use this measure, and it would be a blemish on his record.

The dispatcher must have realized that O.P. was concerned about what he had been forced into and assured him that other diker crews had also said there were problems with pushers. "I'm sending a memo to the road foreman," said the dispatcher, "instructing him to investigate why pusher crews are causing these delays by not properly handling their assignments." Tired, O.P. returned to the L1 to wait for the relief crew.

The eastbound passenger roared by, then the following extra approached and slowed almost to a stop. Two men piled off and approached the engine, but in the semi-darkness they were not recognizable. It wasn't until the back curtain was parted that O.P. saw who had been sent in relief—none other than the self-proclaimed Elmira Branch's hotshot engineer and his fireman. After the usual greetings, the first thing the relief engineer said to O.P. was,

"I understand you had a little trouble trying to get started, Oscar." Then he added another barb: "Don't worry, I'll have you in Ralston in a few minutes."

O.P. felt as if he'd been knocked down and kicked, but he only replied, "You'd better reverse and take up the slack before you try to get out of here."

The block came up clear, and according to instructions the slack was taken. Whistling off, the L1 was set in motion. Laboring down to about its last breath, the engine got a gentle nudge and the 2-8-2 started emitting sharp exhausts. The pusher had picked them up. The start had been accomplished with one try.

O.P. had some misgivings. As the train was smoothly leaving the siding onto the main, he could just imagine this engineer's remarks in the local bars when the crews were washing away their cinders: "When Oscar Orr couldn't get his train started at Bergen and ran out of time trying they called *me*. I showed him how the Elmira Branch men do things. I got going on the first try."

Mulling over what could turn into continuing embarrassment, O.P. made a decision, one that was against all Company rules and regulations. He announced that because there was nothing more for him to do on the engine, he was dropping off and would board the cabin as they snaked out of the siding. Once on the ground, and after allowing twenty or more cars to pass, he reached up and pulled an angle cock. This simple gesture applied the brakes on the loaded hopper and brought the train to a halt, at which point O.P. reset the device. Walking toward the cabin, he came upon the conductor and flagman conducting a car-by-car inspection, one man on each side of the train. The conductor was surprised to see him and asked, "Where you going, Oscar?"

O.P. replied that he was tired and that there was no reason to stay on the engine so he was going back to the cabin and sleep until they reached the terminal.

The conductor responded, "I can't imagine what's wrong with this train. You couldn't get rolling, and now the relief has come to an unexplained stop. We must be having air problems."

Nodding in agreement, O.P. continued to walk until he reached the cabin, where he was determined to stay awake to see what the next move would produce. He knew the train inspection must have been completed when he was nearly jarred off his seat by the slack being rammed back. Opening the door, he heard the head end's whistle signal.

Now the important part of the start had to be accomplished by the pusher, ready to open up when enough slack was run out to allow his forward motion, but that didn't happen. It wasn't until the slack jerked the rear end that the engine was opened up, and it ended up in a wide-open slip, producing another stall. After the second try failed to get them started, O.P. had a notion to go aboard the pusher and instruct the engineer in the proper way to set up, but then he reasoned he had no authority to do so. Besides, his suggestions might breed resentment.

When the third attempt ended as the previous two did, in failure, he went to sleep, until the conductor awakened him in the wee hours of the morning. The relief engineer had taken more than three hours to get started, and as a result all eastbound and westbound movements were tied up, and the early morning passenger was involved too. From this time on, the self-proclaimed engineer who claimed to be the Elmira Branch's finest never offered any slurs or jibes in O.P.'s direction, nor did O.P. mention anything about that engineer's lack of prowess.

An incident in which a crew member expressed a fear of falling off the locomotive occurred only one more time in O.P.'s career, shortly after he started on the diker runs. Early in the winter of 1928 a fireman "bumped" on the crew wearing a neck brace. When he made no mention of why he had to wear the brace, curiosity got the best of O.P., who asked. The fireman explained that it was the result of an accident nearly two years earlier, when he was firing on an Altoona-to-Harrisburg passenger run via the Bald Eagle Branch and down the Williamsport Division. One afternoon, while backing the train from Milesburg into Bellefonte at the lower end of the Bellefonte yard, the engine's trailing truck wheel had caught a switch point, causing the K4 to derail, then upset on its side and slide down an embankment to the edge of Spring Creek. The engineer was unhurt, but the fireman sustained a fractured vertebra in his neck. Now, the relief doctor had determined that he had mended enough to return to work but that the neck brace should be worn on duty. He further divulged that because he now had mixed feelings about running at fast speeds, he'd elected the diker job because it was a slow drag run, rather than bumping back on the passenger crew.

O.P. listened, but didn't reveal that this wasn't exactly a drag run. More than 85 miles was on a single-track main. Frequent siding stops and waiting for meets took up time, but when blocks were properly aligned no grass grew under his locomotive. It didn't take long before that was demonstrated. Leaving Ralston with a clear block to Trout Run, the L1 was set at running speed in only a little more than a mile, and the string of empties was rattling along at speeds of 50 or more miles an hour. Watching out of the corner of his eye, O.P. noticed the fireman casting furtive glances in his direction, then suddenly get off the seat box and cross the deck to the right side to assert himself. "You can sit there with that pipe in your mouth grinning at me when you have this engine going like you're hauling a limited," he said. "You can do that. You've never been on an engine that rolled over."

O.P. expected the man would next ask to stop and be let off, but the fireman merely went over to the coal pile, picked up the scoop shovel, and commenced the firing chores. He fired for O.P. for more than two years, never again mentioning speed. Obviously he had come to terms with his fear, for as quickly as it arose he had overcome it. This was not the first time O.P. had heard perfectly rational individuals express fear openly and without hesitation when aboard a steam locomotive.

A different situation that involved a person who had doubts about O.P.'s ability to operate an engine while hauling a tonnage train over the rails came about in the spring of 1928. In this case, the concern had to do with his interpretation of written train orders, not with speed. When the road foreman of engines on the Williamsport Division retired at the end of 1927, the Company selected an engineman serving as a "special duty man" on the flatlands west of Pittsburgh as his successor. This change in supervisory management did not alter any of the normal operations on the division, but it was not long before this new road foreman issued a directive to all engineers: henceforth engineers had to set their engines once running speed was achieved, and from that point on to control the locomotive by using the throttle while keeping the valve gear in a fixed position.

O.P. agreed in principle with the authority the new man commanded in issuing such a directive, but he had reservations about how it could be applied effectively. The expressed reasoning for using this method was to conserve fuel and water, but the new road foreman had evidently not taken topography within this division into consideration. It could be applied on the double-track river-level section from Harrisburg to Renovo, but on the single-track secondary lines, O.P.'s experience had taught him, both the throttle and the reverse gear had to be used.

So, from the time this directive was received O.P. did not comply with it—not in defiance, but because he wanted to stick with the proven way to get the dikers over the railroad. Everything he could gather about the new boss through the grapevine, and from men who had the opportunity to meet him, had indicated he was a fair man, that he seemed to be aware of the problems engine crews confronted, was ready to listen, and a friendly sort of person capable of doing his job.

But one bleak, overcast afternoon that was producing a mixture of light rain and wet snow while O.P. was waiting for clearance to depart the yards of

East Altoona, he spotted a man clad in clean overclothes carrying a traveling grip and approaching the L1. Just the way he looked and dressed signified that he was some sort of official, and the fireman was cautioned that they were about to be blessed with a visitor. Sure enough, the man came alongside the locomotive, tossed up his bag, and climbed aboard. Introducing himself as the new road foreman of engines, the new arrival explained that he was in Altoona to acquaint himself with this terminal. O.P. got the impression that he was indeed a friendly person. The ensuing conversation revealed that he was aware of the large volume of coal transported out of this point over the Williamsport Division and that, having already inspected the facilities at Altoona he was going to ride as a passenger on the trip to Ralston. O.P. assured him that it was an honor to have him aboard, and offered to explain anything about the run. The road foreman replied, "I'm glad you said that. I've been checking the enginemen's records, and in your years of service with the Company, you've established an enviable sheet. Also, I've had a brief tour of the shops here, and the head engineer informed me that the test data you've been turning in are highly regarded by his department. It seems they were pleased with the attention to detail you've shown in your reports." He added, "It was only logical to choose one of the best freight engineers on the division if I wanted to find out how these coal trains are handled, so I scheduled my time to make the trip with you and your crew."

While these compliments were more than appreciated by O.P., one of the most gratifying things he learned from the exchange was that the Engineering Department actually valued the findings he had been returning in all those manila folders. Up to now, he had never known where they went. In fact, he'd had a strong suspicion that they were merely discarded.

The wet rails didn't present any problems in getting the train out of the yard, but O.P. pointed out to the road foreman the many pot signals, plus the overhead boards that had to be closely watched as the train entered the main line. He also explained that in inclement weather, such as in fog or heavy snow, extreme care had to be exercised in following these signals.

Running down the main line was uneventful, and a clear signal gave them permission to cross over onto the Bald Eagle Branch at Tyrone. Once they were in the yard and spotted under the water plug, another explanation was in order: this stop necessitated coupling on a pusher, which was at best time-consuming. Orders at this point gave them clear blocks to Milesburg. Their only meet was with the late-afternoon westbound passenger ordered to take the siding at a determined time at Julian. O.P. gave a copy of these orders to the road foreman and commented that if they could follow such a pattern it would be a rather fast run.

After the pusher was cut off at Vail, the L1 was set up for the long drift down the Bald Eagle. Timing his movement with the meet in mind, O.P. calculated that if the sixty-five-car train was held at a speed of 35 to 40 miles an hour on this descent, the opposing westbound would be in the siding at Julian and a stop to wait for it to clear would not be necessary. But as they started down the valley the inclement weather suddenly turned into an early spring blizzard. Wet snow was so dense that it obliterated the marker lamps atop the front of the engine. The storm became so intense that landmarks used to gauge how a train was being handled on this section were difficult to see, or not visible at all. It felt as if they were running in a cloud, alone in the world.

This storm was no cause for any particular alarm, but on the other side of the cab O.P. saw the road foreman take the orders out of his pocket, then pull out his watch to check the time. Having finished reading what was governing their authority to occupy this single-track main, he came over to the right side and said, "How in the hell do you know where you're at?" then asked, "What if that passenger is late and doesn't clear by the specified time?"

Taken aback at being questioned, O.P. gave the only answer he could truthfully give: "I know where I'm at. I've spent almost eighteen years on this run, and besides, I have orders giving this extra movement precedence over all trains on this main as far as Milesburg. What the opposing train crew does is not anything I can control." That apparently was not the reply the road foreman expected. It seemed to increase his doubts that this was not a very safe passage in this snowstorm, and he began pacing across the deck, peering out both sides of the gangway.

As he saw what was transpiring, O.P. began to feel uneasy. Checking the time, he still had four minutes before he reached the meet designation. But something he didn't have a chance to explain would prevent any complications: if the meet was not in the clear, the operator at Julian would have to place a red block signal to stop the extra's eastbound progress.

In anticipation of this stop signal, an additional reduction was made on the automatic brake valve, but just as that took place the storm parted for an instant, and during that intermission O.P. saw the rear marker lights of the passenger bending into the siding, and the switch target flash from red to green. Although they had not crossed the switch at the west end of the siding, the passenger had cleared at least a mile ahead of their position on the main. Placing the brake valve in full release, O.P. reached up and opened the throttle three notches to pick up running speed.

Hearing the 2-8-2 coming to life with the blast of the exhaust, the road foreman made a dash to the right side, almost as if to seize the controls, but he stopped short. With eyes as wide as saucers and a complexion like a ghost, he stood facing O.P. shouting, "You G—— d—— fool! You're not running this engine, this engine's running you!"

The outburst did not allow time to explain why the engine had been opened up, and O.P. was not pleased at being cursed at for doing what was necessary to get a train over the road. Standing there with a blank expression, the road foreman must have realized that he had just shown he was afraid. Without another word, he turned and crossed the deck to the fireman's seat, and there he remained until they reached the coaling station at Linden, where he departed. He never uttered another word to any of the crewmen; he just sat in a daze. This road foreman never again set foot on an engine O.P. controlled, and although the two men maintained an amiable relationship there was always some reserve. (Ironically, this road foreman met his demise aboard a steam locomotive in the early 1940s. He was at the controls of a K4 hauling No. 575, the early-morning Buffalo Express, when, between Watsontown and Montgomery, a low-boy trailer hung up on a private crossing. Hitting this obstacle at an estimated speed of 75 to 80 miles an hour, the K4 derailed and turned over on its side, killing both the road foreman and the engineer; the fireman sustained serious injuries but recovered.)

Nearly four years had passed since I had come into O.P.'s life, and perhaps the first vivid recollection I have about my father was the whistle signal he used on a steam engine to signify he was coming home. Instead of the normal sounds issued by freight trains approaching the crossing located in South Ralston, his screecher whistle would start at its highest pitch and from that point decrease without a waver, lowering until it was barely audible. At the end there would be two short, sharp blasts. This whistle signal had been O.P.'s personal means of identification for many years, and it also notified my mother to start preparing a meal, whether it be day or night. Only once in the many years O.P. used that signal was my mother fooled by other engineers attempting to duplicate it. She avowed that it didn't sound quite right but that she wasn't paying too close attention and went ahead and prepared the meal. O.P. didn't show up until the next day. Another sound identified with my father was the whistle of a bird, the whippoorwill, which O.P. would imitate as he walked up the driveway at the rear of our home.

In the early fall of 1928, O.P. took me along to the yard office, where he was checking his standing on the board. This evening jaunt led us to a side visit to the coal hoist, where he put me aboard one of the many L1's lined up there. I was awed by the interior of a dimly lit cab, as O.P. explained the features and pointed out the seat he rode on. At the tender age when you believed everything, I was most impressed by the wheel directly in front of his seat. This, he said, was the steering wheel (years later I learned that it controlled the valve settings). Being introduced to the steam engine made me want to watch these machines performing their duties more closely, but my grandstand on the hill overlooking all the railroad activities was too far away for that. Too young to change that situation, all I could do was keep my hill seat and bide my time.

The winter months passed, and on a late spring afternoon in 1929, O.P. sounded the whistle as he entered town. At this signal my mother announced we would go down to meet him—something new. There was just a trio at the time. My oldest sister had graduated from business college and departed to accept a position as a secretary in the Fisher Body Company at Detroit, Michigan, leaving only myself and my youngest sister, who was seventeen months older than I, at home. We waited for O.P. at the end of the wye next to a huge oak tree that served as a natural built-in bumper block. After this meeting, which was an opportunity for me to get nearer to the railroad, I got permission to go alone as far as the oak tree but no farther.

At the next daylight sounding of the whistle signal, I exercised that privilege. Off and running at the cue, it didn't take long to learn a lesson, much to my dismay. The first part, going down the hill, was taken in stride, but after rounding a curve at the steepest part I discovered my body's momentum was greater than my legs could keep up with. I ended up in a headlong slide on the dirt road. The torn skin on my knees and elbows didn't stop me, though.

I was waiting at the oak tree when O.P. walked up the wye. He took one look at my skinned-up appearance and offered sympathy, but then he advised me sternly that if this would be the result of coming down to meet him it would be better if I stayed at home. Seeing my condition when we arrived home, my mother agreed: I was too young, and besides, running down the hill could cause more serious injury. While my scrapes were being cared for, I did some persuading, and with the assurance that I wouldn't run the next time, my privilege wasn't taken away.

During my vigil at the oak tree as the summer passed, the only important thing I could see from this spot, and at close range, was the occasional engine being wyed. I could see down the left side of the wye to the yard office, but this narrow aperture provided only a glimpse of passing trains. An unloading arrangement constructed in the middle of the wye at flatcar level was obstructing my view. The purpose of this dock was to store materials used by the track maintenance crews—rails, ties, and other assorted items to meet their needs. But as necessary as it was for the Company's operations, it continued to be an aggravation to me because it blocked my view.

One day in the fall my desire to see more of what was going on led me to abandon my designated waiting-place at the oak tree, cross the main highway, and walk down the right side of the wye, passing the dock, to the track where the cabins were sitting. There the whole picture unfolded. I could now see what this business of railroading was all about. What I saw was the entire coal hoist, a line of waiting engines, and all the surrounding activities. One thing that awed me most, of all things, was a crane with a clamshell bucket placing coal onto the tender of a waiting engine.

An enthralled five-year-old trying to take in everything going on before me, I scarcely saw an engine passing by, towing a cabin. The next thing I saw was the same engine again, now pushing the cabin up the wye track toward me. I soon could see that the person standing in the gangway was none other than O.P., who had spotted me in the brush along the track, dropped off the engine, and come over to where I stood. I expected that my discovery was about to be forbidden and that I'd be reprimanded for overstepping my bounds. But O.P. agreed that I had chosen a better spot from which to view all the activity, although he cautioned me about the dangers of crossing the highway and, above all, of getting too close to the tracks.

Then came another unexpected surprise. He took my hand and we walked over to the cabin that had just been set off, where he explained to the conductor and flagman who I was, and stated, "As soon as we get the engine on the pit and mark off, I'll be back to pick up the boy. Don't let him get away."

The two crewmen took me inside and showed me the many things their home on wheels contained, even putting me up on the seat in the cupola that gave an extended view of the surroundings. The best part, however, was when the conductor went to a cupboard, took out a tin cup, and poured me a drink of ice water.

Now that I was permitted to advance to a perfect place to meet O.P., however, inclement weather or nighttime arrivals prevented me from going there, and the arrival of winter ended everything.

During the early fall of 1929 the diker crews were enjoying the prosperity of a booming coal market. O.P., now a confirmed auto enthusiast, decided that the boxy Dodge sedan he was driving should be replaced with a sleeker 1930 model—more or less a way to invest some of the earnings that were being reaped. According to literature available and word-of-mouth information, one of the finest American luxury cars being produced was the Auburn. Two features made the Auburn a little more enticing: it was powered by a straight eight-cylinder engine, and it was manufactured by the local Lycoming Motors plant in Williamsport, also a producer of airplane engines.

Presenting his plan to buy this new automobile brought an immediate rejection from my mother, but that was something he'd expected. She contended that everything about his idea for buying a new car was wrong: the car they had already was well suited for their limited needs, and less than 6,000 miles had registered on the speedometer in just over four years. Moreover, to pay more than $1,700 for a car was unthinkable; a house and lot could be purchased for even less.

O.P. was prepared for her objections though, and my mother gave her approval when he produced his hold card. Instead of using their savings or submitting to a payment plan, he was going to cash in his Pennsylvania Railroad stock, which now had a high market value. So my father purchased a slate-gray Auburn sedan with red wheels, and enough cash remained to buy an electric washing machine for my mother—more or less a peace offering.

Just a few days after this transaction, the stock market crashed, and instead of having next-to-worthless stock certificates on hand the Orrs had some valuable material possessions. Years later my mother said that was one of the smartest moves O.P. ever made, but what prompted him to do so we do not know.

The impact of what happened to the nation's economy during the last days of October 1929 did not immediately affect operations in and out of the terminal of Ralston. Rather, things slowed gradually. Coal was still the most widely used fuel for producing heat, and even though the nation was at the beginning of a severe depression, the winter of 1929/30 brought little change in demand for this product. However, the spring of 1930 reflected an abrupt slowing in the demand for fuel, and the Company initiated austerity measures to cope with the shrinking economic conditions. Over-the-road crews, including most of the dikers, were eliminated, and personnel in every operational phase were laid off (furloughed). That was just the beginning of the hard times. O.P. was more fortunate than a great many of his fellow workers. Twenty-four years on the roster allowed him to hold on to one of the few remaining diker crews.

At the age of five, I was not able to comprehend what was transpiring. The only thing that meant anything to me was the familiar whistle signal that O.P. was coming home.

Spring weather again allowed me to resume my rituals of meeting him, watching what was going on at the coal hoist, and boarding the cabin. One afternoon, after hearing the arrival whistle call and positioning myself at my viewpoint, I watched as the cabin was towed down the siding. After crossing over the main, it was pushed up the wye to my location and as usual set off on the cabin track. But something was different: it was the only cabin there. When the engine was cut off and backed away, the conductor welcomed me aboard, and, genial hosts that he and the flagman were, entertained me with idle conversation. Just as my ice-water treat was being poured the cabin gave a sudden lurch.

Without a doubt, something was amiss. We were no longer setting on a level plane, but rather tilted at a sharp angle. An inspection outside revealed that we had rolled off the end of the rails and that the rear trucks were on the ground. The yard office was only about 100 feet away, and before we had a chance to survey the situation the yardmaster was on the scene. He determined that the only solution was to get O.P. and the L1 back over and to round up the section gang to provide jacks and blocks. Noting my presence, he instructed me to leave the area for a safer spot atop the loading area between the wye. Watching from this raised platform, I saw O.P.'s engine ease onto the pit and, after a brief hesitation, move back, cross over, and come up the wye to the cabin track.

About the time the L1 arrived, the section gang was also coming in with their motor car on the opposite side of the wye. Coupled to this was a trailer car loaded with blocks and jacks. When jacked to the height of the rails the blocks were set, the engine coupled on and, at the signal, pulled the trucks back to their proper position.

As the engine eased away, I decided I'd seen enough and went back to my oak tree to wait for O.P. to appear. When he did, I was all aglow at what had transpired, but somehow O.P. didn't seem to share my enthusiasm. The walk up the hill was mostly in silence, and I wasn't able to relate my version of this experience until we walked into our kitchen.

My mother greeted us, and naturally asked what had held us up, commenting that it had been more than two hours since the whistle signal had sounded. To this O.P. gave a laconic reply: "Just ask Jack. He can tell you."

Welcoming the opportunity, I excitedly recounted what had happened, plus everything I had witnessed. O.P. commented: "If the conductor and flagman hadn't been fooling around with you, Jack, they would have been attending to their duties, and at least they probably would have set the hand brake so the cabin would remain where I set it off." And to my mother he said, "When I come in again, don't let him out of your sight. Tie him to the porch post if you have to, but don't let him come down to the yards anymore."

Why it was the only caboose on the cabin siding, or why a bumper block wasn't affixed at the end of the tracks was something I never did learn. Perhaps it was a sign of the times.

Only a short time later, O.P. told us that the Company had announced that the terminal at Ralston would be permanently shut down. The closing of this facility reduced Ralston from a bustling terminal to a tank town, and it ended services that began on one of the first American railroads. Ralston had been established ninety-three years earlier, in 1837, as the northern terminus of the Williamsport & Elmira Railroad. Undoubtedly the Depression caused the demise of the town, but its role as a terminal would have been phased out eventually—the victim of modern technology. Members of the work force that had been keeping every aspect of Ralston operating were forced to transfer to other terminals. Those with enough seniority went to Williamsport, Southport, or Renovo; those less fortunate were furloughed and, unable to go elsewhere, stayed in Ralston. All in all, there was no mass exodus from Ralston, which remained a town comprised of railroad workers, employed or unemployed, for many more years.

When the official notice of the closing was posted, O.P. began surveying the bid board, and what he learned was not exactly pleasing. The merger of the Williamsport and Elmira divisions in 1921 did not seem important at the time, but now its full impact was being felt. The closest terminal to Ralston was Williamsport, but the bid board there had no position for O.P., even with his twenty-six years seniority. The passengers, fast freights, even the locals plying the Elmira Branch, were definitely out of his reach. Men who had hired out before the 1921 merger and who outranked him in seniority on this branch were now furloughed. Turning to runs emanating out of this point on the Williamsport Division, O.P. found that these runs were held by old-timers residing in that city, except for a few second- or third-trick yard jobs. Further study revealed that the only over-the-road job he could hold presently was with the now-extended diker crews set up to run from Altoona to the terminal at Southport (Elmira, New York). This extension went only 50 miles farther north (west) of Ralston, and adequate passenger trains would afford easy access to return home from this new terminal. O.P. bid on and received one of the new runs, even getting the same conductor he had hauled for the past twenty years out of Ralston.

Marking up in the yard office in Altoona for the first trip on this new, or at least extended, run, O.P. discovered to his dismay that the motive power he was assigned was the 2-10-0 I1 class. If this engine performed like the I1's on the test run in 1923, it would be nearly impossible to grind out 175 miles in the allotted sixteen hours. However, there was a slight difference in the classification: it was now designated as an I1sa. According to discussions with enginemen that had used this locomotive, modifications to the valve motion gave it more speed.

Starting out of Altoona eastbound with a train of more than 4,000 tons, O.P. found that, other than having power, the I1sa was also producing speed.

Before reaching Tyrone on the Middle Division main, he was running at 50 miles an hour. Another element the I1 possessed but hadn't displayed previously was that it could be set back toward center and still steam freely. Although this 2-10-0 performed entirely differently from previous I1's O.P. had handled, it did retain several undesirable original features, which became evident on the long drift toward Milesburg after cresting the summit at Vail. Rod noise was still very much present; up-and-down and side-to-side gyrations still made it ride like a lumber wagon without springs; and it was still equipped with the small tender that made frequent water stops a necessity. The only improvement was the placement of a cabin, or "monkey house," at the rear of the tender facing backward for the head brakeman to ride in, supposedly to give him a view over the entire train while in motion. Orr was to learn that all cabins were not affixed in the same place; some were tight against the coal-bunker slope, others were at the extreme end of the tender.

Considering all the water stops, plus coaling at Linden, they made decent running time to Newberry Junction, where a pilot came aboard to qualify O.P. on the new segment from Ralston to Southport. In addition, and instead of the usual single pusher, two L1's were placed on the rear of the train. The pilot explained that with the tonnage now being hauled one pusher was sufficient to handle the train to Ralston, but that beyond this point it would take all the power of three engines to get up grades encountered on the rest of the run. The pusher would be attached for some 65 miles to Snedekerville (block designation: Sned). The initial 24-mile portion of the run up the Elmira Branch to Ralston, as before, was made with the usual ease. Even with a clear block to Leolyn, the pilot advised O.P. that it was mandatory to stop here for water. Engine crews in the past had established that to get up the hill to Leolyn required a tank of water, even though it was only nine miles in actual distance. Pulling to the upper (west) end of the yards, O.P. made his stop at the now-unattended block-limit call box designated as "Max."

When the yard was closed the Company also eliminated the station block operator's position that formerly controlled movements in and out of Ralston. Then, if movements from here to the next block were not in written form, perhaps taken on from an operator at Newberry Junction, Trout Run, or Bergen, crews would copy orders issued from dispatchers on a "K" card in their own handwriting.

The train occupied the main, but the I1 had to be cut off, enter the siding, and backed down along the standing train to the water plug at Ralston, a distance of almost a mile. One thing favorable about this location was the two separate water plugs, one for the main and one for the siding. Thus the pushers followed suit, cutting off but backing down the main to replenish their water supply. Then the engines recoupled, a maneuver that took some forty-five minutes, and they were ready to assault the Leolyn hill. Before they started, the pilot cautioned the fireman to have his fire clean and above all to be ready to keep the pops singing.

Starting out from Max, O.P. widened out on the powerful 2-10-0, attempting to pick up as much speed as possible, but in a little more than three miles, at the town of Roaring Branch, he was running at only approximately 20 miles an hour. Here, the valley narrowed and the railroad's roadbed was carved out of the side of the mountain. In addition, the grade increased sharply and speed started dropping off. Soon less than 10 miles an hour was the speed maintained. About two miles out of Roaring Branch, the pilot announced they were at Rock Cut and now had a 3 percent grade to contend with. To compound things, they were entering a short-radius double "S" curve. He further advised keeping plenty of sand on the rails. If a slip was made before the spinning could be stopped under wide open conditions, a stall would result, and it was next to impossible to get the train started again. The only solution would be to cut off about twenty cars and double the train to Leolyn.

O.P. held the I1 down for the next two and a half miles before reaching the summit, even around the sharp "S" curve at the very top. It amazed him that he had never worked a locomotive wide open for such a long period of time. That the fireman kept the steam gauge at 250 pounds for the last five miles was no small feat. At Leolyn O.P. again had to cut off and back down a siding to take water. Recoupled and ready to resume the trip, he checked the time: two hours and twenty minutes had elapsed since stopping at Ralston, but he was only nine miles closer to his destination. At this point, the pilot assured him that the remainder of the run would be accomplished much faster, but that the terrain they were about to cover was akin to a roller coaster. He also provided some facts about the geography of the region, explaining that though they weren't exactly on top of the mountain, the valley they were in would broaden, and that before reaching Southport they would be surrounded by rolling hills. He also pointed out that the swamp to the right of the railroad was a dividing line for the headwaters of two streams. Lycoming Creek started there and flowed south to empty into the West Branch of the Susquehanna at Williamsport; Towanda Creek started and flowed north to empty into the north branch of the Susquehanna River at Towanda.

Leaving Leolyn was no problem, as the head end was on a two-and-a-half-mile long one percent downgrade through the Grover Cut to Cedar Ledge. In this distance a speed of more than 40 miles an hour was attained before an ascending grade carried them through the borough of Canton.

Although this grade was nearly 2 percent, the track was straight, and O.P. blasted through the community at 30 miles an hour. Just north of Canton he encountered nearly level track, perhaps on a slight downgrade, for more than two miles, to the village of Alba. The next three miles, to the block station at Cowley, presented an upgrade of about one percent. Just past Cowley a drift of more than seven miles on a one percent downgrade began, taking them past the tower block station at Troy. Following the contours of this area on this grade, they rounded an unusually large-radius curvature, allowing the head end to look across this swell to view the cabin and pushers snaking along directly above them.

A short distance past the tower at Troy, another ascending grade began, and in the next 14 miles to the block station at Sned it had increased to 1.5 percent. This was a relatively straight stretch, and with the speed gained coming off the Troy hill, nearly 40 miles an hour was maintained the entire distance. Just past Sned the pushers were uncoupled on the fly. They backed down and were wyed to begin running light to their terminal at Williamsport, some 65 miles away. From Sned to the broad Chemung Valley and yards at Southport, it was all downhill on a ruling grade of one percent.

At the Pennsylvania–New York border, the pilot instructed O.P. to stop at a small structure resembling a telephone call box, where, he explained, they would pick up a brakeman to comply with the New York State law that required all trains to have a "full crew." On the pit at Southport, O.P. checked his time and found that nearly five hours had elapsed since the Ralston stop, that an average of 10 miles an hour was made on the 50-mile run, and that it had taken him more than fourteen hours to complete the trip from Altoona. The last 50 miles had been over terrain that was as rugged as the Company could offer anywhere in the entire system. There wasn't any time to relax, either. Use of the throttle, reverse lever, and automatic brake valve were needed to coordinate handling a tonnage train with two engines constantly pushing on the rear end.

O.P. regarded this new experience as a challenge. Eastbound out of Southport with more than 100 empties also required expertise in train-handling on this roller-coaster portion. Learning when to shut off and open up again was the most important factor, because if it was not done properly a pulled drawhead would result. In addition, taking a train down the long, steep grade from the block station at Leolyn to Max was no easy chore. The pilot on the return trip advised O.P. that the Company rule was to set retainers on twenty cars before leaving Leolyn, but that crews seemed to bypass this requirement and instead controlled their trains with the automatic brake system. Also, the pilot advised, the safe running speed dropping a train down this heavy grade was 35 miles an hour. Keeping more than 100 cars at a steady speed for eight miles with the automatic brake valve, especially countering the 3 percent downgrade portion, proved to be quite a chore and required exacting brake applications.

Finally, a short way north of Max, the pilot gave the instructions to place the braking system in full release, noting that the marker bearing the lettering "ABL" (Approaching Block Limits) was the proper spot to perform this function. Speed should be picked up to around 40 miles an hour, which would carry them through Ralston slowly enough to handle the 35-mile-per-hour restriction caused by a dogleg curve where the siding from the yard and the main intersected. This drift lasted for more than four miles to Marsh Hill (Bergen Tower), where the engine was opened up a couple of notches to maintain running speed for the remainder of the distance to Newberry Junction.

After completing the first round-trip on this extended run, O.P. started to figure out what he could do to make this run easier to accomplish. On the next eastbound trip out of Southport, he decided to try a method used by engineers descending the slope around the Horseshoe Curve on their way to Altoona. Layovers in Altoona allowed associations with engine crews from all divisions working out of this large terminal, and discussions among these men somehow always centered on the principles of railroading. During one of these enlightening conversations, O.P. asked a Pittsburgh Division man how they handled their trains from the curve down to Altoona. He was surprised when it was revealed that they simply took a monkey wrench and adjusted the feed valve on the automatic brake line to bleed off enough air to keep the train under control. The engineman added that, as effective as this method was, it was contrary to Company rules and violated Interstate Commerce Commission (ICC) regulations to tamper with the brake system, but because it didn't create any problems the officials never bothered to enforce these rules.

Putting this long-remembered illegal principle into practice, O.P. came down the hill without touching the brake lever, and perhaps smoother than if retainers had been set. He had equal braking power on every car in the train. On the next westbound trip up the Elmira Branch, he used this method to descend the Troy hill with two pushers attached, and achieved the same smooth descent. A conductor related many years later, "I rode down the Leolyn-Ralston hill behind lots of engineers, but Oscar Orr was the only one that could bring a train down this grade without upsetting my coffeepot."

Able to handle the descending grades with ease, O.P. began concentrating on finding a solution to the time-consuming method used to get up the hill from Ralston to Leolyn. He could not dispute the finding of the Elmira Division men that it took a tank of water to surmount this grade. Thinking it through, he figured out that they based this fact on a standing start out of the yard where they began their trip for years on the run to Southport. Honoring this time-established principle, O.P. stopped at Ralston on a westbound trip and personally checked the water level to determine how much remained in the tank since it had been replenished at Linden. The 27-mile run had only reduced his supply to around the three-quarter level, so he reasoned that this stop was unnecessary. If he ran by Ralston, enough speed could be maintained to carry him well into the grade instead of hitting it at a crawl.

Discussing his plan with the conductor before leaving Altoona, O.P. told him that they would take no water at Ralston if a clear block was handed on at Bergen, and that when the conductor got his orders at Bergen he should give the highball signal to the pusher engineers, to prevent them from slacking off as they neared Ralston. To further ensure the success of this unprecedented move, he dropped off the head brakeman at Newberry Junction to personally tell the waiting pusher engineers what he was going to do. The brakeman returned somewhat disturbed, and without further ado announced the reaction of the pusher engineers.

"Oscar," he said, "they told me you were crazy to attempt to go up the hill without stopping at Ralston for water. You'll run out of water before getting all the way up, and things will be in a helluva mess. The whole branch will be tied up."

But O.P. told the brakeman he was going to give it a try anyway. He knew that the grade out of Newberry Junction was less than one percent as it followed Lycoming Creek and that after running speed was maintained the pushers could throttle back to less than full power to save fuel. The exception to this was when the train took a siding, in which case the pushers again had to work hard to get it started and up to speed. After World War II, when many of the I1's were equipped with coast-to-coast tenders, the pusher hauling such a tender was the lead locomotive, and the second pusher was the one with the smaller tender. Orders were that the second pusher would work only until the train was started, then not work again until the train reached Ralston. This eliminated a water stop and still made it possible to maintain a decent speed for assaulting the Leolyn hill.

When they reached Bergen, the operator handed on orders that gave O.P. a clear block to Leolyn, and he was on his way. Observing the 35-mile-per-hour restriction passing through Ralston, he waited until the entire train had passed that point before opening up in preparation for the coming grade. Crowding everything he could get out of the 2-10-0, they started up the heavy grade at Roaring Branch at better than 40 miles an hour. By the time he reached Rock Cut, everything was in full forward, but he still was making at least 20 miles an hour. Rounding the last curve as the block operator's shanty was approached, he still had the I1 roaring along at better than 15 miles an hour.

They stopped at the upper end of Leolyn, where a time check showed it had been twenty-two minutes since they had passed Max. They had saved more than an hour and a half. After cutting off and backing down the siding to the water plug, O.P. climbed onto the tender to check how low the water tank was, and was pleasantly surprised to find that almost a quarter of a tank was left. He estimated that, by running through with the speed he maintained, only half a tank was used on the hill.

While taking water, he approached the pusher engines sitting on the main and engaged the engine crews in conversation about to how they felt about bypassing the stop at Ralston. Without any reservations, they admitted that to attempt such a run was risky but that it had been a pleasure to come up the hill at a respectable rate of speed instead of at the usual grinding crawl. One fireman offered a compliment, in a fashion, saying, "You know, Oscar, I've been firing out of Ralston since I hired out, and this was the easiest trip I ever had coming up the hill."

Word of this accomplishment spread by the grapevine but failed to convince other engine crews. They remained skeptical, and most would not attempt this time-saving method, preferring to stick to precedent and assault this heavy grade only after topping off the water tank.

Ralston, although it was no longer a terminal, was still an important part of the Elmira Branch. The long siding, plus the convenient water plugs, made it an excellent place for meets. This prevented O.P., more often than not, from running through. He would often be placed in the siding either for an opposing meet or to clear for passenger movements. Also, on many trips the dikers would have only one pusher from Newberry Junction; the second would be picked up at Ralston. Trains with lesser tonnage needed two pushers to get up the hill but could continue their run from Leolyn to Sned with just one unit. The unneeded pusher would cut off and back down the hill, laying at Ralston to make another shove. When traffic was heavy, this pusher would make at least three shoves up the hill in a day, then run backward some 35 miles to its terminal in Williamsport. It seemed that no matter what O.P. did to expedite his movements, it seemed that 75-mile trip on the single-track Elmira Branch to Southport was always time-consuming.

Toward the end of the summer of 1930, effects of what was happening to the nation's economy were apparent, if only in the rows of stored dead engines and yards filled with empty cars within the Altoona complex. The only encouraging thing O.P. saw for quite some time was a brand-new engine setting outside the shops. At first glance it looked like the M1 class, but he was to learn that it was a modified version classified as an M1a. One thing about this new engine that was different from anything he had ever seen on the Pennsylvania was the attached tender. It was huge, just like one he would have designed years ago. Tapping the grapevine, O.P. learned that the M1a was intended to haul symbol fast freights over the entire system. Perhaps the better part of what he learned was that, other than equipping M1a's with the new larger tenders, the I1sa's might be getting the larger tender.

Before long, marking up at the yard office for another Southport run, O.P. was presented with one of those manila folders, the first one he'd seen for quite some time. The instructions were not out of the ordinary: he was to closely monitor coal and water consumption on an I1sa-class engine numbered 4612. As he neared the ready track, I1 No. 4612 wasn't hard to find. Unlike its many counterparts setting in this area, it was all shined up, fresh out of the shop. But the feature that set it apart from the others was its huge tender. The workers had already dubbed this the "coast-to-coast" model. Taking it out of the yards and eastbound on the Middle Division main, O.P. determined that, other than being equipped with a tender holding 21,000 gallons of water and some 25 tons of coal, this locomotive was performing better than any of the other 2-10-0's previously assigned him on this run. It was producing steam freely—much like an L1 class, not like the usually contrary I1—and it seemed to be exceptionally fast. Before shutting off to cross over at Tyrone, he was running at more than 50 miles an hour. But despite its fine attributes, the 4612 still rode rough, the same as the rest of the vast number of engines in its class.

At Tyrone while waiting for the pusher to couple on, the tank was topped off with water, which permitted bypassing the normal water stops at Milesburg and Lock Haven. Reaching Linden, more than half the coal supply had been used. Perhaps enough remained to reach Southport, but trying to reach that point would require pulling the slides and shoveling forward to the stoker screw opening, and in the cavernous bunker of this large tender, that would be a monumental task, so O.P. took advantage of the facilities available at Linden and replenished both coal and water. On the Elmira Branch, despite a stop for a meet at Ralston, no water was taken, but after working the hill the tank was filled at Leolyn.

Arriving at Southport, O.P. recorded on his sheet that the large tender had made it possible to eliminate three water stops en route. He also noted that if Ralston was bypassed the report for this large tender would have been more favorable: at least running time would have been one and a half hours shorter and there would have been a savings of four or five tons of coal.

On the return trip to Altoona, water was taken at Ralston, not out of necessity but because they took the siding for a westbound meet, and once more in Lock Haven, resulting in shortening running time by almost two hours on this 175-mile trip. Recording all the facts on his sheet, O.P. commented that the use of engines equipped with these large tenders on this particular run would result in savings not only in fuel but also in running time between the terminals. Only a few other I1's were equipped with "coast-to-coast" tenders at this location, and it would be many years before they received this treatment. The 4612 from this time on was used almost exclusively for hauling diker trains in this central region until the end of the steam era.

During the fall and winter of 1930 into 1931, the diker crews were getting three or four round-trips a "half" (a two-week pay period, paid on the seventh and twenty-first day each month), and layovers at Altoona or Southport would sometimes last more than forty-eight hours. O.P. could come home for a layover from Southport with no problems; three passengers each way and at evenly spaced intervals during the day and night solved the layover situation. Altoona posed a greater problem in coming home during the layovers, though, for there were only two passengers each way down the Bald Eagle Branch, and only in the morning or afternoon. This could be quite restrictive if his arrival or calling time did not coincide with those schedules because he could not return home for a layover. Although it was costly to lay over, it was better than missing a call, which the Company did not appreciate. Besides, he couldn't afford to miss a trip. However, as the summer of 1931 neared, the Depression had slowed the economy to a mere crawl and the dikers were down to only two, seldom three, round-trips a "half." Faced with 72-hour layovers, O.P. couldn't afford to stay away from home for such an extended period, even if it wasn't convenient in and out of Altoona. He was forced to come home.

Arriving in East Altoona early one evening, O.P. was resigned to spending another night spent in the cabin awaiting the departure of the passenger train to Williamsport the following morning. While he was marking off in the yard office, an acquaintance from the earlier Tyrone terminal days who was a Middle Division engineer happened to be marking up. They exchanged greetings, and in the ensuing conversation the engineer stated he was running an express train from Altoona to Harrisburg and would be leaving in less than an hour. As in the past, he chided O.P. that he should get out on the Middle Division to see what railroading was all about and now was inviting O.P. to ride along to Harrisburg. First checking the Harrisburg arrival time, then his timetable, O.P. found he could catch the night version of the Buffalo Flyer, Train 575, and make a connection in Williamsport with the early-morning Elmira Branch passenger to be in Ralston at 3:30 A.M.—twelve hours earlier than waiting until the following morning. Although this was a roundabout way of getting home, including an additional 130 miles, O.P. agreed to go along.

The two engineers and fireman picked up the assigned K4 and backed to the passenger terminal, where, while waiting for the express to come in, the fireman began tending the fire. When an ample supply of coal had been placed in the firebox, however, the fireman continued shoveling, which prompted O.P. to ask his friend what the fireman was doing. The engineer explained he was placing a large amount of coal on each side and in the rear of the firebox, especially in the corners, but would leave a bright fire in the middle. This unorthodox method, he said, was referred to as "bank-firing." Although the Company did not condone this practice, they made no attempt to discourage it. Officials were aware that this method made it possible to haul heavy passenger and express trains on long runs at high speeds, which was next to impossible using regular hand-firing methods. The engineer added that the only disadvantage of this method would occur if they were forced to make a lengthy stop, in which case such a large amount of green coal in the firebox would cause coking and make the burning coal one solid mass—and result in one helluva mess.

After leaving the station, while the K4 was still being worked hard, the fireman placed a few shovelfuls in the middle of the bright area, then returned to join O.P. and share the seat on the left side. He explained that their normal running speed was between 75 and 80 miles an hour and that the only additional firing he would do was to place a little coal on the bright area when they slowed for restricted speed signals, and that otherwise he would ride the seat box. As they traveled along, O.P. watched the steam gauge and was surprised at how steady it was holding at just a little more than 200 pounds. If it neared the pop-off point of 205 pounds, the injector was opened, not only cooling things down but keeping the waterglass full. At one point they scooped water using a device that was lowered from under the tender to gather water from a trough between the rails while running. This too was something O.P. had never witnessed before. A brief stop was made at Lewistown, and at this point the fireman took the shaker bar to clean the grates—not sustained shaking, but just enough to ensure that no obstructions were blocking the grates.

Things were operated in the same manner the rest of the way down the

Juniata Valley, and after a short sprint along the Susquehanna River they began slowing as they approached the Rockville Bridge. While crossing this bridge at a slower pace, the fireman placed a few shovelfuls of coal into the firebox—the final application he would make before reaching Harrisburg. When he was finished shoveling, he showed O.P. what the firebox looked like. Rather than a jumbled mess, which he was expecting, O.P. saw a level, even-burning fire, almost like the one that would have been hand-fired carefully for the entire distance. The fireman pointed out that the most essential part of this firing method was speed; not only did the speed create the necessary draft, but the vibration induced by running fast allowed the coal to shake down gradually before it could coke, thus ensuring even burning.

Uncoupling at the station in Harrisburg, they moved the K4 to the pit track area to finish the run. Before getting off, O.P. took one more look into the firebox. If he hadn't been a witness to this performance, he wouldn't have believed the fine shape the fire was in. He thanked his friend the engineer and told him the trip had been an educational experience.

Awaiting the westbound passenger train for the next segment of his journey home, O.P. reviewed what had transpired while riding aboard the express run from Altoona. For many years he had been aware that "bank-firing" was used on the main lines and on the western divisions, but he never knew that one large application of coal could last over such a long distance. Initially the fireman spent a lot of energy correctly loading the proper areas of the firebox, but afterward he was able to ride the seat box most of the time—something that was not possible on a hand-fired locomotive. In fact, the fireman paid less attention to the fire than he would have if a stoker was used. This method of firing also unraveled a bit of the mystery behind the stories of the fast, long-distance runs that various types of passenger engines had made over the years. It had always puzzled O.P. how the fireman could keep steam up on such runs, not so much when the smaller-class passenger engines were in use but when the K4 became the prime power. How the big boiler supplied steam to run constantly was something he hadn't been able to figure out. He knew he could crowd any L1—an engine with a boiler identical to the K4's—to a point where it was impossible for a fireman to keep steam up with a scoop shovel. Now he realized why the Williamsport Division never adopted "bank-firing": its trackage, with frequent slow orders, siding stops, and curves that prevented running at a constant speed for long distances, was not suited for the method.

Through the summer of 1931, diker crews were still subjected to few trips and long terminal layovers, but nothing came up on the bid board that O.P.

could handle with his seniority. His only consolation was that he still had a road job in these difficult economic times. Usually fall brought about an increase in coal movements, but even the change in seasons did not have much effect this time. Only occasionally would the crews get an additional trip in a "half."

Regardless of economic conditions, O.P. finished his run at Southport one Friday—the one before the start of deer season the following Monday—and marked off. For years he had spent this time with former working cohorts from the Sunbury area in their hunting cabin near Hyner. Recently, though, due to the increased deer population in the Ralston area, he chose to take this December holiday and hunt in the mountains around home. The first three days of this hunting season proved to be fruitless, but on Thursday afternoon his luck changed and he managed to shoot a large buck: a big-bodied white-tail adorned with a heavy set of antlers, a perfectly symmetrical eight-point rack. Now that he had this fine specimen, the problem of how to get it home from the remote mountain area arose; there was no snow, and it would be an all-day chore for him to drag it out alone. He had to have help.

Timing seemed to be a factor. He arrived home the same time I got home from school, and, not giving out too many details other than that he had shot a big buck, he sent me downtown to round up some help. I had no trouble enlisting the aid of three husky young men and, as instructed, I also solicited the aid of a grocer to bring his Model-T pickup to the water trough on the Red Run road in forty-five minutes. With only an hour of daylight left, O.P. and the helpers (I was allowed to go along) hurried up the steep mountain-side, which proved to be the hardest part, to the location of the felled deer. Dragging it down didn't pose any great problem, and we reached the waiting pickup just as darkness was setting in. Once the deer was delivered, it was hung on a convenient apple limb in our backyard. In a small town, word of mouth announcing that O.P.'s prize buck was on display caused an influx of townspeople visiting our home that evening to view the fine specimen.

The following morning, O.P. used the Company's telephone system from the call box at the water plug to notify the crew clerk at Southport that he was marking up and to place his name back on the board. Checking on his crew's standing, he was informed that they had completed a round-trip and marked off Thursday morning. Presently he was three times out. The way things were moving, he should be ready to accept a call early Saturday morning.

That evening he told my sister and me that he was going back to work and would leave while we were asleep because he had to catch the early morning passenger at 3:15 A.M. to Southport. I asked when he expected to be coming through Ralston, and after deliberation he said it probably would be soon after the 8:30 A.M. westbound passenger movement but before the eastbound

12:01 P.M. passenger. Angling a little, and because he would be going through on a day I wasn't in school, I asked if it was permissible for me to come down to the tracks to watch his passage through town. (I had been forbidden to go near the railroad or any part of it since the cabin incident more than a year and a half ago.) I was pleasantly surprised when he said it would be all right, if I stayed back and didn't get too close to the tracks.

On Saturday morning I was dressed and ready to go when the 8:30 A.M. passenger left town. All I had to do was put on my cap and heavy jacket to be off and running. About half an hour had passed when I heard an eastbound coming down the valley; its screecher whistle for the crossing at the upper end of the yard could be plainly heard almost a mile in the distance. Wasting no time, I was at trackside sitting on a pile of ties near the water tower when an I1 slowly approached the water plug. I was surprised and rather disappointed to see that O.P. wasn't sitting on the right side, but I used the occasion to watch what this train was doing. As it slowly ground to a halt, a man emerged from the monkey house on the tender and opened a lid, then let it drop with a loud clang.

Just before the engine stopped, another man appeared in the gangway and climbed down the steps, dropped off at the base of the water plug, and lifted the large rod-shaped handle used to swing the spout around to the top of the tender. With the spout positioned in the proper place, the man atop the tender reached up and pulled a lever, and a solid stream of water poured into the tank. After swinging the spout around, the man on the ground came over to where I was sitting and asked, "What are you doing here? Aren't you cold?"

Replying in the negative, I stated my reason: "I'm waiting for my dad to come through."

"So that's what you're up to," he said. "Who's your dad?"

"Oscar Orr," I told him.

He chuckled a little bit and said, "So you're Oscar's boy. I know him real well." He chuckled again and added: "But he's no good. I wouldn't wait out in this cold for anyone like him." As this man turned to head back to the engine he assured me, "Oscar was about ready to get under motion when we left Southport, and the way he runs you won't have to wait too long."

Watching the man on the tender then became the focus of my interest, and when enough water had been put in the tank he released the lever he had pulled open, which shut off the water, and then he gave the spout a hard shove, returning it to its original position. The engineer who had dropped off with his oil can must have found everything in order as he went around the locomotive, for soon he was back peering out the right cab window. I almost jumped off the tie pile when the shrill, ear-splitting whistle sounded a long blast, forcing me to instinctively cover my ears—which was good, because three more long blasts were about to be emitted. Then there was silence for a few seconds. The next sound that came from the engine was the bell ringing, followed by two short, quick blasts of the whistle.

All this took place in rapid succession, and I was completely enthralled by the performance. At the sound of air escaping, I saw the movement of mechanism on the outside of the driving wheels, and immediately the engine gave a long, heavy huff, like a deep sigh. Suddenly, what seemed to be a controllable steam engine went awry. A column of black smoke erupted from the smokestack straight up toward the sky, and the wheels were spinning rapidly, issuing a stream of bright sparks. Startled by this violent action, and unknowing as a seven-year-old, I was afraid this tremendous machine was about to tear itself to pieces. I was just ready to leave my grandstand perch for a safer area when the commotion abruptly stopped. The engine gave a heavy chug and started to move without slipping. The motion caused the couplings between the cars to start rattling, much like a falling domino effect, passing along between each car in rapid succession until it reached the end of the train. The exhausts grew steadily stronger as the train started picking up speed, and in a short time the cars were going by at a decent rate.

Engrossed in watching the train passing before me, I almost forgot the reason I was in this spot, but just as the cabin passed out of my view I was brought back to my senses by a whistle sounding for the crossing up the valley near the end of the siding. Something wasn't in order. It was a passenger engine's whistle, and it was too early for the noon passenger. Why was a passenger coming through in the middle of the morning? This was both thought-provoking and confusing. I knew O.P. didn't run a passenger train, but the man who had just talked to me said that O.P. was following their train.

As much as I wanted to go over and peer up the tracks to see what was going on as the train approached, I obeyed my orders and sat still. The section gang's shanty and the icehouse were blocking my view up the tracks, but the approaching train seemed to be coming fast. I heard the grinding of brake shoes, an indication that it was preparing to stop—and it did, but out of my view. I heard a load discharge of air, and at the same time I heard the engine start. When it came into view, I saw that it had a large red number plate up front and that it was shiny black with a red cab roof. Best of all, O.P. was seated in the cab window.

The same scenario as the train that had just passed was played out. The only differences this time were that a man rode the footboard on the rear of the tender, dropping off to swing the waterspout; that the man atop the tender didn't have a monkey house; and that O.P. was the person coming down the cab steps carrying the oil can. Alighting, he beckoned me over. As he began his inspection and oiling duties, I started asking about everything I'd seen that I didn't understand. Why did he have a passenger engine to pull a freight train? Why did they give him a brand-new engine? Why did he leave his train so far back instead of bringing it up to the water plug? Why did he seem to be in such a hurry? And on and on.

Continuing with his duties, O.P. explained that this type of engine was used not only for passenger service but also for heavy passenger trains and fast freight service, and that it had been assigned to this run for test purposes. It wasn't brand-new, either. Pointing to a plate on the boiler above the cylinders, he showed me the date it was built. It was nearly as old as I was, but it had just been put through the shops and overhauled. This plate, O.P. noted, identified the locomotive as one of the M1 class. The reason he had cut off from the train was to save time; he and the crew were going up home to examine his buck.

Now that the pertinent questions were answered, I proceeded to tell him what I had seen while I awaited his arrival. Of course, the highlight was the frightening, wildly spinning locomotive that seemed ready to fly apart. This interpretation brought a smile to his face, assuring me that this was common. The engineer had only given the engine a little too much steam and hadn't shut off the throttle quickly enough. The spinning didn't usually damage anything. I really made him laugh when I told him what the man who came off the engine said that also caused me some concern: "He told me you're no good!"

"That had to be the fireman," my father replied. "I know that jasper. Wait till I catch up to him in Altoona. I'll show him whether I'm any good or not."

When the tour around the M1 was completed, we ended up under the cab on the left side, where O.P. told me to climb the steps to get aboard. When we were on the engine, he parted the back curtain, allowing entry into the cab, and once inside I spotted my old friend the conductor sitting on the fireman's seat. He greeted me and explained that he'd come forward when they were in the siding at Cowley. He too would go along to inspect the big buck O.P. had hanging in his backyard.

As the crew was leaving the engine (all except the flagman, who was guarding the rear of the train, according to regulations), O.P. told me I could stay in the cab and watch the engine while they were gone. Naturally this met with my approval. He assured me that there was nothing to be afraid of, that everything with the engine was in order, but he gave me firm instructions: "You can sit on my seat and open or shut the window, but don't touch anything else. And if any other kids come around, don't allow them to get on the engine."

As I sat alone in the cab, I listened to the many different sounds the idled engine was making and tried to determine the different odors it was emitting. Perhaps it was hot oil or steam, but the prevalent smell was that of burning soft coal. Peering out the cab window of this exceptionally fine-looking locomotive, I found myself imagining I was in control of the large machine and racing down the tracks. Reality soon brought me back to my senses. I couldn't do that. I didn't even know how to ring the bell or blow the whistle.

Looking out the front cab window, I only saw a few people walking by in the street leading to the station not far from the water plug. But other than gazing in the direction of this new engine, no one bothered to even stop. Finally, a more venturesome person came across the playground in back of the water tank and showed interest in this different kind of locomotive. As he came nearer, I recognized him to be a railroad employee, and also a friend of our family. When he came alongside the engine, I slid open the cab window and leaned out to watch what he was doing. Spotting my presence he exclaimed, "Jack, what the hell are you doing on this engine?" and in the next breath asked, "Where did the crew get to?"

Bursting with pride now that I had been recognized in my exalted position, I hollered back, "I'm watching the engine for my dad. He and the crew went up home to look at his deer." That seemed to satisfy his curiosity. He spent a little more time looking over the big engine and left.

I wasn't sure how long the crew was gone, but it was at least fifteen minutes before they returned, and the first thing O.P. asked was, "Did anyone bother you while we were gone?" I replied that only one person came by, and after learning what I was doing he left. At this he said, "Since you did such a good job looking after the engine, I'll give you a little reward. You can stay aboard and ride back to where we'll couple up."

Elated to have the privilege of taking a ride on a locomotive, I almost jumped for joy. I did jump, but it wasn't for joy. As I was backing up to let O.P. get to his seat, I inadvertently stepped on the foot treadle. With a hiss of air, the fire door clanged open, exposing the raging inferno within. I didn't realize I had stepped on anything until I jumped back, and instantly my fear turned to despair. Without a doubt, I surely had broken something.

O.P. must have seen the expression of fear on my face, for he immediately told me, "You didn't do anything. All the pedal does is open the fire door. Go ahead and tramp on it again."

Obeying his command, I deliberately stepped on the pedal, and almost like magic the door parted in the middle, half going to either side.

"Hold your foot on it for a little bit," he said. "I'll lock it open so you can see in the firebox." And he adjusted a valve so the doors remained stationary when I removed my foot. "Now," he said, "look in there and you'll see what kind of fire keeps the engine running."

I looked into the firebox, but the heat and the intense shimmering glow made it difficult for me to see the entire length of this immense cavity. "How can you see in there and tell what's going on?" I asked.

He replied, "It takes a little while to get used to this condition, but after a little practice, you don't have any problems."

I learned even more about the fundamentals of a steam engine when O.P. pulled back on a lever as he positioned himself on the seat box and announced, "The lever I just adjusted makes the engine go either backward or forward." He then turned a valve and said, "This makes the bell ring," and as he moved a short brass lever he reported, "I just released the brakes. We're ready to move." Leaning out the cab window looking to the rear, O.P. reached up with his gloved right hand and placed it on a long lever. "This is the throttle," he said. "I'll give her a shot of steam, and as we start moving I'll close it, then open up again—just enough to get us back to the train."

Fascinated, I watched the deft, quick motions he made, even pulling a cord to blow the whistle. I was thinking it would be easy to run one of these monsters if I was big enough to reach the controls. Only a few exhausts were made before O.P., his hand remaining on the throttle, pushed it closed. Then, still looking back, he reached down to take hold of the brass brake lever. Slight movements on this lever started slowing the engine, and finally, moving it farther around, set up a grinding on the wheels that brought us nearly to a stop. The full stop came when the tender's coupler met the one on the standing train with a crunch, producing a minor jolt.

Next O.P. pointed to a gauge and explained that it indicated the proper amount of air pressure on the train's braking system. "Watch the hand," he said. "When the brakeman couples the air hoses and cuts in the air, the needle will flicker." Upon receiving a signal from the brakeman that everything was coupled, he then started moving the bottom brass air lever, explaining, "I'm making an air test on the train. Watch that gauge. When it holds steady we'll be ready to leave." Just as he was completing the test, there came a sudden roar of escaping steam. "The fireman got her too hot," he said. "That's the safety valves letting off the steam pressure. See that big gauge by the throttle? It shows we've got a little over 250 pounds, and things are set to pop off at 250 pounds boiler pressure."

O.P. casually reached for a lever above the brake pedestal and below the throttle and gave it a slight jerk. This initiated a growing noise beneath the cab, and when he pulled it more, wisps of steam began rising outside the cab window. "I just opened the injector," he explained. "This will put some water in the boiler, cooling things down and reducing the pressure." As soon as the safety valves closed, O.P. shut off the injector and pointed to a long gauge that held a long tube: "That's the water glass. It indicates how much water is in the boiler. As you can see, it's full right now." It had taken less than five minutes, but I had been able to observe some of the fundamentals involved in running a steam engine.

It was the final part that fascinated me most, though: I was allowed to participate. O.P. got off his seat box and picked me up, explaining, "Before we leave, we have to signal the flagman to get back on the cabin. Grab that cord and pull it down. I'll tell you when to stop whistling." Although the noise the whistle created was deafening in the confines of the cab, I held it down until O.P. told me to let up. I repeated this action three more times. Finished with the calling of the flag, O.P. parted the curtain, placed me on the deck, and said, "We're ready to leave. You'll have to get off now. Just be careful going down the steps."

I scampered down the vertical steps. Before I reached the last one, the bell started ringing, and with the sound of air the reversing rods were moving. As I alighted on the ground, two short, sharp whistle blasts sounded, the wheels started moving, and the couplers between the cars started to rattle. The exhausts grew more rapidly at each turn of the wheels, and the sharp sound it made on the cold December morning caused reverberations between the mountains. It was apparent that O.P. had control of the shiny M1. He never slipped a wheel.

As I stood next to the tracks watching the train pass, I heard the whistle blowing for the crossing in South Ralston. On the last blast, O.P., evidently proud of the M1, finished by lowing it off, identifying himself as the engineer. The sound of the passenger whistle was much more pleasing than the sound of freight locomotive whistles.

When I returned home my mother remarked, "Your dad told me that while he and the crew were looking over the deer, you were watching the engine for him. Did you have any problems?" In response, I explained in detail everything I'd witnessed, plus what O.P. had shown me, elaborating that the best part was riding on the locomotive and blowing the whistle. I then related something that troubled me. "The fireman on the other train told me he knew my dad but said he was no good." My mother, amused, laughed and said: "Maybe he knows something we don't, but I honestly believe he was just kidding you."

As O.P. had explained, the M1 was a test engine, and he had been given one of those manila folders in which to record the results of its performance on the Altoona-Southport run. However, when the Engineering Department sent the engine and folder out, they didn't check whether he had laid off; they just assigned the engine to his crew. So the extra engineer who took his place didn't do too much recording, other than the tonnage he was hauling and the time intervals. O.P. logged all the details on the Southport-Altoona segment of the run with an empty train, noting that coal and water consumption was similar to the amount used by the I1sa class, that the locomotive produced steam adequately under all conditions, that starts had to be made slowly to avoid slipping, that at more than 10 miles an hour it accelerated rapidly, that it developed enough power for ease in train handling, and that its ride was excellent. However, he concluded that this big high-drivered 4-8-2 locomotive could not be used to its utmost efficiency on this particular segment of the railroad. The branch lines with their speed restrictions, particularly the Elmira portion with the many hills and curves, kept the engine from reaching its full speed potential. It could achieve maximum performance only on long stretches found on the main lines. But if the Company were to assign him an M1 on every run, he wouldn't offer any objections.

This was the last engine on which O.P. would record data for the Engineering Department. The austerity program under which the Company was operating had curtailed most equipment development, and the Company made only a few modifications to existing steam power during the Depression era. Before this, the Company had made an effort to steadily increase the size, power, and efficiency of the steam locomotive. In a little more than twenty-seven years, since he hired on in 1904, O.P. had been a part of this transition, especially in the engines used in freight service. Starting with the then large Class R H3 Consolidation (2-8-0); advancing to the larger Consolidations, the H6a, H6b, H8, and H9; and, as the engines increased in size and wheel arrangement, to the L1's (2-8-2), I1's (2-10-0), N1's and N2's (2-10-2), and now the most modern M1's (4-8-2). Even the passenger classes had been sampled on their break-in runs, fresh out of the Renovo shops. The only production model to elude his gloved hand on the throttle was the G5 (4-6-0). The only other engines he never throttled were one-of-a-kind classes, and ones used primarily in yard service, the B8 and B6 series (0-6-0) and the large C1 (0-8-0).

Evaluating the freight engines, O.P. would advocate that the best all-purpose locomotive that had been developed thus far was the L1s. It could run fast, steam easily, ride well, and, despite its rather large size for a Mikado, it was economical to operate. However, the Company had always used this engine without receiving the full benefit of its potential, because it failed to make any of the modifications necessary to achieve high performance. The first time O.P. brought an L1s into Ralston, he determined that it needed a stoker. Then, after running the I1s's, he decided it also needed a feedwater heater and, above all, an attached tender that held approximately 14,000 gallons of water.

A Pennsylvania Railroad Class "R" H3 Consolidation (2-8-0), pictured at an unknown location sometime between 1904 and 1910. O.P. Orr began his career as a fireman and an engineer operating these locomotives.

TRAIN TIME. BELLEFONTE, PA.

A Pennsylvania Railroad local passenger train, headed by Class P (later Class D) 4-4-0 #1381, is readied for departure from the Bellefonte, Pennsylvania, railroad station early in the twentieth century. On a locomotive like this, and from this location, O.P. Orr got his first job firing on a passenger train in 1907.

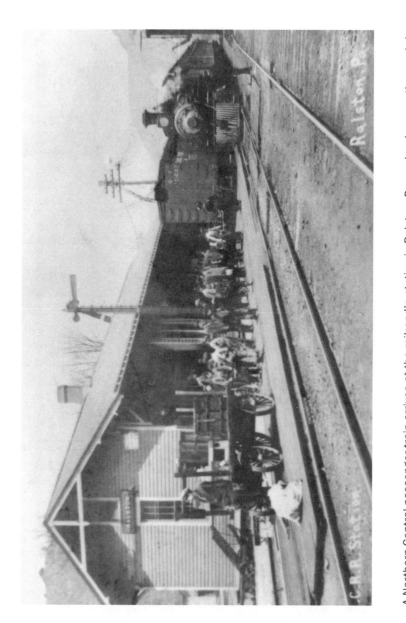

A Northern Central passenger train arrives at the railroad's station in Ralston, Pennsylvania, sometime early in the 1900s. This is where O.P. Orr detrained upon his arrival in 1910 to begin work as a Pennsylvania Railroad over-the-road locomotive engineer.

Oscar P. Orr (left), circa 1914, with his fireman Wesley Kerr, resting against the boiler handrail of a Class H6b Consolidation assigned to him.

O.P. Orr, in his classic pose, straddles the rails for an unidentified photographer taking a picture of his special train at the Trout Run siding. White flags atop a locomotive's boiler signify an "extra" movement. In this case, additional flags have been mounted across the middle of the smoke box. O.P., along with fireman A. P. Thomas (standing on the running board), was bringing in the first 2-8-2 L1s Mikado to reach Ralston in 1921.

One of the Pennsylvania Railroad's fabled 4-6-2 Pacific-type locomotives, shown trailing a milk car in Sunbury, Pennsylvania, in February 1936. O.P. Orr's experience with these locomotives, intended for the Pennsy's fastest passenger trains, required him to do switching maneuvers on local passenger service in 1933–34 that included picking up the morning's milk in milk cars at milk plants along the route.

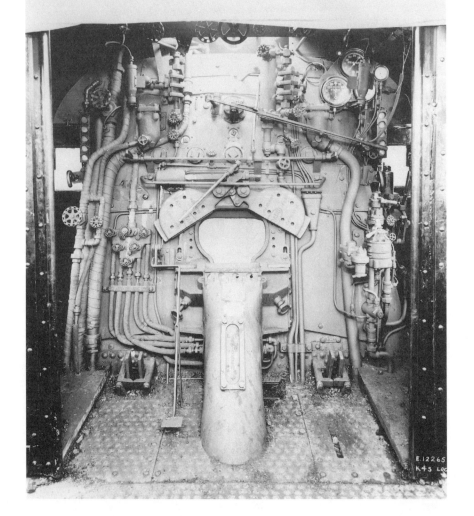

Opposite page | The backhead of Pennsylvania Railroad K4s 4-6-2 #3746 (built 1914–27). This typically was the workspace of O.P. Orr and his fireman while the crew was moving a train along the railroad. The engineer sat to the right, behind the partition visible along the right foreground. The fireman sat in an identical position to the left. The long lever extending from the upper middle of the backhead to the right is the throttle. The lever that appears to be resting against the partition on the right, about midway up, is the reversing gear. The two levers, the upper of which is pointing right and the lower, pointing left, are the train and locomotive air brakes, respectively. Also visible are the firebox doors, swung open by stepping on the foot treadle set to the left of the stoker; the stoker column leading to the firebox; the blower (the upper horizontal bar in mid-picture with levers on each end); the injector (above the brake pedestal); and the receptacles for the grate-shaking bar (the two parallel projections on the floor to the right and left of the stoker column). The myriad knobs and gauges were used to monitor and correct water, steam, and air-pressure levels; to lubricate the valve mechanism; and to read distant signals on main lines.

Looking down the Red Run Coal Company incline plane just west of Ralston, Pennsylvania, from atop Red Run Mountain. Taken in the early 1900s, this view shows the Pennsylvania Railroad's engine house, coal hoist, and other engine-servicing facilities in the background. The wye used to turn locomotives is visible among the sidings leading to the coal tipple and brick factory.

The B-6sb switcher, an 0-6-0, with its "swallow-tailed dinky" slope-backed tender, doing its work at the Williamsport roundhouse within the Pennsylvania Railroad system. O.P. Orr operated these locomotives during his tenure on a yard and transfer crew between 1937 and 1947.

An M1a 4-8-2 locomotive. O.P. Orr operated these locomotives when he moved scheduled freight trains, mostly on runs from Enola to Southport.

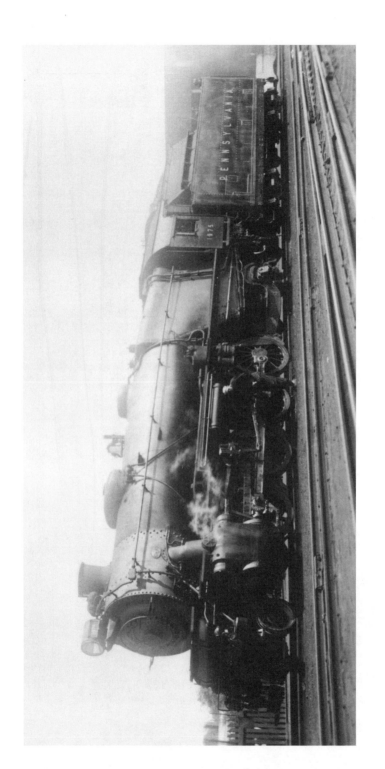

The 2-8-2 L1 locomotive, known as a "Mikado," was O.P. Orr's favorite for combining power with ease of operation in hauling freight trains. The L1 here, #1975, came to Williamsport in 1943 to handle switching chores in Newberry Yard. It is equipped with a Lines West tender called a "Prairie Schooner" to afford the crew better visibility during switching maneuvers. It was one of the many such locomotives that O.P. operated during his career.

The Pennsylvania Railroad's massive I1sa, a 2-10-0, at rest between assignments, is sporting a tender of the type O.P. always thought inadequate for the assignments given to these behemoths. He ran them off and on between 1930 and 1949. Note the "doghouse" behind the coal bunker on the tender.

FIVE

THE DEPRESSION YEARS

During the winter of 1931 and into 1932, the demand for coal, the all-important commodity hauled by diker crews, seemed to decline, and two round-trips per half was all that could be expected. During one of his long layovers at home, O.P. advised the family that before conditions worsened, as they usually did with the coming of spring, he would look for a better-paying run. He also explained that no matter what run was available, he would have to spend more time away from home, that at present there was no other alternative.

One thing was certain: no other engineer with more seniority on the roster was about to bump him off a diker run. He only had to find a suitable run advertised on the bid board. But that wouldn't be lucrative either. Engineers who had decent jobs were hanging on to them, and the Company was eliminating jobs, not adding new ones. The few jobs that did appear on the board were mostly on yard crews, or jobs the older men bid in, leaving O.P. with the Altoona-Southport run.

After waiting and watching, O.P. found a job advertised in the spring of 1932: a new symbol fast freight CSBY 1 and 2 running from Altoona to Wilkes-Barre via the Bald Eagle Branch through South Williamsport, Sunbury, and up (east) on the Wilkes-Barre Branch. The job posting noted that the run was set up as a "pool crew" (first in, first out), that there was no scheduled calling time, and that it was a 196-mile trip one way, making it the longest run on the Williamsport Division. Figuring that the mileage pay rate on this lengthy run would have to be high and would be bid in by older men on the roster, O.P. decided the only thing he had to lose by bidding was the time it took to fill out the form. Placing his bid, he found that when the awarding day came he had beat the odds and had been awarded one of the crews.

Now that he had a CSBY crew, O.P. delved into the new job and found that his was not an ordinary fast freight but a "hotshot." The entire train consisted of perishable merchandise—meat, fruit, and vegetables coming from the Midwest and Far West. Chicago was the assembly point. When the train was made up ready to leave, first-out crews were alerted that within fifteen hours they would be called for duty. This made it necessary to have a telephone installed at home. Previously call boys, then the Company's phone system, had sufficed.

Signing up for his first trip, O.P. was notified that he had been allocated six hours to run from Altoona to Wilkes-Barre, a distance of nearly 200 miles. If he didn't adhere to this schedule, the ire of officialdom would descend on him. O.P. agreed with the officials in the Motive Power Department about the type of engine to be used on that run. Speed restrictions on the Bald Eagle and Wilkes-Barre branches ruled out speeds the M1 or M1a could attain, making it an unnecessary waste under these conditions. Their choice of the all-purpose L1s was more in order.

At the engine house, O.P. made another discovery. The L1s assigned was not the usual run-of-the-mill engine, but one that, along with several others of this class, had been modified and set aside for use exclusively on these runs. They were improved versions, equipped with stokers and air-power reverse gear. Furthermore, the shop had explicit orders to keep these engines in top mechanical condition for use on the CSBY freights.

Out of the engine house, the 2-8-2 was positioned in readiness, and as soon as the "hotshot" came off the Pittsburgh Division and stopped, the engine was uncoupled. O.P. moved back across a switch to couple on. While the engines were changed, two car inspectors, one on either side, made their check of the train, and a switching crew transferred the cabins. This maneuver was much the same as the services afforded passenger movements, and orders received read as ones the first-class named trains operated under.

The CSBY-1 eastbound had precedence over all movements from Altoona to Wilkes-Barre. Starting out, the consist of nearly seventy cars was soon brought up to a running speed of 60 miles an hour. O.P. could work the L1s with the assistance of the stoker and not worry about harming his fireman. The sprint on the Middle Division four-track main ended at the crossover to the Bald Eagle Branch, forcing the first slow move. Entering Tyrone, they made a stop to allow the awaiting pusher to be coupled on. After pounding up the stiff grade out of Tyrone and cutting off the pusher at Vail, passenger speed of 60 miles an hour was maintained on the descent to Milesburg, where a stop to take water was made. The remaining miles on the Bald Eagle were run at passenger speeds, and on the double track from Lock Haven to Linden O.P. was able to crowd better than 60 miles an hour out of the 2-8-2.

Linden, nearing the halfway point on this long haul, was scheduled as a refueling and water stop. The scene at this facility was hard to believe. The track to the coaling tower was clear, allowing him to pull in without the usual waiting period, and in less than five minutes the engine had been serviced. From there on, O.P. was under the guidance of a pilot—not that he was a stranger on the south side single-track cutoff or the double track at Allens Tower, but this was the first he had been east of Allens Tower since 1907.

More than 45 miles of double-track running added to his average running speed. The only slowing was to observe the 35-mile-per-hour restriction while passing through Milton, and again as he passed through Northumberland before reaching Sunbury. At Sunbury he again stopped to take water and pick up a pilot for the remainder of the trip up the north branch of the Susquehanna River to Wilkes-Barre. Crossing over the Williamsport Division main to enter the Wilkes-Barre Branch was reminiscent of the same move some twenty-five years previous, but once beyond the line leading to Mount Carmel, O.P. was in first-time territory.

The single track followed the river on the south bank, and a slight ascending grade would be present the entire distance, nearly 60 miles. Setting the L1s at running speed, O.P. found that the grade limited his progress to less than 55 miles an hour, and despite different settings this was the maximum speed he could coax out of the 2-8-2. Using the engine in this manner made it necessary to make one more water stop, this time at Nescopeck, about midway on the run.

As they entered the Buttonwood yard at Wilkes-Barre, switches were set to enter the track designated to become an interchange with the Central of New Jersey Railroad, much like the one in Altoona. A Jersey Central locomotive was waiting to take over where the L1s was uncoupled, and a switch engine took care of transferring the cabins. From departure to arrival, five hours and twenty minutes had elapsed, making the average running time on this long haul 37.5 miles an hour.

Why would the powerful Pennsylvania Railroad expedite a hotshot freight movement from Chicago to Altoona on its main lines and then, within 300 miles of its New York City destination, switch it to a secondary route? And why would it turn this perishable merchandise special over to a foreign railroad for the remaining 100 or so miles? Unraveling this puzzle, O.P. decided that this secondary segment routing and transfer to another railroad created the shortest distance between Altoona and New York. Cost-conscious shippers of this Depression era could care less about how their merchandise traveled as long as they realized a savings on transportation costs.

On the other side of the picture, the Jersey Central's terminal in New

York was designated by the shippers as their distribution and loading point. Rather than accepting transfer charges at their designated terminal, the Jersey Central, with its command position at this site, opted for and received over-the-road revenue from Wilkes-Barre. The reverse of this arrangement worked effectively for the Jersey Central; perishables from Long Island and the New England states, and imports, were assembled at that terminal to be shipped westward to Wilkes-Barre on their rails. At this point, the CSBY-2 picked up the train of refrigerator cars to be hurried to Chicago for Midwest distribution. (In fact, this joint transportation venture proved to be successful enough to outlast the Depression, steam engines, and into the use of diesel power, until the demise of the Pennsylvania Railroad.)

The CSBY runs allowed O.P. to use his skills as an engineer moving trains of refrigerator cars over the rails, using the speed and power a steam engine was capable of developing when clear blocks were offered all the way. This fast running was exactly the way O.P. always thought a railroad should operate. When a train was dispatched from a terminal, its purpose was to reach the established destination as quickly as possible.

Nevertheless, as he had on previous runs, O.P. again created for himself a certain challenge. He was determined to get the hotshot from Altoona to Wilkes-Barre in five hours or less, but the runs always took just a few minutes longer. Although he was averaging between 38 and 39 miles an hour, there were too many deterrents to contend with: slow orders for track maintenance, restricted distant signals for meets that were late in clearing, slow pusher hookups in Tyrone, and, above all, the L1s's tender, which did not hold enough water for long-distance travel.

Seasonal changes did not interfere with the number of trips the CSBY crews ran. When a perishable product was out of season on either coast, another took its place, and meat shipments seemed to remain constant. Layovers at either terminal were usually around forty-eight hours, and crews made at least three round-trips the half pay period, with an extra one part of the round-trip sometimes included. A comparison of earnings of crews handling these trains with the earnings of the better-paying runs anywhere in the entire Company system would reveal that they were receiving top wages.

One of the biggest drawbacks for the crews was getting home during layovers at either terminal. Passenger train service on both branches left much to be desired. Even under adverse travel conditions, though, O.P. and his crew, mostly men from the Williamsport area, did manage to get home, often resorting to riding cabins on trains traveling in the proper direction.

In the spring of 1933, on a routine run in weather typical of this time of year—a mixture of wet snow and rain—O.P. was keeping the eastbound

CSBY-1, nicknamed "Sea Biscuit" by the crews, on schedule despite adverse conditions. Nearing the community of Milton, he shut the 2-8-2 off and began slowing to observe the 35-mile-per-hour speed restriction. Although the weather was less than ideal, it was not obstructing his vision, and as they approached the American Car & Foundry factory, manufacturers of railroad tank cars, he noticed that automobiles coming from the factory complex were crossing the tracks.

A check of the time on his watch confirmed that these cars were carrying homeward-bound workers who had just completed their day's work. Sensing that this crossing could be dangerous at that time of the day, O.P. made another reduction on the automatic brake system, a more-or-less precautionary measure to make sure he wasn't exceeding the speed limit. At the proper distance from the crossing, he activated the bell and started giving the necessary whistle signals. Apparently all the workers had left, for there was no traffic using the crossing, but just before he came upon that point he saw two cars approaching at a rapid rate: one a sedan, the other a coupe. Alarmed, O.P. immediately pulled the whistle wide open, to warn the cars to stop before entering the crossing, but even though they evidently heard the warning signal, they seemed to accelerate. It was obvious that they were going to attempt to beat the train instead of waiting for its passage.

The sedan did manage to get across safely with inches to spare, but the coupe could never make it. At the last second, O.P. slammed the train into emergency, realizing it was too late to stop. From what he could see, the car would slam into the side of the engine, and that moving force would in turn cast the car aside. His calculations were just a hair off. The coupe made it onto the crossing and was struck by the pilot coupling midway on the auto's engine compartment.

The impact of the collision, and the ensuing dragging effect before the train was halted, smashed the coupe into the pilot and footboards, killing its two occupants instantly. This was the kind of tragedy O.P. had hoped he would never be involved in—hitting an automobile at a grade crossing—but after it happened he resolved that all his afterthoughts about how it might have been averted were useless, that nothing could change the outcome once the accident had occurred.

The accident caused a lengthy delay for this train that was carrying perishables. The eastbound main was closed, as Company officials, law enforcement personnel, and the coroner conducted their investigations, examined the scene, took measurements, and gathered statements from each crew member, all before the bodies and wreckage could be removed. Nearly three hours passed before orders were received to resume the trip, and the Sea Biscuit arrived in Wilkes-Barre more than two hours late for its connection. No official reprimands were given for failing to reach the destination within the six-hour limit on this particular day.

Many years later, I met the person who was the head brakeman on the CSBY-1 and was aboard the L1 on the day of the Milton accident. He asked whether O.P. had ever mentioned anything about the unfortunate incident, and I assured him it had been discussed and that I was aware of most of the details, even the weather conditions. Then he added something I didn't know: "The entire time we were tied up, Oscar never got off the engine. He just sat on his seat box smoking his pipe. Even the officials had to climb on the engine for his statement."

Later I told O.P. that I'd met the brakeman on the Sea Biscuit run, and described the topic of our conversation, the crossing accident in Milton. This prompted me to ask, "Why didn't you get off the engine?" I received a short reply, probably explaining his feeling at that time, and even at the present time: "I knew what I did. There was no reason for me to get off and look at the mess I created."

During the remainder of the spring and through most of the summer of 1933, everything on the Sea Biscuit was run in a normal manner, but O.P. was again watching the bid board. Not that he was dissatisfied with this run, but the problems getting back and forth from terminals, and the short periods of time spent at home, were becoming aggravating. Another factor was the uncertainty of his calling time at the Altoona terminal. It compelled him not to stray far from the telephone, lest he miss a call and lose a round-trip, which would significantly reduce his earnings.

The only job on the board that he was interested in was a passenger run, trains 510 and 511 between Altoona and Harrisburg via the Bald Eagle Branch to Lock Haven, then down the Susquehanna River through Williamsport and Sunbury. This too was a lengthy run, almost the same mileage as he was getting on the Sea Biscuit, but at least he would have a regular calling time. When he bid on this job, it was with the same feeling he'd had about the CSBY 1 and 2 hotshot: perhaps the older men on the roster working out of Williamsport wouldn't opt for this Altoona-based passenger run. So far the odds had favored him; no one with more seniority had ever bumped him off the Altoona-Southport dikers, and he had retained the prime Sea Biscuit crew for the past year and a half without being bumped.

O.P.'s theory proved correct. Near the end of September 1933 he was awarded the bid, and for the first time since he was set up as an engineer in

1909 he was about to become a passenger engineer. But before he assumed his new position, the office of the road foreman of engines asked him to appear for a personal consultation at his earliest convenience. That came as a surprise. He had no idea why such a meeting was necessary. To the best of his knowledge he hadn't committed any infractions in the line of duty.

Appearing as ordered, he learned that the meeting had to do with his physical condition. The road foreman, referring to a copy of the yearly physical exam O.P. had had just days earlier, said, "Oscar, your blood pressure's on the high side. It's within limits for freight service, but it's higher than the Medical Department will allow for a passenger engineer. There's nothing anyone can do about it, because you passed your physical this year. Next year, though, if the reading is this high they'll take you out of service. The Company isn't making any exception either. As you know, they have more people furloughed than they have working. Personally I wish you'd forget about this passenger run and stay in freight service while this condition persists. Your smartest move under these circumstances would be to withdraw your bid."

Mulling over what the road foreman had said, and knowing that everything he'd said was true, O.P. thanked him for his concern but announced that he wasn't going to withdraw his bid. A whole year remained to bring his high blood pressure down.

During our evening meal, O.P. told my mother, sister, and me about his visit to the road foreman's office, stating that he was taking the passenger job but that before he went back to the doctor next year he'd have to get his blood pressure down. My mother, concerned, then interjected that she could offer a suggestion that surely would help: "I've been telling you for some time that you're drinking too much, and if you don't slow down or stop, you're going to end up just like your former conductor did." (The conductor who rode behind O.P. for more than twenty-one years on the dikers had dropped dead of a heart attack while climbing the stairs leading to a walkway over the yards in the Altoona complex during the past summer.) O.P.'s response promptly ended the discussion: "You can't compare me with that conductor. All he ever did was ride on the cushions in the cabin. At least when I'm on an engine I do work, and I try to keep myself in good physical condition."

Assuming the prestigious position of a passenger engineer had been one of O.P.'s aspirations from the time he was "set up running" twenty-four years ago. Now that he had advanced to such a sought-after position, and even though it wasn't one of the named flyers, he would be hauling trains 510 and 511 according to a published schedule. The timetable for these runs indicated that it was a leisurely schedule, but on the first trip with the 510 eastbound he learned that the timetable was misleading. Before reaching Harrisburg, he was constantly having to make up time.

The power used on this roundabout run was the now famous K4s-class engine, but not the more modern version. The ones assigned were still equipped with the manual screw reverse mechanism, were hand-fired, and hauled modified original-style tenders with built-up coal bunkers. Although these engines lacked the more modern attachments, that did not affect their operating performance; they had all the basic needs.

Departing the Altoona station almost mid-morning for his initial trip, O.P. had in tow what was to be the normal consist of this passenger run: an express, a baggage, a railway postal car, and three coaches, a total of six cars. Coupled to such a light train, the K4s took this in stride, and the sprint down the Middle Division main to the Tyrone cutoff was made at better than 70 miles an hour, resulting in an early station stop in Tyrone. Out of there, the pace on the Bald Eagle became slower. The hill to Vail, including a stop after reaching the summit, was the first obstacle.

After descending on the Bald Eagle, a succession of station stops followed: Warriors Mark, Port Matilda, Julian, and Milesburg. Milesburg required not only a station stop but also a stop for water, followed by an unusual movement: the entire train was backed up the L&T Branch for two and a half miles to Bellefonte. That did not improve his scheduled time, as speed restrictions coming forward off this branch were set at 30 miles an hour.

Out on the main again, he picked up his running speed quickly, but the Howard hill slowed this somewhat, and as he descended he had to prepare for the station stop at Howard. At this point he completed the first of many switching maneuvers that were to follow. The train was parked at the station, the K4 was uncoupled, and a dash of more than a half-mile was made to the Sheffield Farm dairy plant to pick up a loaded refrigerated milk car. Here, the brakeman began performing chores usually associated with yard crews: uncoupling, opening and closing the plant's switch, and, once the race back to the train was made, the coupling-up procedures.

The addition of one car did not impede the big Pacific's start or running, but the short distance between stations limited the speed that could be reached. Less than five miles east of Howard, a station stop at Blanchard (Beech Creek) was followed by another pickup move at the milk plant, then a station stop in Mill Hall and the addition of yet another milk car. Not much speed was gained in the three miles remaining on the Bald Eagle Branch. O.P. arrived in Lock Haven on time.

From Lock Haven, the trip would now be on a double-track main, which was supposedly conducive to faster running. But that was not to happen. Just after getting the 4-6-2 stretched out, a station stop was made at McElhattan, and in less than five miles repeated at Antes Fort (Jersey Shore), where the third milk car was added. Running for approximately the same distance, a station stop was made at Nesbit, then the tower at Linden was approached. This stop was time-consuming; the engine was again uncoupled, as this was the midpoint of the run and a move to the coaling tower to refuel was necessary.

While the coal was loaded, the grates were shaken and the ash pan was emptied. From there, the four miles of single track to the Park Hotel station in Williamsport was almost arrow straight. This allowed for fast running, enabling O.P. to arrive on time.

As soon as the train stopped, the engine was again uncoupled and moved forward to take water, a step not performed at Linden. This was the longest station stop on the run, with twelve minutes allowed on the schedule. During this time a waiting yard crew backed up with a B6, split the train, and set out the express car brought in from Altoona. Following this, they picked up two Harrisburg-destined express cars and placed them against four Sheffield Farm milk cars that had just arrived via the Elmira Branch passenger. Moving by this string of cars, they pushed the 510's milk cars onto it, pulled forward to the crossover switch, and placed these cars in a backing move to the awaiting section. After this switching move, the B6 moved out and O.P. again coupled the K4 to this now-heavy train of fourteen cars. The time spent here gave the fireman a chance to further clean his fire so everything was in readiness for the remaining 100 miles to Harrisburg.

The train was barely getting started when a stop was made at the downtown Market Street station. Passengers off the Elmira Branch train that was timetabled to meet the 510 used this train as a shuttle to Downtown Williamsport, and some passengers boarded at this location. Continuing eastbound out of the city on single track did not permit picking up much speed. A slight grade was encountered while crossing over the Reading Railroad's main, and continued onto the bridge crossing the Susquehanna River. On the other side, at Allens Tower, when double track again started, the K4 responded with what it was designed to do by coming up to speed very quickly, even with a heavy train in tow. This speed didn't last long; a station stop had to be made in Montgomery.

Not far from Montgomery the West Branch of the Susquehanna was again crossed to the eastern side, and the tracks remained on this side of the river into Harrisburg. Just on the other side of this bridging, O.P. stopped at Dewart, not only at the station but again to uncouple and pick up the final milk car. From here to Sunbury, three more station stops had to be made:

Watsontown, Milton, and Northumberland. Distances between these points did not offer enough room for the 4-6-2 to build up too much speed, especially when a train of fifteen cars had to be started. As a result, the 510 arrived in Sunbury a little behind schedule.

At Sunbury, a ten-minute stop was on the schedule, the time needed to conduct the last of the switching maneuvers. The train was split back at the railway postal car and moved forward to the water plug, and the tender was filled before again making up the train. Only four more station stops were left before reaching the final destination—Herndon, Dalmatia, Millersburg, and Halifax—with enough spacing between each to allow some time to be made up, even though the consist was now seventeen cars.

Out of Halifax, O.P. put an old teamster's saying—"When nearing the barn, let the horses have their head"—into play and opened up the K4 for his last lap. After crowding everything this engine could muster on the start, it was finally set up for sustained running on this portion of nearly straight track with no speed restriction on the slight curves. Soon he was handling the train at better than 80 miles an hour. On this last dash he picked up enough time to arrive at Harrisburg on time. Sometimes, K4's seemed to run faster than others, although they were all built the same. With one exceptionally fast 4-6-2, O.P. timed himself by the mileposts, and for two miles he was clocking 93 miles an hour.

Contemplating the activities of this run, O.P. decided that he was not running a passenger train, but something akin to a high-speed "local freight job." He had been uncoupled and coupled seven times, and five of these times switching moves had to be made with a locomotive not specifically designed for this type of chore. He had always maintained that the screw mechanism was the optimal in valve control, but he now had reason to believe it also had limitations, especially when it involved switching. At the milk plants at Williamsport and Sunbury, he not only pulled away from the train to the sidings, but also reversed to enter and pick up cars, pulled out in the forward motion, reversed to back to the awaiting train, and then again placed the engine in forward motion to get under way. Turning the reverse gear wheel to reverse and back to forward ten times on this run was enough to create some arm fatigue.

There was not much of a layover in Harrisburg. The 510 arrived in the mid-afternoon, and the westbound 511 had an early-morning calling time. The early departure from Harrisburg was required because the train distributed morning newspapers from the major eastern cities, and hence was nicknamed "the paper train." It also carried a variety of high-class perishables, such as seafood and berries in season.

Like the brakeman who got a workout on the 510, the baggage master on the 511 worked at every station stop. The fireman didn't have any idle time regardless of the direction traveled. Hand-firing the big-boilered K4 for nearly 200 miles required putting more than 15 tons of coal into the firebox. Normally the 511 had a train of ten or eleven cars leaving Harrisburg: railway postal and express cars that were switched off in Sunbury for the awaiting Wilkes-Barre Branch passenger; and three express cars for Williamsport that were taken out by a yard crew, one of which went north (west) on the connecting Elmira Branch passenger. Out of Williamsport westbound, the train was whittled down to the railway postal and express cars and four coaches. It remained unchanged until reaching Altoona in mid-morning. Water again was taken at Sunbury, Williamsport, and Milesburg, and coal was replenished at Linden. With only three uncoupling and coupling motions, the 511 schedule, even with the Bellefonte stop, was easier to run. O.P. could post on-time performance for the entire distance to Altoona.

The 510 and 511 trips, other than being long-distance runs, were not easy to make, but after making the rounds a few times O.P. was satisfied with this job. From the first time he was "set up running" and assigned to a yard crew in 1909, he had been at the mercy of call boys or compelled to remain near a telephone. Now he knew when he was going to work and when he would be off duty. Then too, this job afforded him a reasonable amount of time at home, because after making a round-trip he would be off for a trip. Handling a K4 was a pleasure too, and he found the prowess this locomotive could display amazing.

He even had the opportunity to handle the other rather large Pacific class the Company had in its stable. Instead of always being assigned the K4, he occasionally drew its predecessor class, K2. On the first trip out of Altoona with this older-class locomotive, O.P. had no trouble handling the train of six cars. It rode rougher than the K4, but it had the same fine steaming characteristics. On the stiff grade out of Tyrone it was a little short on the power end, but there were no difficulties, and the run down the Bald Eagle was made according to schedule. Even with nine cars going into Williamsport, he arrived on time.

Leaving Williamsport with the usual fifteen cars, he found that the K2 could start this heavy train with relative ease, but once started he discovered it was nearly impossible to develop his average running speed. It was even more difficult out of Sunbury with seventeen cars. On stretches where he usually made up time with a K4, he was now losing time. On the last segment between Halifax and Harrisburg—what he'd used as a race track—all the speed the K2 could muster was just a little more than 60 miles an hour. He arrived late.

The engine used on the 510 was usually the same one dispatched on the 511, so O.P. was saddled with the K2 on the way back to Altoona. On this side of the run, however, the train wasn't as heavy. While this allowed him to keep within the scheduled time, it did require a lot of coaxing. At the end of the trip, in Altoona, he reasoned that the K2 was a sluggish locomotive. Perhaps if this was the only class of Pacific available, and it couldn't compare with the high-performance qualities of the K4, he might have been less critical.

In the interim, while O.P. was running the hotshot Sea Biscuit and now the passenger run, I had advanced far enough in age to develop a profound interest in the more intricate factors concerning railroading. In the narrow valley in which Ralston was located, one could not escape the railroad activities. Consciously or unconsciously, the railroad was a part of the daily life of this community—especially the passenger train movements—and to some extent played a large part in day-to-day activities.

Every morning at 8:30 A.M., the westbound (north) passenger's arrival served notice that it was time to prepare to leave for another day at school. At noon, the eastbound (south) arrived, signaling lunchtime. Then the 3:30 P.M. westbound gave notice that only fifteen minutes remained until school was dismissed for the day. The coming of the 5:30 P.M. eastbound train alerted us that it was time to stop playing and to go home for supper. Two other passengers passed through town—an eastbound at midnight and a westbound at 3:30 A.M.—both stopping only if someone wanted to get off or get on. Ralston was a "flag stop" for these Pullman car trains. Even in the summertime, my mother issued orders to be at home after the daytime trains had passed through, and we couldn't use the excuse that we didn't know what time it was.

As long as these passengers helped frame my life, I was curious about where they came from and where they were going, and O.P. was my main source of information. He explained that the westbounds left Williamsport and made a 175-mile run to Upstate New York, connecting with the Erie Railroad (the Pennsylvania used the Erie's terminal in Elmira), then continuing north through Watkins Glen and terminated at Canandaigua, where they made connections with the New York Central; passengers transferred to the Central to reach their destinations at Rochester or Syracuse. This too, I learned, was the northern point of the Williamsport Division. Also at this terminal, Pullman cars as well as passengers coming in on the westbound night trains were transferred to the Central for passage to Rochester and Syracuse. Eastbound Pullmans from these two cities carried passengers bound for Philadelphia, Baltimore, and Washington.

The proximity of the school building to the railroad provided an excellent spot from which to observe passing trains. Less than 200 feet separated the two. I was close enough to read the lettering on the passing rail cars. Some adjacent buildings obstructed my view, but there were enough open places to let me see past them. In the classroom that housed both the third and the fourth grades, part of my education evolved around watching what was taking place in the passing daily parade. At first it all looked the same, a locomotive pulling strings of cars, but as time passed I could see that all these trains were not the same. There was a distinct difference in the cars they were hauling, and the number of cars hauled varied with each train.

One thing gave me a distinct advantage. I had been operating a Lionel electric freight train set that I had received for Christmas some two years earlier, and this had helped me to be able to identify most of the cars: box, tank, gondola, hopper, flat, and the red cabin. However, there were variations among the cars. Most notably, some of the boxcars had raised hatches at either end, and some of the flatcars had five ribbed metal boxes affixed to them, with round holes at either end, and occasionally there was a short, stubby car that was always hauled next to the cabin.

When he was home, O.P. helped me identify the cars I described and told me how I could classify the trains that hauled them. These lessons complemented the hours I was spending at school, and the general pattern of movements he outlined took place on a daily basis.

The westbound passenger that went through each morning was followed by the local freight, which hardly ever had more than twenty-five cars. This freight hauled the stubby car next to the cabin, which was a "weigh car," used from time to time to test the accuracy of the railroad's scales. It started out from Williamsport working its way toward Southport, dropping off or picking up loaded and unloaded cars and delivering less-than-carload freight items en route. Seldom did this train have enough tonnage to need the assistance of a pusher. Crews laid overnight at Southport, returning the following day on the eastbound local. Many times an eastbound would be in the siding for the passenger and the local, and once they cleared, it moved out. This train could be identified by the mixture of cars near the head end, followed by a string of empty hoppers. This train was a "diker" and was coming from Southport bound for Altoona.

As the morning wore on, light pusher engines would pass on their eastbound run to Williamsport. Usually they were paired, but at times as many as five or six locomotives coupled together thundered by. Then too a westbound diker from Altoona with loaded coal-hopper cars and two pushers in the rear was not unusual. Often they took the siding to clear for the noon eastbound passenger.

During the afternoon school session, O.P. informed me, I could expect to see the eastbound local, and soon after there would be a fast-freight movement, also going east. The fast freight would be made up mostly of boxcars with the open hatches on either end. These were, in fact, refrigerated cars, and the hatches were where ice was loaded at icing stations along the route of the train. The ribbed steel boxes on flatcars also would be on the fast freights. These were specialized container units, and the round holes on top were fashioned for hooks used by overhead cranes to load and off-load these units. To positively establish that this train was a fast freight, I was instructed to read the lettering on the cars: "Fruit Growers Express," "Morton Salt," "Swift & Co.," "Texaco Tank Cars," and a host of other names were the tip-off. A diker going in either direction usually came on the scene, and on occasion a work train with a crane aboard a flatcar was part of the parade. A stranger appeared only rarely, hauling a smoking steam crane and boxcars with windows cut in the sides. This was classified as a wreck train.

O.P. explained that even though the 3:30 P.M. westbound passenger meant the school day was over, the railroad did not cease operations, and what I witnessed was only a part of the Company's twenty-four-hour routine. During the night, other than the two passengers, three fast freights plied this single-track cinder-bed main, and as many as three dikers went by in each direction. Light pusher engines too were always present on their way back to Williamsport. Of all the movements, the dikers were the most prevalent, and during peak coal-hauling seasons it was not unusual for seven or eight of these trains to go through in each direction within a twenty-four-hour period.

The passing of these trains during school hours did not disturb the normal routine other than brief interruptions, mostly caused by whistling for the station crossing or the south Ralston crossing. This always took place when they were alongside the school building. We were used to the noise, but how I escaped reprimand as I gazed intently out the windows as each train passed, even reading the logos and lettering on foreign railroads' cars, remains a mystery. (Perhaps because my grades never suffered.) Eventually I could readily classify the trains, and beyond that I didn't even have to read the lettering. Most of the cars being hauled were identified by their paint schemes; even the different hopper cars on the dikers fell into this category.

I also learned that not all trains used the same type of locomotive to haul their consists. Trying to identify the different classes of locomotives was perplexing, and here too I relied on O.P.'s tutoring. First he explained that the engine seen most often would be the I1sa, and that this particular class was easy to distinguish. It was the largest engine the Company had in everyday use. I was to look for the twin air cylinders up front on the pilot, and for the "doghouse" under the coal slide on the tender. Another clue to the class would be the numbers under the cab window. Most were in the 4200's, but the numbers went to 4699, and other engines built by the Company had various other numbers. But the best way to positively identify the I1 class was to count the wheels. Each had a small pony truck with one wheel up front followed by five large driving wheels, on each side.

Next in line, in frequency of appearance, were the L1s-class locomotives. The L1 would probably, at one time or another, be on the head end of any of the trains passing through Ralston, even on the rear end as a pusher. Again, if I were to count the wheels on the facing side, I would find a pony truck wheel, four drivers, and a trailer truck wheel under the cab. L1s engine numbers didn't mean a thing; they were supposedly picked at random.

The daily local freights were usually powered by either an H8sa or an H9s. Almost identical in build, these locomotives had a pony truck wheel and four driving wheels on a side. The manner in which steam was supplied to the cylinders distinguished the two. The H9 had an outside delivery system, with the pipe from on top of the cylinder to the boiler clearly visible, while the H8 was fed on the inside by a pipe that was not visible. This seemed like a simple way to distinguish between the two classes, but I couldn't quite get the picture until O.P. used a book to illustrate the difference. The daylight passenger trains would normally have an E6s engine, which was easily identified: on each side it would have two pony wheels, two large-diameter drivers, and a trailer wheel under the cab.

My gazing out school windows now had a new dimension, but I found that determining the class of a locomotive was no small challenge. Trying to remember the wheel arrangements and to apply them to the proper class of engine was not easy. To find out whether I was right, I started checking the oval brass builder's plate above the cylinders on engines when they stopped at the water plug. It was somewhat like looking at the answer sheet in the back of a textbook.

The water plug was a choice location to be near the railroad. It was just off the playground the Company had donated to Ralston years earlier, a rectangular plot running from the back of the station to the now abandoned bunkhouse, and it was separated from the main by a spur track. After school and on off-school days, a large amount of my time was spent here.

Reading builder's plates on the engines for verification purposes caused more confusion, which led to a spelling lesson from O.P. All seemed to have "Baldwin" implanted in bold lettering, but one day I came across one that, according to my interpretation, read "Juanita." This odd name appearing on a locomotive seemed strange. It was the name of an Indian maiden we often sang about in school singing period, so I asked, "Why did they put a name like that on an engine?" At first O.P. was amused, then he took a pencil and a piece of paper and spelled "Juanita," then "Juniata," and explained that I had read the name incorrectly. The name was "Juniata," the name on many engines the Company built in their own shops in Altoona.

Before I had mastered the everyday locomotive classes that O.P. had outlined, I found myself side-tracked by engines that he had not yet described. In the middle of the local as it passed eastbound one afternoon, I spotted a locomotive that was distinctly different from anything I had previously seen. It was a small engine that had no pony truck wheel or trailing truck. All that appeared on one side were three small drivers and, rather than the usual tender, the one attached sloped sharply toward the rear.

O.P. wasn't available for consultation at the time, so I more or less forgot about this engine until I saw it once again one morning, when I heard its shrill freight whistle announcing the approach of a westbound movement. It didn't seem quite as shrill as usual, but instead was rather muted. What came into view was a shiny engine with only three driving wheels on the left side and the sloped tender. It was poking along with no train attached. Details of this unorthodox small locomotive did not escape my memory the second time I sighted it, and I was able to ask O.P. about it. O.P. explained that what I'd seen was undoubtedly a B6-class engine, used mainly for switching cars around terminal yards. It was known as a "swallow-tailed dinky" because of its sloping-shaped tender. When I had seen it in the middle of the eastbound local it was a "dead engine"; the fire was knocked out, and the main rods and eccentric rods had been removed, because it was being transported to the shops for overhauling. The rods were removed to prevent damage to the cylinders, because the piston and valve chambers were not lubricated unless the engine was under steam. And when this type of engine was being towed, there would be a 35-mile-per-hour speed restriction on the train handling it because there were no pony truck wheels. To compensate for the lack of a front axle, the B6 had been built with an equalizer bar to stabilize vertical motion. However, when its front coupler was attached to a car, as when it was being hauled "dead," this added to its stability.

Although the 0-6-0 looked small in comparison with other locomotives, it was a powerful piece of machinery, and this could be attributed to its design. The entire engine weight was placed on the small driving wheels. But it was making its way slowly westbound as a light engine because after being completely rebuilt and steamed up it would not be practical to knock the fire and remove the rods to tow it "dead." Besides, this trip from the shop to the Southport yards served as a break-in run. Fifteen to 20 miles an hour was the top speed it could travel running light, without using steam to pull cars or having the pilot coupling attached to a car. Otherwise, it would bob up and down and put undue strain on the equalizer bar, even to a point that could cause it to break. That would disable the engine.

Noting discrepancies in train movements and the items these trains were carrying, and trying to classify the locomotives correctly, brought so many questions to my mind that O.P. wondered where all the questions were coming from. But he was always patient and answered my questions. To help, he obtained a book that depicted the Pennsylvania's locomotives in a side-view silhouette, showing the wheel arrangements and the boiler-top configurations. "I've been noticing that in your drawing class you've been portraying trains and engines," he said. "When you see a locomotive you can't identify, just make a sketch, then compare it with the profiles in this book when you come home."

Even with the book at hand, I could not always be sure I'd identified the class correctly. My first attempt to use the book came near the Christmas holiday. Instead of the regular E6s power on the head end of the afternoon passenger, the train came into town with a much larger locomotive, and it was pulling seven cars rather than the usual four. A glimpse of this strange power easing in for the station stop revealed two pony truck wheels, three large drivers, and a trailer wheel on its left side. Consulting the book, I found two engines that had the same wheel arrangement; one was the K2 class, the other was the K4 class. So I consulted O.P., who reasoned that the change of power was due to increased holiday demand, or perhaps that one of the E6 engines had broken down and this was the only substitute available at the Williamsport roundhouse.

But, he added, it was more than likely a K2, because the K4's were used on more important passenger runs, such as the one he was presently handling. The features that distinguished an engine as a K2 were its inside steam-delivery pipes to the cylinders (the K4's had outside pipes); its odd type of trailer truck, which displayed the spring arrangement it was attached to (the K4's trailer truck was a curved arrangement, like that used on the E6 and the L1); and, finally, the K2 had a larger cab with two windows (the K4 had only one cab window).

The unidentified engine came back through town on the usual rotation slot as the power for the eastbound passenger train from Canandaigua, but school had been dismissed for lunch so I failed to get a close look again at this engine. The following afternoon, again in rotation, this engine was on the head end of the westbound passenger, and O.P.'s assumptions were, as always, correct: it was a K2.

Soon after, I was confronted with identifying the locomotive that was hauling the eastbound local. It stopped parallel to my window viewing area, but in a position that didn't give me a look at the entire engine. At a glance, it appeared to be an L1, but something seemed different, and when it began moving I counted the drivers: it had a total of five, plus a trailer truck arrangement similar to the one used under the K4's cab. As the locomotive moved forward, I could see that it was towing a car with smoke coming from the wheels on the rear truck axle, and after passing the switch for the siding, it reversed and came back, giving me another chance to see it in detail.

This move in and out of the siding to set off the car allowed me time to make a sketch of the engine, even the boiler-top features. In my inexperienced reasoning, the locomotive was big enough to be an I1, but the trailer truck made it look somewhat like an overgrown L1. Maybe it was a cross between these two engines. The book failed to help me. This could be either an N1 or an N2.

Before O.P. arrived home from his run, I picked out this type of engine again, this time working as the second pusher on a westbound diker, and when he arrived I gave him my sketch and showed him how the book had only added to my confusion. He complimented me on my observations and admitted that the book didn't define these two classes closely enough for me to make the correct choice. He added: "I've been waiting for you to spot this engine. It's an N2sa class. At one time there were a few of these working out of the Williamsport roundhouse, but presently only a couple remain. They're now used principally as a utility engine. When you saw the N2 on the local, it was probably because of heavy tonnage going to Southport the previous day—more than an H9 or an L1 could handle without a pusher, and it was returning eastbound in normal rotation."

O.P. told me that the Company had constructed quite a large number of N2's and its sister N1's, a government National Railroad Administration type. Both types, though, stayed in service mostly on divisions west of Pittsburgh, because though they were reasonably powerful their extremely slow speed limited their use as all-around freight haulers. He said he'd used both these classes on the head end and that in his opinion they were worthless, not only in this capacity but in pusher service as well. "When I got an N2 out of Newberry as a pusher for my westbound runs up the Elmira Branch," he said, "the only assistance they gave me was starting and going up the hill out of Ralston. Otherwise, when I got things 'set up running' at better than 35 miles an hour I was actually pulling the pusher."

Satisfied that I now knew about two other classes of locomotives, I still had another question for O.P.—this one about the smoking wheels on the car set off by the N2. "One of two things could cause smoke around the wheels," he began. "A broken rod might have caused the brake shoes to drag on the wheels, but most likely it was a hotbox." His reasoning was that the train crew could block up the brake shoes and temporarily relieve that problem, but that a "hotbox" required more attention. This overheating occurred when the journal or bearing in which the axle was seated wasn't properly lubricated or was badly worn.

It could also have been a combination of both factors. At the end of each car axle was a round disk that held the axle in place, and the disk was housed in a journal box that was packed with waste, cotton threads saturated with oil. This allowed the axle to run cool under ordinary circumstances. The journal on the car probably overheated on one of the through movements and was placed on a main siding for pickup by the local, probably at Leolyn. Once this crew got it to Ralston, it would be put on the spur track near the water plug to await the attention of car repairmen from Williamsport before it would again be moved to some location for further repairs. O.P. also showed me how to signal a train crew if I ever happened to spot a hotbox on a passing movement. "Just hold your nose and keep pointing at the wheels. They'll know what you mean." (It worked too. Many years later I gave this signal to a conductor, who stopped the train and set off the car with the smoking journal box, and profoundly thanked me for this observation.)

I thought I had reached the point where I could place all the locomotives that passed by my schoolroom window in the proper category according to classes, but I was wrong. One day, soon after the start of another day in school, a shrill whistle below town announced the approach of a westbound movement. It wasn't as high-pitched as an I1, and sounded similar to the whistle of a B6 that I had heard on a previous occasion. Before it came into my view it stopped, and a man walked forward, apparently to throw the switch for it to enter the siding. The bell sounded, followed by two short whistle blasts and the sound of muffled exhausts.

Before long, a strange engine appeared, and I immediately saw that it was a small engine with prominent features on top of the broiler. It offered a high stack, and the sand and steam domes too were higher than the other classes carried, plus they were almost identical in size. In some respects it resembled a diminutive H9: it had double cab windows and sported the same wheel arrangement. Four small drivers on a side were led by a pony truck. As the little engine eased into the siding, it was followed by a variety of cars: two hoppers, a crane on a flatcar, several gondolas, and, last, a cabin. Where it was going, or for what purpose, was a mystery to me, but before school was dismissed that afternoon this train reappeared, running backward, presumably heading for Williamsport. Judging from the cars and the crane aboard the flatcar, I determined that this was a work train.

At home after school, I checked my sketch with the reference book and decided this time that the locomotive hauling the work train was an H6 class. When I approached O.P. about my newest sighting, he agreed that my identification was correct. The engine was an H6, and it was a work train. "It's hard to believe when you compare this engine to an I1," he elaborated, "but when I went to work for the railroad the H6 was the biggest freight engine the Company was using, and it was only on the main lines. The secondary lines didn't get this class until some years later. I was assigned an engine in this class on my first running job out of Ralston, and for nearly eight years I had one of these 2-8-0's regularly—first the slide-valve H6a and later the piston-valve type H6b."

With these remarks, he took out our picture album and showed me three different poses taken aboard an H6b: one with him and the fireman standing on the pilot, the other two in different positions on the running board. "I had these pictures taken in Tyrone around 1915," he said.

O.P. explained that the primary function of work trains in the Ralston area was to meet the needs of the five section gang crews located along the line from Newberry to Leolyn. Ties, rail, spikes, and various other supplies would be dropped off, and scrap materials with salvage value picked up. The clamshell bucket the crane was equipped with would be used to load piles of cinders that the section crews had cleaned from the ends of sidings and at the water plugs into a hopper car. Then, if tracks needed to be raised while the work train and hopper car with cinders were in the area, the pockets on the car would be opened and the cinders would be spread on the roadbed at points designated by the section crew foreman. Normally, O.P. noted, work trains would be handled by an extra crew, but if more-extensive track or rehabilitation work was needed, the job would be bid in for an allotted time period.

One July morning in 1934 the work train became a unit of destruction instead of a rehabilitation unit. The 8:30 A.M. westbound passenger had just cleared town when another engine with a passenger whistle announced its approach by signaling for the South Ralston grade crossing. It too was traveling west. Not wanting to miss seeing what this extra movement was doing in town, I wasted no time getting to my vantage point at the water plug. Just as I arrived, I saw a locomotive running in reverse entering the siding. As it neared my position, I identified the engine as an E6, but it wasn't pulling passenger cars. Instead, it had a crane on a flatcar plus a string of empty gondolas, a boxcar, one passenger car, and a cabin. Seeing it stop almost at the siding water plug, my first thought was that it was going to take water, but that didn't happen. A brakeman hurried forward to open the switch to the former pit track, and upon his signal the train entered this unused section of rails.

Once on this track, the train moved slowly until all the cars had cleared the switch, finally coming to a stop adjacent to the coal hoist. As if on cue, workmen descended from the passenger car, proceeded to the boxcar, unloaded demolition tools, and began to methodically rip portions of the coal hoist apart. On the elevated coal trestle, spikes holding the rails were removed, and splice joint bolts were burned off with welder's torches, and then the crane lifted the loosened rails and placed them in a gondola. Inside the engine-house building, other workers with cutting torches reduced machinery and equipment that had been left behind when the facility was closed into pieces of scrap, which in turn were carried outside. Once everything was removed, the crane loaded it all onto an empty gondola. At the end of the day, the E6 made a few switching moves to set out the loaded gondolas and arrange the passenger car so it was ahead of the cabin, then it picked up the loaded cars and assembled the train for the trip back to Williamsport. Empty gondolas and the crane were left standing on the pit track.

In the days that followed, the E6 came back to town as regularly as clockwork, each afternoon leaving with gondolas filled to the brim, hauling away remnants of a railroad terminal that was among the earliest terminals in the nation. Workers completed the job of removing the contents of the coal hoist and moved on to destroy the yard office, the icehouse, the bunkhouse, and more. The only structures left standing were the section house, the station, the water tank, and two water plugs, one for the siding and one for the main.

Demolishing the coal-hoist building was left to the crane, which attacked it with a vengeance, commencing with all its wrath on the coal trestle. The cross ties were torn loose, the supporting timbers were jerked out, and the ones that resisted were torn to shreds—all with the clam shovel bucket. Then the crane was moved to the track located to the rear of the building, where the first order of business was to pull down the steel smokestack. Workers had mounted the roof and affixed a cable around this high appendage, which was in turn hooked onto the bucket. A few tugs caused the smokestack to crash to the ground. Pieces of the building were also destroyed, but the stack was now positioned so that welders could cut it into short sections, which would make loading the remains easier.

Next the crane used its clamshell bucket as a combination wrecking ball and giant pincer to level the building. In a short time, all that was left was a pile of rubble—that is, except for one item: a stationary boiler, which was uncovered and still set on its concrete base. There was something unusual about this boiler—a closer scan revealed that it had the same flat top as the boilers on Pennsylvania Railroad locomotives. Whatever it was or wherever it originated did not cause the workmen any concern. Torches reduced the atypical stationary boiler to small pieces, which, along with the smokestack, were loaded into a gondola as scrap.

From the onset, I kept O.P. informed about the work train's activities, who the engineer was, and even that his former, fun-loving fireman was on the left side. But I kept asking him questions about things I didn't understand. First, it didn't seem right to be using a passenger-class engine on a lowly work train assignment. About this O.P. reasoned, "Probably all the smaller-class freight engines not in storage are on other jobs. The summertime keeps most of them busy. Then too, this job doesn't require any heavy switching, just moving the crane around. Most of the time is spent setting around waiting. Also, there's a 24-mile run to and from Williamsport each day, and an E6 can do that easier and faster than a freight locomotive."

Another thing bothering me was the demolition carried out without trying to save anything. O.P. explained: "Ralston isn't the only terminal the Company closed. This same thing happened all over the system. If everything was saved, there would be a problem trying to store it all. Besides, all the equipment in these older terminals is either worn-out or outdated, and the Company can use every nickel it can garnish, even if it comes from scrap."

The boiler I had seen uncovered at the coal hoist did come from a locomotive. O.P. said it had once belonged to a class R (H3) engine and that when the engine was scrapped its salvaged boiler was put into service at Ralston. It had been installed shortly after he arrived in 1910, and during the twenty or so years that it was used it provided an essential service for this terminal. The steam it produced had operated a steam ram used to hoist coal buggies filled with coal to replenish the fuel on the tenders (hence the name "coal hoist" instead of "engine house") and to power an engine that powered a line shaft for the shop. Another engine was used to operate a large air compressor, plus steam was used on a pump that kept the water tower filled. In addition, the steam was used to blow a large whistle that sounded each morning at 7:00 A.M., at 12:00 noon, and again at 6:00 in the evening, and at other times for emergencies like fires.

The rubble from all the structures that had been demolished was assembled on a large pile at the coal hoist site and set on fire to reduce it to ashes. The crane was moved to what had been the tracks in the rear of the coal hoist to finish the job: concrete bases and what had been the concrete floor were smashed with the clamshell bucket, which in turn picked up the litter and cast it over the nearby creek bank. Cinders were used to fill the holes and level the ground, leaving a lasting scar on the landscape.

As the crane was moved out, the rails were lifted onto a gondola, the ties were placed haphazardly in a pile. Finished with this section, the E6 then moved around the train, and the same procedure followed on the pit track. The switch to the siding was removed at the upper end, and the tracks were taken out to a point just beyond the concrete pit. This pit was filled in but left intact; it now was a short spur, the entrance switch near the water plug serving as access. Like everything else, ties that had been removed were burned.

The final phase on the work train's agenda began as it attacked the wye and the cabin storage tracks. This operation reduced the number of workmen needed, so the passenger car was eliminated. The trips to and from Williamsport were a light move, with just the cabin. Work on this project began with cutting off the rails that crossed the highway but leaving them in place there. Then the rails down to the dividing switch were removed, and then the rails down the left side facing the main. The loading dock in the middle that was framed up with ties was torn apart, as were the switch and the rails that once led to a coal tipple and brickyard. Advancing to the intersection of the main, the E6 had to be cut off to clear this track; it moved to the station siding, where it would wait until it was needed again.

On my way to enjoy an afternoon at the Boom swimming hole located behind the now former coal hoist, I detoured through town and around the station. Approaching the water tower and the parked E6, I saw the crew sitting in the shade, taking time out for lunch. O.P.'s fireman greeted me with "Looks like you're going swimming, Jack. If I wasn't on duty I'd go along with you." (Our families paid each other social visits, and on occasion the fireman, with his family, would come to our house for Sunday dinner, so I was well acquainted with him.) Confirming that he was correct in his assumption but that because it was too soon after lunch to go into the water I was just idling some time away, I stayed and chatted with the crew.

After a while the engineer interrupted us, saying, "I'm going down to the hotel for some dessert and coffee." No sooner had he left than the conductor came by and announced, "The crane operator notified me that he needs to be moved, and he also wants an empty car. I called the dispatcher, and we can occupy the main for more than an hour. This will give us enough time to get things switched around so we'll be ready to pull out at quitting time." Then he exclaimed, "Where the hell is the engineer?"

When we told him he'd gone to the hotel, the conductor said, "We can't go chasing and waiting on him. We'll have to work without him." And as the fireman started to move toward the engine, he turned around and asked me, "How would you like to ride along, Jack? Or would you rather go swimming?"

Without any hesitation I told him I'd be pleased to go along, as most nearly any ten-year-old boy would say, but then I remembered my instructions. "I'm not sure I should go along. My dad said it was all right to watch what was going on if I didn't get too close to the equipment."

The fireman smiled. "It'll be all right to go with me," he said, "and if Oscar says anything, tell him to get ahold of me. I'll straighten him out." With these words of assurance I climbed aboard and was instructed to get up on the left seat box. "You can be the fireman until we get back," he said.

Our first move was a short one. Going only about the length of the engine, we coupled onto the cabin setting ahead on the same siding and pushed it into an empty gondola. Coupled up, we moved out of the siding onto the main and up to the work area, where we coupled to the loaded car. Backing out with this car, and after the switch was closed, we pushed it a short distance down the main, where it was uncoupled. Again we backed back past the switch, entered the upper end of the wye, coupled the empty gondola to the crane's flatcar, and moved this assemblage back a short distance. Uncoupling, we again moved out on the main, shoving the cabin forward until it was coupled to the loaded car.

At this point the conductor came aboard the engine to explain what he intended to accomplish. "We'll back up the main to Max," he said, "come down through the siding, pick up two loaded cars on the pit track, come out on the main again, and go back to pick up the other loaded car and the cabins. We'll have everything arranged in order when we get ready to leave."

The fireman didn't waste any time backing up to Max as we moved at a pretty fast clip, but the return trip down the siding was slower. The fireman explained: "We can't run too fast. There's a speed restriction on this track. You can feel it too. The E6 wants to rock around a little bit." After getting the loaded cars out of the pit track, the fireman hollered down to the conductor: "When I come back up the main I'll stop and take water. Swing the plug around when I get there."

Moving down the siding, we went by the hotel, and when we came back up the main I expected the engineer to get aboard, but he was nowhere in sight. I surmised he was still enjoying his dessert and coffee. Spotting the E6 at the water plug, the fireman made his way over the coal pile and disappeared, then reappeared moments later, announcing that the tender was filled to the brim. From here we backed up to the parked loaded car and cabin, coupled up, and moved down to our originating point, again entering the short station siding.

I had thoroughly enjoyed the entire experience of riding aboard a passenger engine, but I found it amusing too. The fireman was an exceptionally large man, and the large belly he had developed complemented his stature. That was not an asset though, as we were making the many forward and reverse moves while carrying out the work the conductor had scheduled. Each move required using the screw-reversing mechanism, and as the fireman sat on the seat box rapidly turning the wheel controlling this device, his belly would jump up and down with each turn. I had a terrible time keeping myself from bursting out in laughter, but I suppressed the urge rather than cause embarrassment. I did wonder, though, why his stomach didn't start hurting. It was surely being shaken up.

When the trip was over and we were parked in the sanctuary of the siding, I remained aboard the E6 a while longer and learned more about railroading. After activating the injector and filling the boiler, the fireman came across the deck and said, "Since you didn't bother to do any firing, I'd better see if there's any fire left." When the fire door was opened he added, "I was just kidding. It doesn't take much firing to keep an E6 hot, especially when it's not being used hard."

Placing a few shovelfuls of coal down each side, a few in the middle, and finishing off at the back of the firebox, he closed the door and began to reminisce: "This engine has the same boiler as the H8's and H9's your dad and I started getting at the tail end of the war [World War I], but they were a little more contrary to fire. Once in a while we'd get one that I'd have trouble keeping the steam up. Oscar could see by the steam gauge that I was having problems, and he'd holler, 'Get up here. You run for a little bit. I'll see if I can help out.' He'd fiddle around, shake the grates a little, throw in a few shovelfuls of coal now and then, and without fail it wouldn't be long until the pops would start singing. It was hard to believe, but there wasn't a time he took over that he couldn't show me how to get one hot. He'd even do the same thing with the L1's after we started using them."

Almost thinking out loud, the fireman continued: "Oscar had another special knack. He could set an engine up so it would go faster and still steam good. It didn't matter either whether we had empties or were pulling a loaded train. Other engineers I worked with might go like hell, but they couldn't run fast and still make steam. It was an easy job firing for him, and if I could I'd like to be working with him on the passenger run right now. I'll betcha he really has those K4's flying up and down the river." Mopping the sweat off his brow he concluded: "It's too damn hot up here in the cab. I'm going to get off and sit in the shade with the rest of the crew." Before we left the cab, he pulled out his watch and said, "It's only a little after two. You'll have plenty of time to get your swimming in. Enjoy it, because someday you'll be old like I am and have to work for a living."

Paying my respects and telling him how much I appreciated my ride, I then made my way toward the Boom swimming hole. As I walked along, I realized I couldn't quite agree with the fireman. If I had a choice, I knew I'd rather be working on a steam engine than wasting my time swimming.

When O.P. arrived home from a round-trip, I told him everything I'd been doing while he was away, everything about my ride on the E6, but not all the fireman had said, stating only that he'd like to be firing on the 510-511 passenger run. I expected my father to reprimand me for disobeying his orders, but he didn't.

The work train had most of its intended job finished as the month of July was drawing to a close. All that remained on the right side of the wye was a few sections of track and the switch to the main. This work was progressing one Saturday morning—the E6 occupying the main at a now dead-end street that formerly led to the coal hoist—when by coincidence it became involved in a wedding party. An event of this nature was a major social happening in small towns like Ralston, so both invited guests and curious onlookers were gathered at the bride's residence, the last house on the street.

I was among the crowd that greeted the bride and groom as they returned from the church after the ceremony. Standing where I could watch what was going on without being an intrusion, I saw O.P.'s fun-loving fireman get off the engine, and although he was clad in grimy work clothes no one seemed concerned. He was a local, and everyone present knew he was on the job.

Mingling with the gathering almost like an invited guest, the fireman finally approached the bride and groom and offered his congratulations, but as he and the bride started heading in the direction of the engine, heads began turning to follow this strange move. Reaching the engine, the fireman and the bride scrambled aboard, full white bridal attire and all. Positioned in the gangway with both hands on the hand rails, and as the E6 started off down the main with the bell ringing and the whistle tooting loudly, she gave a parting wave, almost as if in triumph.

The assembled crowd stood in stunned silence listening to the whistling as this unorthodox trip went through town and continued into South Ralston. Not too much time had elapsed until the bride was whistled back. As she climbed down from the cab, the party came alive. Her return was honored with a resounding cheer, and the lawn reception got under way. Being an un-invited guest, I decided I had seen enough. Besides, it was nearly lunchtime, and the tables of food were making me hungry. I left for home.

On that particular day, O.P. happened to be home, and when I related what I had just witnessed he burst into laughter. My mother, however, didn't think it was funny, and even accused me of making up the whole story. "No bride would get on a dirty steam engine in her wedding gown," she ex-claimed. O.P., still laughing, came to my aid, though, and confirmed that he had heard the whistling. "At first I thought one of the workmen had an acci-dent and they were making an emergency run to Williamsport, but when the whistling came back I figured there were some kind of shenanigans going on." He continued, "I worked with that fireman long enough. I should've realized he'd be pulling off a stunt like this. He always did find a way to amuse himself. I don't think that jasper will ever grow up."

When the work train made its final departure at the end of July, all ves-tiges of what had made Ralston a terminal for almost one hundred years had not been entirely removed. The five-track ladder yard, open at either end to the main siding, and just north of the bridge spanning Lycoming Creek, remained intact. The two inside tracks could accommodate the entire train that an L1-headed diker would bring in, but as this storage area curved toward the mountain, it reduced accordingly, bringing the capacity of the outside tracks down to less than twenty-five cars. Why this yard was spared was more than obvious: it was still being used—though not actively, but rather as a rest-ing place for a rusting horde of empty, unused boxcars that completely filled all the tracks. This condition arose at the onset of the Depression: nothing moved in or out of this yard.

Almost a year had passed, and O.P. was still running on one side of the 510-511 passenger job. This alone was enough to establish his theory that the Williamsport Division engineers with more seniority did not like working out of Altoona. With this thought in mind, O.P. felt sure that he wouldn't be bumped off this high-mileage good-paying run. Soon, however, a factor that he failed to consider arose.

As scheduled, he made the required visit to the relief doctor for his annual physical exam during the last week of August 1934, and he left the office feeling that he had passed satisfactorily, as the physician had made no negative remarks. This feeling of satisfaction was short-lived, however. After the visit, he made a complete round-trip, and when he was marking off after bringing the westbound 511 into Altoona, the crew clerk handed him an enve-lope from the office of the road foreman of engines.

The message it contained was terse, and no lengthy explanation was necessary. It merely stated that his physical exam revealed that his blood pressure was higher than set standards. Effective immediately, it advised, he was suspended from active duty. But there was one glimmer of hope for O.P. in this letter: the doctor's findings were not binding. To confirm the results of his examination, it would be necessary to appear before the medical examiners at the Company's headquarters in Philadelphia. An appointment for this exam was provided.

O.P. had no alternative but to return home and begin a waiting game. The first part, waiting for the day he was to go to Philadelphia for the reexamination, was enough to elevate his blood pressure more, but the wait after the reexamination was the most traumatic. Everything he had worked for since hiring out seemed to be disintegrating. The examining physicians had told him he would hear the results of their tests by mail and word was not long coming. My sister and I always picked up the family mail, which had arrived on the 3:30 P.M. westbound passenger, at the close of school each day, and the letter we brought home soon after the reexamination was not to his liking. Frowning as he read it, it must have been what he expected.

Sitting at his spot at the kitchen table after thoroughly perusing the contents, he put the letter down and said: "Well, after all these years, it looks as though the Company doesn't need me anymore due to my physical condition. I'm no longer qualified for road service, either passenger or freight runs. I can still remain on the board, but I'll be restricted to yard service. That's exactly what they want to do. If they put me in the yard now, I'll be there until I retire. I'll never get out on the road again. What they'll do is make me an 8-A-1 man and permanently keep me in the yards."

It was obvious that O.P. was more than a little upset when he continued: "If this is what the Company and all their officials want, I'll quit the railroad. My dad always wanted me to take over the farm, so that's what I'm going to do. In fact, I guess this is about all I have left anymore."

We had listened without any interruptions, more or less shocked that he had been taken out of service, and even shocked by his decision to become a farmer. My mother then interjected, with her ability to arrive at a logical solution for any given situation. "Oscar," she said, "nobody is to be blamed for the predicament you're in. You brought the whole thing on yourself, and in no way can you deny it. Last year the road foreman warned you not to take the passenger run. He even told you what would happen, but you didn't take his advice. Instead, you assured him you'd correct the blood pressure problem. Of course, you didn't do that, but rather made no attempt to watch your diet or give up drinking, and now because of it they took you out of service."

Without hesitating, she continued: "If you quit the railroad now you would give up everything you worked for all these years, and there's no cause to do this. They didn't take you out of road service permanently, merely until you can regulate your blood pressure to the proper level. There isn't anything wrong with taking over the farm, either. The only thing is we don't have enough money to get started. Besides, the condition the country is in, the people that are farming can't sell their crops, so what would we do?"

This made O.P. stammer a bit, but my mother wasn't finished. "Another thing, what would we do with our house here? You know very well since they took the yards out no one wants to buy a house in Ralston. In fact, I don't think we could give it away. Everyone that can is moving out. But whatever you decide to do in regards to quitting and starting farming, you'll have to do it by yourself. The children and I are going to stay here in Ralston."

O.P. stammered and muttered a few words as he listened to this response from my mother: "The only sensible thing to do in your case is to go and see either the road foreman or the relief doctor to find out exactly what your standing is. They should be able to tell you if you qualify to receive benefits from the railroad relief fund. You've paid into it every payday for years, and it's supposed to take care of you when you're sick or disabled."

O.P. seemed to brighten. Maybe he had been too hasty in admitting defeat, he admitted, and he promised to follow my mother's suggestion to consult with the Williamsport officials. "I'll find out if I'm eligible to draw on the relief fund, but under no circumstances will I take a yard job," he asserted. The fund O.P. was referring to was actually a contributory fund, with the class of fund and the amount withheld for it from each paycheck being chosen by the employee. It was not a donated fund, as the word "relief" might imply.

O.P. made the trip to Williamsport, where the relief doctor's office was his only stop. According to the physician, his high blood pressure was a medical condition that entitled him to receive full benefits. Fortunately, O.P. had paid into the highest class of the fund, which allowed him to draw $4.53 a day, seven days a week, for as long as he had the present condition. The only restriction was that he was compelled to submit to a medical examination once every month as long as he was drawing from the fund. There was no limit to how long he could receive benefits.

The allocated benefit amount was considerably less than what he was accustomed to earning, but taking the Depression economy into consideration, the average worker received around thirty-five cents an hour, if a job could be found, and furloughed railroaders received nothing at all. At the supper table, O.P. expressed concern that drawing the benefit was like accepting charity, adding: "I won't be taking this kind of money very long. The relief doctor interceded and made an appointment with a specialist in blood disorders. He'll have me back in shape in no time."

It was an entirely new experience for O.P. to be at home every day, in the morning before we went to school, at lunchtime, and in the evening. My sister and I welcomed the assistance he gave us with homework. We discovered that he had a very good memory for historical events, that geography posed him no problems, and that he was especially adept at solving arithmetic problems. He didn't do the lessons for us, but his explanations were most helpful. And now, of course, if I had questions from my train-watching, I didn't have to wait for him to come home to get an explanation. He was always available.

My mother didn't allow him to remain idle for long. Many things around home needed attending to, and even though many of those tasks weren't exactly to his liking—such as painting, finish carpentry, odd jobs—he managed to get them all done.

In the early fall, when the temperature cooled down, he occupied himself cutting firewood for the kitchen range, because my mother refused to burn coal in her stove. Although this was hard work, he took pleasure in the chore. And he could be selective in choosing the trees best suited for firewood—oak, hard maple, and beech, and even a few chestnut trees for kindling—for only a short distance in back of our house, on the mountainside, was an abundance of dead, seasoned wood. Six years earlier a forest fire had burned off the debris left behind when the mountain was timbered, and killed the smaller trees that remained.

Afternoons, at the end of the school day, and on Saturdays, I was O.P.'s assistant—not that I could accomplish much at my age other than ride on the end of the two-man crosscut saw to keep the blade straight, or help carry the tools. There wasn't anything compulsory about my helping—no orders were given that I should do this—it was just natural as a member of the family for me to be involved. I never considered this a chore, but rather a pleasant pastime and a learning experience as well. O.P. taught me how to identify the many different species of trees by the configuration of their leaves and by the structure of the bark when no leaves were present. In addition, he pointed out how to select the ones best suited for firewood or for use in lumber products.

One day we both gained from a lesson in nature, witnessing something neither of us had ever seen and would never see again, and it was provided by a dead tree. It stood near the area where the forest fire had been brought under control, about 20 inches across the stump and 30 feet tall. Not that it was particularly impressive, but to me it looked as if it should be cut down.

O.P., however, didn't think so. He explained that it was soft maple (red maple) and that this type of tree didn't make very good firewood. About the only thing it was good for, he told me, was kindling, and we had plenty of dead chestnut wood for that.

After a little pleading on my part, he finally agreed to cut it down, but added that we were just wasting time. After the proper notch was cut so that it would fall in the correct direction, we started to saw with the crosscut. It was much easier than the oak or hard maple we had been cutting. In fact, with a relatively few strokes of the saw it began to fall, then hit the ground with a resounding crash. Dead branches flew every which way. The top main structure broke into pieces down to where the limbs had been attached. As he sized up what remained of the tree, O.P. declared, "See, I tried to tell you it wasn't any good. The whole thing is probably rotten."

Nevertheless, I felt compelled to examine what was left of the tree, and made a strange discovery. "Hey, Pop!" I hollered, "there's a bunch of bees coming out of this crack." Coming over to where I was standing, my father not only saw the bees but made another discovery. "I'll be Joe Tinkered!" he exclaimed. "We cut down a bee tree. Look at the honey oozing out."

Noting that the bees were almost dormant due to the cold weather and would therefore not harm us, he said: "Skin down home and get Mom's dishpan and something to scoop out the honey. While you're gone, I'll take the wedges and split this section open."

Returning with the necessary utensils, O.P. had everything ready for removal of the honey. The large comb structure within the hollow cavity, now exposed, had withstood the force of the fall and remained mostly intact. The contents almost filled our dishpan. As we were removing the comb, O.P. explained that the wild bees used hollow trees as their home and that it was difficult to locate their hideaways. The honey produced was stored in the comb to be used as their food during the winter, enabling them to survive until they could once again start the entire process in the spring when things started blooming. Talking about our good fortune on the way home, O.P. conceded that we wouldn't get much firewood out of the tree, but we did come up with a winter's supply of fine tasting wild honey.

In this and other ways, I realized one of the better things about cutting wood: the relationship I had with O.P., something I'd been deprived of until now. During this fall interlude out on the steep mountainside, as we worked we spent much of the time talking. We covered many topics, and usually O.P. did most of the talking. He told me about his boyhood on the farm in Centre County and shared tales of his hunting and fishing adventures, and, of primary interest to me, his railroading experiences.

When we were cutting we were on "benches," level portions of ground in the otherwise rugged contour that prevailed on the west side of the mountain. We could hear trains running on the Pennsylvania, but we couldn't see them in the valley below. Across the valley on the east side, however, was the other railroad serving Ralston, and we could see its grade clearly.

That railroad, the Susquehanna & New York (S&NY), followed along the mountainside higher than the valley floor as it approached from the south, gradually descending to valley level in South Ralston. There, I had seen while roaming around South Ralston, was what looked like a four- or five-track yard arrangement near the burned-out remains of the former tannery, a boarded up combination station and freight house, tracks that had once connected to the Pennsylvania, and a wye. The track that closed the top of the wye continued north at valley level, crossed Rock Run Creek on a wooden trestle directly across from Ralston, then ascended sharply until it was more than 30 feet up on the mountainside, and continued for half a mile on a level tangent until it ended just beyond at a coal tipple.

The only movement on this line seldom occurred more than once a week; it brought two or three empty hoppers to the tipple, and took the same number of hoppers loaded with coal away from the tipple. All that I could see of this from my schoolroom viewing point was smoke from the engine, and I could hear the whistle soundings. The S&NY engines I could see were generally at a distance across the valley, but during the summer one of these locomotives would occasionally pass close by on its way to the coal tipple while I was swimming. It would blast up the grade from the trestle pushing empty hoppers and pass some 25 feet directly above our swimming hole on track laid on a narrow ledge that had been blasted out of solid rock. Just watching this action gave me an uncomfortable feeling as the engine passed over on the precarious perch, and I always made sure I got out of the water to view it from the opposite bank, lest the whole train came tumbling down into the creek.

The only engine used to make this run, according to my observations, was a small, antiquated 2-6-0 that had a rather high stack, its headlight centered on the smoke-box door, with high domes, an electric generator mounted on the boiler top in front of the cab, and a cab that was itself unusual-looking— nothing like the Pennsylvania engines I was used to.

All in all, the S&NY and its infrequent trips to Ralston did not interest me very much. In fact, I never talked about that railroad with my father until, one afternoon, as the little 2-6-0 was pushing its empties along the mountainside opposite our location, O.P. spotted the movement. "Looks like the S&NY is heading up to the tipple for a charge of coal," he said.

I agreed with him knowingly, adding, "It's not much of a railroad, though.

Different times I've walked along the tracks from Rock Run Creek up toward where it ends, and from the way the ties are rotted and sunk in the cinder roadbed, I can't understand why the engine doesn't jump the track."

"That's just a spur line," he explained, "and it's not kept up very good, probably because it doesn't earn them enough to keep it in good repair."

"Is it the only locomotive the railroad has?" I asked.

"No," he replied. "They must have half a dozen or so locomotives all together. This one probably is kept at Marsh Hill as a spare engine for this type of duty, or for switching in their yard or for pusher engine work if they need one."

Still not convinced that there was much merit in this operation, I asked, "If their other engines look like this one, they're not in very good shape. About the only good thing, it has a pretty whistle sound. Do all their engines have this kind of whistle?"

"As far as I know," O.P. said, "they all have this steamboat-type whistle, and the engines they use running over the Pennsylvania's tracks from Newberry to Marsh Hill, and over their main to Towanda, are in better shape. Nothing to get excited over, though."

As long as we were on the whistle subject, I posed another question, "If a small railroad like the S&NY has pretty whistles on all its locomotives, why doesn't the Pennsy put nicer sounding ones on the freight locomotives?"

O.P. smiled. "I'm not sure I can give you a correct answer to that question," he said, "other than that the Company has been using the small screecher whistles as a standard item on freight locomotives for a long time—long before I hired out—and as far as I could ever determine the main purpose was to identify the engine as either a freight or passenger class without actually seeing it. But then I could be wrong. The only other railroad in these parts using this same method of whistles is the P&R (Reading). Only their freight whistles aren't quite so shrill." Musing a bit, he then remarked, "I prefer the large-type whistles, and if I had my say I'd install them on all the engines."

Then O.P. provided some background about this line, reminiscing at the same time. When he came to Ralston in 1910, he explained, the Susquehanna & New York was about the same size as it was then, 1934, mileage-wise, but it was a relatively new venture. In addition to doing a large volume of freight business, it had two scheduled passenger trains in each direction between Newberry and Towanda daily. These trains also served Ralston, discharging their passengers either at the railroad's own station in South Ralston or at the Pennsylvania's station. The schedule was set to the Pennsylvania's movements for the convenience of boarding or departing passengers.

Two American-type 4-4-0's were used in this service, similar in size to the ones the Pennsylvania used on the Elmira Division passenger trains. A distinguishing feature of one of the S&NY locomotives was its ornate headlight. It was not unusually fancy, but its enclosure contained an oil pot and reflector that cast an exceptionally bright beam of light. Laying at the Ralston station one evening while it awaited the connecting movement, a Pennsylvania engineer must have deemed it a better arrangement than the interior assembly on his engine, because when the S&NY was ready to depart they discovered nothing remained inside the headlight. The shopmen from the coal hoist had to jury-rig an assembly to alleviate this embarrassing situation before the train could continue on its journey. No one ever learned the identity of the culprit responsible for this dastardly deed.

O.P. went on to relate that his first observations of the S&NY freight locomotives revealed them to be mostly Consolidations, much the same size as the 2-8-0 H6a class the Pennsylvania had him running. The only exception was that they had round-topped boilers. From what he could gather from talking with their crews when both his and their trains were occupying the same siding, the 2-8-0 types they used were purchased new from Baldwin. The odd types, such as 2-6-0's, 4-4-0's, and geared locomotives, came used from other rail lines.

One Consolidation they acquired new from Baldwin sometime around World War I outclassed the Pennsylvania engines in one respect: it was delivered equipped with a new innovation—a steam generator operating an electrical system that included an electric headlight. The electric headlight caused quite a stir among local railroaders, who were awed when they spotted it in use at night. It gave a brilliant light, and its beam cast out a considerable distance.

Hearing this, and thinking of the light a kerosene lamp gave off in homes not yet wired for electricity, I said: "The old oil headlights probably weren't too good. I don't imagine you could see very much with them."

But O.P. responded, "Nothing was wrong with an oil headlight if you took proper care maintaining it. You had to keep the reflector polished, the lens clean, and the wick trimmed properly, and mix a little camphor with the kerosene. It produced a bright, white light that gave you good visibility, but the beam wasn't as concentrated, and it wouldn't project out as far as the electric counterpart."

With darkness descending, we ceased our woodcutting chores and our railroading for the day—or at least that was what I thought. Later, as we finished our evening meal, my mother asked how we were progressing and then addressed O.P.: "I suppose Jack had you busy again answering his questions?" Evidently he had told my mother that I had been keeping him occupied with my many questions.

"We're getting quite a bit of wood ready to bring home," O.P. said, "but today we had a little different situation. I did most of the talking. We were thrashing out some of the S&NY's operations. However, I never did finish giving him the background on that railroad."

My mother, my sister, and I listened intently as he explained that this line had started because of a common tree, a hemlock, which played an important role in the development of the leather industries during the later part of the 1800's and into the twentieth century. Without dates or other facts, he gave us a general review: Before that period, the leather industry was centered in the New England states, because it depended on the trees in that region that were a source of tannic acid rendered from their bark. Hides were immersed in vats containing this liquor, which was a basic step in curing and in the process for dying the leather.

When it was discovered that hemlock bark yielded tannic acid too, and that hemlocks were also abundant in North Central and Northwestern Pennsylvania, small tanneries began springing up in this area. The huge tracts of hemlocks were virtually all virgin growth because of the nature of their wood—a type of softwood that as lumber had a long grain structure that made it difficult to plane into finished boards; the grain would raise, making it splintery. The large lumbering firms operating in Williamsport, once the lumbering capital of the world, were therefore not interested in this low-grade lumber, and the hemlocks were left to grow. When the small tannery operations began, however, these large hemlocks were felled, their bark was peeled and hauled to the tannery sites, and the logs were left where they were cut to rot away.

This wanton waste ended when a large leather-manufacturing firm chose Ralston as the site for a sole-leather tannery and formed a separate lumber company with headquarters in Williamsport. Under the enterprising direction of the capable men heading the parent leather company, their lumber subsidiary either bought, leased, or formed long-term contract arrangements on thousands of acres of virgin timberland in North Central Pennsylvania.

In conjunction with the building of the tannery, the lumber company began constructing a rail line to supply the needed bark. The line ran south out of Ralston along the eastern side of the mountain on an ascending grade—the present S&NY tracks—for nearly a mile, where a trestle was erected to span the valley. This trestle, more than a quarter of a mile long, crossed over Lycoming Creek, the Pennsylvania Railroad main, and the highway and was constructed entirely from wooden timbers. On the west side of the creek it continued in a southerly direction parallel with the Pennsylvania Railroad, but at a higher elevation, for another six miles to Grays Run, in order to facilitate the shipment of lumber sawed by a sawmill at this location. The tannery, too, built a rail system to serve in and around different buildings, as well as a small yard and a shop to service the 0-4-0 tank locomotive it purchased for switching chores.

From the outset, the lumber company's engines shared this yard and servicing area, and for their logging operations they brought in locomotives that were not the conventional type. Rather than turning the driving wheels by rod arrangements, the wheels on the engines were powered by a long shaft that ran from the cylinders to mesh with a spline gear and pinion, and were dubbed "stem winders."

The first phase of the logging operation on the west side down the Lycoming Valley wasn't exactly the type of work these powerful low-wheeled engines were designed to perform. Nonetheless, they plodded slowly to and from Ralston to the Grays Run Mill site. It was soon evident that the stem winders played a part in enlarging and modernizing the Grays Run Mill.

After renovations, this sawmill was capable of producing nearly 100,000 board feet of lumber daily. To supply a mill of this size was no small undertaking, and to meet the mill's needs the rail line was extended beyond the mill up the narrowing valley until the standard-gauge tracks reached the top of the mountain. At this elevation, access to thousands of acres of timber was possible. The mountain stretched from the Lycoming Valley west nearly six miles to the next valley division, what is known as Steam Valley. On this triangular plot of mountaintop, tracks were also laid south to near the Trout Run area. Off these main arteries, a web of tracks covered the entire region.

Interrupting O.P.'s story, I interjected: "That must have cost a lot of money to build a railroad up and across the mountain, plus they must have had to use pretty big equipment. How was this done?"

O.P. explained, "The leather company must have planned this all out well in advance of actual construction."

Although the story now drifted a little off course, how the rail lines were actually laid was an important part of the development of the entire operation. O.P. went on to explain that elaborate grades weren't necessary for these trains, and that only the main arteries were built with cuts, fills, and wooden trestles to span hollows or streams. On the wedges (spur tracks), about the only thing they were concerned with was keeping the roadbed on a level plane; gullies and small runs were merely filled with logs. The whole system was just temporary. Once a section was cut off and the logs were removed, rails and ties were taken up—only to be relaid at another section.

The geared locomotive, able to ascend the mountain grades, moved as well on the rolling mountaintop terrain and around sharp curves. It seemed they could go anywhere a set of rails could be laid. Although it might have been faster to use mechanized equipment to lay the track, only very limited lengths of the roadbed, if any, were constructed with this aid. Manual labor, using picks and shovels and, when necessary, generous amounts of blasting powder, carved out the roadbeds.

One would think that using manpower for this type of construction would be quite expensive, but the men in charge of these combined ventures showed their resourcefulness and kept building costs at a minimum. Through agencies specializing in recruiting European workers eager to come to America at the turn of the century, they found an unlimited supply of workers. The country chosen to supply this work force was Italy, and to meet immigration requirements these workers were provided with documents declaring they had gainful employment waiting for them in America, guaranteed by the lumber company. What wasn't immediately clear was that these men agreed to work for the Company for a specified time to pay for their ship passage, transportation, and lodgings. In a sense, they could be classified as bonded or indentured slaves. It must have been disheartening for these workers who believed that this country was the land of opportunity, especially when they found themselves transported to the middle of a vast wilderness completely isolated from civilization and forced to live in crude, makeshift temporary camps.

But these workers accepted these conditions with little or no dissension. After working out their debt to the Company, few remained in the woods. Most drifted to surrounding towns, and many to the larger city of Williamsport, where they had no trouble finding employment in factories or as track workers on section gangs of the Pennsylvania, Reading, or New York Central. A few applied trades learned in the old country and started their own businesses. But the loss of these workers caused the lumber company no problems; they merely recruited a new group.

When the tanning and lumber operations began as planned, the officials of the parent leather company went on to develop their vast land holdings and chartered a railroad to tie everything in the region together. This new subsidiary was incorporated as the Susquehanna & New York Railroad, and for many years it served to enhance the profit structure of these diversified ventures.

The roadbed for this new railroad was started where the trestle crossed the valley below Ralston. Continuing around the point of the mountain, part of the Allegheny chain, where it entered Pleasant Stream Creek Valley, it followed above stream level in a northeasterly direction. As in building the logging rail segments, Italian immigrant labor was chosen as the main work force for this project, but the roadbed had to be graded in a more precise manner to accommodate rod-driven locomotives. In order to accomplish this, the line was laid along the mountainsides up this valley, crossing the creek at many intervals.

Building the rail line up this valley opened the vast timber and bark resources held by the leather company. The first point of any importance the railroad reached was a lease- contract operation sawmill at Masten, served by a narrow-gauge logging railroad coming into this location from the east. Now that lumber could be easily shipped out, the mill was enlarged, and a second mill was built to saw hemlock logs.

O.P. noted that somewhere along the way someone in the organization learned that hemlock lumber weathered well, even without the use of preservatives or paint, and with this one important advantage introduced the cheap grade of lumber to authorities of ports along the eastern seaboard. The ports created a demand when they found hemlock was durable for dock planking, timbers, and rough boards for a multitude of uses. This proved to be most beneficial to the leather company's growth for they now had a market for hemlock lumber.

The S&NY did not stop at Masten, but went beyond the headwaters of Pleasant Stream to the summit of the mountain. On top, at an elevation of more than 2,000 feet, the line passed through the small farming community of Ellenton and began a descending grade into another wilderness of virgin timber on the other side. It went a short distance farther to pass through another small settlement, Wheelerville, before following Schrader Creek Valley to Laquin (Lay-Quinn), the site of a lease-contract sawmill. From here it ran along the valley floor to Barclay Junction, where it connected with an existing rail line that had been built to serve coal-mining on the Barclay Mountain, since purchased by the Company. The line then passed through the village of Powell, where the leather company had an established tannery, continued on to Monroeton, and then into Towanda, where it terminated despite a proposal to continue into southern New York. A yard, shops, and engine-servicing facility were constructed. Here too this line connected with the Lehigh Valley Railroad.

In conjunction with the building of the main line, the officials of this conglomerate demonstrated their determination to succeed by constructing a spur line to a coal tipple north of Ralston. This short segment provided a source of coal right on the line to supply the needs of not only the road engines and logging locomotives but also the tannery, thus eliminating buying coal from outside mines and paying shipping charges to the Pennsylvania Railroad.

The terminal facilities at Ralston proved inadequate once the S&NY was in full operation, so a portion of level land was purchased at Marsh Hill, about three miles south of Ralston, near the mouth of Pleasant Stream. Here a yard and engine-servicing facilities were built, and a connecting track to the Pennsylvania's main line was laid. The new terminal was labeled Marsh Hill Junction. However, the S&NY did not end there. Trackage rights over the Pennsylvania were acquired, to cover movements on the Elmira Division from Marsh Hill Junction to Newberry Junction, and on to the west end of Williamsport over the Williamsport Division main.

In the west end of the Newberry section of Williamsport, sufficient land was purchased to build a fair-size yard, shops, and engine-servicing and repair facilities. One obstacle hindered the S&NY from reaching its terminal in Newberry without a time-consuming move. Coming off the Elmira Division, trains were required to go into the Rose Street area of Williamsport before getting on the Williamsport Division tracks, where the engine would have to uncouple, run around the train, couple up, and pull it backward to Newberry. Departing movements would be required to repeat this performance. A connecting spur from the Elmira Division to the Williamsport Division main along Lycoming Creek would eliminate this drawback.

A plan to circumvent this problem again demonstrated the thinking of the leather company's hierarchy, who had proposed to the Williamsport city council that the S&NY build a cutoff spur, which would also create a dike. This dike would prevent flooding of the Newberry section, which occurred when the Lycoming Creek overflowed its bank. Whether it was political influence or the flood-control factor, the city council granted the S&NY's request.

This short spur also became important to the Pennsylvania Railroad, because it allowed easy access to the Elmira Division for movements to and from the west. O.P. surmised that gaining this short piece of cutoff track must have been the real reason the Pennsylvania granted trackage rights to the S&NY, for without that the Pennsylvania had nothing to gain. Before, they had the S&NY sewed up in Ralston. The Pennsylvania Railroad was bringing in green hides for the tanneries ("green" or unprocessed hides originated in slaughterhouses all over the United States and with foreign sources, mainly South America) and sundry supplies for the tannery, the town, and its engine facilities, and it was receiving cars filled with tanned leather, lumber, and various by-products of the sawmills and transporting passengers that originated on this line. Also, when the yard was established in the west end of Newberry, the S&NY was able to interchange shipments with two other rail lines—the New York Central and the Philadelphia & Reading—taking another bite out of the Pennsylvania's freight revenues.

Such a move was not in accord with proper business management. What the railroad lost in freight revenues certainly could not be generated in charges assessed the foreign line for use of their tracks. It even had to contend with four passenger trains, and at least the same number of freight trains on the busy Elmira Division main. Thus O.P. reasoned that the only logical answer was that the Pennsy must have decided that the dike spur was essential to its operation and paid the price.

Another venture the leather company entered into that complemented the tanneries it had established over the entire area was a glue factory constructed at the west end of the S&NY's yard in the Newberry district. The major ingredient in the glue-manufacturing process was residue removed from green hides before they entered the tanning vats. This by-product consisted of flesh and hair scraped from hides, which would be placed in gondola cars for transport. Although a generous amount of lime was scattered over this material, it was still a smelly mess. About the only thing related to leather that this company didn't construct in our area was a factory to manufacture finished leather products.

For a short line, the S&NY was a prosperous venture from its inception, but being dependent on the subsidiary companies of the parent organization for the majority of its revenues, activities beyond its control limited the railroad's growth. Interchange passenger and freight revenues from connections with the Pennsylvania, the Lehigh Valley, the New York Central, and the Reading were sources of income, but never enough to sustain its total operation.

Less than two years after he arrived in Ralston, O.P. related, the logging project in the Rock Run Valley, east of town, was completed, and with that the sawmill at Grays Run was without a supply of logs and therefore ceased operations. The rail line, the trestle below town, the Grays Run connection on the Pennsylvania's main, and the village of Grays Run soon became things of the past. This closing did not significantly hurt the S&NY's operations, for it still had the tannery at Ralston, which had become one of the largest sole-leather producers in the nation. It also had the mills at Masten and Laquin, and the tannery at Powell, all producing enough freight volume to keep the line more than busy. A large volume of passenger traffic came from sizeable towns at the mill sites. In fact, the railroad had a captive ridership; it was the only feasible means of travel in and out of this wilderness area.

Throughout the second decade of the twentieth century, during World War I, and into the early 1920s, the S&NY was a busy short-line railroad. Improvements were made to the roadbed during the war under government control and the leadership of the Lehigh Valley. Because bridges were never upgraded, however, weight restrictions limiting the use of large locomotives were applied. In fact, it even prohibited the use of double heading on the steep grades from Marsh Hill to Ellenton and from Laquin to Ellenton, resulting in costly double movements to get more than eight or ten cars at one time over the mountain in either direction.

A slowing of the economy in the early 1920s did not help the S&NY, and a disastrous fire that completely destroyed the Ralston tannery in the summer of 1923 started a decline in business that couldn't be stopped. O.P. in fact noted that other tanneries in the area seldom actually ceased operations; instead, most of them just burned down. The supplies of timber and bark also began a rapid decline during this period, forcing the largest sawmill on the line at Laquin to close during the mid-1920s. Soon after this closing and the loss of most of the town's population, passenger service was cut back to one train a day. The tannery at Powell also suspended production, leaving Masten with the only mills on the line still in operation.

In the early 1930s when the effects of the Depression took over and the timber supplies were finally exhausted, the Masten mills closed and that sawmill town too was abandoned. Today, O.P. explained, the only products that originate along the line are a few cars of pulpwood and an occasional shipment of coal, which generally doesn't leave the S&NY but is used at either the glue factory or the electric generation station in Towanda, or as fuel for the line's locomotives. Interchange traffic between the other railroads it connects with supplies some freight revenue, but not nearly enough to be profitable.

O.P. closed his narrative by observing that the S&NY still runs a scheduled passenger movement each way every day. This, however, is a mixed train, with a combination passenger-mail car attached to freight cars. He added that probably the entire railroad would be abandoned if the parent company had its choice, but that the Interstate Commerce Commission still deems the Susquehanna & New York Railroad necessary to the region it covers and won't permit it to end operations at the present time.

My mother was surprised at how much O.P. knew, not only about Ralston but also about the entire area. "How did you manage to gather all these details?" she inquired.

"Actually this was much like putting a puzzle together," said O.P. "Over the years I've talked with officials in charge in some of the companies, and others who have worked with the companies in various capacities, and read newspaper articles pertaining to Company ventures, and of course I personally witnessed much of what was taking place."

In school the following day, I couldn't help thinking about my father's narrative of Ralston's past, and by the time I joined him that afternoon on the mountainside, I had questions that needed answering. One of the biggest questions had to do with how the logging locomotives were cared for and serviced so far out in the wilderness.

That was not too much of a problem, according to O.P. At the end of each work day, the log trains returned to the mills, where facilities to service, coal, and water the locomotives were available. If they were working quite a distance from the mill and remained out in the woods, shuttle crews would take the log trains in at different intervals. Meanwhile, temporary facilities were set up where the engines were actually working. A siding on an elevation would be built, and a hopper car of coal would be placed on this and dumped; coal would then be shoveled into wheelbarrows, wheeled out on a ramp, and dumped into the tenders. The same method was used to coal the steam-powered log loader.

The engine crews took care of the locomotive to keep it in working order, and at night a person would be on duty to fill the lubricators, grease, and keep steam up so everything would be ready to go the next morning. Mechanics from the mills could be summoned to handle breakdowns. Major repairs required the engines to be towed to the shops in either Newberry or Towanda. The engines had to be taken to these locations for boiler washes.

There were never any water tanks or waterspouts along the tracks, because the stem winders had a siphon system that permitted them to obtain water from a stream that would be partially dammed up by throwing a couple of logs to form a small pond. At such sources, a hose attached to the tender would be dropped, and water was sucked up to fill the tank. The log loader also could get its water in this manner, either from a pond or from the engine's tank.

I was wondering why the Susquehanna & New York Railroad, once so prosperous, could be in such a deplorable state at this present time. "Could it be that they pay the crews too much money to run their trains?" I asked.

"No, that's not the cause," O.P. replied. "The government's agency, the ICC, won't permit them to cease operations, mainly because of the mail contracts. This contract doesn't pay enough, nor do they haul enough freight to keep going. At one time the crew probably made as much money as our crews, but the Brotherhoods never unionized this line, and through the years when our pay was increased, they, as independent employees, never got these raises; they worked for what the company was willing to pay. Today, probably the section gang workers on the Pennsylvania's track gangs make more money per hour than the train or engine crews on the S&NY."

Railroading in general continued to be an important topic of discussion for my father and me while we were cutting wood together. One afternoon I heard what I supposed was the eastbound local performing a rather commonplace move that I had watched many times from the school window. The engine pushing a car would go down the main to a point somewhere in South Ralston and stop; then the engine would open up as if it was making a passenger start; then it would shut off just for a moment, then really open up, passing by my window like it was running away from the devil himself, minus the car.

Soon the car would go coasting by going up the siding, and presently the engine would come back, enter the siding to retrieve the car, and come back out on the main with one car behind the engine. I could understand what was being accomplished by this move, but it just seemed simpler to push the car to the destination in Williamsport. This was a good opportunity to ask O.P. why the local did this type of switching.

"The maneuver you just heard the local making is called a 'flying switch,' and, by the way, according to the rule book, it's an illegal move," he responded, and when I asked why, he explained: "The main thing is it's too risky. You have to execute the move properly and gain enough speed before shutting off to allow the brakeman to pull the coupling pin. Then, the engine has to speed up to run by the switch to allow the coasting car enough time to enter and clear the switch."

O.P. clarified this further, with a few of the pitfalls. "There have been cases where the man throwing the switch did it too soon and the engine was either derailed or upset. Then too, sometimes the same thing happens to the car if the switch is not thrown soon enough. Another important part is the speed. The car must enter the siding far enough to clear or the railroad would be tied up. Also, in cases of a stub end siding, if the car is kicked too fast it has a tendency to go over the bumper block, either upsetting or landing on the ground.

"The legal way to make this move in compliance with the rule book would be for the engine to cut off above the siding at Max, come down the main to Ralston, pick up the car, back up to Max, and place it in the siding. The engine then would have to come down through Ralston, enter the siding, back up and pick up the car and push it out of the siding so it would be in the proper position to couple up to the train. But this takes too much time, so the crews 'fly' the car, not only here, but all over the system, and, I would imagine, on the other roads as well."

"Pushing the car in front of the engine is also not permitted, according to the safety rules, unless the train stops at all public grade crossings and a crew member goes forward to flag traffic," O.P. continued. "This wouldn't be practical, especially from here to Williamsport. There is an alternative. An air whistle attached to a hose can be coupled onto the air line at the front of the car, but doing this means a crew member would have to ride out in the open to blow the whistle at all the crossings." A fellow railroader he knew had been in France with the American Expeditionary Forces during World War I as a member of a railroad battalion and was assigned to an engine crew there. It turned out that after learning the basics of the French system and adjusting to the strange locomotives, the soldiers didn't experience too many problems getting trains to and from their destinations. One day while making a routine trip, they were dispatched to pick up two cars from a stub siding en route, which placed them in front of the locomotive. To deal with this situation, the soldier crew found a convenient siding and proceeded to make a flying switch. The French railroaders on board began jabbering and gesturing excitedly, thinking this was some sort of magic because they had never seen such a procedure before. "These Americans are not only wild, they're also crazy," they were saying.

Although O.P. had scheduled our woodcutting project to be finished by the first of November so it wouldn't interfere with hunting season, it ended early. He was working alone when he stepped on a rock covered with wet leaves, throwing him to the ground with such force that he broke three ribs. After being treated by our local physician, he was in no condition to do this heavy work, so he hired a teamster and had the pole lengths and log-size wood we'd assembled hauled to our backyard. There we cut it into stove-size wood and put the finished product in our woodshed for future use.

The arrival of hunting season found O.P. spending quite a bit of time enjoying this sport, and our table that fall was graced with a generous amount of wild game. One evening after a day's hunt he remarked, "This is the most I've been able to hunt in my entire life. Even when I was a boy back on the farm, I could only spend a small amount of time hunting, and from that time on I've always been working. Of course, when I hunted with the Sunbury crew at Hyner I laid off for deer season, but that was about all the time I ever got."

Although I wasn't old enough to have a hunting license or carry a firearm, I did accompany him on various occasions, either after school or on Saturdays. On these hunts, he gave me the honor of being his dog. My part was to jump on brush piles to chase out rabbits, or go through heavy cover to roust out grouse and rabbits. It didn't take me long to learn that whatever species I could chase out, whether it was running or flying, O.P. rarely missed anything. In deer season I wasn't permitted to go along, but he did get a large-rack buck without my assistance.

After hunting season was over, it was just a short time until the Christmas holidays and the new year of 1935. There had been no significant change in O.P.'s blood pressure over the four months since he had been taken out of service. Even under treatment by the Williamsport specialist, he failed to reduce it, so he pretty much gave up. The only medical attention he continued with came from our town doctor, who was taking his blood pressure at least once a week. This doctor, who also was a personal friend, told O.P. from the onset that the only way to get his blood pressure down and keep it normal was to lose weight and exercise. The doctor said he wouldn't prescribe any medication for this particular condition.

The exercise part was no problem. He was active most of the time, and he did a lot of walking—something he always enjoyed. But losing weight was different. He admitted that the more he exercised the more he wanted to eat, and in this category my mother's excellent cooking was something he couldn't resist. So he wasn't successful in reducing his weight at all. But he did try garlic, having heard that garlic was effective in reducing blood pressure. By this time he was willing to try anything, so he purchased a bottle of concentrated garlic tablets and began taking a self-prescribed dose. After a week he had ingested enough garlic into his system that he began to reek like a freshly crushed garlic clove. One only had to enter a room he occupied to detect the odor he was emitting.

He continued to take these tablets for nearly a month, and when he went for his weekly blood pressure checkup at the end of this period there was no change in his condition. When he told the doctor what he was taking, the doctor smiled and told him he could smell his self-prescription. Garlic just might be effective over time to control high blood pressure, the doctor explained, but it would not result in any quick reduction. With that in mind, O.P. discontinued this rather offensive smelling self-cure.

One evening during the winter, snow began to fall, continuing until mid-afternoon the following day until it had accumulated to more than fifteen inches. This made for excellent sled-riding, and after school that day most of the kids in town were out sledding on the hill where we lived, myself included.

I was coming back to the starting point on the curve below our home when an S&NY engine whistled its approach. When it came into view it was already working hard on the stiff grade that rose from the valley floor. It was shoving three empty hoppers on its trip to the tipple, and I assumed that the heavy snow cover was not going to help. My only thought was that this little engine would never be able to push the cars through all the snow to the top of the crest, but with a cloud of black smoke coming from the stack with each sharp exhaust, it went over the top onto level track. Watching this movement across the valley, as the little train smoked along the opposite mountainside and clouded the perfectly white background, it looked like a picture an artist might portray.

Awhile later, as I was resting after a sled ride, I spotted the same locomotive coming back with three hoppers loaded with coal. Nearing the point where it was to start descending the grade, an unusual thing happened: the last car uncoupled and was left sitting as the train went on down the hill. The crew apparently discovered that their train was shy one of its cars somewhere in South Ralston—exactly where was out of my sight, but moments later I heard it coming back and when it came into view it was pushing the two loaded cars. The grade didn't seem to be slowing its progress either, until it got to within six or seven car lengths of the errant car it was attempting to retrieve. Then a column of smoke erupted from the stack toward the sky, and the train came to an abrupt halt. An attempt was made to start again, but it just resulted in a violent spin, sending another column of smoke straight up.

Realizing that wasn't going to work, the crew reversed and went back down the grade to the level for another try. This time, although more speed was attained, the same thing again took place near the place where it had slipped out on the first try. When they left after the second try, I figured the crew found out it was impossible to reach the dropped car and would go back to Marsh Hill yard with the two loaded cars. But I was wrong, for I heard the engine coming back, and when it appeared I could see that it was running light. The crew must have dug out a switch from the heavy snow cover at the South Ralston yard and set off the two loaded cars. Running light, and charging as fast as the tracks would permit, the little engine still couldn't reach the errant car, spinning out as if an invisible barrier was keeping it from reaching the top of the grade.

The crew was undoubtedly determined to retrieve this coal car, so I rode my sled down to the bottom of the hill and ran over to the Cemetery Road grade crossing to see the action close up, at trackside. Just as I reached the crossing, the engine passed, and from the sounds it was making the engineer was using all the power he had at his command. Peering up this straight section of track, I saw the engine spin out short of its goal again. As the engine went by, going up and down the grade, I noticed something unusual: the engineer was standing in the cab going up, but sitting down at the controls, the engine facing forward, when he came back down. The same was the case in the next attempt: the engineer was in a standing position on the way up but sitting down on the return. It was nearly dark as I watched the engine cross the trestle heading for South Ralston, finally giving up on what turned out to be a losing cause.

That evening at the supper table I gave O.P. a blow-by-blow description of the hardship the S&NY crew had encountered on its coal run. And I asked him why the engineer was standing up in the cab when the engine was running backward up the grade, but sitting down when he came back down. That wasn't unusual, O.P. explained, saying, "This engine was probably an older slide-valve type locomotive whose forward-reverse motion is controlled by a large manually operated lever called a Johnson Bar. On some of these engines, when the Johnson Bar was moved to the reverse position it extended back far enough to require the engineer to drop his seat, meaning he had to stand while running backward."

To give me a clearer understanding, he got out a book with a cutaway diagram showing the box-type flat slide-valve motion, and also the round cylinder-type piston valve. He pointed out that the slide-valve motion was activated by an inside mechanism attached to one of the drive axles, whereas the piston valve was moved by an outside eccentric rod. He noted too that the older-type slide-valve-equipped locomotive used saturated or wet steam. The piston valve, when it was first developed, also used wet steam, but when the superheater came into the picture, it removed the moisture content of the steam, more or less drying it, providing more efficient power for the engine.

Years ago, O.P. went on, the Pennsylvania's engines all had slide valves, but as they were constructed for more power and speed, the piston valve was used. Through the years, the older engines came to be outfitted more and more with piston valves and also superheated, and when this transformation took place the manually operated Johnson Bar was usually removed. They were then fitted with a screw device or an air-operated cylinder that controlled the valve motion. About the only class on the roster equipped with slide valves were the B8's 0-6-0 switch engines.

So I also learned how steam was transmitted to power a locomotive, but I still wondered why a rail car would come loose while the train was moving. O.P. explained that this could happen for a variety of reasons. "A pretty good guess," he said, "would be that the couplers between those cars weren't locked. Or it could be the fault of the train crew, who perhaps didn't make a proper inspection, or perhaps didn't hook up the air lines before leaving the tipple." It is especially important, he explained, that the air lines be hooked up, so that the train would go into emergency when the cars parted and would stop almost on the spot. "Since this didn't occur," he continued, "the only logical explanation I can come up with is that the engineer must have made a reduction with the independent brake valve so he could regulate the speed going down the grade. This braking action only on the engine and tender wheels allowed the cars to come forward, giving the couplers slack enough to open up the one on the rear."

Then he added, "You know, the S&NY crew were really lucky they lost that car on level ground while it was being pulled. Had the car stayed coupled until they rounded the mountain on this spur and came out on their main, a backing move would have taken place. From this switch to Marsh Hill, it's well over a mile, plus it's a straight heavy downgrade. If the car had uncoupled here, it would have run away with nothing to stop it until it reached their yards. Being loaded, it would have gained a lot of speed and, to say the least, would have caused a considerable amount of damage someplace."

In the cold and inclement weather, O.P. wasn't too actively engaged in physical exercise. About the only thing he accomplished was tending the furnace, taking out ashes, keeping the kitchen stove supplied with wood, and shoveling snow when needed. Around our large house there were always things in need of repair or refurbishing, but he always left painting, varnishing, or carpentry jobs to a hired contractor. Whether this was because he wasn't adept at that kind of work or that it did not interest him, I never learned. There was one exception: he would make plumbing repairs, and from what I could see he was good at this.

During these long winter months he seemed more relaxed, or perhaps he had accepted the fact that there wouldn't be any substantial change in his blood pressure; the relief doctor's finding would be the same after each visit to his office. He spent much of his spare time reading books, plus *National Geographic* magazine, a few magazines relating to outdoor activities, and the daily and Sunday newspapers. It wasn't long before I discovered that O.P. regarded reading as more than just spare-time activity. To him it was part of the learning process, and whatever he read he would be able to recall almost verbatim.

When the snow finally melted and the weather started warming, it was a time for outdoor activities again. The initial project was to trim all the shrubbery to perfection and to rake the yard clean—all under my mother's supervision. Then he began pruning the many fruit trees on our property. Helping to gather the brush and limbs that had been removed and placing them on a bonfire, I asked, "Is this the best time of the year to prune trees?"

"It's as good a time as any," my father responded, "and actually may be better to do it in the spring, or at least when the leaves aren't on the trees. You don't have as much of a mess to clean up." But then he added: "Really, there are only fifty-two days a year when you're not supposed to prune trees."

Puzzled, I inquired: "What time of the year do these days occur?"

"Sundays, of course," he replied. "That's the number of them in a year, isn't it?" He went on, "You never do this kind of work on Sunday, but if you have a job on the railroad, you have to work. The trains run whether it's a Sunday or a holiday. Those days are the same as any other day, as far as the Company's concerned."

I realized then that resting on Sundays was a part of my father's philosophy of life and that our family never did any of the usual weekday things on Sunday. We might take a long walk through the mountains on our side of the valley, or an automobile ride through the surrounding countryside, or an occasional visit to my oldest sister's home in Williamsport, but little else.

One day after the spring rains ended and the ground firmed up, O.P. decided that it was time to level our lawn, so he rented a dump truck from the local Ford dealer and took it to a place two miles north of Ralston, where suitable topsoil could be found at creek level. After hauling a few loads for our yard, he decided the soil was of such fine quality that he would use it to enrich soil in our garden as well. So, what started as a small job became a lengthy hauling venture that lasted most of the week, including Saturday.

I rode along for a couple of loads that day, and though I wasn't old enough to evaluate his truck-driving skills, he did demonstrate his shoveling talents. At the loading site, his first move was to fill his pipe and light it, then, picking up a round-pointed garden shovel, he began to put the dirt in the truck's dump box. He used a rhythmic motion, never pausing or stopping for a rest until the box was heaping full. I was amazed. I couldn't understand how he or anyone else could shovel that much dirt without at least stopping for a rest. Although the truck was the largest standard model Ford had in its line, and was rated at a capacity of around four tons, this still was a substantial amount of dirt to shovel by hand without pausing.

Between outside chores, O.P. spent some time fishing—something else he was good at. After an evening thundershower, when the creeks would rise, he would often spend half the night fishing, and the result was some extraordinary catches. Unlike hunting, I could participate in this sport—not at night, but mostly in the afternoons or early evening hours. Most of the places we fished were near the railroad. Its roadbed paralleled Lycoming Creek all the way to Williamsport, so fishing also provided a good opportunity to do some train-watching.

As the trains passed in both directions, O.P. could tell me many interesting things about the characteristics and operations of the railroad. As the 3:30 P.M. passenger train passed our location, he pointed out the E6 heading the four cars in tow, and the number it carried: "That's the Four and a Quarter, No. 425. She and her sister E6, the 666, known as the Three Sixes, have been on the Williamsport to Canandaigua runs daily for quite a while. There isn't any difference between these two engines and the rest of the E6's, except these two have a built-up coal bunker on their tenders so they can carry enough coal for this 175-mile trip. They make this run six days a week—up one day and back the next." (Watching for these numbers after they came to my attention, I could see that they appeared regularly for many years after this, on the same trains.)

Another thing I had noticed for some time was that these trains—the 8:30 A.M. westbound, the 12:00 P.M. eastbound, the 3:30 P.M. westbound, and the 5:30 P.M. eastbound—never seemed to have many passengers on board. O.P. explained: "About the biggest share of the passengers on this line are Company employees, mostly over-the-road crews going to and from terminals. The Company is aware of this too, but the ICC rules the operation of these trains and deems them necessary. Even if they don't make any money, they are still required to continue these runs." He then said something rather strange: "The Company would get rid of all their passenger trains, maybe keeping a few of the named crack flyers on the main lines, but on the secondary lines they'd relegate their operations to hauling freight exclusively. That's where they can make money. Naturally, the government won't permit this to happen, but they're always working toward that end."

History showed him to be right, but at the time, 1935, I found it difficult to believe that the railroad would ever get to a point where it no longer ran passenger trains.

Often the places we chose to go fishing were accessible only by walking along the railroad tracks, and that was where I learned that caution should be used while on railroad property. One day a freight movement approached us as we were heading toward our spot. O.P. moved back off the roadbed a few feet and instructed me to join him. "Never stand close to a moving train," he said. "There're many things that might injure you when they're passing. For example, a brake rigging could be loose, and one of the rods could be dragging outside, or a load might have shifted, and pieces could be hanging over the side. And you can't rule out the possibility that the whole damn thing might derail." He then added, "When I'm working, and off the engine when another train passes, I always get back a respectable distance. Even in the cab I always pull my head in."

Another time, when we were crossing the tracks I stepped on the rail and I immediately received a reprimand: "That's something you should never do. Step over the rail, but not on it. The rails can be very slippery, especially if some oil has been leaked on them, or even if they're just wet—and you can't always tell their condition by looking at them." He went on, "It's against a safety rule to step on a rail like you just did, and if you were working for the Company and an official saw you do that, you'd probably get a few days off without pay."

The spring weather improved, and near the end of May we had our garden plowed, but this year an additional plot of grass was also readied for planting. This was directly related to his blood-pressure problem—not that it was alarmingly high, but it did remain high enough, after all these months, that the relief doctor was keeping him out of service.

Not able to foresee any immediate change in his condition, we held in reserve whatever produce we raised, to help in our present limited financial circumstances. O.P. and my mother went about the gardening in a teamlike fashion. The soil was prepared and rows made, straight ones, by my father; the seeds were planted with her green thumb, then covered by him. I was obliged to pick up the stones that were in abundance on our hillside plot. It wasn't long after planting that the cultivating had to be done. This, along with mowing our large lawn with a reel-type mower, occupied a portion of his time.

Another aid to our existence was a small flock of chickens. They supplied us with fresh eggs and an occasional Sunday dinner. O.P. decided that it would be better if we increased the flock; eggs we didn't use could always be sold, plus there would be more chicken for the table.

We had a convenient source for peeps too. A chicken-raiser located below us on the same hill incubated 12,000 eggs at a time during the spring season, and our family purchased one hundred of these peeps from a regular hatching of unsexed eggs, which the raiser assured us would produce about an equal number of pullets and roosters. To raise and house this increased number of chickens, additional facilities would be needed. So O.P. constructed two coops: one to house the pullets and one for the roosters, who would be separated out when combs developed and sexes could be determined. To keep costs down, my father found a source for the heavier framing timbers and some lumber at no cost: he tore down a small shed located on the former tannery site, one of the structures spared when the main buildings were destroyed by fire.

But my mother was afraid that these boards and timbers could still be contaminated with the deadly anthrax germ, a disease transmitted from hides of affected cattle that originated in foreign countries that entered into the human body's bloodstream through cuts or skin abrasions and had proved fatal to many tannery workers that contacted the germ until our local physician developed a cure. My father explained that the germ was probably no longer present as a germ, and that even if it was there was a cure, but my mother wasn't totally convinced that it was safe to handle the lumber. She forbade me to go along and help with the procurement chore, and further warned me never to play around the old tannery site. I wasn't even allowed to help with the framing work. O.P. himself may have been somewhat leery of the material he could have only for the taking, because he elected to purchase boards for the roofs and sidewalls from a nearby sawmill. When the two coops were completed, his skill at carpentry work was apparent. They were well suited to the intended purpose.

Our chicken-raising venture made it necessary for O.P. and me to travel to Roaring Branch for starting mash, to ensure proper growth of the new chicks. Just as we were leaving the feed mill after our purchase, we heard a hardworking freight approaching. Standing with me on the loading dock to watch it pass, O.P. all of a sudden began hollering, "That's the way to do it, buddy! Pull 'er out, pull it out all the way." He then started laughing so hard he couldn't speak, but just pointed toward the engine. I was dumbfounded at his sudden outburst—that is, until I looked up into the cab. There, instead of sitting on the seat box, the engineer was standing on it, both gloved hands on the throttle, apparently pulling for all he was worth.

O.P. exclaimed, "Did you see that?" and then in the same breath said, "I've seen some fellows do some strange things in the cab, but this one tops them all."

I asked, "Why would the engineer stand on the seat box?"

O.P. explained, laughing: "That engineer isn't very much bigger than you are, and he's skinny as a rail. A sudden windstorm would probably blow him away. His L1 probably has a sticky throttle. Most generally you can open a throttle easy enough, but usually they're harder to close. This, plus his small size making it impossible to reach standing on the deck, and without a doubt a limited amount of strength, made him get up on the seat box. He had to get the throttle opened up too. From here to Leolyn, the grade really gets steep, and you have to use about all the power an engine can develop."

I had another question. "If the engineer is that small, how did he ever get a job working on an engine?"

"That's something I have always wondered, but it's sort of a mystery to me," O.P. said. "Nobody else seems to have the answer either. He's older than I am and even though the engines were much smaller a few years back, they still required a lot of hand-firing. How he got around this function before he was promoted and set up running, I can't figure out." He added: "Evidently he manages to get along all right. He's had one side of the local for quite a few years, down from Southport one day and back up from Williamsport the next without any trouble I've ever heard of." (Another time, I saw this engineer off the engine at the water plug, and he resembled a boy dressed in railroader garb.)

Our spacious front porch was always cool during the warm weather months, and at the end of the day and on Sundays, O.P. relaxed and read the newspaper there before the evening meal. When I joined him, which I frequently did, I tried not to interrupt his solitude, but on many occasions we ended up discussing railroading.

One Sunday afternoon on the porch a westbound movement came whistling into town, and O.P. remarked that it had to be a diker because no other trains would be running at that time of day. We could hear the exhausts of the working engine, but the foliage at this time of the year blocked our view of the train. It passed through town and into the vicinity of the former yard office. The head-end locomotive shut off. "He's going to stop for water," commented O.P. "He'll drift now until reaching Max. This allows the pushers to shove in the slack between the cars. They'll keep working until the head end sets the air on them."

It happened as he said. The pushers were exhausting hard when they came by, but their slowing was audible. As they stopped, we heard their gasp, somewhere in the vicinity of the yard. Everything was quiet for a moment, then the pushers started backing down to the water plug. We knew they had reached this oasis when the brake shoes grated and we heard the sound of a tank lid being thrown open. Soon after, we heard the head-end engine clanking down the siding to join the pushers and fill its tank. A bell signaled that the pushers were leaving, and we heard the dull thud that told us they had again coupled onto the cabin. The head-end locomotive did not move out as quickly as the pushers, so I wondered why it was spending so much time there. O.P. said the fireman was probably shaking the grates and cleaning the fire after the 125-mile run from Altoona. When we heard a loud banging noise, like someone hammering on the engine, O.P. remarked, "Not only was he cleaning the fire, the fireman is also dumping the ash pan. It must have been full too."

The engine must have been at the water plug for nearly an hour when the bell started ringing, and it moved back up the siding to resume the trip to Southport. "How can that crew spend so much time fooling around?" I asked. "Won't the officials get after them?"

His reply surprised me: "They probably would like to, but there's nothing they can do about it. Work rules established between the Company and the Brotherhoods allow an engine crew to take water, clean the fires, even drop the ash pan if necessary. But nothing can be said because there were no expectations about how long these chores should take. I'll admit that this crew did quite a bit of fiddling around. I suspect the engineer knows he's getting pretty close to his sixteen-hour limit and he's figuring on getting in just shy of outlawing. This will give him about another hour's pay over the trip mileage rate. Some of the fellows do this pretty regularly, but I can't quite see their reasoning. I'd rather make a run well under the mileage rate. It's just like getting paid extra for not working a full day."

Not too long after leaving the water plug, we heard the head-end locomotive issue a series of long, shrill whistle blasts, and then, a short time later, two short blasts. The couplers rattled for a moment, then simultaneous exhausts from the pushers showed that the train was finally on its way.

"Why do these trains always do all this whistling?" I asked my father.

"It's a means of communication," O.P. replied, "but around the railroad you use the whistle so much it becomes automatic, and I guess I never bothered to tell you about the importance of this means of signaling." He explained that before becoming a promoted engineer every man had to demonstrate, among other things, that he was familiar with every signal the whistle was intended to sound. The Pennsylvania had these signals incorporated in their Book of Rules, but federal regulations required all to use the same whistle sounds.

He left the porch, went into the house, and came back with his copy of the Book of Rules opened to the pages that listed all whistle signals an engineman had to be familiar with. The long whistle sounds were indicated by a straight bar, "———," and the short signals by a zero, "0." Pointing to five bars and to the explanation that that signal was used to call the flag when a movement was westbound, he told me that was the signal the diker had just used before departing. If we had heard an engine sounding four long blasts, it would have been an eastbound calling the flag.

"What does 'calling the flag' mean?" I inquired.

Leafing through the book, O.P. found the section that explained that any stopped movement occupying a main, regardless of the direction it was traveling, had to deploy a flagman approximately twenty car lengths to the rear, for train protection. In daylight hours he must carry a red flag, at night, a red lantern. A proper whistle signal must be given, and enough time must be allotted for him to board the train. In addition, the flagman is required to place two torpedoes on the rails before boarding. At night he must also set a five-minute fusee, a slow-burning tube of cardboard filled with flammable chemicals that warns a following train of a stopped or slow-moving train ahead. If a movement following comes upon a burning fusee, it must stop and wait until the device burns out before proceeding.

Instead of getting a clear understanding of all the whistle signals and what they communicated, I was becoming befuddled. "I didn't expect you to grasp the meaning of these signals right now," O.P. assured me, "but if you keep paying attention, and refer to the book, you'll be able to tell what a train is doing without seeing its actual movements."

Following his advice, and with lots of referring to the book, I could soon tell not only the east and west flag calls but also that two short whistle blasts meant the engine was about to move forward, that three short blasts meant a reverse move, and that a long, short, long, and short signaled a road crossing. The crossing whistles, though, seemed to vary, for every individual engineer seemed to have his own version of how he sounded the warning at this point.

The locomotive's bell was used in conjunction with the whistle, and O.P. advised listening to it as well. The bell would be rung before an engine moved in either direction and at all grade crossings, and by passenger engines when they were pulling into a station. I learned more about whistle signals on another evening while we were awaiting the call for supper. The eastbound passenger, due into town at 5:30 P.M., whistled for the crossing at Max. I wasn't paying any attention to its approach when O.P. cautioned that I should listen for the signal it gave before it reached the station. In the vicinity of the bridge over Lycoming Creek, three short whistle blasts were sounded. "The conductor has notified the engineer that it's necessary to make this station stop," O.P. told me, "and the three short whistles were an acknowledgment that the order would be followed."

When I asked how the conductor gave that order, O.P. responded with a question: "You've seen the conductor pulling on a cord in a passenger car vestibule? That cord opens a valve on an air line running to the engine cab, where it activates a small air whistle, called a cab signal, to let the engineer know what he's supposed to do by the number of times it's pulled. Three times means to make a station stop, two times means it's time to leave the station."

He continued, "A passenger train can arrive early at a station, but according to regulations it's not permitted to leave before the time published in the timetable. Sometime when you're watching the passenger trains come in and leave, notice the conductor. He'll check his watch for the correct departure time before he pulls the cord."

The next day found me at the station when the noon eastbound passenger rolled in. I was anxious to see all these communications in practice. Walking forward to the stopped E6, I positioned myself at the gangway steps so I had a partial view of the cab's interior. The engineer watched back along the train until the brakeman boarded, and the engineer then turned around and looked straight ahead. Just as O.P. had said, I heard two plaintive beeps from within the cab, then two short, sharp whistles. The bell began to ring. Air was released from the train and locomotive with a hiss. Sand began flowing in front of the drivers. The engineer opened the throttle, closed it, and started notching out again. The passenger was under way.

I was satisfied that the communication system really worked as a signal for the engineer to start the train, but to observe the other half of the process, I met the westbound passenger at 3:30 P.M. and concentrated on the trainmen's part and on exactly how the message was relayed. The first person to get off the train was the brakeman, whose primary responsibility seemed to be assisting the departing passengers as they alighted, and doing the same for those boarding. When the last person went up the steps, he followed, slamming down the metal plate that covered this entrance. The conductor was standing in the vestibule, watch in hand, and evidently at the exact moment he reached up and gave the cord above his head two short tugs. The engineer replied, and the train began moving. There was now no mystery about how a passenger train made its start.

On a Sunday afternoon in mid-July, O.P.'s former, fun-loving fireman paid an unexpected visit and joined us on the front porch. After exchanging the usual pleasantries, he told us that he and many other Pennsylvania Railroad employees had been furloughed, and that although they would probably be called back in the fall, there wasn't any assurance that he'd even get on the extra board at this time. Rather than be unemployed for more than two months, and perhaps longer, he'd decided to go into business for himself. With financial help from a relative, plus a mortgage on his home, he had been able to lease some land about 18 miles southwest of Ralston. The property was atop a mountain, and, according to natives of the area, there were coal deposits beneath it. He intended to remove the coal and sell it in the Williamsport area, which was only some 12 miles south, paying the property owner a royalty on every ton mined. But first a mine shaft or the main drift had to be opened, the road up the mountain needed improvements, timber props to hold up the mine roof had to be cut, mine rails and cars had to be procured, and, if the coal was there, a loading platform would need to be built. And all these and many other things would require supervision of some sort.

The fireman concluded, "Oscar, you helped me quite a bit when I started firing, and you also spent a lot of time tutoring me for promotion exams. Now I need your help again to make this venture a paying business." He had miners to open the drift, and three other men to do the related work, but trying to keep everybody working was proving too much to handle alone. "If you could sort of keep these men busy doing the odd things, I'd be able to get the coal out sooner, and I have to do that or I'll run short of money. And that's another thing. I can't afford to pay you what you're used to making on the railroad. Thirty-five cents an hour would be all I could manage, but I don't expect you to do too much work other than supervise."

O.P. had listened carefully and gave an immediate answer: "It suits me fine. I'm not doing anything anyway. This'll give me something to do till I get my blood pressure back to normal."

As O.P.'s about-to-be new employer was leaving, he said, "I forgot to tell you, we're working ten hours a day, six days a week. I'll pick you up tomorrow morning a little after 6:00 A.M. Tell Amelia I'll have you home by 6:00 P.M." There was no mention of time-and-a-half for overtime.

At the end of the first few days on his new job, O.P. was visibly tired when he sat down at the supper table. "You must be working pretty hard," my mother said. "I thought you were supposed to just see that the men were doing the work."

"I can't stand around and do nothing," O.P. retorted. "Besides, if I'm not working, these fellows think they should stop too."

This new experience was interesting to O.P. though, and each evening at suppertime he would keep us informed of his daily activities. The only mechanized piece of equipment in the operation was a small Ford dump truck, and O.P. was the designated driver. Fill was loaded by hand onto the truck to be distributed on the road, but the widening and ditching was done with picks and shovels, and sledgehammers were used for removing large stones. When not constructing the road, the crew cut props and hauled them to the mine site.

Not too many days passed before the miners had their drift past the outlying crop line and they hit a seam of coal measuring nearly three feet deep. It proved to be a good grade of bituminous, or soft, coal. What had been a wildcat venture turned out exactly as the natives had predicted. When the first coal was hauled out of the mine, it was stockpiled on the ground, but before long O.P. and his crew began building a loading ramp that would enable coal from the cars to be dumped into waiting trucks. This led to another project for the crew: erecting a scale and a scale house/office.

Once coal was being produced in marketable amounts, Williamsport haulers, as hoped, picked up the nearness of this supply, and a steady stream of trucks were present every day. Digging the shaft farther into the hill, they found that the coal seam increased in depth until it measured six feet deep, and the coal was free of binders or foreign materials. With this find, additional miners were hired and sales increased. Two commercial firms were added to the customer list—a brewery and a large greenhouse—becoming house accounts to which O.P. hauled several loads in the dump truck every week.

The family had become accustomed to having O.P. around all the time, so his absence while he was helping to get the mining operation into production created a real void. Understanding that this was something he needed to do, I did my best to watch what was happening on the railroad, and tried to keep him informed. Nothing out of the ordinary transpired during the summer, until one morning a strange whistle echoed in the valley north of town, sounding the warning for the grade crossing at Max. From the sound of the whistle, my first thought was it belonged to an S&NY engine at the coal tipple, then I realized this spur didn't have a crossing up that far, and that it had to be a movement approaching on the Pennsylvania main. Hurrying down to my viewing spot at the water plug, I was just in time to see a shiny engine with a headlight centered on the smoke-box door slowing to a stop.

When this engine came to a full stop, I had an opportunity to give it a closer inspection. Up on top of the smoke box, in front of the stack, was a cylindrical appendage that gave it a husky look. The front of the cylinders were covered with a shiny metal, and a silver star adorned each piston-valve front. The tires as well as the rods on this 4-6-2 type were painted white. Examining it further, on a tender larger than most Pennsylvania engines hauled was a large yellow-tinted diamond with the word "ERIE" inscribed within. Attached to the tender were dark-green passenger cars, all lettered "ERIE."

Moving closer so I could look into the cab, I made another discovery. The throttle was suspended from the roof of the cab on a vertical quadrant, rather than the slightly angled quadrant attached to the boiler backhead, as on Pennsylvania locomotives. The brass builder's plate above the cylinders wasn't the same either. It gave an unfamiliar class designation and showed that it wasn't built by Baldwin or Juniata either, but by Alco Locomotive Works. The fireman's side of the cab had two seats, one in front of the other. The water-plug routine was conducted by the Erie crew as I had witnessed many times before, and as this eastbound foreigner was ready to depart it even gave the same whistle signals and rang the bell before moving.

Blasting away from the water plug, this powerful-appearing locomotive hauled mail and baggage cars, coaches with white cloths on the seatbacks, a diner, and Pullmans. These cars were shiny too, and the people aboard waved friendly greetings. The cars were clean, and none of the windows was open on this warm summer morning. This was completely different from passenger cars the Pennsylvania ran through town.

After this train—as nearly perfect as my imagination would allow—had passed out of view, and the melodious whistle sounded a farewell as it blew for the South Ralston crossing, I figured that would be the last such fabulous sight on the rails of our isolated valley, and when the shrill screeching whistle of the morning local announced its westbound approach, I knew I was correct. But before long the stillness was again interrupted by the sound of a foreign intruder, this time westbound. It turned out to be another Erie passenger, and up front two of the impressive 4-6-2's were in charge, each as resplendent as the one that had just gone the other direction. To my inexperienced thinking, this was an unusual way to haul a train—or at least it was a sight I had never seen before. On this line there were never any heavy passenger movements; freight trains westbound, needing extra power, always used one or two pusher engines on the rear end. The lead engine of this duo had another odd feature: its tender had angled sides for the coal-bunker section, and behind this the tank was rounded, much like a tank car. Again, all the cars in the consist were immaculate, and all the windows also closed.

This parade of Erie power, both passenger and freight trains, continued all day long, sandwiched between the normal Pennsylvania movements. Eastbound, only one locomotive headed each train, passenger or freight. Westbound, two engines were always used. The passenger engines were 4-6-2's. The freights were handled either by 4-8-2's or by a wheel arrangement that was unfamiliar to me: 2-8-4's. All had the cylindrical adornment in front of the stack, and a few had the odd tank-car type tenders. They were all shining. One of the westbounds had an exceptionally long train made up mostly of refrigerator cars. Up front were two Eries in charge, and on the rear end it had a Pennsylvania L1 pusher. Evidently it had too much tonnage to get up the hill, but this time the L1 was coupled on differently: it was pushing hooked up to a car, and the cabin was attached to the tender so it was being pulled along.

All these new and different sightings made it an exceptional day for train-watching, and by the time O.P. got home from the mines I had lots of questions. He wasn't surprised that the Erie had been running trains through town all day long. "I know," he said, "one of them was laying in the siding at Trout Run when I came through on my way home. It must have been holed up for the 5:30 P.M. eastbound passenger and it'll probably be coming through pretty soon."

At least this opened a new avenue of questioning. I asked, "Did it have two engines on the head end?"

"I don't know," he replied. "All I saw was the cabin just beyond the station. I couldn't see what was up front from the highway. But why do you ask?"

My explanation was that the Pennsylvania never used two engines on the front of their trains in our area, but that the Erie had that amount of power on both its passengers and its freights when they were going west up the valley. But O.P. pointed out that on divisions operating over areas where there were no exceptionally heavy grades, the Pennsylvania also used two engines, on heavy passenger and freight movements. This method, called "double-heading," wasn't used on the Elmira Branch because of the heavy grade out of Ralston and the roller-coaster grades beyond Leolyn to Southport. Pushers on the rear of freight trains allowed for better train control by keeping the slack together and thus reducing the risk of pulling the cars apart.

He went on to answer another question I had before I even asked it: "They probably had a bad wreck or a washout on the Erie in New York somewhere between Elmira and Olean and are rerouting the preference trains down this way, or vice versa, through to Newberry Junction, west to Renovo, on to Emporium, and into Olean, where the Pennsylvania intersects the Erie. That's the Erie's main line between New York and Chicago. You've no doubt been seeing the best trains they have to offer."

I assured him they were all nice-looking trains: the engines were all shined up, and the passenger cars were like new, plus all the windows were closed. They were better than anything the Pennsylvania had to run, I added. At this he was somewhat amused and countered my findings: "You've been watching the best equipment the Erie has to offer. If you could watch the Pennsy's main line, you'd see their finest and it would look every bit as good. The windows are closed because the cars are air-conditioned to keep them cool regardless of how hot it gets outside."

Even though everything O.P. said seemed logical, I still believed the Erie engines were more powerful, but he again wasn't going to let me belittle the Pennsylvania, though he did concede that the Erie had some excellent locomotives and that he had seen them many times from the station platform these railroads shared as they high-balled through Elmira.

The cylindrical object mounted on Erie locomotives in front of the stack on top of the smoke box, O.P. explained, was a "feedwater" heater, a device that heated the water coming from the tender before it was injected into the boiler to make it more efficient at producing steam. But I asked, "If this is such a good device, why doesn't the Pennsy have it on their engines?"

To my surprise he replied, "They do." "It's a different design, but it serves the same purpose. The next time you see an I1 or an M1a at the water plug, walk around to the left side. About halfway back, above and below the footboards, you'll see a large, rectangular object. That's the feedwater heater. They never installed them on the older-class engines, though, because the boiler and firebox designs gave them enough capacity to make steam to serve the goals they were built to achieve." The Pennsylvania's locomotives were forerunners in the power department because of their capabilities in producing steam, he continued, and few other railroads had anything to equal them. The Company might be a little lax when it came to polishing their engines, but generally it kept them in good mechanical condition, which enabled them to get the trains over the road without breakdowns.

The different features the Erie locomotives had were installed out of necessity. Double seats on the left side, for example, provided a place for the head brakeman to ride. The Pennsylvania, when it went to smaller cabs, got around this by putting the "monkey house" on the tender. Larger tenders were an advantage too, for they eliminated coal and water stops. The Erie did not have track pans to scoop water on the fly on the main line. The rounded tenders that resembled tank cars were "Vanderbilt tenders," and what specific advantage they had he couldn't ascertain. Evidently the train with the L1 pushing had too much tonnage for the two head-end engines to handle going up the hill, and the cabin probably was not constructed to be pushed, so they had to tow it. After the movement O.P. had observed at Trout Run went by, the only other Erie to go through was a westbound passenger, soon after dark. We watched it passing with its long string of lighted cars from our side yard. Whether any other Eries used this branch line detour to reach their destinations during the night I never knew, but none was to be seen the following day. The parade was over.

Following the Erie's intrusion, the remainder of the summer went by with just normal Pennsylvania movements, and then I was back watching them from a school window. O.P. continued to labor at the developing mining operation, improving his physical condition to the point that during his mid-September visit to the relief doctor the physician remarked that his blood pressure was showing definite signs of improvement. On his subsequent visit to the medical examiner in October, he was told: "Orr, you're in better shape now than you've been for a long time, plus your blood pressure reading is normal. I'll set up an appointment in Philadelphia. There's no reason for them to hold you out of service anymore."

O.P. was thankful for the confidence the doctor had in his condition, but he asked to wait another month before scheduling a reexamination at headquarters in Philadelphia, just in case things didn't stay the same. His mid-November examination by the relief doctor was again in O.P.'s favor— his blood pressure was normal—so he was given an appointment for an exam by the main medical board. Our local physician too found that his blood pressure was normal, and that pleased O.P., but he asked the doctor, "Is there anything I can do to keep it that way? How can I go to Philadelphia knowing for sure that everything will check out favorably?"

The only sure way, according to the doctor, was to have a pint of blood removed three days before his appointment, but the nearest place to get that done was 11 miles south, in the neighboring town of Trout Run. O.P. set up an appointment for himself there three days before his trip to Philadelphia, and, figuring that if removing a pint of blood was the answer, a quart would be better still. That's the amount he had removed.

For the scheduled appointment, O.P. traveled to Philadelphia for another complete physical exam conducted by a team of Company doctors. A younger member of the staff compiled all the results and took the personal medical history. At the end of this session, although not exactly revealing of any results, he complimented O.P.: "You're in real fine shape for a man of your age. You must engage in some pretty strenuous physical activities."

O.P. confirmed that, explaining how he'd been helping a friend start a coal-mining operation and had been doing quite a bit of hard labor for the past three or four months. Then the doctor asked, "I see you have a puncture wound on your right arm. How did that occur?"

Thinking quickly, O.P. answered: "As I just told you, I help at this mine, and while we were constructing a tipple I slipped and grabbed a timber to keep from falling, inadvertently running a spike into my arm."

The young doctor smiled a little and responded, "I have a pretty good idea what kind of spike it was too, but don't worry. That was just my own observation. It won't be entered on your records."

As O.P. departed, the only thing he knew for sure was that his division road foreman and the division relief doctor would get a copy of the exam results and the medical board's determination regarding his physical condition.

After a week, O.P. finally received a letter from the road foreman, and it contained exactly what he wanted to hear: he was again qualified to reenter any type of service as an engineman.

Ready to resume working as an engineman again, the day after he got authorization to be placed back on the board, O.P. journeyed to the Walnut Street yard office in Williamsport and signed the register. When he returned home late that afternoon, however, he told us there were very few jobs working out of Williamsport but that he could exercise the "bump" he had coming to procure a run. All the road freight jobs and passengers were held by men with more seniority. In fact, the only jobs on the entire division where he could be home at least part of the time were the Altoona-Southport dikers, and at this particular time they were only getting two or three trips a half.

Rather than taking a diker run and incurring the expenses of laying over at either of the terminals, he explained, he had opted to take an 11:00 P.M. to 7:00 A.M. yard job in Williamsport. At least he would be working six days a week until something better suited became available. Another reason he had selected this trick was that he could share driving expenses with two machinists who lived right in town and worked the same number of days at the engine house.

O.P. started back to work on a very appropriate day, especially during the Depression—Thanksgiving Day 1935. That evening, as he was assembling all the items he would need to be an engineer once again, I asked a question that was troubling me: "Pop, do you think you'll know how to run an engine again?" That brought forth a chuckle, but he answered with confidence, "Oh, I might be a little rusty for a while, but I'm sure everything will come back to me with a little practice."

One thing about the third-trick yard job was that we were able to enjoy O.P.'s company. He was always home in the morning for breakfast before we departed for school, and every evening after our meal until he left for work, and every Sunday, which he had off.

It had been twenty-six years since he had worked in the Williamsport yards, and he found that things were quite different there. Instead of switching with a road engine relegated to yard service, he had an 0-6-0 B6sb specially designed for that chore and equipped with all the modern devices. One of the most useful devices the "swallow-tailed dinky" sported was the air reverse mechanism. O.P. had also noted that the B6 was easy to handle and had a remarkable amount of power for its size.

During the time he was with this yard crew he said little about the work hours or the conditions, other than to complain about having to ride to and from work with one of the machinists. The car he rode in was an older-model Dodge sedan that lacked a heater and was fitted with leather seats. On cold winter mornings after working all night, O.P. said, it was worse than climbing into an icebox, especially when the temperature was zero or below.

The yard job did not last very long. In mid-January 1936 O.P. bid on a job advertised as a yard and transfer job that paid a local freight rate. He would be working out of Lykens, Pennsylvania, which was at the southern end of the anthracite coal fields. He had talked with some people he knew who worked out of the Sunbury/Northumberland area and said that it was a good-paying job. The only drawback was its remote location. The crew worked six days a week, which meant he would have to come home on Saturday evenings and return to Lykens on Sunday evenings. The pay justified this move, he explained, and it was better than the Williamsport yard—until something better came up on the bid board. He also explained that the location of this job would be like Altoona was to the older engineers on the division with more seniority: none of them particularly wanted to handle runs that removed them from their homes. This assumption again proved correct, as he was awarded the bid.

On the Sunday afternoon he left home to take over this new job, he departed in his Auburn automobile. He left early because he had never traveled to the area, and he wanted to arrive before dark so he had time to find suitable accommodations. The trip followed the Susquehanna River from Williamsport through Sunbury, and then at Millersburg turned almost due east for nearly 20 miles, to Lykens. It took more than three hours. He could have taken a passenger train as far as Millersburg on the Williamsport Division main, but there were no passenger trains running to the Lykens Branch, and on Sundays not even a freight movement, so the only way to get there was by automobile. Toward the end of the first week we received a short letter from him telling us he was doing well and that he would be home as scheduled on Saturday evening. He arrived a little earlier than expected. Mining operations did not run a full shift on Saturday, so he got an earlier marking-off time and was home for the evening meal, at which time he gave us the details about his new job.

He had found comfortable lodgings at a small hotel within easy walking distance of the engine terminal. There he also took his meals, plus there was a bar where he could wash the cinders from his throat. Best of all, the prices were reasonable for all the services. The motive power assigned to this crew was an H9, a 2-8-0 in excellent shape. It had been in this area for only a short time after it came out of the shops, according to his fireman, who had held that job for nearly two years. Because of this heavy Consolidation, the engine crew was given a higher rate of pay than an 0-6-0 switch engine would have afforded. The Consolidation had almost as much weight on the drivers as an L1-class engine, which was the basis of the pay scale. This rate of pay, combined with a local freight rate, O.P. figured, meant that he was averaging more than twenty dollars a day for the six working days—very good pay during the Depression. Of course, he was putting in long days too. The crew was called for 7:00 A.M., but there was no established marking-off time. Often it was 7:00 P.M. or later when they put the engine on the pit. That didn't bother him, though. As long as he had to stay away from home, he explained, he might as well be working. Besides, he didn't have to idle away a lot of leisure time.

During the day, the switching chores were easy: taking empty hoppers to the breakers (coal tipple), spotting them on the loading tracks, removing the loaded ones, which were then assembled into a train. One good thing the fireman had going for himself was that every morning, at a particular breaker, a certain worker he knew was controlling the loading chutes, so when he spotted the H9's tender beneath it he opened it up and put three or four tons of nut-grade anthracite coal into the bunker. The fireman then put a generous amount of this hard coal in the firebox and got on the seat box. Using this quality fuel, the 2-8-0's pop would sing for around two hours before the fireman had to replenish the fire. The hard coal caused very little smoke, and there was little ash and no clinkers.

After the breakers ceased operations in the late afternoon, their cabin was attached to the waiting assembled train, which usually consisted of thirty-five to forty loaded cars, and a 20-mile trek to the main line at Millersburg began. This was an easy haul for the H9. Most of the trip was on a descending grade, and it wasn't a fast run either. The top speed on this cinder-bed track was set at 30 miles an hour, and there were areas where speeds were restricted further.

At Millersburg the loads were set off on a siding, the cabin was uncoupled, and a similar number of empty hoppers were picked up. Occasionally, other than the empties, cars filled with general merchandise, fuel, mining supplies, and mining equipment would be attached to the consist. Once this drag was placed properly for the return trip, the cabin would be coupled on and the return trip to Lykens would begin. It was a little different on the return, for some of the grades were very heavy and the 2-8-0 did a little straining. At least no speed limits were exceeded.

Like all jobs, there was a main drawback—it was seasonal. In the late spring, in the summer, and in the early fall, the crew members told him, things slowed down to five days a week, and there were only one or two trips to Millersburg during that period. When the weather turned colder, as it was now, and the demand for hard coal increased, so did the workload. All things considered, O.P. conceded, it was a good job, and he concluded his description of his new working circumstances with this confession: "A fellow makes some foolish decisions, and I really made a big one. I could have been working this job all the time I was off instead of just drawing from the relief fund."

O.P. didn't work out of Lykens as long as he had anticipated. The Saturday afternoon after completing the second week at this remote terminal, he stopped at the yard office in Williamsport on the way home to pick up his paycheck for the previous half—and almost automatically reviewed the bid board. He was surprised to find two jobs that he thought worth his bidding on, which he did. During the evening meal, though, he told us he thought his chances for getting one of those crews were slim because the symbol fast freights were prized runs, coveted by enginemen working out of Williamsport for years as the best jobs on the entire division.

These runs were the EC1 and 2 and EC3 and 6 (the symbols were E for Enola and C for Canandaigua [New York] in the northern section of the division). The EC1 and 3 were westbounds, while the EC2 and 6 ran east. Since the inception of these runs many years ago, crews ran from Williamsport, either as EC2 or EC6, to Enola and back to Williamsport, as EC1 or EC3. The Elmira Branch crews (former Elmira Division men with seniority dating to hiring on prior to 1921) ran from Williamsport to Southport, where they terminated. At Southport cars were interchanged with the Erie, the Delaware, the Lackawanna & Western, and the New York Central.

The Central had trackage rights on the Pennsylvania and ran its own trains into Southport, handling the cars destined for Upstate New York along their main line and bringing cars into this terminal. This method of transfer made the C symbol a misnomer, for cars were no longer hauled to and transferred at Canandaigua.

The reason these jobs had been advertised was that the Company, operating on its austerity program in keeping with Depression-era conditions, was eliminating Williamsport as a terminal for these fast freights. Instead of a 75-mile run from Southport to Williamsport and another 100-mile run to Enola, the crew would cover the entire 175 miles as one trip. The move would eliminate two Elmira Branch crews and two Williamsport Division crews. This new operating plan for these fast freights would be divided: two Elmira Branch crews on one side of the runs, and two Williamsport Division crews on the other side. Enola was the designated terminal for the Williamsport crews, and O.P. had a good chance to get one of these crews because the older engineers would be reluctant to give up their homes and move to another point on the division.

During O.P.'s third week at Lykens he was notified that his bid had been accepted and that he now had one of the EC3 and 6 crews. He had regained his status as an over-the-road engineman. Before taking over this road crew, though, he had one requirement to meet. Having run over the Williamsport Division to Harrisburg and over the Elmira Branch between Williamsport and Southport during the past five years, he was qualified on those portions, but 1907 was the last time he'd crossed the Rockville Bridge to enter the Enola yard, so now he had to qualify on that segment.

Leaving home a day before he had to qualify and take over the new crew, he spent the entire day learning how to leave and enter the west end of the huge Enola yard, and learning the procedure for crossing the Rockville Bridge to and from the Williamsport Division main. Then he rented a room at a boardinghouse near the passenger station in Harrisburg, preferring that to accommodations at the Enola bunkhouse. Whichever the facility, however, he would have to ride the jitney services back and forth between the yard and the passenger station.

All the EC's had a scheduled calling time, both at Enola and at Southport; there was no set time for their arrival at either terminal. O.P.'s EC was called to leave Enola in the early evening, and to his dismay he discovered that the power assigned for all these fast freight runs was the I1sa, 2-10-0 class. He did not agree with that selection of a slow, rough-riding class of locomotive for a 175-mile trip.

Coming out of the large Enola yard presented no problems, but getting clearance to cross the Rockville Bridge slowed his movement. He had to occupy one of the eastbound tracks to cross this lengthy stone-arched structure, but there were other complications also. Going east on the bridge, he had to cross over its two westbound tracks to reach the spur that led to the Williamsport Division main. Then, at that point, he had to cross over the eastbound main before occupying the westbound track for the trip up the Susquehanna Valley. When the clearance came and the crossing was made, his orders were to perform that maneuver without delay.

Hauling some eighty cars in the train, mostly refrigerator cars and preference merchandise boxcars, was not difficult for the 2-10-0 going up the nearly level river grade, and before too long O.P. had the large locomotive pounding along at a steady 50-mile-per-hour clip. Running on clear blocks to Sunbury and still in the clear, he made a stop to replenish the water in the small tender. While stopped, he called and received orders to take a siding at Northumberland, to clear the westbound track he was using for a following passenger train. After that movement passed on the double-track main, he was cleared to Allens Tower at the south end of the bridge leading into Williamsport, which controlled the single track leading to this point. Orders handed on at Allens cleared the EC3 into the yard to occupy the siding set by the switch tender at this location. Then there was a long delay. The train had to be cut to clear city grade crossings, and cars destined for Buffalo and Erie were set off. After this move was completed, the I1 was backed to the roundhouse, where coal, water, and sand were replenished in order to complete the next 75 miles.

While the I1 was being serviced, a yard crew added cars to the train that were also bound for Upstate New York, and an L1 pusher was coupled onto the rear end. Williamsport was a busy place between 11:00 P.M. and 3:00 A.M. Passenger trains, both from the east and from the west, plus two off the

Elmira Branch, were entering and leaving. O.P. had entered the yards in between these movements at around midnight, and it was nearly 2:00 A.M. before he got clearance to clear the yards and occupy the Elmira Branch. In less than an hour a westbound express was due to leave and follow on this branch line. Running clear to Leolyn, they passed Ralston around 2:45 A.M. without a stop for water. O.P. did, however, give his lowed-off whistle signal as he blasted through town.

Sufficient speed was maintained for the assault on the Leolyn hill, and they crested the top thirty minutes ahead of the following early morning passenger. As expected, the operator at Leolyn was displaying a red board, and orders designated that he was to occupy the siding at this point until the passenger movement went through. Taking advantage of the time remaining before this movement, O.P. cut off and ran up the main to the water plug to fill the tank before entering the siding. The pusher could cut off and do that chore while in the siding. If he had entered the siding and waited for the movement to pass before filling his tank, he would have had to cut loose and enter the main to back down to the water plug. That would have involved a longer delay.

One advantage of Leolyn was that, at the west end of this siding, after bring cleared to occupy the main, a device called a spring switch allowed the train to pass onto the main and then would automatically close after the pusher passed through it. This made it possible to leave the siding while gaining speed, instead of running out slow, waiting for the switch to be closed manually, and getting the trainman back aboard before building speed.

From Leolyn the remaining 40-odd miles of the trip was a series of downhill and uphill grades. The amount of tonnage O.P. was hauling could have been handled over these roller-coaster grades with the 2-10-0 alone, but controlling a train of more than eighty cars with a pusher keeping the slack pushed in was easier, and faster running speeds could be maintained. Also, following the passenger movement gave him clear blocks to stations at Cowley, Troy, and Snedekerville (Sned), the last block. At Sned, orders were handed on that he was clear to enter the yard at Southport. At this point the pusher was cut off on the fly, and the only slow order came at State Line Junction, where the additional trainman was picked up to comply with the New York State full crew regulation.

In the yard at Southport, the EC3 was placed on a siding aligned as it entered. The I1 was cut off and taken to the engine house, where it was put on the pit track. Marking off at the yard office around 6:00 A.M., O.P. noted that he had been on duty nearly eleven hours. Figuring his time for the 175-mile trip, he found that he had run at an average speed of only 16 miles an hour. This, he concluded, was more akin to a local movement than to a symbol fast freight.

The layover at Southport was at least twenty-four hours, usually longer, but it depended upon his arrival time, and transportation was waiting when he marked off, allowing him to travel the 50 miles to home in about an hour and a half. His transportation home was provided by his flagman, who lived a short distance south of Ralston. When the EC was tied up in Williamsport, the flagman would call his wife, notifying her that he was on the way through and to listen for a whistle signal as they passed. Then, as prearranged, she would be at the yard office with the car three hours later to take him home.

Returning to Southport after spending twenty-four hours at home was also convenient. The 8:30 A.M. westbound passenger train through Ralston arrived at this terminal well ahead of the EC6 mid-morning call. Marking up at the yard office, O.P. learned that he was assigned the same I1 locomotive he had brought in on the EC3, a consist of ninety-odd cars, mostly merchandise boxcars, and running orders cleared him out of the yard after the eastbound passenger passed at 10:45 A.M.

Leaving Southport eastbound, he had a clear block at Sned, Troy, and Cowley, but orders handed on instructed him to take the siding at Leolyn for a westbound diker movement. While in the siding waiting for this loaded coal train to clear, he took water, a necessity with the small tender attached to the 2-10-0, and something he had planned to do regardless of this meet. It was easier to start a train on the descending grade out of this location, and it would have been impossible to run the rest of the distance to Williamsport without making this water stop. This meet slowed his progress, and it was around 1:30 P.M. when the whistle signal echoed in the valley as the EC6 passed through Ralston.

Running on clear blocks to Williamsport, he entered the yard and was placed on a siding until both the eastbound and westbound Buffalo Flyers cleared the station. After his train was split so the grade crossings were not blocked, O.P. pulled to the water plug to fill the tank again. He found it unnecessary to replenish the coal or sand, though, and no cars had to be set off or picked up, which saved more time. The EC2 did this work as it passed through earlier in the day. It was nearly 3:00 P.M. before the board showed clear and he managed to get out of the city. After crossing the river, and as he was about to hit the double tracks, the tower at Allens gave him a clear block, providing clear running to Northumberland.

Running the I1 at nearly its top speed, he hammered out the miles to Northumberland in less than an hour. As he approached this point he found he still had a clear block. Continuing on, he made another water stop at neighboring Sunbury. This stop might have been bypassed, but O.P. wanted insurance in case there was a lengthy delay before reaching Enola. Notifying the dispatcher while at this water stop, he was told that he could run clear all the way to the tower controlling the intersection at the Middle Division's main at Rockville. The remainder of the run down the river to this busy intersection also required less than an hour's time, but, as expected, the tower there displayed a stop signal.

At this control point he was notified that he would not be held very long, and he received orders clearing him to the bridge approach track, over the bridge, and into the yards. After a westbound movement passed, he got the clear signal, crossed the bridge, crossed over the eastbound tracks, and entered the yard approach to the siding properly aligned for the EC6. His time on duty for this eastbound trip was less than nine hours, a little more respectable for a fast freight run.

After marking off, the crew figured that a twenty-five-hour layover in Enola was too long to spend at this terminal, and there was plenty of time before the nine o'clock departure of a westbound passenger to Williamsport, so they elected to return home. Taking advantage of the time remaining before the evening passenger's departure, O.P. first used his rented room in Harrisburg to clean up and change into his travel clothes, then stopped at a nearby restaurant for his evening meal and went on to Peanut Joe's bar for a few beers to wash away the cinders.

Once aboard the train, his journey back to Williamsport only took two hours and he arrived at that terminal at 11:00 P.M. The crew, except for O.P. and his flagman, were home. O.P. and the flagman had an additional twenty-four miles to travel. Anticipating this when he went to Enola to qualify before making this round-trip on the ECs, O.P. had left his car in a 24-hour storage garage two blocks from the station in Williamsport. Retrieving his car, he was back in Ralston before midnight. On this end of the trip not as much time was spent at home. To be back in Enola for the evening call, it was necessary to catch the eastbound Buffalo Flyer in Williamsport at 2:30 the next afternoon.

Although it involved quite a bit of traveling, O.P. appreciated being able to spend time at home at the end of each trip. On subsequent days, much the same routine run—EC3 to Southport and home, E6 to Enola and home—was followed. He was always able to get from home to Southport, and on the eastbound EC6 runs, if there were delays and he arrived at Enola too late to catch the 9:00 P.M. westbound passenger, he spent the layover at his room in Harrisburg.

For the EC6 runs, there was a slight deviation in the scheduled calling time at Southport. On Sundays their calling time was an hour earlier than usual because there was no weekly eastbound passenger train on that day. The EC6 left Southport at 10:45 A.M., running on the passenger's scheduled time in order to pick up Sheffield Farm milk cars at Troy, Canton, Grover, and Hepburnville and set them off at Williamsport. When O.P.'s crew had this Sunday run every third week, he laid over in Harrisburg, because the 9:00 P.M. westbound passenger did not operate that day either.

The Sunday before O.P. took over the EC job, he and I walked to the top of the mountain on our side of the valley to inspect a recently begun venture in strip-mining, a new practice in the area for removing coal deposits. It wasn't very pleasant walking; the sky was overcast, and it was warm enough to cause the snow to melt, resulting in sloppy, slippery footing. Typical for late January.

On the way back I experienced pain in my leg, but it wasn't severe enough to be overly concerned. When I awoke the next morning, however, the pain was still there and I was having difficulty walking. At the breakfast table I explained that my leg was hurting badly and that I didn't feel good either and that perhaps I should stay home from school. That idea was quickly put aside, though. My problem was attributed to growing pains or a cramp from walking too much. Besides, O.P. said, it would ruin the record I'd maintained for nearly five years: perfect attendance, and never once being tardy.

Instead of improving during the school day, as my parents had assured me I would, however, the pain in my leg increased, and when I returned home that afternoon I'd developed a fever. My mother put me to bed immediately and plied me with home remedies, but her good intentions proved to be in vain. The next morning I was unable to walk and was burning with fever.

The local doctor was summoned, and his initial examination confirmed that my temperature was dangerously high, although he was unable to determine the cause. He couldn't determine the source of the extreme pain in my right leg either, and after his second visit, with no improvement in my condition, he decided that I was suffering from rheumatic fever. To receive proper treatment, he said, I should be hospitalized, but he warned that, with no ambulance service available, transporting me by automobile would be dangerous due to the extremely cold weather. Furthermore, he said, there was little that could be done to arrest this affliction whether I was at home or in the hospital. Complete bed rest and medications to reduce the fever and control the pain were the only treatments he could prescribe.

I was treated daily at home by the local doctor, but for more than three weeks I didn't respond to this course of treatment. My condition deteriorated to the point where pain medicine taken orally had no effect and the doctor visited twice daily to inject a pain killer with a hypodermic needle. Then sometime during the fifth week my fever went away as suddenly as it had stricken me. Although very weak, I finally began to recover. The pain also began to ease, but not as rapidly as the fever, and I was still unable to use my right leg. First I was allowed out of bed to sit in a chair in the bedroom, and then to go to an overstuffed chair in the living room. Sitting all bundled up in this chair was the most comfort I had experienced since becoming ill, so instead of going back to bed I pleaded to remain in that position and was allowed to stay there temporarily.

Seated in front of the bay window, I had an almost unobstructed view of the railroad and could watch the trains passing through not only during the daylight hours but also at night. Sleeping soundly was another thing I was unable to do, and it seemed that every whistle the trains sounded would wake me up. It wasn't only an occasional movement, either. Much to my surprise, trains ran in a steady procession during the entire night: two express passengers, the fast freights EC3, EC2, and EC1, dikers in both directions, and two or three different pusher movements running light back to Williamsport.

You could almost tell time by these trains. The eastbound passenger went through at midnight and the westbound went through at 3:15 A.M. Usually before either of the passengers was due, trains would occupy the siding and take water during their wait. I couldn't see the crew's movements, but I could see the flames of their handheld kerosene illuminating torches as they oiled around and cleaned the ash pan, and I could also see the glow of their lanterns and the beam of the engine's headlights, the cab lights, and the markers. The sounds they created seemed very loud on the still winter nights: the banging of water-tank lids as they were opened and closed, the pounding on the ash pans when the fires were cleaned, the bells ringing, and the necessary whistling. Then too, as they were departing, the sharp roar of the locomotive's exhaust, the rattling of the cars, especially the empty hoppers hauled by the eastbound dikers, and the cannon boom of torpedoes if the train had stopped on the main track. How I ever slept through this din before I became ill was hard to imagine. Even more difficult to understand was how people living close to the tracks managed to get any rest. I surmised it was a noise one became accustomed to.

My train-watching was interrupted for part of one day at the recommendation of the doctor. I was taken to the hospital in Williamsport to be x-rayed to determine if something other than rheumatic fever was causing my illness. The x-rays failed to show any abnormalities in the bone structure of my leg, but the doctor still wasn't satisfied with his original diagnosis because of the pain I was still experiencing.

During the two weeks or so that I spent in the easy chair, I had the unexpected pleasure of watching something other than trains. One morning the local freight stopped below the station, and when it came into my view it was towing five gondolas with an odd assortment on the cars. At first it looked like they contained two sheds plus an assortment of equipment. The local moved up on the main track, which was puzzling, but after a short time it came back down the siding and stopped in the vicinity of the water plug. The L1 was cut off of these cars, went back up the siding, and came back down the main, entering the siding at the lower end. It then coupled onto the standing cars and pushed them into the dump track that was formerly the pit track at the engine house.

For a while I couldn't understand why the local went to all this trouble when a flying switch would have been much simpler to execute. Fortunately O.P. was at home that morning, and he explained that certain materials being transported were posted with "Do Not Hump" signs. If so labeled, crews wouldn't make a flying switch, either. After a trip downtown, O.P. was able to tell me what was being transported. On the gondolas were the parts and pieces of two 80-ton Bucyrus-Erie earth-moving machines that had arrived from the factory as rebuilt units, now owned by the Ralston Coal Company. They were going to be used to expand the recently started strip-mining operation.

From my viewing point, it was too far to see exactly what was taking place as the first machine was reassembled, but it was nearly a week before smoke came rolling out of the stack and I was astonished at the shrill whistle that sounded. This unit had a bright-red shedlike enclosure that housed the boiler and internal machinery. On the outside on either side were catwalks and a large bunker for its coal supply. Wide metal tracks were under the main frame that held the turntable and the unit was fitted with a shovel front that had a steam engine mounted on the boom to operate the dipper stick.

After it was completely assembled, O.P. took me to the site and we watched how this shovel was being used to help assemble the second unit, which turned out to be exactly the same as the first one. The only difference was that the house was painted black. It had an 80-foot boom mounted up front, and a drag line bucket was affixed to the extended cables. (I later learned that these machines had horizontal boilers that carried 125 pounds of steam pressure and were operated not by control levers but by a rocker-arm throttle similar to those used on locomotives.) In less than two weeks, both of these large machines chugged over the siding and main tracks, up the old wye roadbed, across Red Run Creek and the main highway to the base of the mountain, where they were parked to await melting of the winter's snow before continuing to the mountaintop.

Gradually my strength returned, and the kindly doctor who had once visited daily now made only infrequent visits. On one of his visits he brought along a pair of crutches, advising that they should be used to help me to learn to walk again. His intentions were worthy—these devices helped me to stand and allowed me to become mobile, at least around the household, but I still was unable to use my right leg.

O.P. kept his EC crew rolling, coming home from both terminals on an almost daily basis. This pattern was interrupted during the middle of March, but not by his choosing. The weather had turned warm, causing a rapid melting of the heavy snow cover of the past winter. When he arrived home from Enola late one night, it had started to rain hard, which, coupled with the warming trend, created an excessive amount of runoff water. These conditions prevailed during the night, and by midday the Lycoming Creek was running bank-full in our section of the valley. That prompted O.P. to call the yard office in Williamsport, from which he learned that the creek was already overflowing its banks in the areas below Cogan Station and that the flooding was temporarily halting all movements using the Elmira Branch.

Furthermore, he was told that the West Branch of the Susquehanna was also dangerously high and that if this condition continued the Williamsport Division would soon be shut down. He then contacted the dispatcher's office, referred to by trainmen as "Number 9" (Room 9, the official headquarters of the Williamsport Division, located on the second floor of the Park Hotel station building), and informed a dispatcher that in light of the present situation he was marking off and that the yard office in Enola should be notified. The dispatcher replied that this probably would not be necessary. The Susquehanna River was now running bank-full and all movements not presently out on the road were being annulled.

After O.P. had placed his calls using the Company telephone line at the water plug, the rains slackened, and he wondered whether he had made an unwise decision. Early in the evening of March 16, the rain again intensified, and before we drove by to pick up my mother and sister, who had attended a church banquet in honor of Saint Patrick, we went by the creek to check on it. It was running wild, ready to spill over the banks, and sometime the next morning, that's what happened.

On Saint Patrick's Day, March 17, 1936, our town of Ralston was flooded, as were other communities below us along Lycoming Creek. The Susquehanna River valley was also being flooded. Williamsport was inundated by even higher water than any flooding since 1889. All means of transportation were halted, and our only communication with the outside world was news received by radio.

The rain ended before noon on March 17, and Lycoming Creek receded almost as quickly as it had risen. It was running within its banks by nightfall. The following morning, O.P. and I toured around to view what damage the water had caused and were surprised to find that, other than depositing large amounts of mud and a lot of debris, nothing much had been destroyed. Talking with some of the residents that had watched this catastrophe as it took place, we learned that the railroad roadbed served as a barrier preventing the water from entering the town with any force. However, most of the damage caused was not from the main stream but from its tributary, Red Run Creek. This was a result of the recent fording of the stream by the steam shovels. Where the bank had been cut down to allow these machines to pass, it also allowed the floodwaters to flow down the old wye and along the main, washing out the roadbed for about 200 feet to the vicinity of the section house, and from here down an alley through town. By word of mouth we learned too that south of Ralston there were numerous washouts the entire distance to Williamsport. North of town the railroad left the valley floor, and although small washouts occurred, there were none of any serious consequence the rest of the way to Southport.

On the second day after the flood, O.P. decided the family should go to Williamsport to see how my married sister and her family were faring, or perhaps he was curious to see what the situation was in the river valley. The main highway to this city was closed, forcing us to travel a roundabout route through the hills to reach our destination. There wasn't any danger of the waters reaching their residence. The concern was their food supply and adequate heating. Finding everything in fine shape, we decided to take a tour to view how things were within the city. My brother-in-law acted as chauffeur.

Our first destination was the yard office, but when we got to High Street two blocks away, water was flowing, and although it was less than curb high, O.P. warned that we should not proceed any further: a manhole cover might pop up, and if we were to drop into the a hole it would inflict serious damage on the car. Backtracking, we went to the top of the Grampian hills, from which vantage point we could scan the city and the valley below. What we saw resembled a large, mud-colored lake that covered the entire valley. From this distance it even seemed to be placid, but evidence of its destruction could be seen. In the mid-city area, smoke was rising from structures that caught fire and burned during the height of the flood.

Returning from our visit to Williamsport, we spotted signs that the railroad was being put back into shape. A short distance south of Ralston there was a work train with gondolas loaded with heavy riprap, hoppers containing cinders, a tool car, a passenger car, the clamshell-equipped crane on a flatcar, and a cabin, all being pushed by an H9. Later that evening the 2-8-0 whistled the announcement that it was coming back to town, and after what sounded like some switching movements it left heading west (north). O.P. reasoned that the crew was getting close to the sixteen-hour outlaw limit and was heading back to Southport before the time expired. This was the pattern the work train was to follow for the next few days—arriving early each morning and leaving again late each evening.

Five days had passed since the flood, and O.P. announced that on the following day he was going to journey to Williamsport to find out how long it would be before the division would be in operation. If he did not have to leave for Enola within the next day or so, we would travel to Howard to visit his parents. O.P. and I went to the Williamsport yard office the next morning, and although everything was covered with mud it was evident that things were getting ready to run again. Engines were steamed up around the roundhouse, a B6 swallow-tailed dinky was in the yard switching cars, and the office was open. O.P. learned that the Elmira Branch was to be running by that afternoon. Passenger trains also would be run through on the Williamsport Division, but it probably would be at least two days before the Enola yards would again be functioning.

We continued our journey to Howard, where, other than the ever-present mud and debris, the western area of Williamsport seemed to be in fairly decent shape. That wasn't the case when we passed through the river towns of Jersey Shore and Lock Haven, though. Water marks showed that this flood had reached the second stories of homes and businesses. Household furnishings were stacked in the yards of these dwellings, and merchandise from stores was piled on the curbs. Everything was wet and covered with mud. West of Lock Haven, after passing over the Bald Eagle Creek out of Mill Hall, there was hardly any evidence of a flood, other than standing pools of water in the fields. Howard was located on a knoll and had experienced no damage whatsoever.

We left my grandfather's house in the afternoon, early enough so we would be back in Ralston before dark. Not far north of Williamsport we caught up to a diker heading up the Lycoming Valley with two pushers—proof that the Elmira Branch was open for traffic once again.

The next morning, O.P. used the railroad call box to contact Number 9 and check on when he could expect to be called for duty. The answer the dispatcher gave him came as a shock. He had missed a call while we were visiting at Howard. Trying to justify missing a call, the second one he had missed in his thirty-two years of service, he explained that the yard office had misinformed him. The dispatcher commented that he should continue to enjoy the time off as EC3 wasn't making very good progress; presently it was still east of Sunbury, and without a doubt would outlaw at Northumberland. Relating that the main east of Williamsport was in deplorable condition, the dispatcher noted that most areas were running under slow orders and that in many places, with only one track open, movements were having difficulty getting through.

The next day, O.P. learned that the EC3 had made it as far as Williamsport and was being held there for another eight hours rest; it was expected to be in Southport in time for the regular calling time the next day to resume its schedule as EC6. With this information, O.P. took the 8:30 A.M. westbound passenger the following morning to pick up his crew and start working, again after spending ten days at home on a vacation without pay. It was nearly two weeks before things returned to normal. Each trip, regardless of the direction, took up almost all the sixteen hours allotted, but on none of those trips was he forced to outlaw. During the rebuilding period he was able to get home from the Southport end, but he laid over on the Enola side, using his room in Harrisburg to good advantage.

CHAPTER SIX | CONSTANT CHANGES DURING THE MID-1930s

Instead of spending my time in front of the bay window, I started going to the kitchen where I could enjoy my mother's company. Here too it was easier to do the schoolwork my sister brought home each day, so I wouldn't slide too far behind my classmates. My teacher also sent books she had selected for me from the school library, and I used them to full advantage, not only to further my education but also to please my mother by reading aloud as she went about her household chores, particularly in the evenings as she ironed in the adjoining laundry room. This also made me aware that keeping our family supplied with clean clothing and linens was a never-ending process.

Monday was always wash day, rain or shine. On nice days clothes were hung on an outside clothesline. During inclement weather they were taken to our spacious attic for drying, the only thing this portion of our house was ever used for. A wringer-type washing machine performed the washing operation, after which the clothes went through the wringer into a tub of rinse water, then were finally wrung again to be hung for drying. There were a few exceptions; some of the items received additional treatment in a pan of starch, including O.P.'s bib overalls and his overall jacket. Curious about why the overclothes O.P. wore while running a locomotive were given this treatment, I asked my mother, who explained that the starch prevented some of the grease and grime from entering the fabric, making it easier to get them clean in the washing process. Before washing these overclothes, O.P. had to take the buckles off the straps on the bib overalls, empty all the pockets, and turn them inside out. But he wasn't always thorough, so occasionally a handful of wooden matches would be found floating in the wash water, or his cake of Bon Ami might be crushed as it went through the wringer.

Another item of his attire would be put through the washer at the end of the wash cycle, and only on rare occasions: his greasy leather gauntlet gloves.

My mother didn't like to do this, because it left a deposit of oily scum in the washer that was difficult to clean out. Also, she was careful about drying these gloves, to keep them from becoming hard and stiff by applying hand cream every so often to keep them pliable.

Evenings after wash days were spent ironing almost every item washed, even O.P.'s overalls. Watching as the overall jacket was carefully pressed, I noticed that the jacket bore stains that looked like streams of rust. When I asked why, my mother said she didn't know and that washing wouldn't remove it. Later, when O.P. was assembling his clean overalls to pack in his travel bag (almost a ritual, which took place every week as he carefully laid out each item on the kitchen floor and folded on the ironed crease), I asked him what caused the stain on his jacket. It was a result of atmospheric conditions, not a regular occurrence, O.P. told me. When it was extremely cold and the cab was fully enclosed with the back curtain dropped and all the windows closed, a certain amount of steam was always present in the cab. It would rise, penetrate behind the tongue-and-groove boards that lined the cab roof, and condense when it came in contact with the cold metal. The result was rain: water would run down the curvature of the roof and leak out of the liner directly over his seat. There was no way to stop or escape these rusty drippings.

The first step in packing was to lay out the bib overalls, folded so the creases matched on each leg; then the jacket was placed on top, also folded so the creases matched. The last items were his neckerchief and cap, which he carefully rolled up to form a round bundle about 6 inches in diameter and 18 inches in length, tying it with a shoestring as the final step. The overclothes were placed in the leather traveling bag among the other items stored there. A separate area was used for a change of clothes needed when laying over and for gauntlet gloves, goggles, pant straps, overshoes, a monkey wrench, and the folder that held the timetable, the time book, and the Book of Rules.

Equally well organized thought had to be given to sustenance. It hadn't taken O.P. long after hiring out as a fireman to discover that over-the-road crews could not have regular eating habits. Crews working a trip board were subject to being called out whenever a train was made up and ready to depart; it didn't matter whether it was night or day. When his runs originated in a home terminal city, he chose to stay in a room-and-board establishment; meals there were provided at normal times. During layovers at other terminals, all meals had to be taken at either hotels or twenty-four-hour restaurants, and their timing depended on arrival and departure times. Most eateries catering to trainmen did not feature gourmet cuisine, but rather substantial fare that was affordable for railroad crews.

Meals to be carried along were another matter. If he was called out during daylight when he was staying at a boardinghouse, a substantial lunch could be packed for him, but for calls that came during the night he would have to seek out a nearby all-night restaurant to pack the lunch. O.P. learned to ration these packed meals carefully. Most of the sidings where his train would be detained were in remote locations and offered no opportunity to purchase food. Whatever he packed had to sustain him for the duration of his run.

O.P. was generally not a finicky eater, but he was choosy about what went into his sandwiches. He insisted on some type of roasted beef, pork, or chicken, and cheese, and refused to eat processed lunchmeats. On one occasion he came home from a run grumbling. The only thing his fireman had in his lunch was cucumber sandwiches. "I don't see how a woman could send a man on a run with only cucumber sandwiches and expect him to fire a steam engine," he exclaimed.

Meanwhile, on one occasion, when O.P. was emptying the pockets of his dirty overalls, out came matches, a bundle of waste, a cake of Bon Ami, and a number of folded onionskin copies of train orders and "K" card forms. He selected one of the copies and handed it to me, saying, "If they handed you this order, what would you do?"

Looking at the train order almost in disbelief, all I could see were abbreviations and X's in front of what appeared to be engine numbers. Not any of it seemed to have any meaning. It was like trying to decipher hieroglyphics. I admitted that I couldn't understand the message this order conveyed. I expected O.P. to be upset that I couldn't translate a common, everyday train order, but it was just the opposite. He said with a small chuckle, "Don't feel bad. I know some engineers that can't read them either. If it wasn't for other members of the crew helping, they, like you, would be lost."

O.P. took a blank piece of paper and began writing out in full all the abbreviations on the order, and that made it easy to interpret what a movement should be doing. He then left me with all the orders for me to write out without using the abbreviations, with instructions that if there were things I couldn't understand he would help me later. My first attempts weren't too accurate, but under his patient tutelage I was finally able to get his train to its designated spot according to orders, and without any head-on collisions. The exceptions were the orders written in O.P.'s own handwriting with a large letter "K" at the top of the form.

I asked about that, and my father explained that the "K" card method was used at unattended blocks, where there was no longer an operator at the location. A movement was prohibited from going beyond an unattended block without written orders, so the engineer had to telephone the operator at the next tower in the direction he was traveling, have orders dictated, and copy the message on this form to document that the movement was being controlled.

With the coming of spring, the trees began to leaf out and the foliage obstructed my view of the railroad. All I could do was listen to the sounds of the trains. During the layover time O.P. spent at home in between the EC trips, he kept me abreast of the happenings on these runs.

On one westbound EC3 trip he encountered numerous delays, the longest of which was getting in and out of the Williamsport bottleneck. After setting off the cars destined for other division points and receiving cars added by the yard crew, plus getting his I1 serviced at the roundhouse, he contacted the dispatcher for clearance to leave the yard. What the dispatcher had to relate wasn't encouraging at all. "Oscar," he said, "I've got problems. All the pushers are out, the house doesn't have any unassigned power bigger than an H6, and to top it all off, there are no extra crews available. They're all out too. Adding to my woes, you've got more tonnage than your I1 can take up the hill on the Elmira Branch, and according to my orders we're not permitted to split your train to reduce the tonnage. All the cars in the consist out of Enola and Williamsport must remain intact until they reach Southport. About all I can do is hold you here until we get a pusher back."

O.P. acknowledged there was a predicament but advised the dispatcher he couldn't wait too long or he would outlaw before reaching Southport. The idea of an additional delay, plus outlawing, was not to his liking, so he made the dispatcher a proposition: "I've got a good I1 and she's steaming better than most of them. I know I can make it to Ralston without a pusher, and if I could have clear blocks to Leolyn, maybe I could make it up the hill without help. The operators at Trout Run and Bergen (Marsh Hill) will be able to let you know how I'm progressing. If I see I can't make it, I'll take the siding at Ralston and wait there for a pusher."

The dispatcher agreed to the proposal and said: "I won't have any trouble clearing you to Leolyn. All the congestion tonight is west of there. I'm holding the EC2 at Troy for a meet that's just now by Cowley, and I'll hold them at Leolyn until you get there. If you should stall on the hill, don't cut your train to double over. Just cut off and run light to Leolyn. I'll advise the EC2 crew to cut off and go back down with you to help get your train the rest of the way up the hill."

It was after 6:00 A.M. when clearance was given to leave Williamsport. The weather was clear, but it was colder than usual for a spring morning, and a heavy frost covered the ground. The train was stiff as O.P. moved out of the yard, but once he was on the branch he got the 2-10-0 set up and managed to maintain a speed of more than 40 miles an hour up the valley. As he whistled through Ralston in the daylight, he saw that the frost was heavy enough to resemble a light snowfall. There wasn't any deviation in his speed until the grade started getting heavier out of Roaring Branch, then he started slowing down.

Rounding the curves at Rock Cut at the steepest part of the hill, his speed was reduced to around 10 miles an hour, but the I1 was operating smoothly with the gear in the bottom notch and the throttle wide open. Holding that pace, he rounded the "S" curve at the top of the grade and was still hauling the heavy train at a respectable speed. Seeing the morning sun shining on the flat land ahead gave him a surge of confidence. He had accomplished what he had promised the dispatcher. He also was thinking that now he would be able to reach Southport without outlawing. Just then he emerged into the sunshine and his thoughts were shattered. The 2-10-0, without any warning, went into a wide-open spin, so violent that he thought it would surely strip the rods before he got it shut off. He had experienced slipping action many times in the past, usually as a result of inclement weather, but hardly ever when the weather was this clear or when operating with a wide-open throttle. At the time, though, he couldn't focus on the cause; he was too busy applying sand to the rails and getting the I1 opened up again.

By the time he had the engine working, the forward momentum had nearly stopped. Fortunately there was no more slipping, and he was still hauling the train—barely, though, and just from one labored exhaust until the next. The operator's shanty was in full view, so if a stall did occur the EC2 crew could come to his rescue without too much delay.

Almost to his surprise he kept the train moving, and then it dawned on him why he'd commenced slipping: the sun. It had melted the frost on the rails, making them wet and slippery, almost as if they had been greased. A clear block was displayed as he thundered by the block operator, still only barely moving, and although he needed water he went by the water plug to the intersection of the siding at the west end, reasoning that there he'd have the train on level ground, which would allow him to get started again.

After a backing move down the siding to take water, he notified the dispatcher that he was proceeding. The dispatcher complimented him for his accomplishment and told him that the branch was now pretty well relieved of its earlier congestion and that clear blocks would be showing all the way to Southport. It wasn't exactly an easy run from Leolyn—the rest of the distance was over undulating grades—but he arrived at Southport with just over an hour remaining on his sixteen-hour limit.

O.P. had formed his opinion of the I1 class after the first trip on a 2-10-0 back in 1923, and it didn't change after he ran them on the dikers from Altoona to Southport during part of the 1930s and into 1931. The 175-mile EC assignment, when he ran them as the power for a symbol fast freight, did not do anything to increase his fondness for this class of engine, but he would admit that they did have two virtues: They were powerful and reliable.

He thought he knew everything about those locomotives, until suddenly one of them almost shook him off the seat box. Eastbound on EC6, somewhere between Sunbury and Rockville, he was running along at the top speed of about 50 miles an hour with the valve gear set back as close to center as good steaming would allow and with the throttle pulled out a few notches to maintain a steady speed, when for no apparent reason the I1 began shuddering. And it was not just a mild shudder, but one with enough force that it seemed the boiler was about to part from the frame, or the running gear was going to disintegrate.

Closing the throttle immediately and making a hard reduction with the automatic brake valve, just shy of going into emergency, O.P. reduced his speed to around 15 miles an hour before the shuddering stopped. As the speed was being reduced, he leaned out the cab window looking for something broken on the running gear, but everything was intact. He then hollered across the cab for the fireman to inspect his side, which also turned out to be in one piece. The only other time anything like this had happened was soon after World War I when he was running the H8 as a test engine and the valve motion went out of square. The difference was that this time nothing was being blown out of the firebox, and there was no eruption coming out the stack.

Assuming that their visual inspection from the cab was sufficient, O.P. opted to continue and not to come to a full stop on the main to check the engine. Dropping the reverse lever farther forward, he began notching out on the throttle, and as speed was gained everything was working exactly as it should. Continuing down the river, his first stop was at the junction to the track leading to the Rockville Bridge, where a complete on-the-ground examination was conducted. It revealed that all parts were still in place and everything was tight.

When the engine was put on the pit track at Enola, O.P. didn't file a report on the unusual performance the I1 had displayed. There wasn't anything he could find amiss with the locomotive, but he was curious whether any such thing had happened when other engineers were running a 2-10-0, and after some questioning among his cohorts a Middle Division man told about experiencing the same shuddering condition while running down the

Juniata River. His reaction had been the same as O.P.'s, shutting off and bringing the I1 almost to a complete stop. But, he stated, someone else had informed him this wasn't the solution to this problem, that the most effective solution was to open the throttle a couple of notches.

The fact that other engineers had found the same idiosyncrasy with the I1 made O.P. realize his I1 was not one of a kind. He still had no idea what caused the shuddering, but after analyzing how the 2-10-0 was set up to run, his speed at the time, and the location, he theorized that somehow he had reached a point of equilibrium. Without realizing that the engine was at a neutral position, neither pulling the train nor coasting, at just the precise moment, on a slight downgrade, enough slack ran in and this inertia pushed the I1 beyond this neutral zone, causing it to start working against itself. (The idea to give the engine steam was apparently a logical solution, and at a much later date O.P. applied that theory and the shuddering stopped as if by magic.)

There were doubts at first that the extended Enola-Southport EC runs would be practical. In railroading circles these runs were too long, and the many bottlenecks along the way would result in numerous outlawings. After more than three months of successful operation, however, those jobs became permanent, so the men working out of Williamsport with seniority in their favor began bumping onto their crews. First the EC1 and the EC2 seemed to suit these older men better, but soon others selected the EC3 and the EC6.

All turned out to be runs that paid well, but O.P. became one of the victims of this turn of events. The board at Williamsport offered nothing he could take but yard jobs. The best-paying local crew he could bump onto was an 11:00 P.M. to 7:00 A.M. yard and transfer job at Lock Haven. The only road job presently on the board that he could hold was the Altoona-Southport dikers, but he still didn't want any part of these coal drags.

Selecting the Lock Haven crew gave him the benefit of being home each day though, and it wasn't a bad job. After performing the assigned switching chores for the night, the crew was permitted to mark off, so usually O.P. had an early quit. But it did involve a drive of more than an hour each way to cover the nearly 60-mile journey to and from Ralston.

Bumping seemed to be the vogue once it started on the division. O.P. had figured his yard job would last until he could bid on a road job, but that proved to be wrong because he himself bumped in less than three weeks. Back at the yard office in Williamsport, scanning the board to find out how to exercise his bump, he got a surprise. The man one position below him on the roster had somehow latched on to the EC3 and EC6 crew and was running this job. All this illustrates how the bid system was almost like playing poker:

O.P. had one card better in the deal, and he used it to get the EC3 and EC6 run back.

Meanwhile, the local doctor's visits had become infrequent, and toward the end of May my physical condition had improved to normal, but there was no improvement in my right leg. At that point the doctor suggested that my parents take me either to New York or to Philadelphia to a specialist, who might be able to diagnose what was causing my condition. So O.P. contacted his sister, a nurse at the Jefferson Hospital in Philadelphia, to see if she could offer any help in this direction. She said that the Children's Hospital in Philadelphia could probably provide the treatment I needed and that treatment there would be free because it was operated by the Masonic Order for crippled children of members of this organization.

An appointment was set up for mid-June, and as the time for the appointment neared, O.P. calculated that rather than laying off for a round-trip, we could make the journey during his layover at Enola. He then would be back home in Ralston around midnight, giving him plenty of time to clean up and rest before catching the 6:30 A.M. eastbound passenger in Williamsport for Philadelphia.

The day before our scheduled trip he left Southport with the eastbound EC6. After a normal departure, however, numerous delays arose on the Elmira Branch and he was behind schedule reaching Williamsport. There, too, longer delays than usual occurred, and things did not improve when he left that terminal. At Northumberland he was held in a siding for a lengthy period, and during that wait the westbound passenger he should have boarded in Harrisburg passed. By the time he was cleared to occupy the main, he wasn't sure he would be able to reach Enola and get back to Harrisburg to catch the next passenger, the 12:30 A.M. westbound Buffalo Flyer, so he could get to Williamsport, get his car, drive to Ralston, and clean up and change clothes in order to catch the 6:30 A.M. eastbound.

Before he reached Millersburg there wasn't enough time left to make this move, so he made a decision that would have caused him a great deal of trouble if the proper authorities were aware of what he was to do. He commanded the fireman to take EC6 into Enola with the head brakeman handling the firing chores, and he got off at Millersburg. There he caught the 12:30 A.M. westbound Buffalo Flyer and reached home sometime after 3:00 A.M. He had just time enough to bathe, shave, don his dress attire, have breakfast, and be back in Williamsport at 6:30 A.M. No time for rest.

The passenger train we boarded was made up and waiting at the Williamsport station. We passed forward through the coaches to enter the smoking car, which had only a few occupants, and selected a seat. O.P. was acquainted with the train crew and, acknowledging them, started a conversation with the conductor. Before we departed, O.P. explained to me that this was classified as a local passenger because it would be making stops at most of the communities trackside all the way to Harrisburg.

From the onset the journey was a memorable one for me. It was like traveling with a tour guide. One of the first sights my father brought to my attention was the bright morning sun shining on spiderwebs filled with dew that adorned the adjacent fields. This, he proclaimed, was a sure sign that it would be a pleasant day for our trip.

The train, regardless of all the stops it made, traveled at a much faster speed than the ones on the familiar Elmira Branch. As we approached Northumberland, O.P. explained that this yard complex and engine-house facilities had been established soon after he began firing, in order to relieve congestion at nearby Sunbury. As we passed over the bridge separating Northumberland and Sunbury, he pointed out that we had just crossed the north branch of the Susquehanna River, which in a short distance joined the West Branch, the one we had run along most of the way from Williamsport. From this confluence to the Chesapeake Bay the Susquehanna was just one large river.

When we came into view of the river below Sunbury, it definitely had increased in size, and we saw numerous small stern-wheeled, steam-powered paddleboats pushing flat barges. These boats, I learned, were dredging for coal silt (slack) that had washed down the north branch from the anthracite region's hard-coal breakers, which, when reclaimed, was then shipped to the Harrisburg area for use as fuel for steam boilers.

A little farther down the river I began noticing V-shaped formations constructed of stones in the shallow waters to trap eels during their migration or spawning runs. At the station stop at Millersburg, O.P. said this was where he got off the EC6 during the night to catch the westbound flyer. Also at this point a ferry plied the river, making it the only spot an automobile could cross between Sunbury and Clarks Ferry.

Not far beyond the Clarks Ferry Highway Bridge the railroad right-of-way became narrow, with steep banks on the left and a highway on the right, below which was the Susquehanna River. Along the left side, steel girders supporting a high fence appeared. The purpose of this structure, I found, was to protect trains from rock slides. This protective device was electrically wired, and if the circuit was broken by a slide, a stop signal would be presented regardless of the direction in which a train was traveling.

O.P. then told me about a tragedy that happened in this area soon after the turn of the century. It came about during a winter storm, and it was caused not by a rock slide but by an unusually hard sleet storm. Ice pellets rolled down the ledges and the valley, building up enough on the westbound main that a passenger train running at speed rounded a curve and hit the accumulation. It was packed solid enough to derail the D16-class locomotive and several cars, resulting in the death of the engine crew plus several people in the wrecked cars.

A short distance east of this narrow stretch, O.P. told me to look at the bridge crossing the river ahead: the Rockville Bridge, the largest stone arch bridge in the world. As we passed, he pointed out that it was built wide enough to hold four tracks, two for westbound traffic and two for the eastbounds, and added that his train used to use that bridge going to and from the Enola yards.

As the train was slowing for the Harrisburg stop, one of the trainmen entered our car and announced that passengers for Mt. Joy, Elizabethtown, Lancaster, Coatesville, Downingtown, Paoli, and Philadelphia should remain seated. All passengers for other locations were advised to change trains. The station at Harrisburg was much larger than I had imagined, with people everywhere, a multitude of tracks and passenger equipment, and trains galore. We hadn't been stopped very long before our car was moved forward a short distance, then moved in reverse until the bump of a coupling let us know we were attached to the Philadelphia train.

Our layover lasted less than fifteen minutes and we again were on our way. O.P. informed me that we were now occupying the main line. I secretly began looking for the shiny engines hauling trains that matched the appearance of the Erie's equipment when it ran through Ralston the past summer, remembering O.P.'s saying that the Pennsylvania's trains on the main line were equally well maintained. But most of the engines and passenger equipment I could see in the Harrisburg yard resembled the type of equipment used on the Williamsport Division—nothing really clean or shiny. After passing the yard, we began running faster than I had ever ridden before. The scenery was flashing by. Passing the Steelton-Highspire steel mills, we left the river valley to enter rolling hills and farmland. Mountains were no longer visible. The engineer in charge of our train knew how to take advantage of this terrain, and O.P. estimated we were making between 70 and 80 miles an hour.

It did not seem to take long for us to arrive at Lancaster, and when we made our stop it was apparent that this station was different from any I had ever seen. Instead of the passengers departing and boarding by the vestibule steps, they walked out of the car onto a raised platform that was level with the vestibule.

Not far east of Lancaster my attention was called to troughs filled with water between the tracks. These, I was told, enabled steam engines to drop the scoop found beneath the tenders on all road locomotives, which allowed them to take water on the fly. These track pans were used the entire year too. In cold weather they were heated by steam pipes to keep them from freezing. We also passed what looked like an engine terminal facility, where we saw familiar classes of engines assembled, all in their customary grimy coating. O.P. said this facility mainly served locomotives used in and out of Philadelphia.

Coming into Paoli, we began to see evidence of the electrified system: trackside steel structures with wires suspended to cover all four tracks. On the storage tracks near the station an array of electric locomotives were parked, along with strings of passenger cars with round holes for windows on either end. These cars, O.P. explained, were electrically powered MU (multiple unit) cars that could be used individually or coupled together to form a train, all controlled by one motorman up front. The principal purpose of these cars was to haul commuters to and from the Philadelphia area. Our K4 backed past as we were sitting at the station, and O.P. pointed out that we would be hauled by an electric locomotive for the remainder of the trip, but exactly what type he couldn't determine.

It didn't take long for the electric power to get us rolling at speed. All was real quiet, except for the wheel sounds on the rails and the raucous horn the locomotive used for a whistle. Each time the horn sounded, O.P. shook his head, and I would ask: "What's the matter, Pop? Is something wrong?"

"The Company must have spent hundreds of thousands of dollars designing and developing these electric locomotives," he replied, "and they're perhaps the most modern and powerful in the world. Then probably someone in the Engineering Department came across an idea for saving a few dollars, and so, instead of installing a decent-sounding whistle, a nickel-and-dime air-operated foghorn was selected. It actually cheapens the locomotive's image."

I had to agree. The sound being admitted wasn't a pleasant one, but I reasoned, "How could they use a whistle on an electric locomotive? There's no steam to blow it."

He had an answer for that question too: "Air that's compressed and under pressure has much the same properties as steam. Air can blow a whistle—in fact, the Lehigh Valley uses an air whistle on some of their newer steam engines, and they sound good."

As congestion increased, tall buildings could be seen in the distance and our train began to reduce speed. Soon we were in a large yard complex, in the midst of which was an engine terminal. Although there were more engines assembled there than I had ever seen or thought possible to exist, none that I could pick out as we rushed by were strange to me. Gradually slowing to a very low speed when the station was in view, our train's wheels were directed through a maze of rails, crossing switches and crossover points. It was amazing to me how it could be guided through all the congestion.

All trains coming into the huge Broad Street Station at Philadelphia, our destination, pulled to the end of their track with their power up front, my father pointed out. Trains ready to depart were in reverse of this, and although the entire station was wired to handle electric locomotives, steam was heading some trains. Steam engines took their consists to destinations where electric wires were not in place.

The throngs of people alighting from the train were met on the platform by red-cap porters, ready to handle any passenger luggage. Another novelty for me was that instead of baggage men handling single baggage trucks, the wagons were being towed in multiples by a small, hard-rubber-tired vehicle.

Walking forward alongside our train, we approached the streamlined electric locomotive that had brought us in, designated a GG1. We stopped to look over this strange form of power. I was surprised that my father knew a great deal about this type of locomotive. One of the first things he noted was the absence of rods on the drive wheels, explaining that individual motors supplied power to each axle. He then called my attention to the body design, one cab in the center with controls on either side, which allowed it to run in either direction without turning the locomotive; all the engineer had to do was change controls from one side to the other.

A strange feature of this design was the two parallel bars on each cab window, a safety feature that made it impossible for an engineman to stick his head out. The large raised, diamond-shaped bar structure on top of the roof, I learned, was a pantograph that could be raised or lowered, and there were two such devices on the locomotive. Their function was to pick up electric current from the overhead wire, supplying power through conductors to give the motors their energy. O.P. mentioned that in the Book of Rules pertaining to the operation of electric locomotives, it was prohibited for anyone to get within three feet of the overhead wires with a metal object in hand, lest the high-voltage current be picked up, resulting in possible electrocution.

At the end of the platform we emerged into the main station area, which to me was immense. I was completely befuddled by its size, but it didn't seem to bother O.P. Pointing to a large clock, he mentioned that we had plenty of time to have lunch before our appointment. We found a restaurant located conveniently on this concourse, and I let him choose what to order. He suggested sandwiches with Manhattan-style clam chowder. That was my first taste of this kind of soup, and it was delicious, possibly the best I have ever had the pleasure of enjoying.

After lunch, back in the main concourse area, O.P. informed me that to get a taxi to take us to our destination we'd have to go down the stairs to the ground level. Afraid that we might become lost in the vast complex, and in order to find our way back, I felt it would be prudent to pay attention to distinguishing features along the way, so I carefully noted all the signs and objects along our way until we reached the taxi stand.

Leaving the station in our cab, there was so much to see: tall buildings, trolley cars, and crowds of people. We arrived at the hospital, but how the taxi driver was able to negotiate the feat of getting us there, especially in the congested mass of traffic, amazed me. Entering a large, multistory building we were directed to the proper office for our appointment, at which time I underwent a lengthy interview concerning my condition in the presence of two doctors. Then I was escorted to a room for a complete physical examination, documenting all their findings.

Once the examination was over and we were back in the office, the results were explained to us. The verdict was encouraging: my case could be treated effectively, and I would be able to walk again, but the course of treatment would be lengthy. First, I would be confined to the hospital, then I would be required to become a resident at the "children's home," not only until I was completely healed but until I graduated from the home's high school. In addition to receiving an accredited education, I would be taught a trade of my choosing. The only time I would be permitted to go home was over holidays and vacation periods. It didn't take much to convince myself that I didn't like the idea, but I realized I wasn't old enough to have much say, and, somehow, whatever was required, I wanted to walk again.

O.P. too had listened intently to the proposed plan, and I was worried about what his response might be. But he wasn't ready to give an answer at that time. Without hesitation, he told the doctor that we would let him know our decision at a later date. With this we thanked our host for everything and bade him good-bye.

After we left the hospital, O.P. didn't talk about anything that went on during our visit. We didn't have any trouble finding a taxi; one was parked a short distance away, almost as if we had reserved it. On our way back to the Broad Street Station, O.P. checked the time and said we had plenty of time before our train departed and added that it would be prudent to have our evening meal before boarding. We chose to eat at the same place where we had eaten lunch, because it was convenient, then adjourned to the waiting area, where we could watch all the activities of the busy station, more than enough to occupy our time.

Engrossed in watching everything that was going on, I failed to notice the sign posted on the platform listing the train for Lancaster, Harrisburg, and Williamsport, until my father nudged me and said our train was made up. Even though it would be another half hour before departure time, he said, we should get aboard; at least the seats were more comfortable in the coach than in the waiting area of the station.

On the platform by the train, we were advised that the Williamsport cars were located in the forward section, and after walking past at least eight cars a brakeman supervising the boardings confirmed that we had selected the correct cars. While we were sitting awaiting the departure in the coach, we watched trains on adjacent tracks on either side move in and out. Most were powered by electric locomotives, and not all were using the sleek, streamlined version; some were pulled by square, boxlike bodies.

Just before we left I saw a steam engine approaching about three platforms on the right, and as it neared I could identify it as an E6. It didn't look as if it was in very good condition either. In fact, it was grimier than the ones I was accustomed to seeing on the Elmira Branch. It was a little different from the 666 or 425 in that the tender had straight sides without a built-up coal bunker, and the lettering on it read "PENNSYLVANIA READING SEASHORE LINES." When I called this to O.P.'s attention, he explained that both of the railroads whose names were on the tender had once served most of the same points in southern New Jersey on parallel rails. Rather than compete with each other, they had recently merged into one system as an economy measure.

The cars that followed, twelve in all, matched the engine in appearance: they too were covered with grime. They looked familiar, though, and most of the coach windows were raised, much the same as on cars that passed through Ralston in midsummer.

Normally the E6's running on the Elmira Branch hauled a maximum of four cars westbound and six cars eastbound. At other times, during peak holiday periods, if more cars were added to the consists, a K2- or K4-class engine was on the head end. Seeing an E6 handling a train made up of twelve cars immediately raised a question. "How can they use such a small engine to haul that many cars?" I asked.

O.P. replied, "This is the area the E6 was designed to perform on, and they often handle as many as fifteen cars with no trouble. There aren't any grades to speak of—none like the ones we have back home. About the only drawback is having to start a heavy train, but once they're under way speed is easily maintained, and fast too."

As our train pulled out of Broad Street Station, I again watched intently at the panorama of railroading that surrounded this vast terminal. From what I could see, the B6 switch engines dominated these yards; they were carrying out their switching chores everywhere I could see. Suddenly I spotted a 0-6-0 swallow-tailed dinky that somehow looked different from the others. Taking a closer look, I could see that it was equipped with slide valves instead of the usual piston valves. I had never seen a Pennsy engine with the slide-valve motion. "Look at that old B6 coupled to those passenger cars!" I exclaimed.

O.P. just about missed it, but at the last moment picked out my newest discovery. "You're right in one respect," he said. "It is an old engine." But then he added, "On the other hand, you're wrong. It's a B8 class, forerunner of the B6." He continued by explaining that because this class was a little lighter and not nearly as powerful as the B6, the few still remaining on the roster were relegated to light switching duties, such as in these coach yards. I also learned that a B8 had handled the switching chores at Ralston for many years. In fact, it was the only class swallow-tail ever employed at that terminal.

We hadn't cleared all the yards going out of Philadelphia when I noticed O.P. was nodding off, and that was understandable: he had gone without sleep for a day and a half. It didn't bother me to be without his companionship. There were so many things for me to observe as we raced along the main line. At Paoli, our inbound experience was reversed; we were uncoupled from the electric locomotive, and a K4 was coupled on to take over. It did not take the steam engine long to get our train rolling at a speed as fast or perhaps faster than the electric locomotive maintained coming out of Philadelphia. As I sat watching the landscape flashing by, I discovered I was listening to the mellow sound of the K4's whistle, and I had to silently agree with O.P.: it was certainly more fitting for a locomotive hauling a passenger train on the main line than the electric's "foghorn" version.

Before we reached Lancaster the sun was setting. From my window, it resembled a huge red sphere casting various shades of pink on the horizon as far as my eyes could see. This was a spectacle I couldn't see at home because the steep mountainsides blocked that kind of view. The shades of the sunset could be seen after we left Lancaster, but before we reached Harrisburg, darkness had set in.

Our stop at Harrisburg was different from our stop there on the eastbound journey. Instead of cutting off the section we occupied and switching us onto another train, we remained in one spot while additional cars were added. O.P. awoke during our layover somewhat refreshed and described the moves that were taking place, even pointing out that after all departing passengers had vacated the coaches, no one would be allowed to board until our train was made up again with a different K4 coupled on.

However, someone did come aboard carrying a large tray: a vendor selling sandwiches. This was permitted, and when he reached our seats we sampled his wares. My father bought a cup of coffee for each of us, and although it was served in a paper cup it was rather pleasant-tasting.

It didn't take long for our train to be made up, and passengers assembled on the platform were allowed to board. Several of the people entering our car I judged to be railroaders, based on their attire. Just before we left Harrisburg, one of those men stopped and greeted O.P., expressing surprise at the dress clothing he was wearing. It didn't look like he'd be taking the EC3 out tonight, he said. O.P. explained that we were returning from Philadelphia, where I had been taken for an examination, and that he had marked off for a round-trip. After I was properly introduced, it turned out that this gentleman was the conductor on the EC1 and EC2 runs. He asked if he could sit with us for the trip to Williamsport, and when we welcomed him he pushed the seat in front of us back and sat down facing us.

The ensuing conversation dwelt mostly on topics concerning the railroad. One thing that was perplexing to the conductor was the delays his crew had been experiencing. He said that on the trip just completed they nearly outlawed, and that was the reason he was on this late train. Normally he would have been back in Williamsport hours ago. O.P. added that the same thing was happening to him on the EC3 and EC6 runs, but he didn't say that on the last trip he was running so late he had to get off in Millersburg in order to take me to Philadelphia. It was fascinating to listen to these two men talking about their everyday happenings relating to working on the railroad. Besides, there was little I could see as we sped along in the darkness, other than lights from dwellings, small towns, and the flashing crossing signals.

Somewhere along the line another man, who happened to be the engineer on the Williamsport Division end of the EC1 and EC2 crew, joined us, and it turned out that my father and he had hired out on the railroad just a few days apart. The friendly discussion among these three men was enough to keep my attention as we sped along in the night.

At the station stop in Northumberland, several men boarded and entered our car, and all appeared to be railroaders. Spotting one of the men and announcing that he was an old acquaintance, the engineer who had joined us excused himself to join his friend seated farther back in the car. The conductor sitting with us took that opportunity to strike up a conversation with me and was evidently impressed by how much I knew about railroading. "Where did you learn so much about this railroad?" he asked.

With O.P. sitting beside me, I confessed that he was my teacher, explaining that he talked a lot about the railroad and that he always was willing to answer my many questions.

"I suspected that," the conductor responded, and then he offered a bit of praise: "Your dad is one of the best engineers on the road. I've ridden for years behind all kinds, but none of them can handle a train as smooth as he can. And I'll tell you another thing: he's the only man I've ever had on the head end that can take a heavy train down the Leolyn hill in a way that will allow me to leave my coffeepot on the cabin stove without it being jarred off. In fact, he never slops out a single drip."

I did not divulge that I knew how O.P. accomplished this feat: by a simple adjustment on the feed valve of the automatic brake system. Rather, I thought that as long as we were passing out laurels it would be better to dwell on his ability to take heavy trains up the hill. I was just about to relate how he had managed to get an overtonnage train up that grade and that another engineer with about the same tonnage had stalled even though he had the assistance of not one but two pushers, when the absent engineer rejoined us. O.P. began kicking my leg under the seat, and I took this as a signal to withhold my tale. It was only a short time before we arrived at Williamsport, and I didn't dare do any more bragging or storytelling. I just listened and spoke only when spoken to.

We picked up our car, parked near the station, for the last leg of our journey to Ralston, and we were not far beyond the station when O.P. explained why he had interrupted me on the train. "You must use a little judgment when you start telling strangers things you and I talk about," he said. "You probably would have caused the engineer that sat with us more than a little bit of embarrassment. He was the fellow that stalled going up the hill. It would have embarrassed me too. He'd have known I told you about his dilemma, but other than the stalling part, I don't know what actually caused it. It could have been related to many things—an I1 that wasn't working properly, weather conditions such as wet rails, or even pushers could have let him down. I truthfully can't say why he stalled."

Then he revealed something else that might become a strain on their long relationship: "He's the fellow that's one spot below me on the roster, and I just bumped him off the EC3 and EC6 job."

When we reached home, my mother was waiting up to greet us, anxious to hear what the doctors found. She was more than pleased about the assurance they had offered, and especially that I would be able to walk again without crutches. Everything seemed to meet with her approval until O.P. told her my treatment would require that I be confined as a resident of the institution until graduation from high school. She immediately rejected that arrangement, saying, "He's our son and we're not going to have someone else raise him. We'll have him treated somewhere else, no matter what the expenses will be."

She then asked my father to once more contact his sister for help, this time in finding a private doctor that we could consult. The idea that I wouldn't be taken away from my home was very reassuring.

My aunt again came to our rescue, arranging for an appointment with a prominent orthopedic surgeon associated with the Jefferson Hospital. In less than two weeks I was again bound for Philadelphia, this time accompanied by my mother. This gave me the opportunity to be the tour guide, pointing out the many things that I had previously seen and explaining them to her to the best of my ability. To me, the second trip was as fascinating as the first one. There were numerous things relating to the vast Pennsylvania Railroad system that I overlooked the first time. My mother, however, was only mildly interested in this type of viewing.

When we arrived at the Broad Street Station, I impressed her with my skill in finding the way around, and more so by knowing exactly how to reach the taxi stand. Unlike the previous trip, when O.P. and I had made it in a single day, this time we spent the rest of the day and the night at my aunt's apartment. The following morning, accompanied by my aunt, we arrived at the doctor's office at the appointed time. He didn't waste any time trying to impress us with a pleasing bedside manner. He was strictly professional in his conduct, and after briefly examining me he bluntly informed my aunt and mother that I was not suffering from rheumatic fever but that he would have to take x-rays to determine what the problem was. He wanted to admit me immediately to Jefferson Hospital for the first phase of treatment, and the results would be available when he made his rounds that afternoon.

This doctor scolded my mother because she had, he thought, waited so long before seeking professional help, but she made it clear to him that that had not been the case. I had been under the care of a physician, she explained, but due to the suddenness of my illness it had been recommended that I stay at home. Furthermore, she said, x-rays had been taken when my condition improved and had showed nothing amiss. This doctor only responded that no more time should be wasted.

After I was admitted to the hospital I learned that bed rest wasn't to be part of my treatment. There were x-rays, and then people came and arranged a structure at the foot of my bed, attached to which was a pulley with a rope. Weights were put on the end of the rope, and a harness was fitted around my ankle. None of us knew why this traction method was being used, other than that it had been ordered by the doctor. When the doctor came, he explained that my leg was drawn back because my leg muscles were retracting due to inactivity, and that the traction would bring my leg to its normal position. He then went into detail about what my ailment was and what had caused it.

"According to the x-rays," he said, "a small portion on the side of the hip socket was crushed, resulting in a serious bone infection termed osteomyelitis. Presently," he continued, "there is no sign of any infection. What cured it is a mystery too. No known medicine can combat this disease, and if the affected limb isn't amputated, death is the final result." He continued: "Also, probably from infection, the hip joint is dislocated. The easiest way to adjust this condition would be to operate and clean that portion of the bone structure, but that's too risky. It would probably activate the infection again, and then he'd lose his limb for sure. The first step is this traction, and if it works I'll set the bone back into the hip socket. That's about all I can safely administer."

The doctor asked us how I might have suffered the injury that was severe enough to damage the shell of the socket and crush the small outside portion. The only incident I could recall occurred more than a year and a half earlier, when I'd bruised my hip badly when I fell from a grapevine swing on the mountainside behind our house. That was the only injury my mother could recall too. The doctor discounted that, though, saying that what caused my illness had taken place more recently.

But what my mother really wanted to know she presented as a direct question: "Will you be able to correct this condition so the boy will be able to walk again?"

"I'm not about to make any rash promises," the doctor replied. "The only thing I can truthfully tell you is that it's going to take time and that it depends on how well he responds to my treatment."

Satisfied that I was receiving the proper treatment, my mother announced when she visited me the following afternoon that she was taking the late afternoon train back to Ralston. O.P. and my sister also needed her.

It wasn't as if I had been abandoned entirely to total strangers. My aunt visited me daily, either before going on duty at 7:00 P.M. or when her shift was completed at 7:00 A.M. The traction method was used for three days, but when the doctor saw that it wasn't accomplishing anything he ended that treatment. But relief from the stretching was only temporary. The next morning I was taken to the operating room, where my leg was forcibly straightened, the hip joint was reset, and a cast was applied. When I awoke from the anesthesia, there was a cast on my leg, but it completely encircled my body from my rib cage around the waist area. This plaster of Paris apparatus was wet and clammy and it seemed to weigh a ton, and I had to lie flat on my back hardly able to move. My aunt told me during her evening visit that the doctor had said the operation had been successful. The best news was that in a few days I would be allowed to go home, after the cast was dry and if there was no flare-up of my previous infection.

On the second day after my transformation, the doctor wanted me out of bed and starting to walk with my crutches, and I thought that part would be easy because for the last three months or so I had used these crutches to maneuver around. But I was mistaken. To begin with, I couldn't even get out of bed without the nurse's assistance, and when I did stand the heavy cast was a definite problem. My back was held perfectly rigid, as was my entire right leg. The only free movement I had now was my arms and left leg.

After three days of regular practice, though, I was able to cope with this cumbersome device in which I was encased, even walking the hallways to explore some of the hospital's interior. My doctor was even pleased with my progress, especially since there was no indication that the infection was going to reoccur. Finally, the best thing he had to offer was that if my condition remained stable for the next three days I would be permitted to return home.

My mother was notified and arrived the day I was to be discharged, but when she saw my cast she expressed concern about how I would ever be able to get around while fitted with this device. My aunt and the head nurse on my floor assured her that in a relatively short time I would be able to function much the same way I always did. The doctor's only instructions were that I shouldn't place any body weight on my right leg for a month. Then, after that, I could start putting some pressure on it every day until it would bear my entire weight, and if no pain occurred I could try to walk on it. An appointment was made for me to return in three months for reevaluation and to have the cast changed. If I started experiencing pain or my temperature elevated, I should return to Philadelphia immediately.

The day I left the hospital we spent the night at my aunt's apartment to get acquainted with the outside world once more. My mother's worries were increased when she saw the difficulty I had getting in and out of the taxi and that I was unable to do anything without help. Her primary concern was how she was going to transport me back to Ralston, especially with the long train trip to Williamsport.

The following afternoon we prepared to leave for the Broad Street Station. The taxi driver eased our initial step by taking us to an entrance with a conveniently located elevator that took us from street level to the train platform level, where we entered the gate to the waiting Harrisburg-Williamsport train. We didn't encounter any difficulties, but at the car designated for the Williamsport section my mother worried anew how I was going to manage to get up the coach steps. This problem was solved by the brakeman standing at the entrance to our car, who effortlessly lifted me up to the vestibule.

In the coach, at the seat we selected for the trip, the conductor came forward from the far end of the car and obligingly pushed the seat in front of us back, suggesting it probably would be more comfortable if my leg were placed up on this seat. This arrangement was fairly comfortable, my mother's fears were alleviated, and I was busy again observing all the railroading activities. This undoubtedly was the best train trip I ever took. I was going home satisfied that one day in the near future I would be able to walk again.

When I returned to Philadelphia at the end of three months, I could walk without the aid of crutches, even though it was awkward because of the way the cast restricted my movements. My treatment, however, required that I have casts for nearly two years: for six months the full body arrangement to my ankle, then shorter versions that allowed me to use my knee, and finally a celluloid model fitted with hooks similar to a high-top boot that could be laced up and removed for sleeping or bathing. While wearing these casts I visited the doctor every three months, and after the casts were gone I still was in his care until the beginning of 1941.

The results of this doctor's care were satisfactory. I was able to walk with only a slight limp, but my right shoe required a built-up sole and heel. There wasn't any more pain, and the bone infection never reoccurred. I could engage in almost all playground sports, hunt all day, scale the mountainsides with O.P., ride a bicycle, roller skate, and even learn to dance. Although I had to make the frequent trips to Philadelphia, they were always enjoyable because there were always new things to see or things that I'd missed the previous times. I also watched with interest construction activities related to the electrification system as it was being installed between Paoli and Harrisburg. The entire time I kept looking for a shiny steam engine coupled to a string of really clean cars, comparable to the ones the Erie had run through Ralston. I was sure such trains existed on the Pennsylvania, as O.P. had said, but for some reason they always escaped my sighting.

On these journeys I was accompanied by my mother and, most of the time, my sister. The trips turned out to be vacations in the big city lasting three or four days. My aunt was a gracious host, taking us around the city to many points of interest: movies, department stores at Christmas, and, one of the best parts, when just she and I attended big-league ballgames to see either the Athletics or the Phillies play.

Just traveling around the city produced sights that were always interesting:

steam-powered shovels excavating building foundations, chain-driven Bull-dog Mack trucks equipped with solid rubber tires, and, one of the oddest conveyances, a vehicle that resembled a large horse-drawn delivery wagon, mounted on solid rubber-tire wheels and powered by batteries that were mounted beneath the box, with the operator sitting up front on an open wagon seat with just a straight tiller device to steer. Especially fascinating was riding the trolley cars through the center of Philadelphia right down the middle of each street, or the subway that ran underground and emerged as an elevated system.

In 1937, schedule changes reduced the time the trip from Williamsport took to a flat four hours each way. The train we had heretofore taken was scheduled to leave Williamsport at 6:30 A.M. and arrive in Philadelphia at 11:30 A.M. The return trip departed Broad Street Station shortly after 6:00 P.M. to arrive in Williamsport around 11:15 P.M. The changes began in late spring, providing coach-fare passengers with a fast, almost limited train service. Departure time at the Park Hotel station in Williamsport was now at 7:00 A.M., arriving the Broad Street Station at 11:00 A.M. It left Philadelphia on the return at 6:30 P.M., reaching Williamsport at 10:30 P.M. Publicity given to this new schedule stressed the ease it afforded business people, shoppers, and regular travelers, in that they could be in Harrisburg at 9:00 A.M., spend the entire day in the state capital, and leave this city at 8:30 P.M. to be back in Williamsport at a reasonable hour in the evening. The Philadelphia time was also pointed out, explaining that one could spend an entire afternoon in the city.

This faster schedule was the result of the recently completed electrified system from Paoli to Harrisburg. Electric locomotives would be used to haul passenger trains the entire distance to Philadelphia, starting in 1938. O.P. came up with a different version of why this new abbreviated time schedule had been adopted: it was a calculated move by the Company to lure passengers from its competitor, the Reading, which for some time ran a four-and-a-half-hour train to Philadelphia.

An interesting article appeared in our local daily, the *Williamsport Sun,* about the inaugural trip of the newly established train, named the "Susque-hannock." The reporter had been granted permission to ride in the cab of the locomotive, and he aptly described many things related to his trip, beginning with the engine chosen to haul the train. The engine crew had informed him that the high-drivered locomotive was an Atlantic type, technically classified by the Pennsylvania Railroad as an E6s and capable of handling the attached six cars with ease. What intrigued him most about his cab ride was the fireman's ability to stand on a deck that was bouncing up and down lurching from side to side. It fascinated him that anyone could shovel coal through the narrow fire door to feed a raging inferno under those circumstances, and accomplish this feat at speeds exceeding 75 miles an hour. He described traveling so fast that the trackside telephone poles resembled a high picket fence, and noted that the fireman could do his job without spilling a lump of coal. Without a doubt, the reporter concluded, the man had to have been born an acrobat.

When my turn came to ride on the Susquehannock, I learned how it ran on such a fast schedule. Station stops that the train it replaced used to make were eliminated, and stops at the larger communities were brief. Even the stop at Harrisburg was changed. Instead of switching our cars onto another train, we never moved. Additional cars were coupled both on the back and on the front, and a GG1 was coupled on. This maneuver cut at least ten minutes from the time, and the stop at Paoli no longer required time to change from steam to electric. This train carried me back and forth until I no longer required medical attention, and when I last rode it in 1941, it was still running on the four-hour schedule.

Back home after my initial stay at the hospital in Philadelphia, I learned from O.P. that not much had happened on the railroad during my absence. One thing the Company had done, though, was assign M1- and M1a-class engines to the EC crews, which pleased O.P. They weren't received on a regular basis, but often enough for O.P. to know that they had the appropriate power to haul the fast freight runs. These big 4-8-2's could handle the heavy-tonnage trains common on the EC's faster schedule, and their huge coast-to-coast tenders eliminated some water stops, as well as the time-consuming coaling stop at the roundhouse in Williamsport on the westbound trips. When he was lucky enough to get an M1 out of Enola, he considered it an unexpected vacation, compared with the pounding one received from an I1 on this long trip.

It didn't take him long to form an opinion of the M1 classes either. Every engine he drew steamed easily, rode as smoothly as a K4, and, perhaps most impressive, ran fast. O.P. believed that the river grade on the Williamsport Division main was ideally suited to the design of this type of locomotive, but he found that the 4-8-2's performed equally well on the variety of grades on the Elmira Branch. Although on this branch many factors limited hauling trains at speeds these engines were capable of running, there was nothing that detracted from their overall performance.

About the only weakness the M1's seemed to have, and it was especially noticeable at some locations in both directions on the Williamsport-Southport line, was starting a heavy train. O.P. learned that these starts could sometimes be ticklish. The 4-8-2's couldn't dig in or lug like the 2-10-0 I1's. It wasn't that they couldn't exert the necessary power, but rather the reverse: they had too much power. With their combination of power and high drivers, unless they were opened up carefully with a generous amount of sand applied, these engines could be extremely slippery.

O.P. did conclude that the M1's were about the best all-around freight hauler the Company had on its roster, but he did have some reservations. He would not concede that it was superior to the L1s 2-8-2 class that was particularly well suited for all lines covering this area of Pennsylvania. A vast fleet of these engines had been built, but responsible personnel in the Motive Power Department somehow failed to realize the potentials of this locomotive, and that oversight actually restricted its performance. With the addition of a feedwater heater and stokers, an increase in boiler pressure to 250 pounds, and the addition of a tender large enough to correctly supply adequate coal and water—things that should have been incorporated originally—the L1 would be a masterpiece.

He theorized that the Company would save money if the dependable L1 were used on more freight runs, even if it couldn't haul the long tonnage trains assigned to the I1's or M1's. The 2-8-2 could manage a train of seventy or seventy-five cars at the top allowable freight-car speed, 60 miles an hour, and handling a train of this size was easier than handling a train of 125 cars, the limit imposed by the ICC. Stopping or starting the shorter train resulted in less lost time and fewer cases of mechanical difficulty and car-knuckle breakage. Even if two individual trains had to be used, the Company would be money ahead in the long run. The most important benefactor would be the shippers, who could be offered a faster schedule. Everything considered, O.P., despite his years of service, was still figuring how to get a train between two points the quickest way possible.

During the first week in August, O.P. was bumped off the EC3 and EC6 crew again, and as it happened in the spring, an older engineer was holding down the counterpart run, EC1 and EC2. As usual, the board at the Williamsport yard office had only a few jobs showing where he could exercise his bump privilege, either yard jobs or the Altoona-Southport dikers. One job on the advertised bid board interested him, though: a work train out of Bellefonte scheduled to be opened and awarded on August 15. He didn't make an immediate decision about whether to bump or place a bid, but rather discussed all this with my mother. His best move, he explained, would be to try to bid in the work train crew, because it would be the best-paying job. If he didn't get it, he could then bump on one of the other jobs.

There was a disadvantage, though. The schedule listed it as a six-day-a-week job terminating September 30, 1936, and that would require him to be away the entire week, coming home only on the weekends. But there was a bright side: he could live with his parents in Howard, so he could spend some lengthy time with them—perhaps his last such opportunity because both were advancing in age. My mother agreed.

O.P. put in his bid, and awaiting the opening date gave him a few days' vacation—without pay. While he was off, we took a day's trip to my grand-parents' home, to visit and to tell them of his plans. They both were pleased that he would be spending some time with them, and added it would coin-cide with my aunt's summer vacation. She was expected to be home for a month during the same period.

On the opening day, O.P. used the Company phone at the water plug and learned from the yard office in Williamsport that he had been awarded the bid on the work train. Reporting in at the yard office in Bellefonte at the appointed time, he assumed his duties as an engineer on a work train, one job that he had never handled. Now, after twenty-seven years, his orders revealed he would again be running on the L&T Branch. The job of this work train was to upgrade the roadbed and rails from Bellefonte east to Mifflinburg. Ditches were to be cleaned, and ballast would be spread the entire distance.

At the engine house O.P. picked up the power he was to use: an H9 that had just come out of the shop at Altoona. It looked like a new engine, but already a film of the ever-present lime dust was beginning to coat the newly applied paint. Backing down to the yard area to pick up the ballast hopper cars and the cabin, a stop was first made at another siding to couple onto the only piece of equipment that was to be used: a Jordan Spreader, which was positioned in front of the locomotive. O.P. had seen this boxy-looking affair in yards and on work trains, but never in actual operation. This would be another new experience for him.

When he came home on Saturday evenings each week, he filled me in on most of the details of his new duties. Concerning the work train, a crew of track workers living in camp cars were included in this renovation pro-ject. Their part in the operation was tamping the ballast, raising the track, installing new ties where needed, and replacing worn rails. A few men rode in the cabins and opened the pockets on the hopper cars, evened out the bal-last if mounding occurred, and cleaned debris left by the ditching procedure. The larger number of workmen followed with their own motor cars, pulling their tools, ties, rails, or whatever necessary on trailer cars. When work was being performed on the track, O.P. was to run the train as slowly as possible, at no more than a snail's pace.

The Jordan Spreader was designed by Oswald F. Jordan at the beginning of the twentieth century to cut back overgrowth in ditches built to divert water and debris away from track and roadbed, and, if necessary, to even out any ballast that had been spread. O.P. found it to be an interesting piece of equipment. Its operator was seated high at the forward end of the car and was able to manipulate blades (wings) located on both sides. These attachments were operated by air cylinders, the air supplied by the engine. The blades could be raised or lowered for the depth needed, and also angled for the proper width of the ditch. It took only one push to clear the ditch on both sides of the line. As the train approached an area where the spreader was to be used, the ballast-spreading stopped, the H9 was uncoupled, and the machine was shoved ahead of the engine through for the length of the ditch being cleaned.

Few train movements interrupted this work detail, only the eastbound morning passenger train, one local freight, and the westbound afternoon passenger train. Sidings located at most of the small communities along the L&T made these meets easy and reduced the time lost when the movements did pass through. These sidings also were used at the end of the work day. The nearest one was used to set off the Jordan Spreader, parked so it could be placed on the head end the next morning. At the next siding along the line, the 2-8-0 would be uncoupled, run through the siding, couple to the cabin, and pull it and the empty ballast hoppers back to Bellefonte. The engine did not need to be turned either. It was always run heading east. Not much switching was required either. The local freight took care of advancing the camp cars and their supplies to different locations as the work progressed. The farther they went from Bellefonte, the more travel time they had, and the working day was shorter. At least O.P. had a chance to run the H9 a little faster.

One evening, running backward as usual, O.P. spotted a number of convicts near the prison at Rockview leading their teams back to the barns after spending a day in the fields surrounding this state penitentiary. He had passed by several fine-looking teams, and as he approached the highway grade crossing, a team ahead of this intersection seemed to be in a hurry to get back to their barn.

O.P. was watching the way these horses were prancing and the trouble the prisoner teamster was having holding them at a walk, when he saw a man doing something his father had cautioned him never to do while working horses. The long driving reins, according to his father, should be held firmly with your hands, never tied together. Above all, even if it was easier, never tie them together and place them over your shoulders and under your armpits. That could be dangerous, but that was exactly the way the prisoner had the reins affixed to his body.

Perhaps he could teach this man a lesson when he whistled for the crossing, O.P. thought. His energetic team would rear up and be even more difficult to restrain, and the reins would be dropped. So he didn't give the accepted Book of Rules signal with the high-pitched screecher whistle, but rather just two low-toned calls followed by a wide-open, long blast. The team's reaction was different from what he had expected, though. The horses didn't rear up, but instead broke into a wild gallop, instantly jerking the teamster to the ground and pulling him up the dirt road in a cloud of dust. Unable to undo this unfortunate incident, O.P. regretted that he had caused the runaway as he watched the horses, still dragging their driver, pass out of sight. This man certainly must have sustained injuries, and that wasn't part of the lesson he'd intended to administer. He did, however, get a firsthand demonstration of what his father had always considered a dangerous practice.

On another evening's return trip backing to Bellefonte, O.P. experienced something that was common to the railroads traversing the rural areas of Pennsylvania: he hit a cow. He probably would have been able to stop because the running speed wasn't very fast, but the animal must have been standing on the left side of the tracks out of view. Furthermore, at the time the fireman apparently wasn't looking either. Just striking the cow and throwing it off the tracks was usually all that happened, but not in this case. Somehow the force of the impact threw this bovine into the center of the tracks and it rolled beneath the tender, where a crude butchering process took place, starting at the rear trucks. When the carcass reached the protruding water scoop it must have become entangled. It was at this point that O.P. noticed something was amiss. Parts and pieces of the unfortunate creature were flying out from under the tender as the animal became disemboweled. As the remains came loose, the front tender truck started a cutting action. Meanwhile, the intact portions that had hung up on the piping and couplings between the tender and the engine came loose. From here more grinding than cutting evolved; entrails, meat, and parts of the hide were all picked up by the drivers. The wide tires on the drivers picked up the blood and remains and distributed them liberally on the hot ash pan, under the boiler, and onto the rods.

Bringing the train to a stop, O.P. and his fireman realized that an awful stench was entering the cab. The odor from the blood, flesh, entrails, and other remains was bad enough, but it also was being burned on the hot portions beneath the engine. Under such conditions, they wasted no time getting off the H9, and once they alighted they could see the mess that was left of what had been a cow. The only consolation was that there was nothing remaining to clear from the tracks. The smell in the cab was less penetrating when they again boarded the 2-8-0, and traveling backward seemed to keep what remained of the odor below the deck. They arrived back in Bellefonte without anyone getting sick from the smell.

At the yard office as he was signing off, O.P. also had to fill out a report with full details of his encounter with the cow—milepost number, time, approximate speed, and the like. The data would be needed by the claim agent so settlement could be made with the owner of the animal to cover the loss. Even though this area in the east was considered a fenced range, the Company was liable for livestock killed by a train on their private right-of-way, and this law had been upheld for many years.

Driving to Howard, O.P. felt he could still smell the odor of the carnage, even though the accident was now more than two hours in the past. Later, while at the dinner table, he didn't have any desire for food. My aunt, knowing he had a healthy appetite, noticed his unusual behavior and remarked to their parents, "Oss doesn't seem to be enjoying his meal." Then, with a chuckle, she added, "I bet I know what's ailing him too. I bet he hit a cow today." That untimely remark caused him to end his meal in a hurry.

At the end of the allotted time, the work-train crew was abolished and O.P. was again without a job, but the termination did give him the right to bump. It was the last time he ran over the L&T Branch. Back home, he checked the board at the yard office in Williamsport. The engineer with more seniority was still on the EC3 and 6 run, but the engineer one number below him was holding down the EC1 and EC2 crew. There were no other jobs available, and although the schedule of that fast freight wasn't as convenient as the EC3 and EC6 side, he didn't have any alternative but to take this job.

The EC1 left Enola about four hours later than the EC3 during the early morning hours, and most of the time had no trouble getting as far as Williamsport. As usual, though, while the crew did no switching at this terminal, the yards were congested, causing some delay in the running time. Time was also lost when the I1's were the head-end power. Their small tenders made a trip to the roundhouse for coal and water—a necessity before tackling the grades to be encountered. In addition, the pusher(s) had to be attached, which generally involved losing more time.

Once on the Elmira Branch, the EC1 ran after the early-morning westbound passenger and, providing he didn't run into more delays, O.P. whistled through Ralston sometime around 7:00 A.M. If he could get to Southport early enough, he'd board the eastbound passenger to arrive home at noon. That did not happen often. Instead, he was usually a little late and would have to wait four or five hours, until the next eastbound passenger train departed Elmira around 4:30 P.M. to bring him into Ralston at 5:30 P.M. As an alternative, and if he was marked off in time, he would ride the cabin on the EC6 or, on rare occasions, the cabin on an eastbound diker. That was considerably better than enduring the long wait in Elmira.

Not too much time was spent at home, either. To make his calling time, it was necessary to catch the 3:15 A.M. westbound passenger to get into Southport with just enough of an edge to mark up. Running eastbound on the EC2, he went through Ralston around 7:00 A.M. or earlier, sometimes spending time in the siding to meet the westbound EC1. At Williamsport this crew had to set off and pick up cars before departing for Enola. If things worked out normally, he'd be back home by late in the afternoon. If he was too late arriving in Enola, he would spend the layover in the room he again retained in Harrisburg.

Leaving Southport one exceptionally cold morning during the second week of November with an M1a and a heavy train consisting of 109 cars, he was to run into all sorts of time-consuming delays. To begin with, a pusher was needed to assist him out of the yards at Southport and all the way to Sned. At least he had a clear block for the descent to Troy. Still running a clear block at the tower at Troy, he started hitting the heavy Troy hill grade to Cowley, and that was time-consuming too. It slowed the 4-8-2 to a snail's pace to work up-grade with the heavy tonnage. Fortunately, the grade past Cowley was mostly descending on the remainder of the Elmira Branch.

At the Leolyn block station, a message handed on ordered him to take the siding at Ralston to meet the westbound EC1. After this movement passed, he didn't get permission to proceed until the westbound passenger cleared at 8:30 A.M. That stop used about an hour and a half of running time, and it was around 9:45 A.M. before he reached the yards at Williamsport. On this particular morning there was one thing in favor of the EC1: no cars had to be set off or picked up. All he needed to do was take water and be on his way. But that did not happen. The dispatcher informed him that another eastbound train was just leaving and that a westbound was waiting at Allens Tower to enter the yards. It was more than an hour until the westbound's cabin passed by and the overhead bridge signal displayed a clear block.

In contact with the dispatcher in his office at Number 9, almost directly across the tracks from where he was waiting, O.P. expected to be ordered to extend his delay, especially on a day when tie-ups seemed to be the rule. However, a chance to be off running was offered by the dispatcher, who said, "Oscar, I know you've been held here for quite a while, but the eastbound passenger is about due. If I let you out you'll be ahead of it by ten minutes. Do you think you can run ahead of it to Northumberland?"

O.P. didn't hesitate to assure him that he could do that, adding: "I have an M1a with a big tank. If you keep the blocks clear for me, I'll probably be able to run ahead of the passenger all the way to the Rockville Bridge. On the other hand, if I'm getting behind, pull me in at Northumberland." Accepting this proposal, the dispatcher gave him the order to proceed, informing him that his progress would be closely monitored.

Before O.P. could get started he had to couple the train up. It had been cut to keep the city crossing open while he lay in the yard. Reassembled, and after a hasty air brake test, the train was moving again, sounding two short whistle blasts to the switch tender, acknowledging the signal given that the switches were properly set to occupy the main. When he reached the main he checked his watch and found he was only ten minutes ahead of the passenger's departure schedule. Easing out of the yards, he began to widen out on the throttle when he judged that the long train was all clear of the switches, but there was no response. He was unable to pick up any speed, and it didn't take long to realize why. The prolonged wait and extreme cold had allowed the car journals to stiffen up, so that it was almost like trying to pull a train with all the brake shoes dragging.

Reaching the east end of the city, O.P. began to think that what he had assured the dispatcher he could do might not be possible. His train was barely moving. Here another obstacle had to be overcome: a curve compounded by a slight grade leading to the Reading's main crossover and the approach to the bridge spanning the Susquehanna. With the engine opened as wide as possible without provoking slipping, and under all the sand that could be poured on, he felt uneasy. All he could do was sit on the seat box and listen to the sharp, labored exhausts.

This slow dragging continued across the Reading main and onto the bridge. Midway across the span the big 4-8-2 was down to its last breath. One thing seemed to be certain now: either he would start slipping or the train would grind to a dead stall. Whichever came first, he was about to make a grand mess out of the railroad for a while. He would not only tie up the passenger that was about to follow—which would be a grievous sin—but also have the double-track Reading main blocked. Then too, the dispatcher that allowed him out ahead of this movement would be in trouble, plus the reputation O.P. cherished for many years would be severely tarnished. These thoughts were suddenly exploded when the M1a started to come alive and the train began to roll free.

By the time he was off the bridge and past Allens Tower, entering the double track, his speed was increasing, enabling him to notch out farther on the throttle. It didn't take much time to have the 4-8-2 really barking, and at that he began bringing the reverse lever back toward center, setting up for his running speed. When things were functioning normally, a time check revealed that he was a scant three minutes ahead of the passenger, but still picking up speed at every turn of the drivers. Nearing Northumberland, he examined his watch again and noted that time was being gained: four more minutes were added to his favor.

Still running under the assumption that the dispatcher would probably clear him at this point, he had the fireman crawl over the coal pile and onto the tender to visually inspect the water supply, because even if this engine did have the coast-to-coast tender, it had been used exceptionally hard out of Williamsport. Here, or at Sunbury, was the last place the coal could be replenished. The fireman's report was favorable: more than half a tank remained, enough to get to the Rockville Bridge and a sufficient amount even if they were held up before getting to Enola.

Easing off in obedience to the yard limit speed restriction, and now expecting an order to take a siding because of the short time he had on the following passenger movement, he was mildly surprised when the tower that came into view displayed a clear board. An order handed on by the operator gave him permission to run clear all the way to Rockville. With nothing to stop him now, O.P. picked up running speed in a hurry, never letting off again until an approach signal was displaying as he entered the Rockville block limits. Proceeding at a reduced rate of speed, another thought entered his mind: if he was held up here for any length of time before being allowed to cross the bridge, the journals would once more stiffen up. In that case he might be able to get on the bridge, but he couldn't possibly haul this heavy train all the way around the approach curve and up the grade that was present. A repeat performance of the Williamsport departure would occur, but this time it would surely end in a stall and he would tie up the main line.

Coming into view of the tower, just as he expected, a stop signal was showing. Just before he came to a complete stop, though, the signal changed to clear. Releasing the air, he widened out on the M1a to gain speed before hitting the approach curve. As he thundered by the tower he checked his watch and found that he had gained ten minutes on the passenger's schedule, putting him now twenty minutes ahead of this movement.

O.P. didn't regard this run as anything special, just handling a train in a routine manner, much the same as he would any other time while doing a day's work—except that on this occasion he was awarded quite a bit of publicity in the railroad's newspaper. A double-column spread appeared with bold headline "WILLIAMSPORT DIVISION ENGINEMAN COMPETES WITH AIRLINES." Evidently the dispatcher had monitored the EC2 as he proclaimed he would, and his sheet must have been presented to higher officials, then passed on to the newspaper. O.P. concluded that the article must have been written from the dispatcher's entries. It gave the departure time, listed Engineman O.P. Orr as the man in charge, and mentioned his entire crew, the engine number, and the time the Rockville tower was passed. It was also apparent that the reporter interjected some thoughts of his own, weaving them into the story of this run by stressing the importance of offering shippers fast deliveries.

As he should have been, O.P. was pleased with what had been written, but he didn't think the run was worthy of special recognition because he believed that runs of this nature should be made on a daily basis and in both directions. Other engineers holding the EC crew were equally capable of running in that manner, providing they were given the preference a fast freight should command and were assigned the proper type of motive power. He reasoned that the 11's were a poor choice to handle these 175-mile trips if speed was needed to haul first-class merchandise.

Bumping was still taking place, and during the first week of deer-hunting season in December 1936, O.P. lost the EC1 and EC2 crew. This time he didn't have to make any decisions; he exercised his bump on his friend, only one man below him on the roster, who at the time was holding down the EC3 and EC6 side. Other than the calling time, there was no difference in these runs, except the EC3 and EC6 runs allowed him to spend more time at home.

At the breakfast table the day before Christmas, O.P. remarked that there would be snow for the holiday. Snow had started falling the previous evening and was still coming down, accumulating to more than a foot so far, light and powdery. Bidding us good-bye as he was leaving to catch the 8:30 A.M. westbound passenger, he stated that at least this year he would be able to spend part of Christmas day at home. When he arrived in Southport it was still snowing. In fact, the snow seemed to be intensifying, and by the time he had marked up and was ready to leave, the wind was picking up in force. He encountered no difficulty getting out of the yard or ascending the grade to Sned; in fact, the 11 did not even labor too hard pulling the rather light consist on this first leg of the trip.

Past Sned and descending toward Troy in the broad open valley of farms, the effect of the storm became more evident. Coupled with the heavy snowfall, strong winds were creating large drifts. This created an effect O.P. had never experienced running in a snowstorm, and it gave him an eerie feeling. Most of the time he was unable to see much beyond the front of the boiler. When there was visibility, he had the sensation of being on a white cloud. Nothing ahead assured him that a set of rails was hidden beneath the white expanse on which he was riding. Only the passing telephone poles outlined where the tracks were supposed to be.

The bitter cold, plus a constant swirl of snow from the forward movement of the engine, made it impossible to run with the cab window open. Compounding this situation, the small window on the front of the cab was obstructed most of the time by snow thrown back when large drifts were hit. To make things more uncomfortable, the fine powdery snow infiltrated the cab through every little opening and was sucked in around the loose-fitting back curtain. It wasn't long before the interior, including O.P. and the fireman, was dripping wet.

Nearing Troy, the valley narrowed and drifts were neither as prevalent nor as deep. However, it still was snowing so hard that O.P. had difficulty seeing any distance ahead. Crossing the two highway bridges before entering this northern-tier community, O.P. began slowing, trying to see what signal the tower ahead was displaying. He wasn't surprised to see a red board showing. He had to meet the local at this location. Presumably it hadn't yet cleared.

In the tower the operator informed him that an eastbound movement that had gone through more than an hour ago reported it had run into problems getting through the drifts on the grade between there and Cowley. When the meet was finally in the siding, the local's engineer also checked in at the tower to report clear, and confirmed that drifts were bad in several places coming down the hill. In addition to being deep, they seemed to be packed as solid as concrete.

Permitted to proceed, O.P. was made leery by this news, but figured he had a little advantage now that the local had plowed the tracks open. That was initially correct. From where the local had entered the siding, he ran over open track along a hillside on his left for more than a mile. But things changed abruptly when he left this shelter. Instead of following a well-defined rut in the snow, now there was nothing visible ahead, just a swirling mass of white.

Running close to 30 miles an hour, he ran into a drift that did little to slow the I1. Hitting the next drift, however, he not only slowed but came to a complete halt. This drift was even with the running boards, and in what little distance he could see ahead it looked as if there was a solid wall of snow. About the only course of action was to attempt to back out of this predicament and take his train back to Troy.

He had no difficulty getting the train started in reverse, and when he reached the point where the local had gone into the siding the 2-10-0 was cut off, allowing him to run around the train on the siding track to the tower. Notifying the dispatcher of his plight, he then suggested that a plow be sent to clear the drifts or it would be impossible to get a train through this stretch in either direction. The dispatcher acknowledged that the situation certainly warranted the use of a plow and advised him that he would try to send one out of Southport as soon as possible. Notification would be given when to expect its arrival.

After a short period of waiting, O.P. received the dispatcher's answer, which wasn't encouraging. The plow had already been sent out of Southport and was on its way west (north) to open the tracks through the Lake Region to the terminus in Canandaigua. Williamsport was in a state of chaos on the eve of this holiday. All the extra men available had been called out to replace men laying off, and as help on movements requiring additional power to combat the storm. The only order he could issue, and he apologized for doing so, was for O.P. to use his I1 as a plow and attempt to get through the drifts.

Complying as ordered, O.P. set out with the light engine around 2:30 P.M. Beyond the sheltered hillside he found things hadn't changed. If anything, they had worsened. He wasn't even able to determine the spot where the previous stall had occurred. It didn't take long to realize how ineffective the big 2-10-0 was when it came to removing snowdrifts without a plow, and how solid a pile of snow became after it was blown into a sizeable drift. Rather than a soft, fluffy mass, it was more like running into a stone wall.

Marking his position by a large tree close to where the tracks should be, he saw his efforts did not indicate a great deal of forward progress. During the ramming-and-stalling process, O.P. conjured several thoughts, most relating to the negative aspects of this unusual task. One of the main concerns was getting the I1 stuck out in the middle of nowhere. Another was how long the pilot would stand this kind of punishment. But foremost was the two large air-reservoir cylinders mounted on the pilot. If the force of these impacts dislodged either of them, it would result in a broken air line, bringing this venture to a screeching halt—not that he needed the braking power, but it would mean it would be impossible to reverse the locomotive.

After a few passes into the drifts, he decided that perhaps more speed would allow him to gain more headway in opening the right-of-way. To do this he would have to back off a little farther for a fast charge. He had not backed far when, to his dismay, he ran into a solid wall of snow back of the tender. The trench cleaned just a few minutes earlier was again drifted full. That brought the 2-10-0 to a shuddering stop and caused an entirely new worry. If he began ramming into this drift with full power, the tender would probably be lifted, resulting in a derailment. He had no other option left than to get back through this obstacle. A bit of good fortune was present, though, for on the second try he broke through and was able to reach the sheltered area. Now it was necessary to back a longer distance, and making this maneuver before advancing slowed his forward progress almost to a standstill.

Bucking snowdrifts proved to be strenuous work, not only for O.P. and the fireman but also for the engine. In less than two hours the tank of water was exhausted and the coal supply was dwindling. Returning to Troy to fill the tank, he telephoned the dispatcher to explain that very little progress was being made. About the only thing he was accomplishing was burning coal at an alarming rate. Furthermore, bucking into drifts, coming to jarring stops, and spinning the drivers all raised havoc in the firebox. In order to keep a full head of steam, the stoker and the blower had to be used most of the time. At this rate the coal supply would be used up in less than two hours. Sand too was getting low, but the trial-and-error method he'd adopted proved that sand was unimportant in the snow.

Listening to O.P.'s problems, the only solution the dispatcher could offer was to send a replacement engine out of Southport, provided an extra engine crew could be found on Christmas Eve. The dispatcher did find a bit of additional help though. The section crew had been called out, and they would accompany him as an insurance measure in case the I1 became stuck in a drift.

Darkness had fallen by the time O.P. and the section crew jammed into the cab and started out for another round, not that the absence of light made much difference, for all afternoon it had been impossible to see in the raging blizzard. The services of the section gang weren't needed to shovel snow. The upgrade that was present eased things when backing out of the drifts. He had yet to get into a drift that held the engine fast. This crew of men did, however, help the fireman and head brakeman. When the slides were opened on the coal pile, they were put to work shoveling coal forward to keep the stoker screw covered.

Low on water, and with what he estimated was a sufficient amount of coal to get the locomotive safely back to Southport, O.P. once again returned to Troy. Reporting to the dispatcher, he was advised that another I1 was being sent out from Southport and that when it arrived he was to continue bucking snowdrifts until he got through to Cowley. He was also told that his crew, including the section gang, should go to the passenger station, where arrangements had been made with a local restaurant to provide hot meals for each of them.

The warmth of the station and the food made this an enjoyable respite, but it lasted only a short while: the replacement engine rolled in too soon. Briefly discussing the storm with the extra engineer, O.P. learned that the snowplow was keeping the north end open, but even it was having a difficult time, and that the afternoon eastbound passenger had made it into Elmira, where it was annulled. All other movements were canceled too. Rumors also persisted that the eastbound night express passenger might be annulled before it left Canandaigua.

Heading back out with the fresh engine, O.P. discovered that the wind had ceased blowing at hurricane force and the snow wasn't falling as hard. Better still, the trench he had opened partway up the hill hadn't drifted shut during the break. With no worries now about being blocked, the long backing moves were eliminated. For the first time his efforts at clearing the tracks began improving.

For more than an hour his plowing continued. The weather too began cooperating: it had stopped snowing and the stars were shining. All that remained of the storm was the bitter cold. Nearing the summit of the long grade, he ran into his last major obstacle—a long cut drifted full—where the inevitable happened. After he had bucked his way to about the midpoint of the cut, the I1 became hopelessly stuck.

It took the section gang almost an hour of industrious shoveling before he was able to back the 2-10-0 out of its confinement, then plowing began again. Finally, around 11:00 P.M., he reached the summit at Cowley. Contacting the dispatcher from the operator's station to report that the rails were cleared, he was ordered to return to Troy, pick up his train, and once again begin his eastbound trip. When he asked the dispatcher how much time he had on the eastbound express passenger movement, he was told that this train was running late, that presently it was somewhere west of Elmira. Running orders would be received from the block operators along the line.

After returning to Troy, O.P. made a stop for water, coupled onto the train, and was off once more. Not much speed was attained ascending the hill, even with the light consist attached, and orders were handed on at Cowley. He had a clear block to Leolyn, but a meet was to be made at Canton. The westbound afternoon passenger had been held at Canton since 4:00 P.M. waiting for the EC6 to open things up to Troy. On the downgrade, other than running through heavy snow cover and an occasional drift, he didn't run into any problems getting to Leolyn, but it wasn't a pleasant Christmas Eve to be at the controls of a steam engine. The powdery snow churned up by the train reduced visibility and filtered into the cab to produce a bone-chilling dampness.

Another clear block was displayed at Leolyn, and no orders were handed on. Dropping down the hill in the narrow valley, he ran out of the drifts, and snow still hid the rails. When he reached Ralston, O.P. decided to stop for water, although he didn't have an urgent need for it. It was a protective measure. Anything could happen before he reached Williamsport.

At this stop he got off as usual to oil around and inspect the running gear. Not much oil was used, however, nor could he see very much. The entire undercarriage was encrusted with snow and ice. The front of the I1 was packed with snow up to the smoke-box door, the dual air cylinders were covered, and where the footboards should have been nothing remained but some splintered pieces hanging from twisted metal straps. Just before he got back on board, realizing he was cold, wet, tired, and hungry, he had a sudden urge to leave everything parked on the main and walk home. But he resisted that urge and stayed on the job.

On his way again, another clear block was showing at Bergen (Marsh Hill). An order handed on noted that he was to meet an extra that was being held in the siding at Trout Run. As he assumed, the block was also clear when he reached this position, but orders handed on instructed him to take the siding at Cogan Station to clear for the following eastbound express. He entered the siding as ordered, and after the passenger passed he requested permission to occupy the main. But permission was not granted. Instead, he was to hold the EC1 until the westbound express cleared, and that train wasn't scheduled to leave the Williamsport station until 2:45 A.M.

While not objecting to this order, O.P. did call the dispatcher's attention to the limited amount of time remaining before he would outlaw. There was a brief pause, perhaps the time sheet was checked, and when the conversation resumed he got an order that allowed him to assume the main after the westbound cleared. He was also given clearance to enter the yard and assigned a track, where the train was to be set off and the engine would be taken to the roundhouse. When all this had been accomplished, he was to mark off for the mandatory eight-hour rest period. Everything went exactly as ordered, and O.P. was in the yard office with just a few minutes remaining on the sixteen-hour duty limitation.

All the members of O.P.'s crew lived in or around Williamsport, so this break allowed them to return home, but for O.P. to attempt to go to Ralston was out of the question; highway conditions wouldn't permit it. So he went across the tracks from the yard office to the conveniently located "Pennsy Lunch," had an early breakfast, and then retired to the bunkhouse located near the Park Hotel station.

With less than six hours sleep, he was called with instructions to report for duty again "right on the eight"—that is, at the end of his allowed eight hours of rest. After a quick meal at the Pennsy Lunch, he marked up, received another I1, coupled up to his parked train, and resumed the trip to Enola. Reaching this terminal early Christmas evening, he was instructed when he marked off that the EC3 would remain in its proper rotation, and again he was allowed only the minimum eight-hour rest period. That short time did not give him enough of a break to go to his room in Harrisburg, so another rest was spent in the bunkhouse.

Leaving Enola somewhat later than his regular EC3 calling time, he still was able to arrive in Southport in time to catch the eastbound passenger to Ralston. He was back home at noon on the day after Christmas, thinking that wasn't the proper way to spend a holiday.

The bumping pattern was still in vogue at the beginning of 1937, and once more O.P. was the victim, a lucky victim. The man on the EC1 and EC2 crew was below him on the roster, so all O.P. did was put his seniority to work. The net effect was nothing more than a change in his calling time. Freight traffic during the winter months seemed to be increasing, especially from fruit and other produce cars coming from the south. Both EC westbounds were hauling their share of those commodities, and it did not slack off with the coming of the spring. Most of the cars hauled were destined for upstate New York cities.

When reporting for duty at the yard office in Enola late one spring evening, O.P. was notified that his calling time was respited for four hours due to a mishap that tied up both the mains on the Williamsport Division. A respite meant he was not to go on the time card, and thus held to sixteen hours on duty from that time, for another four hours. When his waiting time was up, he reported for duty, and after marking up he received orders to circumvent the accident site with EC1. He was rerouted over the Middle Division to Tyrone, down the Bald Eagle Branch to Lock Haven, back on the double-track main to Linden, over the single track to Newberry Junction, and from here onto the Elmira Branch, a detour of more than 115 miles. An M1a with a large tender was the assigned power, and the train was made up entirely of refrigerator cars, less than sixty all told.

Preparing to leave the yard, his pilot for the Middle Division segment boarded the engine, and asked, "Do you want me to run, or would you like to handle it?"

O.P.'s answer was almost a confession, telling the pilot that for years he had harbored a desire to run a train on the four-track system over a long distance. The pilot was very congenial about this request, allowing that he preferred to just ride along for a change. Once under way, O.P. had the M1a set to run at about 60 miles an hour on tracks that could accommodate this constant speed, and without worrying about making speed reductions normally found on the Williamsport Division's double-track main. Cab signals also indicated the positions of the block's distant signals at all times. Another convenience never before experienced was scooping water from the track pans.

Running at sustained speeds with a light-tonnage train that was easy for the 4-8-2 to handle, it did not take long to cover many miles. Somewhere beyond Huntington, the pilot suddenly gave an urgent command: "Get this train stopped, and do it in a hurry. I almost forgot that we have an order to load ice for the cars. If we run by this station, all hell will break loose."

Following the pilot's directive, O.P. made as much of a reduction on the automatic braking system as possible without going into emergency. Just shy of a complete stop, the pilot directed him to run through the icing facility at about two or three miles an hour and ice would be loaded into the cars' chutes on the fly. This was another learning example of railroading on the main lines.

Arriving at Tyrone, the EC1 was switched off the Middle Division onto the Williamsport Division's Bald Eagle Branch. In the familiar yard, O.P. spotted the 4-8-2 at the water plug to replenish the tank. While this chore was being performed, he went to the block tower for running orders to cover him to Lock Haven. (This was the last time O.P. would handle a train over the Bald Eagle Branch.)

He didn't get the orders he'd expected, though. Instead, the operator told him to contact the dispatcher, who commended O.P. for the fine run he had just made coming up the Middle Division and told him that the EC1's movement was being watched closely not only by local officials but also by the main offices in Philadelphia. The perishables in the consist had to be in Southport by 9:00 P.M. in order to comply with contractual agreements with the foreign rail lines. An interchange had to be made so the fruits and produce in the consist would be at their distribution points early the following morning. To expedite this movement, clear blocks were to be displayed all the way to Linden (Nesbit), where another crew with an I1 would relieve the EC1 crew.

O.P. immediately questioned such an arrangement, informing the dispatcher he had been respited for four hours, that he still had plenty of time to reach Southport before his sixteen hours would be up. It turned out that somehow the sheet showed him running on the regular calling time, so a correction was made and he was given the go-ahead to handle the train the entire distance.

With that settled, the dispatcher then informed O.P. that a serviced I1 would be waiting and that he should change engines when he reached Linden. In addition, a pusher would be waiting at Newberry Junction to assist him to Leolyn. Countering this order, O.P. declared that the M1 he had would be the best choice to make the best time, since time was the important issue, and that if he would be running under clear blocks a pusher would only be a hindrance. All he actually required was a man to help with cleaning the fire when he stopped at Linden for coal, water, and sand. That plan was accepted, and two and a half hours later, when he came to a stop at the

Linden tower and before the engine was uncoupled, a machinist accompanied by two helpers came aboard.

Pulling down to the coaling station, these men began filling the lubricator, cleaning the fire, and inspecting the engine. In this cooperative effort, the 4-8-2 was coupled to the train, ready for the remainder of the run in a minimal amount of time. All that O.P. had to do now was get to Southport before 9:00 P.M.

While he was making this roundabout trip on a different time schedule, his activity caused more than a small amount of concern at home. During breakfast, my mother mentioned that she hadn't heard my father's whistle that morning and wondered if I might have heard it. I replied that I hadn't heard it either, but added that this wasn't unusual. He had been late on other occasions. At school that morning I watched all the westbounds, and none of them had the familiar refrigerator cars the EC's handled.

The morning passed, and by the time I came home for lunch my mother was more worried, thinking that he must be involved in some sort of accident. Trying to dispel this idea, I reasoned that an engine failure was probably the cause of his running late. The afternoon went by without a sign of the EC1. When I returned home around 4:00 P.M., my mother was certain that my father had had an accident. Without a doubt, he was lying badly hurt somewhere along the line. Attempting to calm her, I pointed out that if that were the case we would have been notified by now. I still maintained that the engine had broken down.

We usually had our evening meal around 6:00 P.M. but it wasn't a very pleasant mealtime on this particular day. My mother was insisting that she wasn't going to wait any longer. She wanted to request the aid of our next-door neighbor, also an engineer, and have him contact the yard office in Williamsport to confirm her suspicions. But before she could do that, as I was attending to one of my evening chores, feeding the dog in the backyard, I heard a faint passenger whistle from farther down in the valley. It wasn't long before I heard the rapid exhausts approaching, and when the whistle sounded for the South Ralston grade crossing it started lowing down. O.P. had finally let us know he wasn't disabled, and he was doing it in a grand manner too. His big M1a was really barking, running faster than any other westbound I'd ever seen going up the valley. This evening he didn't finish the whistle signal with the two short blasts until the engine was leaving town.

It was around 6:30 P.M. when he blasted through Ralston, and the only stop made on the Elmira Branch was at Leolyn to take water. Arriving in Southport before 8:00 P.M., O.P. was an hour ahead of the deadline. Later he told me that the 4-8-2 he had on this run had astonished him with the power it could develop, even when hauling a little over the maximum tonnage allowed on this branch, and from Newberry Junction he could accelerate to speeds faster than restrictions would permit without working the engine wide open.

He hit the stiff grade out of Ralston with enough speed to crest the 3 percent part of the hill, and, as he described his ascent, it was fast enough that a person would have been unable to get off and then get back on the train again. After a water stop at Leolyn, he was able to handle the roller-coaster grades to Southport without any difficulty. But no news item ever appeared in the Pennsy's Williamsport Division newspaper about this unusual trip, nor was there any word of commendation ever accorded O.P.

A few days later, with clouds hanging low in the valley and producing a light spring rain, O.P. was running late again. Around mid-morning he whistled for the South Ralston crossing. This time he was finished whistling before he reached my view from school. As he drew nearer, it was apparent that a problem existed. Only muffled exhausts were coming from the engine, and after traveling a short distance O.P.'s forward progress was interrupted by slipping.

As he passed my viewing area, I observed that the I1 he had was grimier than most engines of this class, and that even the round shaft from the piston connecting it to the main rod on the left side appeared to be rusty, not shiny as usual. The slipping continued as long as the sound was audible. I concluded that at the slow speed the train was moving O.P. would probably stop to pick up a pusher and come back down the siding for water, but I was wrong. No pusher came out of the siding, and in a short time he whistled for the crossing north of town at Max.

Later that afternoon I was at the station to meet the 5:30 P.M. eastbound passenger, and, as I suspected, O.P. disembarked. Walking home, I deluged him with questions about the strange performance he had displayed earlier in the day. Addressing my questions in proper sequence, he covered relevant details relating to this trip from the onset:

A longer delay than usual getting out of the Enola yard and across the Rockville Bridge put him behind his schedule. When he reached Williamsport, he was held up getting into the yards, and, once there, he couldn't get clearance to occupy the Elmira Branch. About the only thing in his favor was a light-tonnage train. He didn't need a pusher, and he didn't need to have the 2-10-0 serviced at the roundhouse in Williamsport. All he did was take water. A short time later, and to his dismay, he discovered that he had made a mistake by not going to the roundhouse.

Eventually he was cleared out of Williamsport to occupy the branch. The misty rain was making the rails slick, requiring generous use of sand. After traveling a short way, he discovered that the sand flow to the drivers seemed to be restricted. Running orders gave him a clear block all the way to Leolyn, but at Trout Run an eastbound meet failed to clear the main, and he was presented with a red board.

Waiting for this extra movement to get into the siding gave him the opportunity to check the sand dome for what he believed to be some sort of obstruction, probably caused by wet sand that had caked from the boiler heat after the engine was serviced at Enola. Lifting the lid on the sand dome, however, he learned that wasn't the cause. It was nearly empty. Evidently someone had neglected to fill the sand dome in Enola. This disturbing revelation required O.P. to make an immediate decision: either he could notify the dispatcher and request the assistance of a pusher at Ralston, or he could attempt getting up the hill to Leolyn with the marginal amount of sand still in the dome. If he went to Ralston and waited for a pusher to be called out of Williamsport, or if he stalled on the hill, he would outlaw before reaching Southport. He decided to risk going up the hill unassisted, reasoning that help would come to his rescue sooner if he stalled, tying up the railroad, and that he might be able to make it all the way to Southport before the sixteen-hour limit ended. This situation would have been averted had he taken the time to have the engine serviced as usual in Williamsport.

After the meet and starting out at Trout Run, just enough sand was put down to get the train rolling, but he couldn't pick up much speed because wet rails prevented him from using any amount of power. All the I1 wanted to do was slip. Running in this manner until he was north (west) of Ralston, he didn't use any sand. Then, before the grade increased, a small amount of sand was applied—just enough to gather some momentum for the 3 percent climb that remained.

I interrupted him at this point, asking, "Wasn't your arm most worn out by then, from opening up and shutting off the throttle all this distance?"

"No," he replied, "I didn't touch the throttle once I was moving. After I found out how much power could be used, I used the independent brake to slow down the drivers when slipping occurred, then released the air to pick back up again."

Somehow he managed to get up the hill without stalling, but at Leolyn he was switched into the siding. Orders handed up informed him he would be held there until the eastbound noon passenger passed. He could then proceed, with further running orders to be received at Cowley.

Easing out of Leolyn on the downgrade and through the Grover Hole gave him swing enough to go up the Cedar Ledge hill and through Canton at a reasonable speed. At Cowley a clear board was displayed, and the orders handed on indicated he was clear through Troy to the next block at Sned. Downgrade all the way to the west end of Troy, he managed to get the train rolling fast enough to surmount the grade to Sned without any problem. A clear block presented at this point permitted him to continue downgrade to the Southport yards ahead of his outlaw deadline.

Eastbound one morning in mid-May on the EC2, O.P. had cleared the yards at Southport soon after his calling time, in charge of an M1a brought in on the previous morning's EC1. As he started down the Elmira Branch, an unusual number of clear blocks were displayed. The weather was warm, and past Leolyn the sun was just breaking over the mountaintops, all of which enhanced the pleasure of running unrestricted with an exceptionally easy-riding locomotive.

Dropping down the hill, he released the air just north (west) of Max, and, to take advantage of the fine riding qualities, he allowed the train to continue drifting a little faster than usual. Entering the old yard area west of Ralston, jammed now with empty, rusting boxcars, he began reminiscing about how it used to appear. Furthermore, as he passed where the yard office once stood, the wye configuration and the bare cinder-covered location of the once-bustling coal hoist (engine house) also brought back vivid memories. In sight of the Ralston station, he was still daydreaming about the past, almost expecting to find a clear board showing, but that wasn't the case. The operator's duties in the station building had been abolished when the terminal closed in 1930.

Suddenly he came back to reality, and found that while reminiscing he had completely forgotten about the speed restriction on the dogleg curve about 200 feet ahead, where the siding intersected with the main, and that he was traveling much too fast. Confronted with something that was now beyond his control, and realizing it would be futile to apply the brakes—even that it was too late to go into emergency, which would be of no help in the short distance remaining—he continued at the same speed. He rounded the first part of the curved section and was almost out of the next part, as though his excessive speed was no problem. Just as he straightened out to the approach leading to the overhead bridge, he could feel the left side of the 4-8-2 lifting up. A thought flashed through his mind: "Oscar, you're about to take an early morning swim in the creek." Fortunately, the raising motion stopped and the locomotive gently settled back down. As he was on the bridge, the right side began coming up, but it also settled back down gently.

This rocking motion continued, first one side, then the other, and each time it occurred the motion became faster until it ended with a violent shudder, causing dust, cinders, and whatever else that shook loose to engulf the interior of the cab. He likened the sensation to a wet dog shaking water from its fur, or perhaps to a spinning coin as it falls over. Each gyration gets faster before it comes to a stop.

By the time the M1a leveled off, his concern turned to the train, and looking back at the swaying cars he watched helplessly, expecting one might swing into the bridge at any time. But that didn't happen either. All followed along in an erratic manner. The entire incident did jar him back to reality, however, and he was left fully aware of how close he had come to causing a major catastrophe simply because he was enjoying a pleasant ride and day-dreaming for a few moments.

The month of May was nearly over, the 1937 school year had ended, and O.P. was bumped again. Once more he was able to bump a younger engineer off the other fast-freight crew, changing only his calling time when he went back on the EC3 and EC6 side. This schedule was to my liking, for I could be at the station, or the water plug, to watch my father as he drifted through town with the eastbound EC6. For some reason he never had to take the siding here, nor did he ever stop to take water. The only contact I had with him was a friendly wave.

During the days that followed in the summer of 1937, I did chores around home in the mornings, so after lunch I was free to enjoy doing whatever I chose. At first I spent some of the time fishing, but the novelty of that soon wore off. The neighborhood kids all were at the swimming hole, but I couldn't yet participate because of the body cast down to my knee. Reading filled some of my time, but even that became boring, and I saved most of it for evenings and rainy days. I was at trackside on the days O.P. passed through going eastbound, and soon I began to spend almost every afternoon watching train movements.

I started concentrating on the different ways the engineers spotted their engines at the water plug. It was mainly the eastbounds that came in with a train and spotted to take water. The westbounds generally had pushers, so this risky stopping at the exact location was rarely attempted. They generally stopped below the crossing in South Ralston, running up to the water plug light or pulling all the way through to Max and coming back down the siding light.

Some eastbounds came in at a crawl, others came to a prompt gliding halt, like a passenger train approaching a station. Still others didn't stop in time, which meant they had to back up. This required a greater effort than usual and resulted in having to pull out the slack. Power spinning and a slamming of the cars into each other, which caused everything to rattle and bang, was not uncommon. Executing this maneuver, some enginemen still stopped short of the tender lid's location. Most, however, pushed back beyond the water plug and pulled back up to the correct spot. This was easier because all they did was pull out the slack that was backed up. The rails, both east and west of the water plug, bore evidence of these mistakes. Round depressions were ground out of the tracks matching the spacing of an I1's ten drivers.

Watching these maneuvers for some time prompted me to ask O.P. why there was no set pattern used when an engine stopped for water. He answered without really committing himself, but said he suspected that some of the errors could be attributed to the type of cars a train was hauling.

He admitted to experiencing problems stopping exactly when tank cars were being transported. After spotting the tender under the spout, he explained, the sloshing action of the liquid caused the entire train to keep moving at least an engine's length beyond the plug. He also made an analogy between a group I was familiar with, school students, and locomotive engineers: both fell into the same types of categories, those at the top of the class, the A students; those that were average; those that were lower in the class but tried; and those who might have had higher grades but did not care. The only time the latter group was interested was when report cards came out. On the railroad, their equivalent was the payday that rolled around every two weeks. Then too there were some engineers who could run an engine capably but couldn't handle a train properly no matter how hard they tried. For them, running a train proved to be a frightening experience. Most men in this category bid themselves into yard jobs or pusher service to keep themselves off head-end runs.

Although I was able to spend as much time around the railroad as I wanted, O.P. was always cautioning me to stay away from Company property or anything relating to it. He would remind me that only Company employees were allowed on Company property and that disregarding that rule could lead to arrest by the Company's policemen for trespassing. I always tried to obey that regulation, but after seeing that nearly every train passing through during these Depression years carried a number of hoboes, I wondered out loud to O.P. why those men weren't apprehended. It was obvious that they did not respect the rules governing Company property; in fact, they could be seen riding in the open doorways of empty boxcars or, in another favorite car, an open gondola during pleasant weather.

They even went so far as to ride free on passenger trains. I once saw one transient board the 3:30 P.M. westbound passenger making it look easy. The

E6 was making the usual fast start from the station with four cars, and in the vicinity of the former yard office, some 200 yards from the depot, it was picking up speed rapidly when the hobo made his move. Running down the upper leg of the old wye roadbed, he grabbed the tender handrail on the fireman's side, swinging onto the footboard as deftly as a veteran crewman, then proceeded up the ladder and across the tank portion and positioned himself beneath the sloping back of the coal bunker. Telling O.P. about what I had seen, I then expressed my concern about how these men could openly defy the regulations, especially hopping passenger trains.

These transients began appearing in numbers soon after the beginning of the Depression, O.P. explained. At first only a few were observed on Company property, as time went on their numbers increased, and soon there were so many it was impossible to control all of them. Most of them at one time had jobs, homes, and families, and probably were upstanding individuals in their own societies, but when the economy collapsed many lost all they had. Consequently they started roaming aimlessly, to the warmer climates of the South or the Far West during the colder months, returning to the northern areas in the summer. Some worked if they could find odd jobs or seasonal employment, others just bummed and begged for food, and none stayed at any one location for long. They would just catch a passing freight to look for some sort of promised land.

In regard to these transients, train and engine crews had an unwritten rule: as long as they stayed away from the engine or the cabins, the riders went undisturbed. Otherwise, the train crews risked retaliation: an air hose might be cut, or a coupling pin pulled, angle cocks opened, or any number of foul deeds devised to interrupt a movement. In addition, if Company rules were enforced and all those hoboes were arrested, the jails couldn't handle everyone. About the only thing the cops did was tell them to get off Company property, mostly in yard areas. But arrests would be made if anyone was caught stealing or destroying property. O.P. concluded, "It would take all day to discuss all the whys and wherefores covering this breed of men the Depression years developed. It would take more than one book to tell their entire story."

As O.P. passed through town one afternoon on the eastbound EC6, he wasn't drifting as usual; he was working the I1, and his position in the cab wasn't the same as usual: he seemed to be riding on his knees. This strange behavior aroused my curiosity, and when he arrived home I asked him to explain.

Commending me for my observation, O.P. at the same time confirmed my suspicions: "I was riding on my knees so I could look back over the train as it rounded the light curve approaching town. After I released the air, coming off the mountain just west of Max, the train wasn't rolling as freely as it should have. That's why I was working the engine to keep up my speed, and I was trying to spot any smoke coming off the wheels, which would indicate brakes that were hanging up."

This explanation satisfied me to a certain extent, but it raised another question: "I thought the reason a monkey house was put on the back of the tender was to allow the head brakeman to watch back over the train. Isn't that his responsibility?"

"You're right in that assumption," O.P. replied, "but you can't always be sure the other fellow is doing his job. For all I knew he might have been back there sleeping or reading. Besides, when you watch what's going on yourself, especially in a case like this, you're making doubly sure there's nothing wrong."

A short time later I was watching a diker rattling through eastbound when I heard the air come on in the vicinity of South Ralston, slowing the train to less than 10 miles an hour. This pace lasted until quite a few cars passed, and then the slack began running out and the train again started picking up speed. I couldn't imagine what had interrupted this train's movement. Nothing of any consequence had occurred, and because it was on a downgrade with a string of empties it didn't seem to have any trouble getting up to running speed. As the cabin came into view, I could see a man standing on the bottom step, and when the cabin passed the water plug coming onto the level area leading to the station the man swung down. He hung onto the grab iron with one hand, but his legs didn't seem to be able to keep up with the now fast-moving train. When he released his hold, I expected to see him start doing flips. Somehow he managed to stay on his feet, however, stopping a short distance from my observation position. When he was at a complete halt, a traveling grip was thrown off, followed by a wave from the conductor. Engrossed in watching this performance, I did not recognize who had gotten off until the grip was picked up and the man walked closer. It was none other than O.P.

After our greetings, I said, "That train was going too fast to get off safely. Why did you do that?"

O.P. smiled and said, "You're probably right, I shouldn't have tried what I did, but luckily there wasn't any mishap." He then explained why he chose to come home on the diker. Earlier in the morning, westbound on the EC3, he was running pretty much on schedule until he arrived at Leolyn. There he was put into the siding, not for one but for two meets. This turned into a time-consuming layover. Then, at Cowley, orders handed up indicated that a diker was let out of the siding and was running ahead of the EC3. Before he reached Troy, a restricted board was lit up on the distance signal, and at Troy the operator gave him an order to proceed with caution and be prepared to stop at Sned. Arriving at this block, a stop signal was showing, forcing him to wait until the pushers were cut off and had cleared the main by entering the wye. Finally, before he was allowed to enter the yards at Southport, he experienced another delay. The train ahead had to be put away. Consequently, before his train was in the yard it was too late to catch the eastbound noon passenger to Ralston.

At the roundhouse, after his engine was put away, he ran into an old acquaintance who announced during their conversation that he was heading for Altoona with a string of empties as soon as he picked up his I1. This gave O.P. the opportunity to be on his way home, eliminating the wait of more than five hours for the next eastbound passenger to depart. He informed his friend that he intended to ride the cabin to Ralston, then asked if he could slow the train in the vicinity of the station enough to allow him to get off. Assured that this would pose no problems, O.P. marked off and boarded the cabin.

It turned out to be an easy run for the diker. The only stop was at Leolyn for water, and orders handed on as the cabin passed the operator's station indicated it could run clear to Trout Run, where it was to take the siding for a westbound. Everything went along as it was supposed to, except the engineer started slowing when the cabin was west of the Lycoming Creek bridge, more than a quarter of a mile from the station, in an area where it was nearly impossible to get off. After slowing for a short distance, speed was again starting to build up, and the conductor, now aware of the situation coming up, declared that when they were in the vicinity of the station he would activate the air valve to stop the train, but O.P. said that if he couldn't get off he would ride on to Trout Run and catch the afternoon westbound passenger back to Ralston. If the emergency procedure was used, he realized, it would make the train late for the scheduled meet, and someone would be held responsible for this action.

As it turned out, I saw the rest of the story. Nothing was actually out of order, although it was dangerous. I had my usual questions for my father. "Why," I asked, "didn't the engineer judge the slowing distance more accurately?" and continued by explaining that I'd observed this misjudging quite frequently while watching trains pull out of the siding eastbound. They seemed to pick up speed before the cabin was on the main, making it difficult for the flagman or the conductor to throw the switch and get back on board. Often they had to run really fast for a long way before they could catch the train.

In response, O.P. didn't exactly discredit his friend for misjudging the correct point for slowing down, explaining that judging the length of a train with more than 100 cars, sometimes up to the ICC limit of 125 cars, was difficult. Judging the length of a train, he explained, was similar to spotting an engine under a water plug, in that some engineers could master the function easily while some would always have trouble no matter how hard they tried.

Soon after, a diversion entered my routine of watching only Pennsy movements. It was signaled by the sound of a foreign engine's steamboat-type whistle echoing in the valley above town. Hurrying down to the water plug, I was surprised to see a New York Central locomotive easing in to take water, and when it stopped I scrutinized this stranger. It appeared to be very much like the ones used by the Erie: centered headlight, cylindrical feedwater heater atop the smoke box, large cab with a rocker arm throttle, two seats on the left side, and a large tender. In some respects it resembled the Pennsylvania's M1, but the builder's plate above the cylinders revealed that it was classified as an L1.

Soon after the eastbound stranger left, the daily local arrived and entered the siding. Following this movement came a westbound Central. That was a special treat: it was a double-header and stopped just short of the water plug. The engines cut off and rolled up light to take water.

Another surprise came with the next westbound into town. The whistle sounded much the same as on the previous foreign movements. This engine was smaller, though, and as it neared the water plug I could see the word "ERIE" on the tender. Examining this locomotive as it took water, I could see that while it resembled a Pennsylvania L1 the brass plate designated it as an N2. Those classifications were confusing to me. Neither the Central's nor the Erie's classifications were anything like the Pennsylvania's. During the remainder of the day, two more Central trains were sandwiched among the regular branch movements, and last came another Erie, eastbound.

Later I asked O.P. why New York Central trains would be using the Elmira Branch. Where, I asked, were they coming from, what would be their destination, and why would Erie movements be mixed in with the Central's? O.P. had no trouble explaining the presence of these foreign trains passing through Ralston. The New York Central normally ran trains from the Newberry Yard terminal in West Williamsport up what was termed the Pine Creek Branch to Corning, New York, and from there to Syracuse, New York. The eastbound (south) trains originated at Syracuse and terminated at Newberry. The exception to this pattern was that the Central also hauled a large volume of coal up the Pine Creek line, destined for points in upper New York. This coal originated from the Clearfield, Pennsylvania, yard, coming from feeder lines serving that Western Pennsylvania terminal. It was hauled over either the Beech Creek Branch or Pennsylvania tracks from west of Renovo, to another Central yard located in Avis, Pennsylvania, before heading north over the Pine Creek segment.

Most of the general freight hauled by the Central was interchanged with or from the Reading Railroad, which also had a termination yard in Newberry. A wreck and derailment somewhere between Corning and Newberry disrupted the normal flow of traffic, forcing the Central to reroute its trains over the Pennsylvania's Elmira Branch from west (north) of Elmira through Southport and on to Williamsport.

Erie movements were mixed in with the Central's because there was some kind of agreement between the two railroads to run an Erie train every day each way between Corning and Newberry. How this came about, or why, O.P. was unable to explain. To O.P.'s way of thinking, it would have been more logical if the Erie would have just interchanged their cars with the Central at Corning, where these lines intersected. A similar arrangement was in effect also between the Central and the Pennsylvania. The Central ran trains from a point near Stanley, New York, over the Elmira Branch into Southport every day.

O.P. went on to relate that the Central crews shared the same facilities as the Pennsylvania crews at Southport, even washed the cinders from their throats at the same bar. One Central engineer seemed to delight in telling the Pennsylvania men what a great throttle artist he was, and tried to convince his audiences how superior the Central's locomotives he commanded were when compared with the derelicts the Pennsylvania had in its stables.

The Pennsylvania men tolerated his boasting. Besides, there was little they could do to silence him short of resorting to violence. One day, though, a Pennsylvania conductor slowed him—and his mouth—down. Heading to Southport eastbound out of Canandaigua on an extra movement, this conductor's train had gone only a short way when it was placed in a siding. After the train was cleared off the main, he went to the telephone box to notify the operator, but before he could place his call, he overheard the bragging Central engineer requesting orders to enter the Pennsylvania tracks for his run to Southport.

Granting permission to proceed on Pennsylvania rails, the operator also gave him orders to scoop—that is, run past the extra already in the siding and enter the next siding beyond the Pennsylvania train for the same scheduled meet. Being scooped by another Pennsylvania crew wasn't a favorable happening, but to have a Central crew do such a thing was worse yet, especially so when the braggart on the head end would proclaim this feat to everyone listening at the Southport bar.

The Pennsylvania conductor arrived at an immediate decision to slow down the foreign movement, enough so that perhaps it would be late for the scheduled meet and thus temporarily tie up the single-track main. Hurrying back to the cabin, he grabbed the coal oil can and a broom, walked forward a few car lengths beyond the end of the train, saturated the broom with oil, and proceeded to apply this substance for about thirty car lengths up one side of the rail and back down the other.

Back on board the cabin, the conductor stood on the rear platform and presently heard the Central approaching. It was working hard to keep up speed on the slight upgrade it was encountering. True to form, the engineer, apparently proud of what he was accomplishing, gave a low, taunting whistle blast as he roared by the cabin. The cadence of this exhaust was broken when he hit the coal oiled rails, causing the engine to erupt into a wild power spin. He immediately shut off, and when he opened up again the slipping reoccurred. This kept happening until the train was at a complete standstill. It was stalled on the main.

This unexpected turn of events forced the block operator to change the moves he had set up. The Pennsylvania extra was ordered out of the siding and advanced to the next location farther east; the Central was ordered into the siding that had just been vacated. At the end of the trip, most of the Pennsylvania crew adjourned to their favorite bar to await the arrival of the Central train. As they expected, the engineer soon made his appearance. Ready to hear the wrath this boastful engineer was certainly harboring, they were astounded when he never uttered a word about his stall. Although somewhat disappointed when they were unable to place some barbs, the Pennsylvania men deduced that they at least found a way to shut off the steam that was running this Central man's mouth.

Watching train movements, I discovered another practice the railroad was using in the handling of its pushers. Trains that had enough tonnage to require the assistance of two pushers to get up the hill from Ralston to Leolyn often needed only one pusher from Leolyn to Sned. The rear engine would be cut off at Leolyn, back down the hill to Ralston, enter the siding at Max, and come down to the water plug. The first chore the engine crew performed was to take water. The engineer climbed down off the engine to oil around and swung the spout around to the fireman, who had climbed atop the tender. When the tender was filled, the fireman pushed the spout clear and climbed back over the coal pile into the cab to begin a strenuous chore, cleaning the fire.

Sometimes I would climb aboard to watch this task performed, not as an intruder but as a welcomed guest. Many of the pusher crews were made up of men who lived in Ralston, either currently or before the Depression closed the yards. First the grates were shaken with a large, heavy lever that fit onto protrusions on both sides of the fire door. Then, if clinkers remained, the fire would be pulled to the middle of the firebox with a long steel rod with two prongs, and the grates opened from one side. The rod was then inserted into the firebox to break up the clinkers and force them into the ash pan. This rod required the fireman to insulate his gloved hands with a big wad of waste in each one, and it could not be used in the raging inferno of the firebox very long before it was heated to almost white hot, causing it to bend. A brief exposure necessitated it be brought out and cooled.

Once the clinkers were dispensed with, the grates were closed. The rod was used to level the fire, then placed, still smoking, in its holder along the left side of the tender. It was never perfectly straight. Cracking the blower, the fireman next shoveled coal on either side, down the middle, and to the back of the firebox. The duplex stoker was turned on, the barrels on each side of the firebox alternately turning and augering coal up until the steam gauge climbed back to the normal operating pressure of 250 pounds per square inch. Through this routine, water was injected into the boiler until the glass indicated it was full.

This did not complete the fireman's job. Next, he got off the locomotive armed with the coal pick and began cleaning the shields underneath the grates. Then he dropped the ash pan by prying a sliding bottom shield loose with the coal pick. Residue from the fire dropped between the rails. Pounding vigorously on the sides of the ash pan with his coal pick as the engineer inched the engine along, the fireman watched until nothing more was discharged. Iron plates placed between the rails along the water-plug area prevented the hot ashes from igniting the ties. The fireman restored the ash-pan opening plate to its closed position and climbed back aboard the locomotive.

Now that everything was in readiness for the next shove up the hill, the pusher crew had nothing more to do but wait for the arrival of a westbound in need of their assistance. Once the pusher completed its second assault up the hill, it was cut off again at Leolyn. The crew's work for the shift was done. All that remained was to make a light trip for 35 miles, backing the entire distance to the roundhouse in Williamsport.

CHAPTER SEVEN | END OF THE GREAT DEPRESSION AND THE WORLD WAR II YEARS, 1937–1947

The summer of 1937 was passing too quickly, as most vacation periods have a tendency to do. August was following that pattern. O.P., as usual, left soon after lunch one afternoon to catch the passenger train at Williamsport en route to Enola to pick up his EC3 for another night run back to Southport. Later the same afternoon, I was enjoying a snack before supper when the back screen door opened. Entering our kitchen was O.P.

Before my mother or I could speak, he made an announcement as he set his traveling bag down in the middle of the kitchen floor. "I won't be using that for a while. I've been bumped again, but this time I'm not going to bump on a road job. I figured I've been spending the biggest portion of my life just riding trains back and forth from Enola to Southport, either on a passenger or running my own crew, and I'm getting tired of this routine. I just bumped onto an 11:00 P.M. to 7:00 A.M. yard crew, and I start tonight. At least I'll have a job like a normal working man, plus I'll be off every Sunday. The only bad part is, I won't be bringing home as much money on payday."

After listening to his explanation, my mother agreed with him, adding that she was sure he would bring home enough money for our needs. O.P. then told us that when he was at the station waiting for the train to Harrisburg an employee gave him a message to contact the yard office. With plenty of time before the passenger's departure, he walked to the yard office and learned he had been bumped. Looking over the board, he made the decision to take a yard job. No first- or second-trick crews were within his seniority standing, so he was forced to take the one on the night trick. There was one bright note: a 3:00 P.M. to 11:00 P.M. yard and transfer job was on the bid board and advertised to be awarded September 1, so he placed his name on that list.

Both positive and negative features were connected with O.P.'s newly assumed yard duties. On the positive side, we enjoyed more of his company, and it felt so much better to know exactly when he was leaving home and when he would return. Even on Sundays, his day off, things were different. We might all go to a movie in nearby Canton, one of the only towns in our area that had a theater open on Sunday. Or, on weeknights, he might take my sister and me to a professional Triple-A baseball game played under lights at Bowman Field in Williamsport. After the game, he took us out to our oldest sister's home to spend the night while he worked his trick, and he picked us up the following morning for our return to Ralston. The negative side wasn't too bad. We had to be quieter than usual in the house, and not make too much noise outside either, while O.P. was sleeping during the day.

This routine didn't last long, though. When the bid was awarded on September 1, O.P. had the bid award for the yard and transfer crew, and his hours changed to working from 3:35 P.M. until 11:35 P.M., six days each week, with every Sunday off. We weren't aware of it at the time, but these changes were to affect our lives for many years. Also, O.P.'s familiar whistle signal would never again echo in the valleys surrounding Ralston. He had made his last run on the Elmira Branch. This held true as well for the Bald Eagle Branch. When he brought the EC1 over that line the previous spring, it was the last time he would run between Tyrone and Lock Haven.

The second-trick yard and transfer crew seemed to suit O.P. He wasn't confined to spending eight hours with back-and-forth switching chores, and his assignments took him outside the yard limits for some time each day. Even the pay scale was better than the regular yard job. There were limiting features, though, and one was the B6 he was assigned, which did not rate very high on the pay scale compared with the larger road-class engines he was accustomed to running. All wages were based on the weight a locomotive had on its driving wheels. Another was the pay the yard crews received. According to work rules, the Company did not operate on a forty-hour week, so a crew could work seven eight-hour days and only receive straight hourly wages. The only overtime paid was for more than eight hours on duty during a single work day. Also, in compliance with this working arrangement, holidays were always regular work days and did not allow for extra pay or provide time off with pay.

This job was different from most of the usual yard jobs in another respect: it rated a cabin, but not a very modern cabin, just an old wooden cabin with only four wheels (two per axle). Its main purpose was to shelter the train crew on switching duties outside the perimeter of the actual yard area, and for backing moves on the south-side freight line. A small air whistle was coupled to the brake line and sounded by the brakeman at all unprotected grade crossings when backing. The switching wasn't the usual breaking up or making up of trains all over the yards; it was confined to moving cars in and out of the freight house, mostly working the lower (east) end just west of Hepburn Street, one of the major north-south thoroughfares in Williamsport. The schedule was coordinated with workmen unloading or loading cars at this facility. O.P.'s crew started removing loaded freight cars and spotting empties, or vice versa, when these men ended their work day.

There were seven tracks used at this freight transfer station, and all cars had to be spotted so side doors on the cars were aligned to allow ramps to be placed to bridge the span between tracks. Cars that were removed were set off on yard tracks, where other crews would pick them up to sort them out for their proper destinations, loaded or empty. Replacement cars would be picked up, and the string would be cut onto the designated tracks. This was a coordinated procedure that involved all crew members. One of the brakemen threw the switches, the other rode the cars pulling the coupling pins, and the conductor gave the orders from his handful of waybills. He also gave the signals to O.P., in the daylight with hand motions and after dark with his lantern.

Correct speed was essential when cutting cars: too much could cause damage to merchandise when cut cars rammed into those already set in place; not enough, and the cut cars did not clear the switches. The Company had installed recorders on some cars to measure the amount of shock to which cars were subjected, and reprimands were given to engine crews for rough handling. O.P.'s crew conducted the same maneuvers at the upper end (west) of this freight house, just east of Walnut Street. In all, the freight-handling facility encompassed nearly four city blocks.

O.P. started a schedule that he maintained almost to the minute and held to it every working day. After lunch he generally read for a while, then just before leaving home he shined his shoes. In the summer he performed this shoe-shining ritual on the chopping block in the woodshed; in winter, on the first step of the inside cellarway. He left home at precisely 1:45 P.M. and picked up a machinist who worked the same hours at the roundhouse in Williamsport. It normally took only thirty-five minutes to drive to Williamsport, but he left early to park his car in the storage garage and walk the three blocks to the yard office. There he marked up, donned his work clothes, and went to the engine house to take his B6 out at 3:35 P.M. He reasoned that if he had any problems with the automobile he would still have time to get to work on time. "The railroad," he would say, "doesn't wait on you if you are late."

Once out working at the freight house, O.P. handled the engine until around 5:30 P.M., at which time he would trade positions with the fireman, who took over running until around 8:00 p.m., when the entire crew took their twenty-minute break. While the fireman ran the B6, O.P. ate his lunch. Then, on their break, he poked around, visiting a neighborhood grocery on Hepburn Street to purchase a snack, maybe going to a fish market on Fifth Street near where the engine was parked, or, if they happened to be at Walnut Street, going to a barber shop to get a shave.

He never had to worry about his fireman handling the engine. The men he had on the left side had all worked as engineers until the Depression, when they were set all the way back to firing. And the twenty minutes allowed for break usually extended beyond the time limit, which was not the crew's fault. Their switching chores completed, the train of cars to be set off at locations outside yard limits assembled, they still had to await permission to occupy the main before heading east on their transfer run. By the time clearance was received it was usually 9:00 p.m. or later.

Every night the first place to be served was a large oil and gas pipeline storage-tank terminal located across the river east of Allens Tower. Empty tank cars were set off, and loaded cars were picked up. From there they backed up past Allens, heading west up the south side cut-off branch. The first stop was at Maynard Street in South Williamsport, where they switched at an industrial complex and occasionally at a retail coal dealer's unloading docks. Continuing west up the south side, they arrived at the Linden (Nisbet) coaling facility, where loaded cars of company coal and sand were switched off and empties picked up. When this was completed, all that remained was getting clearance to run east on the main into the city, but sometimes this point became a bottleneck. All other trains had preference over this transfer job. Freights and numerous passenger movements in and out of Williamsport after 11:00 p.m. held O.P. before he could get back to the roundhouse. Many times it was 3:00 or 4:00 a.m. before he marked off.

It didn't take my sister and me long to realize that O.P.'s second-trick job offered us a perfect opportunity to go to the movies in Williamsport on Saturdays. At first we would go out to my oldest sister's home, have our evening meal with her and her family, attend the 7:00 p.m. show, then return to her home. When O.P. marked off, he would retrieve us there. This arrangement didn't last long before O.P. suggested we attend the 9:00 p.m. performance and be waiting for him either at the storage garage or at the Pennsy Lunch restaurant. It suited me best to go to the restaurant, where I could watch the activities of the busy yards at Walnut Street. My sister, not interested in such things, would go instead to the storage garage. O.P. soon extended another privilege: letting me go into the yard office to inquire whether he would be quitting on time. He stressed that I shouldn't bother the clerks or linger within this office.

When O.P. was late coming in, I would make a second visit to check on his whereabouts. During this second inquiry the clerks often invited me to sit down and visit with them. Usually during these early morning hours, things were slow and they had time for conversation. It was enlightening to learn how well versed they were in the behind-the-scenes functions connected with railroad operations, such as calling out crews, notifying crews of the number of the engine they'd been assigned, posting mark-up times, and the like. (Most of the clerks I came to know rose to prominent positions in later years.) Even the yardmasters were friendly, and I became well acquainted with many of these gentlemen. One revealed that he had been a brakeman on O.P.'s first crew in 1909, when he'd worked the Williamsport yards.

Another place I frequented was the crossing watchman's shanty, where I would visit with the man that guarded the busy Walnut Street crossing with a long wooden pole with a Stop sign affixed at the top. Standing in the middle of the street with his sign, he carried a red flag in the daytime hours, and a red lantern after dark, to warn motorists to stop for an approaching train. The place I spent most of the time when O.P. was working late was in the switch tender's shanty, located directly across the tracks from the yard office. This spacious structure had wooden benches attached to three of the walls, a large cabin-type stove, and a multitude of windows that permitted easy viewing of all movements regardless of their direction. Most of the yard train crewmen, conductors, and brakemen used this shanty, hanging their lanterns all around the walls. Before the third-trick crews went on duty, they would fill the lantern's pot with kerosene and meticulously clean the glass globes with wadded-up sheets of dampened newspaper. When the second-trick men completed their work day, they would enter to hang up their lanterns.

I couldn't help but notice that the majority of the lanterns belonging to these trainmen were New York Central issues, which were preferred for the much larger globe than their squat Pennsylvania counterparts. At home we had a couple of New York Central lanterns O.P. had garnered somewhere along the way, and used them when we went fishing at night. They emitted more light than the Company's models. The switch tender, however, carried a lantern similar to the ones used by the car inspectors, which cast a single wide beam of light that was better suited to walking and throwing switches, although he kept a lighted red lantern hung by the door, ready for use in an emergency. Something else drew my attention when I first entered this shanty: inscribed in chalk on one of the walls was a running list of dates that indicated the first snowfall of the season for at least the past fifteen years.

The switch tender was busy most of the time, carrying out the duties his title implied. He knew in advance of all movements coming in and going out of the yards that used the main, and he set the switches for entry to or for leaving the main. Even the passenger trains entering or departing from the Park Hotel station on the eastern end were routed by his switch settings. One of the switches that required the most attention was the inlet track leading to or from the roundhouse. All light engines coming into or going out of the house used this track, with the occasional exception of an engine that would use a track at the eastern end of the facility. Through freights or passengers would acknowledge the switch tender's lantern signal with two short whistle blasts, indicating that the engineers knew the switches were aligned properly.

At the time O.P. began working the yard and transfer crew, four other regular crews worked the yards on all three tricks, six days a week, plus the "basin" yard job that switched on the Canal Branch. This branch left the main traveling east, just west of Rose Street, and switched the industries that were once located on the former canal's basin, so the job description was accurate in this sense. Besides serving the many plants and factories in this area, it also took care of numerous commercial establishments along the line that continued through the lower section of downtown Williamsport to end a few blocks east of Market Street. The entire route, parallel to both the Company's and the Reading's main, ran close to the Reading at some places, but the latter railroad had no access to the industries there. To traverse the light rails on this branch and switch the short, tight switches, this job rated a special-class engine, an A5 0-4-0. It resembled the B6 0-6-0, only in miniature, and was the only engine of this class in the entire region. It was thus easy to remember its number: 1203.

Unlike the other yard jobs, basin crews only worked the first and second tricks. Rose Street wasn't the only way to enter and exit this branch; the crew could also use Hepburn Street, running on tracks embedded in the middle of this downtown artery. It differed from the other yard jobs in another aspect: crews used a four-wheel wooden cabin, a sister to the one O.P. used on out-of-town runs.

The crew that O.P. drew on the newly created job were all veteran rail-roaders who had seniority over almost all the other men performing yard chores. O.P. didn't have to work very long with them to find that they all were congenial and went about their assignments in an efficient manner. He described them according to the way they conducted themselves while working their assignments. One of the brakemen was a slender, slightly built individual who opted to ride the cars to pull the pins when engaged in cutting cars; he was always whistling, whatever he was doing. The other brakeman was a large man, at least six feet four inches tall, who was elected to set and throw all the switches. Side by side, these two men resembled the comic-strip characters Mutt and Jeff. The conductor was of average size and, when working, always wore his false teeth in his vest pocket. The fireman was just a little taller than O.P., and a person who found many things during the work day amusing; he was always laughing about one thing or another.

Soon after O.P. started on his new duties, a matter arose that required an audience with the yardmaster in his office that included the fireman. The yardmaster presented the two men with a message he had received from the superintendent's office but written and composed by his assistant. The subject was unnecessary engine smoke at the east end of the freight house. Several phone calls had been made to Number 9 by the irate owner of a gasoline service station situated on the southwest corner of Hepburn Street, next to the railroad crossing. The yardmaster explained that he was only conveying the message and that this discussion was not to be construed as a reprimand, but from now on they were to avoid causing an excess amount of smoke when working in this area.

After leaving the office, the fireman and O.P. discussed this matter but agreed that a B6 was not a smoky locomotive and that if they were guilty they hadn't been aware of the excess smoke. Between them they determined that usually before pulling a string of cars out of one of the freight-house tracks— sometimes thirty or more cars—a few shovelfuls of coal would be placed in the firebox, in order to get a full head of steam. Because they occupied the single-track main, and also blocked off three major streets leading in and out of downtown Williamsport (Hepburn, Pine, and Market), all the cutting moves had to be made as expeditiously as possible, therefore requiring lots of steam. And enough steam could be generated only by putting coal in the firebox. That was probably when the 0-6-0 exhausted more than a little smoke.

For the next few days the fireman abided by the yardmaster's request, and the service-station owner was evidently pacified, because to the best of their knowledge no more calls were made to Number 9. The truce, however, was short-lived. The fireman came up with a solution of his own to reduce smoke emissions and still keep the boiler hot, and O.P. wasn't consulted. Parked alongside the main loading dock and under the protective overhanging roof of the large freight-house facility, the fireman got off onto the platform, which was level with the deck on the B6, and began gathering large pieces of timber that had been used to shore up materials in the boxcars and arranging them on one side of the coal pile. O.P. didn't seem to regard that as anything out of the ordinary; crew members usually piled discarded boards and timbers on the pilot, on the tender's rear platform, even up the swallow-tailed slope. One brakeman once gathered enough of this material to construct a barn on his farm. O.P. was aware that the fireman had come back on board, but he didn't pay any attention to what he was doing, because he was looking back for the conductor's signal that it was clear to pull the drag out of the freight house.

Just before he got the signal, the fireman came over, and, standing in the gangway, announced, "Oscar, I'm firing with wood instead of coal. That'll keep the smoke down." O.P. didn't say anything as he started pulling the cars out. "See that, Oscar?" the fireman said. "There's hardly any smoke. It's working."

Out of curiosity O.P. looked up at the stack and was alarmed to see a shower of sparks flying out, and increasing with every exhaust. Soon a solid stream of red-hot material was emitted. At this he told the fireman to take a look at the stack and see how well his brilliant idea was working now. "If you don't set that gas station on fire," O.P. said, "you'll probably blow it up."

The fireman's reaction was just the opposite of what O.P. expected. He roared with laughter, exclaiming, "Oscar, that looks better than most of the fireworks they have on the Fourth of July."

Working the 0-6-0 hard, the shower of sparks persisted until they were near Market Street, at which time it was shut off. O.P. instructed the fireman to cover his wood fire with coal before they started cutting cars. Enough sparks had been discharged to start fires anywhere along this three-block area. He also told the fireman, "We're both probably going to be given time off to think about your idea to cut down on smoke. I'll bet the phones in Number 9 are ringing off the hooks about now. At least we'll have an opportunity to talk to the superintendent when he calls us on the carpet."

After a few days their fears abated. No one, it seemed, had seen the display of sparks other than the crew members, and nothing was ever heard from the upper offices. Thoughts that the fireman had given up his shenanigans, however, proved premature. Coming out of the freight house with a string of cars, the fireman pointed out a pile of tires lying on an outside loading platform that ran along Fifth Street. Saying that some of them might fit his automobile, he dropped off to examine them after the cutting procedure was finished. Three of the tires suited him, and O.P. watched as he brought them over to the parked engine and threw them on deck. The tires didn't appear to be too healthy, but O.P. didn't question his selections.

Receiving a signal from the conductor, O.P. backed the B6 into the freight house and coupled to another string of cars. As usual, he leaned out the cab window to look to the rear for the go-ahead motion from the conductor. When the signal was given, he released the independent brake, turned on the bell, opened up on the throttle, and, when he turned around, saw the entire area on his side enveloped in a pall of dense, black smoke. His suspicions were confirmed when he got a whiff of the smoke. It smelled like burning rubber, and he realized then that the fireman had squeezed the just-salvaged tires into the firebox, again while O.P. was preoccupied watching for signals. A light breeze had carried the black cloud right over the service station, completely obscuring it. But the worst part was just beginning. Each exhaust lifted this dense smoke higher, and it started drifting directly toward downtown Williamsport.

This prank not only amused the fireman, it had him convulsing in uproarious laughter. He was laughing so hard it looked like he was going to fall out of the gangway. In between spasms he blurted out, "Look at that, Oscar. That S.O.B. running the service station turned us in for a little coal smoke, so I decided to show him some real smoke for a change!"

Black smoke continued to belch out of the stack until they were in the vicinity of Pine Street. The tires were consumed faster than the wooden timbers, and the fire started burning clean. Realizing what the outcome of this incident could be, O.P. told the fireman, "Somehow you fail to consider how serious your monkeyshines are. As soon as some of the city officials find the business district fouled up with this cloud of rubber smoke, someone will be sent out here to investigate, and when they find out it came from our engine, we'll see a flock of Company men down here. We'll be lucky if they don't can us both."

But again his fears again were unfounded. No one even came near them, nor did they ever hear from any Company officials. But the fireman's attempt to agitate the service station proprietor failed once more.

The vendetta the fireman was having with the gas-station owner seemed to pass, but not entirely. In the days that followed, O.P. occasionally noticed that an excessive amount of smoke would roll out of the stack while the B6 was laying-in on the freight-house tracks and the wind was blowing in the right direction. No other warnings about the smoke problem were ever received. O.P. decided the proprietor had probably given in, perhaps concluding that complaining didn't bring about the results he wanted.

With O.P. home every day, and with regular work hours, we had the opportunity to do more activities as a family. We would accompany him to Williamsport, and there were Sunday walks in the mountains again, and help with homework. For my part, one of the best things was going hunting with O.P. on Saturday mornings.

In the fall of 1937 the Pennsylvania Game Commission changed its hunting regulations, dropping the license age limit from fourteen to twelve years.

Now I qualified, having reached my thirteenth birthday in October. That I had a hunting license and could legally carry a firearm, though, did not make me an expert hunter. There was much to learn about the sport, but O.P. was a good teacher. Somehow he knew almost exactly where to find the quarry we were hunting, whether rabbits or ringneck pheasants. And when we did find them, he rarely missed a shot.

The areas we usually hunted were north of Ralston, starting just beyond the water plug at Leolyn and working our way toward Grover, either along the swampy ground or in the hills along both sides of the railroad. Ringneck pheasants seemed to prefer the low-lying swamp area, while rabbits abounded in the higher regions. Sometimes we traveled farther, to an area between Canton and Alba known locally as Minnequa, where the terrain was similar to that at Leolyn except that on the east side of the tracks there was an apple orchard ideally suited for rabbit cover.

After hunting a few times at both these locations, my curiosity was aroused, and I asked my father how he knew exactly where to find the game we were looking for. He explained that on his many trips up and down the branch, on dikers or the EC's, he had noticed where the pheasants hung out during daylight runs. The rabbits revealed their whereabouts at night, in the powerful beam of his headlight. Now all we had to do was hunt them out.

Hunting in the proximity of the railroad led to other discoveries, and O.P. was available to answer my many questions or call my attention to certain things he thought I should be aware of. One of the first things he pointed out was at the west end of the Leolyn siding attached to the top of the switch target: a yellow sign with the letters "SS," which, I learned, translated into "spring switch." The purpose of the switch was to allow trains to leave the siding at faster speeds, because it automatically sprang shut, eliminating the need to close it manually and wait for the trainman to get back on board. Such a device at this location was important. It allowed trains to leave the siding on the downgrade and to gain more momentum going through Grover Cut to make it easier to ascend the Cedar Ledge grade into Canton.

On a later outing I was able to see how this switch operated. A diker came up the main and stopped, and the head engine cut off. The brakeman manually threw the switch, permitting the I1 to back down through the switch to the water plug. When it came up the siding after taking water, no one touched the switch, and once the engine cleared the siding it closed automatically, allowing the I1 to back down to its train. Once the engine coupled up, air tests were made and the process of calling the flag began.

During the latter procedure, O.P. called my attention to the exhaust steam coming from the shrill screecher whistle, pointing out that it was audible only when it first began sounding. As it was opened to the full extent, there was no sound, for it reached such a high pitch that the human ear couldn't hear the sound. While watching this, he pointed out that this type of whistle was well suited to engines carrying 205 pounds of steam pressure. When the I1's were developed and the steam pressure elevated to 250 pounds, whistles were out-of-date, no longer served their intended purpose, and emitted a sound that was not audible, especially at close range. The Company nevertheless continued to use them.

Once the diker was under motion, O.P. told me to watch how quickly it picked up speed, noting that by the time the pushers went by the milk plant in Grover, less than a mile west, the train would be going better than 40 miles an hour. On another Saturday morning while we were hunting in the Minnequa area, he pointed out that the I1 leading a train heading westbound was drifting. It was on a downgrade after surmounting the grade into Canton and would drift until it reached Alba. The pushers were still working; they never shut off. Their job was to hold the slack in on these roller-coaster grades.

On our way home from a morning hunt north of Ralston, O.P. casually asked whether I was planning to go to Williamsport with him on Saturday afternoon or would spend the rest of the day in the woods in back of our house pursuing squirrels, as had been my routine since the opening of small-game season.

I replied that I'd like to accompany him because there was a movie I'd like to see, so he surprised me by suggesting that if I went to the early-evening show and got back to the Hepburn Street crossing by 9:00 P.M. I could ride along, either with him on the B6 or in the cabin with the train crew. It didn't take me any time to accept, assuring him I'd be there, and, if I could, telling him I'd prefer to ride on the 0-6-0 with him. Only one thing came to mind: "Where will I ride? There's hardly enough room in the cab." That would be no problem, he responded. "You can ride either with the fireman or behind me on my seat box. They're wide enough for two people to ride comfortably."

Following his instructions, I arrived at the Hepburn Street crossing shortly before 9:00 P.M. and found the B6 resting on one of the tracks along Fifth Street. As I climbed aboard, O.P. greeted me as he slid the doors open at the back of the cab. He advised me to sit behind him on the seat box and told me they hadn't completed their work yet. A cut of cars still had to be taken out of the freight house and switched before we would depart on the nightly rounds. We waited for a train to enter the yards, and as soon as it cleared the main the conductor gave his lantern signal for us to back into the freight house to couple onto a string of cars.

Again at his lantern signal we moved out across Hepburn Street and continued on to the main. We moved east across Pine Street all the way to beyond Market Street. All the major streets leading in and out of downtown Williamsport were blocked, and on the busiest night of the week. The stores had just closed, and people were coming from or attempting to reach the four movie theaters. Needless to say, they announced their irritation by blowing their horns. The only one enjoying this blockage was the fireman, who shouted across the deck, "Listen to those silly people, Oscar. You'd think they were going someplace in a hurry." Then he broke into hearty laughter.

The crossings were tied up for some time too. After the first cut we cleared Market Street, but for the others, after making the first cut, we pulled ahead, still blocking Pine Street and Hepburn Street. It wasn't until the cutting was complete that all the crossings were cleared. O.P. pointed out that the crossing watchmen were also getting a workout. Each time the gates were lowered from their tower position they had to pump them back up with a large wooden lever that provided the needed air pressure.

During the entire maneuver, O.P. was leaning out the cab window operating the engine running in reverse motion with his right hand, and it amazed me how he deftly selected each control without even glancing at their position. He turned on the bell valve, changed the position of the reverse lever, opened the throttle to the desired amount of steam, worked the independent air-brake lever, and even applied sand by flickering the sand valve to keep the 0-6-0 from sliding as it came to a stop when the cars were cut off. Once the cars and cabin were made up for the transfer run, no time was lost coupling the B6 onto this consist. We left town running forward eastbound faster than I thought this type of engine could go. After passing Allens Tower, we ran the double-track main for approximately two miles to Sylvan Dell, where we set off six tank cars at the petroleum storage facility there and picked up four loaded cars. Once that was accomplished we started a backing movement, going now in a westerly direction pushing the cabin past Allens and up the south side freight-line cutoff.

At the west end of South Williamsport, two boxcars were placed at an industrial plant and two loaded cars were picked up. From there we continued on to the Company's coaling station at Linden (Nesbit). The cabin had led the train all the way up the south side, and at each grade crossing the plaintive air whistle could be heard sounding its warning. We set off four loaded cars of coal plus a car of sand—enough, O.P. commented, to keep the steam-powered clamshell crane busy until he came back on Monday night. This machine could also move on the rails, positioning cars to be unloaded and setting out the empties for pickup. That night we also picked up four empties, and when these were coupled up to the train it gave us a total of ten cars plus the cabin. Backing up to the tower, O.P. got off to receive orders for the return trip into Williamsport—and he was lucky: he got clearance to occupy the single main into the city. Heading east again, we were running in a forward position at around 30 miles an hour, and at that speed the 0-6-0 rode rather smoothly, with no bobbing or weaving.

One of the best things connected with this last portion of our trip was my being appointed bell-ringer. O.P. let me know when I should operate this valve, but he wouldn't blow the whistle because that was prohibited by city ordinances. When we returned to the yards, I dropped off at the Walnut Street crossing on the side opposite to the yard office, and the train continued down one of the side tracks. The B6 was cut off and headed for the engine house to be parked for the night. After that, I rode with O.P. and his crew on most of my Saturday visits to Williamsport, not always in the cab of the engine but in the cupola on the cabin as well.

One night, just before we left the city on the transfer run, I learned how to make instant coffee. The brakeman, noting that the pot was empty, suggested that I come with him to see how this brew was concocted. Placing the fresh ground coffee in the pot, we went forward to the B6 and he hollered up to O.P. sitting in the cab: "Crack the injector, Oscar. I need some hot water for coffee." When it began to gurgle and live steam and a small amount of water came out of the discharge pipe, the pot was placed where this emission filled it. Taking our product back to the cabin, it was placed on the stove, and a small amount of cold water was poured in to settle the grounds. The coffee was ready to drink.

At the beginning of my train-riding my mother scolded O.P. mildly for taking me along: "Oscar, you shouldn't take him along on that dirty engine when he has his good clothing on. He'll be filthy when he wants to dress up again to go anywhere." But that didn't bother O.P., who countered, saying, "I think we have enough money to get the boy's clothes cleaned if he soils them." Fortunately I never seemed to get dirty; both the cab of the B6 and the cabin were clean.

Although I did not ride with O.P. or the crew on every trip I made to Williamsport, I did go along frequently. On one cold winter day the weather was anything but favorable; it had snowed all day, and it was still snowing when I went to the early movie. When I emerged from the theater at 9:00 P.M. it had stopped, but a different sight greeted me: traffic was jammed on Fourth Street. I soon discovered what was holding up traffic—the basin crew was coming out of the Canal Branch on Hepburn Street. The little A5 had eight cars plus the cabin in tow, and it was tying up not only Fourth Street but also the other major east-west lane, Third Street.

The 0-4-0 was having a difficult time. The some eight or ten inches of snow that had fallen during the day was packed down on the brick pavement of Hepburn Street, completely erasing any signs of the rails embedded in the middle of this means of exit. The train could make only about 15 feet of forward progress before it would end in a spin, then reverse, back about the same distance, and repeat the performance. To watch all this from a different angle, I walked away from the small crowd of people gathered on the corner and took a position alongside the daily newspaper's building on Hepburn Street. From there, with a head-on view of the 1203, I witnessed possibly the strangest thing a locomotive ever accomplished: making a forward charge, the A5 left the middle of the street and came to a stop up against the right curb.

The engine crew got off, surveyed the situation, and got back aboard. Then the engineer reversed the 0-4-0 and, as if on rails, backed it on the "track" it had made in the hardened snow to the middle of the street without slipping a wheel. Realizing that it would take a long time for the basin crew to get out to the main, I left, hoping I hadn't spent too much time watching this maneuver and missed going along with O.P. for the remainder of the Saturday night's outing.

When I approached the Hepburn Street crossing, I was surprised to see the B6 still there, but then I realized no one was in the cab. The cabin, a newer wooden model called a "Mae West" because of the offset cupola, was parked nearby. This cabin, which had four-wheel trucks that replaced the old four-wheel model, was rare in the area, and I wanted to take a closer look. It was called a "Mae West" because it was an N6 model, with an offset cupola. I went straight up to the cabin, and once inside found all the crew members there, except O.P. I was told that he was at the call box getting running orders to leave the city. Most of the seating in the large cabin was taken, so I climbed up onto a seat in the cupola, where I could hear the conversation and my presence wouldn't be a distraction. Before long, O.P. entered, and from the tone of his voice I knew immediately that he was upset: he was using a version of the King's English I had never heard him use. Most of his attention was directed to the yardmaster for bringing the basin crew out by way of Hepburn Street, allowing, in so many words, that this man should have his head examined. What made the matter worse was that they had to wait until this crew was out and cleared. It was bringing a large, oversize boiler that had to be taken up the south-side cutoff to Linden without delay tonight, because of a New York Central bridge in Newberry, and at the rate the A5 was coming it would take another half-hour before he broke a track out to the main.

Next he focused on the yardmaster, telling the crew that if this man had an ounce of sense he would have directed the 1203 out the usual exit at Rose

Street, that they could have picked up the boiler car at that point and would have been on their way by now. About this time he noticed me sitting in the cupola. Greeting me sheepishly, he explained that everything was all messed up that night and that there wasn't much anyone could do about it.

Vacating my lofty perch, I went along with O.P. to climb aboard the waiting 0-6-0, where we sat watching the 1203 struggle against the elements. While we were waiting, he explained that the boiler was too high to be routed through the yards. The New York Central overpass at the west end of New-berry was too low to handle anything over normal freight car sizes. This is where the yard and transfer crew came into the picture. The boiler would be shuffled east to Allens, then west on the southside cutoff to Linden, where a westbound through freight would pick it up for delivery somewhere farther west. The only good thing about this forced delay was that they were not taking cars to Sylvan Dell or conducting any switching on the south side that night. They only had to deliver the boiler plus the usual cars of company coal and sand.

It was nearly 10:00 P.M. before we left the yards, and O.P. didn't waste any time, especially on the backing move up the south-side freight cutoff, running the B6 at least 35 miles an hour all the way. At Linden the coal, sand, and boiler cars were set off, and five empty hoppers and seven boxcars were picked up. With the assembled train and the Mae West cabin, we backed farther, to the tower, where we sat ready to enter the eastbound single track for the trip back into the city.

O.P. climbed off and went to the tower for his running orders, and before long reappeared in a hurry. When he got back aboard the engine, he told the fireman that the dispatcher had given him clearance but that he was allowed only ten minutes to get back into the yards. They had to clear off the main by 11:00 P.M.

After we crossed the river bridge, it was a straight line all the way to Williamsport, and O.P. took advantage of that by really opening up the B6. It wasn't long before we were running faster than I thought an 0-6-0 could manage, at least 40 miles an hour. The maximum allowable speed for a B6 was 35 miles an hour when the engine was proceeding forward. According-ing to the books, the danger of higher speeds was the stress placed on the equalizer bar located beneath the front of the boiler. This bar was designed to take the strain that the pony trucks on a conventional engine absorbed. Too much speed could cause the bar to snap. Knowing this, I asked: "Pop, aren't you traveling faster than you're supposed to with a B6? Won't the equalizer bar break?"

"No," he said, "there's nothing to worry about. We have a good-size train behind us. Besides, I'm giving her plenty of steam. That'll take the load off the equalizer."

We didn't slacken our pace until we neared the Park Hotel passenger station, and during our sprint the B6 acted as O.P. said it would. All it demonstrated was some lateral motion, but it didn't bob up and down much at all—not nearly as badly as one might expect at our speed.

Using an automobile to travel back and forth to work every day caused some problems at first. In the early fall of 1937, the Auburn started to use oil, so we took it to Lycoming Motors, the firm that originally built the engine, for an overhaul. The motor was totally rebuilt, oversizing and reboring valve seats and cylinders. When the job was completed the car ran better than it did new. The only misgiving we had about the oversized assembly was the resultant gas consumption.

Normally, the Auburn averaged about eight miles a gallon of gasoline, but after the overhaul the best it would produce was five miles a gallon, so it used ten gallons of fuel for the 50-mile round-trip daily. Although gasoline only cost 16 or 17 cents a gallon, O.P. determined that the Auburn was costing more than a day's wages each week traveling to and from work. The owner of the garage he patronized in Williamsport offered a solution. He lent O.P. a used 1932 Model-B four-cylinder Ford coupe to try, to see if it would be more economical to operate. This vehicle did operate efficiently. During the week O.P. used the coupe, the cost for gasoline was only $2.50, compared with the $11.00 or more for the eight-cylinder Auburn. But O.P. wasn't satisfied with the Ford so he returned it.

My sister and I weren't happy about that, though. Nearing the age of becoming licensed drivers, we felt that the Ford coupe would be ideal for our purposes. But O.P. solved the fuel economy situation the following March, when he traded the Auburn in on a new 1938 tan four-cylinder, four-door Willys-Overland sedan. This move from a luxury model to one of the smallest cars on the market served his purpose well, and that sedan proved to be a dependable form of transportation.

O.P.'s yard and transfer job was mostly routing, but the improving economy in the latter years of the Depression was reflected in an increased amount of traffic on the railroad. Another change came about in 1938, when more crews were needed to handle the additional freight. Furloughed men were called back, and bumping, especially among firemen, was taking place. Although O.P. still had veteran firemen to work with, none seemed to stay with him very long. During the summer of 1938, movements through Ralston were also on the rise. Dikers loaded with coal heading north, and empty hoppers heading in the opposite direction, dominated the scene.

That summer it was no longer necessary for me to wait at trackside for O.P. to pass through. Besides, I once again was permitted to enjoy the afternoons swimming, so my time was pretty well occupied. However, on cool or overcast days I still idled time away at the water plug, but now with a certain purpose in mind: I was determined to duplicate O.P.'s distinctive whistle signal.

As usual, most of the westbounds pulled through to the upper end of the old yards, making them impractical for my purpose, so I concentrated on the eastbound that stopped to take water. Oiling around the locomotive with the engineer, I would ask him if I could climb aboard the I1, now the exclusive motive power on the through runs. When my request was granted, I would make another request: permission to call the flag. The first question the engineer would ask was, "Do you know how many times to blow for us to whistle off?" and I would reply, "You're eastbound, so I'll blow four long blasts." The response would be, "How do you know that's the right signal?"

When I replied that my father was an engineer and taught me the whistle signals, "What's your dad's name?" was the next question, and I'd answer proudly, "Oscar Orr." I learned to tolerate the stock remark that answer drew: "Oh, I know Oscar, but I'll tell you one thing: he's no good. But go ahead and call the flag."

What I had assumed would be an easy feat—to duplicate O.P.'s whistle—did not turn out as I'd expected. I would blow three longs (in the cab with the roof hatch open, the high-pitched screecher whistle was a deafening sound), and on the fourth blast I'd try to low the whistle off. To my dismay, everything worked just as I wanted until I reached the midpoint, at which time the whistle valve would start chattering and emit a series of staccato toots.

Not giving up, I tried to match the lowed-off whistle on various other occasions but always failed. Somehow I couldn't get the whistle valve to stop chattering. However, I must have been pretty close to sounding something like O.P. My mother noted she often heard someone trying to mimic his whistle, but it wasn't quite right, as usual, and it didn't fool her.

One time I even received a compliment of sorts from an engineer who wasn't as inquisitive as some of the other head-end men. All he wanted to know was whether I knew the proper sequence before calling the flag, and where I learned it. He allowed me to perform the ritual, and as usual it didn't turn out as I'd wanted on the fourth blast. When I finished, the engineer exclaimed, maybe with a hint of scorn, "Boy, you sound just like a Bald Eagle Branch man. They're always trying to play a tune with the whistle," and in the next breath he asked, "Who'd you say your dad was?" When I answered "Oscar Orr" it brought forth a chuckle. "I've known Oscar for years, and I've heard him play that tune lots of times. I guess I should have recognized it." Without any more conversation he gave me the normal command, "You'd better get off. We've got to get this train to Altoona." By the time I reached the bottom step of the gangway, the I1 was already in motion.

Deciding that my attempts to duplicate O.P.'s strange whistle sounds were futile, I gave up. I was at a dead end. My only salvation was to consult my father to learn the proper procedure, but that wasn't productive, either. It was one of the only times he didn't give me the answer I needed. Instead, he just smiled when I told him about the trouble I ran into when the whistle was lowed to just the midpoint, but he did promise that he'd explain one day. "Better still," he said, "I'll show you how to control the whistle valve until it shuts off." (He never revealed the secret, though, despite many promises to do so.)

The times I was associating with engine crews and answering questions about my credentials or ability to correctly call the flag, I often got inquiries about my father. One engineer, upon learning my identity asked, "I haven't seen Oscar for quite a while. Where's he working these days?" Replying that he had the second-trick yard and transfer crew in the Williamsport yards brought about an answer I'd heard previously from one of the local fireman: "I guess I did know he was in the yard. From what I heard, that's where he'll be until he retires. They made him an 8A-1 man."

Those remarks troubled me, and when I told my father what was being said, he didn't react too kindly either, stating firmly, "If I was an 8A-1 man I would have told you. You can believe those fellows if you want to, but I'm telling you now it isn't true. I'd leave the yards today if I could get a run that would allow me to be back home every night. I've told you I was tired of living on the road, working all kinds of ungodly hours, and making do from a traveling bag." That explanation sufficed, and I never again mentioned his status, although from time to time he still expressed a desire to go back out on the road, provided he could be home the same day.

Time seemed to pass rapidly at the end of the 1930s. O.P. still was content with the yard and transfer crew, and nothing out of the ordinary took place. The only mishap on this job came one evening when two elderly women in a brand-new Ford sedan crashed through the crossing gates at Hepburn Street just as a cut of cars was switched off. The automobile was demolished, but no serious injuries resulted.

A monthly magazine that O.P. received became the object of my interest: *The Brotherhood of Locomotive Engineers Journal*. For quite some time I only read the joke section and "True Stories of the Rail," but as I grew older, the technical aspects relating to the development of other railroads for new steam locomotives began to intrigue me. These articles led to discussions about the features being incorporated on new steam locomotives, increased steam pressure, larger combustion chambers, roller bearings, and the like, and how many existing engines were being modernized to incorporate these innovations.

As usual, I had many questions for my father, primarily about the Pennsylvania's seeming lack of interest in many of those features. He was always ready with his understanding of the Company's position. Much of the money they had went into the electrification program and electric locomotives during the Depression era, and because the steam power they had was adequate to handle all the traffic being generated, nothing new was added. Some modifications, such as streamlining a few K4's, installing different valve motions, and making boiler changes on a few engines, were introduced. But nothing really new came out of the erecting shops where engines were built or overhauled the same as new.

Two devices that seemed to be practical were being put on some of the newer engines. Their use on long runs was expected to reduce the cost of operations. One was a back pressure gauge that indicated the proper setting of the valve motion; the other was a speedometer. Much to my surprise, O.P. labeled both these items "gadgets." In his view, they were not a necessity, just something more to break down on an engine and cause the shop men more headaches. In the long run they would be just another worthless attachment, he said. "Besides," he added, "I can put my head out of the cab window to listen to the bark of the exhaust and set my engine up just as close as any gauge they can develop. Plus, I'll go just as far on coal and water as an engineer using this gadget will." He did concede that it might be a help to some of the enginemen who had trouble setting an engine up, though, providing the gauge was accurate at all times.

He also regarded the speedometer as an unnecessary feature. "After you run any of the classes for a period of time, you can pretty well judge the speed you're traveling. A lot depends on the track you have to run on, but mainly you handle an engine so it's steaming good, not using an excessive amount of water, and riding like it should. If you want to know exactly how fast you're going, all you have to do is time yourself between the mileposts." The engineer that designed these gadgets would have lost money trying to sell them to O.P.

As a labor-oriented publication, the primary objective of the *Brotherhood of Locomotive Engineers Journal* was to keep Brotherhood members informed of all activities relating to all railroads and of how their livelihoods were directly affected by various actions. Concern was always expressed about work rules, the need for increased safety, and the federal government's position on all matters pertaining to the railways. One of the most common editorial subjects was how the government was spending tax monies, even the portion railroads contributed, on other forms of transportation, especially waterways, trucks, and buses; airplanes were not yet a concern. The plan to construct the St. Lawrence Seaway with tax dollars seemed to be topmost among editorial objections. Work rules, better working conditions, increased take-home pay, shorter hours, and the like were ongoing topics—as they have been since the beginning of the railroads.

Elsewhere, information on safety measures and safety devices being installed on locomotives to prevent harm to engine crews predominated, and occasionally there were articles describing boiler explosions. Noting that these mishaps always occurred on other lines but never on the Pennsylvania, I approached O.P. for the causes of such tragedies. First, he explained, these accidents were in a sense due to the design of the boilers. They were more likely to occur on engines with a conical rounded top than on the flatter wagon-top Belpaires found on the Pennsylvania. However, when water was injected into any type of boiler that had a portion of the firebox crown sheet exposed, it caused such a sudden expansion of steam that all the built-in safety factors couldn't begin to handle the reaction.

However, human error or negligence was almost always the underlying problem. Engineers whose engine wasn't producing steam as it should were likely to use the injector as sparingly as possible, to keep the train moving, and if extreme care wasn't taken in that procedure, the water level would drop below the rounded crown sheet and result in an explosion. On the other hand, not paying close enough attention to the water bottle could allow the water in the boiler to become too low before the injector was used, with the same result.

By the summer of 1940, the economy was recovering from the throes of the Depression. Business on the railroad was increasing, and many of the men furloughed since 1930 were being called back to take their places on the roster again. But this recall did not affect the yard and transfer's train crew. These trainmen were classified as yard personnel, and there wasn't a better job for them to move up to in the Williamsport yard complex, so they stayed with O.P. Firemen, though, were not in the same category. They were now either being "set up running" or advancing themselves to the better-paying road jobs. The result was that O.P. had men working with him who had not shoveled coal into a firebox for many years.

The increase in freight traffic was reflected in the amount of work the yard and transfer job had to accomplish during a trick. A project that eventually drained an appreciable amount of revenue from the railroad was responsible for a sharp rise in car loadings for the Williamsport area in the late spring of 1940. This project, begun in 1939, was to be the initial highway of the future: the Pennsylvania Turnpike. Necessary in the construction of this elaborate roadway was concrete sand, and a local producer was awarded the contract to supply it from a pit along the river east of Williamsport, near the borough of Montoursville. The logical place to load the sand would have been the Reading Railroad's siding at the plant site, but the operator, in order to defray the interchange charges that would have accrued at the Reading's terminus in Newberry, opted to use the Pennsylvania. The sand was trucked some two miles to the Pennsylvania's Canal Branch and loaded on siding facilities that had been enlarged to handle the operation. This line was an extension of the Canal Branch that ran through the heart of Williamsport, and it paralleled the Reading line from the east end of the city to the west bank of Loyalsock Creek, where it terminated.

O.P.'s yard and transfer crew was assigned to take care of this operation. Every afternoon around 5:30 P.M. they took between twenty and twenty-two empty 70-ton hopper cars to the sand siding and returned with a similar number of loaded cars. This 10-mile round-trip usually took two to three hours, depending on when the main was available. The loaded cars were set off on a yard track, where they would be coupled to a westbound movement for delivery in the Pittsburgh area. In this way more than 120 cars loaded with sand were delivered every six days.

Later in the summer, O.P. acquired another fireman who had been called back after being furloughed for almost ten years, and by chance this man was a resident of Ralston, so they also rode back and forth to work together. On one occasion, this fireman talked about what a pleasure it was to work with O.P. He was not only an easy man to fire for, he said, but also, unlike many engineers, he shared the firing chores and O.P. allowed him to handle the engine. The fireman went on to tell how every afternoon around 5:30 P.M., when they were ready to leave the yard for the sand siding, O.P. would change positions with the fireman, saying it was time for him to eat lunch. Then, before he started eating, he shoveled an enormous amount of coal into the B6's firebox, climbed onto the seat box, and stayed there for about two hours, until they had the loaded sand cars put away in the yard.

O.P.'s firing method amazed this fireman. Pops were singing the entire time he was running the engine, even during an extremely hard drag coming up the stiff grade off the branch before entering the main with more than 1,400 tons behind the 0-6-0. All O.P. did was watch the steam gauge and occasionally open the injector when the pressure was nearing the pop-off degree. The fireman then confessed that when he tried the same firing method it didn't work well for him; he ended up with an unholy mess in the firebox, and it took the rest of the night to get his fire back in shape.

After giving this matter some thought, I reasoned that O.P. was using a version of the "bank-firing" procedure that he had seen used on the K4 when he rode over the Middle Division from Altoona to Harrisburg some years ago. When I asked him about this he immediately asked, "What makes you think that's how I'm firing?" Saying, then, that I was correct in my assumption, he added, "How did you find out what I was doing?"

I told him about my conversation with his fireman, then countered with a question: "Why didn't you explain this method to him and show him how to do it properly?"

He chuckled and said, "He watches me do this firing every evening, but he never asked me to tell him what I was doing or how, so I assumed he wasn't interested. Actually, it took me two or three trips to judge the right amount of coal to use, but the secret of it is that we are moving all the time and that the coal is vibrated enough to burn evenly. I only put the coal on the sides and in back of the firebox, keeping the front and middle light. When the fireman tried it, and I watched him, he put a whole wad of coal in the middle, and he found out to his dismay that this just wouldn't work."

Even my train-watching from school increased during the remainder of 1939 and into 1940. There was a constant daily procession of trains on the Elmira Branch through Ralston: loaded and empty dikers, locals, fast freights, passengers, plus light pushers moving in the midst of this increased flow of traffic. It really made one wonder how this single-track main handled all these movements. Probably the most remarkable factor was the coordination the dispatchers had to maintain with the block operators to keep this traffic constantly flowing.

There was even a very special movement to contend with in 1939. The King and Queen of England came through with their own English consist, engine and all, on their journey from upper New York State to Washington, D.C. This led to a discussion on British railroading, and O.P. was well versed on that subject, relating that in England the engine had not been equipped with a bell and headlight but was to meet American rules, that the rails were laid on concrete ties, and that fewer grades and curves were found in the English structure.

There had been no changes in the motive power the Pennsylvania was using through Ralston. Most of the trains were using I1's, M1's, L1's, or H9's on the locals, with occasionally an H6 on a work train or sometimes substituting for the E6's on the daytime passengers, or even a light B6 heading leisurely on its way to Southport. However, in the summer of 1940 I had the good fortune to see the newest steam engine the Pennsylvania had designed, and one I was sure would never grace the rails of the Elmira Branch. O.P. had acquired a pass for my sister and me to Philadelphia, and another from Philadelphia to New York, so we could attend the World's Fair.

In Philadelphia we stayed with my aunt, who had agreed to accompany us, along with our cousin from Lancaster, to this great event of the century. After spending the night in Philadelphia, we boarded an excursion early in the morning at the Broad Street Station, a train that was scheduled to take us directly onto the Fair site in New York. A restriction on our passes, made out to "The Dependent Son and Daughter of O.P. Orr, Engineman, Williamsport Division," stated that these credentials would not be honored on certain numbered trains listed, or on excursions, so we were ready to pay for the trip just for the convenience it offered, but the conductor never said a word except to tell us to have a good time.

Once out of Philadelphia, our GG1 electric locomotive picked up speed, and according to calculations I made with my Ingersoll pocket watch with the aid of mileposts, I clocked our movement at a steady 96 miles an hour. Arriving at the huge Fair complex, my aunt informed us that it would be impossible to see everything on these vast grounds in one day, so we would go to some of the featured highlights according to an agenda she had mapped out.

After attending some of the main attractions, we neared the area designated for the railroad displays. It was easily located, as coal smoke and steam were visible above the surrounding structures. My suggestion that we visit this display was rejected by my aunt, who explained that our itinerary wouldn't permit this unscheduled stop. Besides, she added, "Why would you want to pay to see some steam engines when you can watch them every day for free?" A wide opening in the fence around the display allowed me to peer in, so I did see the mighty S1 Duplex chugging away on rollers. Our day at the World's Fair ended at the Aquacade, where we saw not only the fabulous Billy Rose water show but also the fireworks display at the conclusion.

Back aboard the excursion late that night, we found many of the occupants in our coach had their windows raised, seeking some relief from the extremely hot and humid weather. Heading toward Philadelphia, and just as we were leaving the lighted skyline of New York City, an unbelievable stench filled the car. Windows were slammed shut, but the odor still persisted. Word passed through the coach that we were passing through an area used to raise pigs but that the pigs weren't the whole cause of the stink; much of it could be attributed to the garbage they were fed.

Back in Ralston, we related our experiences to my mother and O.P. I expressed regret that I did not see the railroad exhibit but added that I did manage to peek through the fence to see the Pennsylvania's new S1. O.P. was well read on that locomotive and, he said, he was not impressed by its qualifications. It was way out of proportion for practical use in hauling trains over the entire system, noting that the only area where it could be run was on the western divisions of the Company. He doubted whether any other locomotives of the class would be constructed. Again, his predictions were correct.

Early in the fall of 1940, I became interested in another form of transportation, the automobile, when I passed my operator's examination to become a licensed driver. Now both my youngest sister, who became eligible to drive in summer 1939, and I were driving O.P.'s car. Although we were novice drivers, few restrictions were imposed. We only had to tell my mother or O.P. what we were using the car for. We never had to request the keys, either. O.P. never locked the garage or removed the keys from the ignition when at home. All we were told was to use caution at all times. If we were to damage the vehicle it would be a hardship on O.P., who used it to get to and from work. In other words, it would jeopardize the livelihood of the family. In addition, he pointed out, the automobile was simply a machine: it could go backward or forward, fast or slow, start or stop, or do anything else you commanded it, except think. That was our responsibility. In the years to come, we drove the family car around our locality and in the city traffic of Williamsport without putting a blemish on its surface. The only thing O.P. ever blamed us for was when a tire went flat. Then he would accuse us of running the back alleys instead of staying on the main streets.

One day during the first week of December in 1940, O.P. presented the family with a present, and although it was a little before Christmas it was a pleasant surprise. Under cover of darkness, after finishing the second trick, he brought home a new 1941 Hudson Sedan. But by a strange quirk he did not have the opportunity to announce his surprise—it was discovered by my mother and sister. The senior class was conducting a soup sale to raise money for their spring graduation trip to Washington, D.C., and my sister had gone home to drive my mother down to the school, as she was selected to help with this venture. When they found this new vehicle in the garage, my mother was reluctant to use it, but my sister reasoned that if it was parked in our garage it belonged to us.

I became aware of this new automobile when I heard a horn blowing and, looking out my school window, saw the shiny maroon Hudson go by.

It didn't take long to figure out who it belonged to, either; horn-soundings were my sister's trademark. With her in the car were other senior-class girls, who, on the pretext of preparing for the soup sale, were riding around with my sister.

The new automobile wasn't exactly a surprise to me. O.P. had discussed the possibility of buying a new car earlier in the fall while we were hunting, and said only that he'd looked over the new model Hudsons at the dealership where he was having the Willys serviced and was favorably impressed. He had even asked me what I thought of this particular make and model, but I told him I knew very little about it, other than what ads in the newspapers and magazines had portrayed as its distinct virtues. No other person in our area owned one of the new Hudsons, so I couldn't offer any objective comparisons.

After the soup sale, which I attended, and with a little persuasion over my sister's objections, my mother permitted me to drive her home in the new automobile before the afternoon classes resumed. When we pulled into our backyard, O.P. had yet another surprise for us. Hanging in the apple tree was a nice buck deer he had bagged on his morning hunt. When congratulations on his successful hunt concluded, my mother questioned his purchase of a new vehicle. O.P. had logical reasons: first, that America was about to become involved in a war, which would probably make it impossible to buy a new car, and second, the Willys wasn't built to last much longer. In conclusion, he stated the real reason for his purchase: he never did like the small Willys; it just wasn't his kind of automobile.

War being waged by nations in many parts of the world was creating a profound surge in the economy due to preparations for America's inevitable involvement in armed conflict. On the railroad, all furloughed firemen had been recalled by the summer of 1941, and new men were being hired. O.P. was getting firemen on their initial trial trips at firing duties, the first new help he had on board an engine since before the Depression began in 1929.

One of these new recruits seemed to draw a special interest from O.P., who in a sense regarded him as his protégé. This man wasn't new on the Company's roll; he had previously worked as a crossing watchman and for some time as the second-trick guard at Walnut Street. Heading for the round-house each afternoon, O.P. had exchanged pleasantries with this young man over a period of time. When new fireman's applications were being accepted, this man, at O.P.'s suggestion, submitted his formal request to be added to the roster. Perhaps it was O.P.'s endorsement of the application that led to the young man's hiring as a fireman, and, once hired, the officials at the yard office gave him the opportunity to make his debut as an engineman on the

Williamsport Division with O.P.'s crew. Not too much time elapsed before this protégé bumped around until he got on as O.P.'s regular fireman.

In 1941 our family life underwent a change. My sister, after her graduation from high school in the spring, was accepted into nursing school at the hospital in Williamsport and began nurse's training that fall. Now, except when she had a day off from her studies, just the three of us were at home. For a time this was a very noticeable void in our household. And in December the life of the entire nation changed suddenly when the United States entered into a global conflict with the Axis countries. Before that, the railroad was operating at almost full capacity, and in order to meet this sudden surge in traffic more working hours were demanded of all employees. All the yard crews at Williamsport were put on a seven-day work week, extra pusher crews were added, and the EC fast freights reverted to a split run: Southport to Williamsport, and Williamsport to Enola. Traffic was so dense that it became impossible to make the 175-mile trip in sixteen hours. From that point on, I could spend only limited time with O.P., at lunchtime when I came home from school and on weekends in the mornings before he left for work. But he was still able to keep me abreast of what was transpiring on the railroad.

In the spring of 1942 the ICC finally gave the Susquehanna & New York permission to abandon its operations, and in the summer all rails were lifted. Ralston was again served by a single railroad. From the inception of this line soon after the turn of the century, it had offered the Pennsylvania competition in a small way, not only in freight that was generated in the vicinity of Ralston but also in handling incoming shipments.

Since the mid-1920s, when forest products and the tanneries in operation were in decline, revenues of the S&NY dropped, and during the Depression years profits became a thing of the past. With nothing in the foreseeable future that would generate car loadings, the only alternative the railroad had was to cease operating. The demise of this ICC-regulated intrastate short line, O.P. believed, actually proved beneficial for the Pennsylvania. The Company acquired the property owned by the S&NY in the Newberry area—not only the buildings but also the yard facilities and tracks. The long-range goal was to relieve the congested Williamsport yards.

A dike (levee) project begun in 1940 to control the course of the Susquehanna River through most of the Williamsport area also entered into the projected plans. Fill dirt used in this flood-control endeavor was removed from a hillside adjacent to the Pennsylvania's main, and the level ground remaining when this project ended, due to the outbreak of World War II, was graded off for the installation of long tracks for switching and making up freight trains. Also included in the S&NY deal were interchange tracks with the New

York Central and Reading railroads. This additional yard project was started in 1942, and by early 1943 it was in full operation.

Meeting wartime demands created a workload from the time it began, but neither the seven-day work week nor the overtime he was working bothered O.P. Rather, by the end of 1942 it was the type of firemen the Company was hiring that he was having trouble with. Many of the men hired in 1941 were called by or volunteered for military service, and those hired to replace them did not seem to have too much interest in railroading. This was especially obvious when these men had to use a scoop shovel to hand-fire a B6. As a consequence, they spent as little time as possible working in the yards, and there was a constant turnover of firemen on the yard and transfer crew. The main objective most of these men had was to get out of the yard and on a road job that had engines equipped with stokers.

Another thing O.P. discovered about most of these newly hired men was that they did not exhibit any desire to learn how to handle an engine. He surmised that they felt running a switch engine wasn't as glamorous as commanding an engine out on the main. One morning while hunting, he expressed his dissatisfaction with the type of men he was getting to work with. "I'm sure," he said, "your sister could do a better job firing than most of the men I've been saddled with, but under the present circumstances I guess I'll have to put up with them."

In late January 1943, O.P., after spending nearly five and a half years on the second-trick yard and transfer crew, was bumped. An older man with a slight edge in seniority who was recuperating from a recent illness and couldn't stand the rigors of his former road job had selected O.P.'s crew as the place to recover. There were road jobs that O.P. could have bumped on because of the wartime conditions, but none suited him. He still maintained that he wasn't going to go back riding passenger trains and living out of his traveling bag. With that thought in mind, he selected the second-trick crew in the newly opened Newberry yard. This job was different from the other yard jobs, and an L1-class road locomotive was used in the switching duties. This particular engine had been sent to the Williamsport roundhouse soon after this new facility began, when management learned that a B6 couldn't handle the task of breaking up the heavy trains brought in by the EC crews. The L1 No. 1975, had been used on the western regions of the railroad and was equipped with inverted coal-bunker sides, which was unusual in this region. It was a tender that crews called a "Prairie Schooner." The resulting increased visibility made it ideal for switching. Furthermore, it was stoker fired.

Every evening, O.P. made a trip to Williamsport, bringing in a string of cars destined for local distribution, and after dropping them off he took the

1975 to the roundhouse for its daily servicing, and got another engine, also a newcomer, H10 No. 7799, which he would use until he finished his trick. It too was stoker fired, and it was brought in to be used as the regularly assigned engine on the Berwick Branch local and as a fill-in engine in the Newberry yard.

Although compared with his long-held yard and transfer job, which paid a road day plus overtime, the Newberry job base pay was just at a yard rate. But the L1's pay rate almost put these jobs on an equal pay basis. Instead of the overtime, O.P. found that this new job had another pay incentive. Every time cars were set off either on the Central's or the Reading's tracks, this interchange move on a foreign line paid the crew four hours time. Such a move happened almost every night.

Actually, he was pleased with the change in his routine. About the only thing that caused him any problem was the new breed of fireman. Regular firemen still didn't last for any extended period of time, so he had a constant flow of men off the extra board, all very inexperienced. This, combined with the fact that the 1975 and the 7799 were stoker fired, meant that the new men, who had a limited acquaintance with the stoker, insisted on using it to fire these engines. From the time he took over the Newberry job, one of O.P.'s foremost concerns was to teach his firemen that these road-class engines would respond better, and in turn their duties would be easier, if they would resort to hand-firing. He stressed that the stoker was intended principally for use on the road, when there was constant running, and not for use in the yard, where the running was intermittent.

But none of the firemen heeded his advice. They still used the stoker. When he was moving a long drag, these firemen always had the stoker wide open, and when the movement stopped to begin switching out cars, either the pop was up or too much coal had been placed into the firebox, requiring use of the blower to keep steam up. The result was a constant conflict between trying to keep the engine working and attending to the duties it was performing. All this did not make O.P.'s job easy. He had to keep monitoring the steam gauge and the water bottle, and use the injector more than necessary or issue a warning to apply the blower.

Once, he attempted to explain to a fireman that he was using an excessive amount of coal and water, but the advice fell on deaf ears. On another occasion, after leaving the roundhouse for Newberry with the light L1 and a perfectly clean firebox, O.P. decided he would show his fireman exactly how this engine should be fired while performing routine switching chores. Arriving at the yards, O.P. opened the fire door and took the scoop shovel, and told the fireman to watch as he fixed the fire for switching. Applying a generous amount of coal to both sides and to the back of the firebox, he explained that the middle portion should be kept clean and burning bright all the time. Furthermore, he said, to keep the boiler hot he only had to occasionally place a few shovelfuls of coal in the middle of the firebox. Then, after working for about three hours, the sides and back should again be built up. Other than that, he could ride on his seat box.

The fireman watched every move, and O.P. believed that this young man might take his advice, so he was astounded at the remark he made: "Your method no doubt works, but personally it's much easier to turn the stoker valve than to bend my back using a scoop shovel."

At that, O.P. decided it was better to maintain a working relationship with these young men and extend advice only if they asked for it, or offer assistance only if they actually needed help. Working under these conditions, though, he said, "I'm ashamed to take the 1975 into the house with the mess that's in the firebox. Every night those fellows cleaning fires probably shudder when they see me coming. I've been expecting the foreman to complain, but I guess other engineers must be bringing in engines that are just as bad. One thing is for certain, they couldn't be any worse." There was one thing in his favor, though. He never had a steam failure with the 1975 or the 7799 while switching in the Newberry yards.

Before the winter ended in 1943, O.P.'s mother died after a lengthy illness, and less than a month later his father died unexpectedly. Things were changing in Ralston too, and the intent was to alleviate a portion of the pusher overload on the Elmira Branch. Fourteen pusher crews were working the board out of Williamsport, and it was not unusual to see a string of five or six light I1's coupled together passing through town on their way back to the roundhouse. Some of the engine crews were outlawed, and the lead engine was dragging them back. Pushers were never given movement priority, and when they were running against westbound wartime traffic they had to go in and out of almost every siding.

Out of Williamsport (Newberry Junction) one I1 pusher could easily handle a maximum 6,000-ton train as far as Ralston. From there to Leolyn, up the ascending grade that reached 3 percent at one point, two I1's were an absolute necessity, and sometimes even they weren't sufficient to get up the hill. From Leolyn to Sned, one I1 pusher could again keep a train moving. To ease congestion and avoid using unnecessary power on tonnage trains, the rear pusher would cut off at Leolyn, come back to Ralston, and many times make three more shoves up the hill before backing light to Williamsport. This procedure was working well, but someone in the Company hierarchy reasoned it would even be better if an I1 was stationed all the time at Ralston. As a result, a work train came to town with the clamshell crane aboard, and the first job this machine performed was to uncover and remove the cinders from the buried concrete pit, the one that had been used until 1930, when the Ralston terminal was closed. After it was opened, rails were unloaded and workers affixed them to the top of the concrete sides. It now was again ready to serve its intended purpose.

As all this was going on, other workers were repairing a coal-loading ramp located across the tracks on the siding that served the former station/freight house, which had burned to the ground in the summer of 1941. This ramp had been built by a local mining company to make it possible for trucks to dump coal into hopper cars, but it wasn't used much, so only a few ties in the riprapped sides had to be replaced. Farther down the siding, a pocket was excavated between the rails, and into this crevice a mechanical elevator was placed so coal could be unloaded from a hopper car into a dump truck.

After finishing the pit work, the work train crossed over and backed down the station siding, where the crane it carried was again put to use. On the north side of the ramp, an assembled angle iron structure was unloaded from a gondola car and atop this framework was affixed a round tank affair. When the assembly was set upright, it was approximately 20 feet tall. Next, a large boxlike bin covered by a lid was unloaded and set beside the steel tower. Workers then ran piping from the bin to the top of the tank. Installed on the bin was a long length of air hose with a brake-line connector at the end. This strange assemblage resembled a miniature water tower, but in working principle it was a quite ingenious device. While the work train was in the siding, oil, grease, an assortment of tools, and a bale of waste were unloaded and stored in the shanty used by the section gang, a small building that was the focal point of the terminal and also served as a lounge area.

The following morning the westbound local put two cars of Company coal in the station siding, and a Company dump truck delivered a load of sand, dumping it in the bin. At this point, everything needed to start the terminal was ready, except the engine and work force to service it. The men that bid on this new operation were from town or its immediate vicinity, and most could walk to work. The work day was broken into three tricks covering twenty-four hours, for machinists and engine crews alike. Machinists at this small terminal handled many chores their ratings did not include. In addition to taking care of mechanical problems, they filled lubricators, greased and oiled, and even assisted when the fires were cleaned. The engine crews also did things not usually associated with their actual responsibilities, but, working together, these men provided a unique service for the Company.

A routine was set up for all crews to follow when backing down the hill from Leolyn to Ralston after the first engine came to town. At the unattended block station, Max, located at the upper end of the former yard, the engine entered the siding, backed down to the water plug, and, after taking water, pulled into the pit siding for servicing: Then the fire was cleaned and, if necessary, the ash pan was dropped. When these chores were completed, the I1 ran out of the siding and backed down to the main, where it went forward to the station siding and reversed and backed down to the ramp. At the ramp, a dump truck loaded with 10 tons of Company coal was waiting, ready to discharge its load into the I1's coal bunker. A local contractor supplied this service on a twenty-four-hour basis. In conjunction with the coaling process, the front air hose on the locomotive was coupled to the air line leading to the sand tower, and when air was energized a machinist on the boiler top filled the sand dome. In less than five minutes coal and sand were loaded and the I1 was again ready for its next shove up the hill.

From the time it started, this small terminal worked quite efficiently. An I1 would only work out of the Ralston facility for two or three days, at which point it was exchanged with a pusher fresh out of the Williamsport engine house. Officials apparently had this operation under their scrutiny, for it was not long before additional work was bestowed on the new venture. Loaded dikers out of Altoona had found servicing at Linden was overcrowded and now passed Linden and went on to Ralston to avoid a long wait. In every respect the move was timesaving. The I1's in charge of these coal trains always stopped for water in Ralston, where in a matter of a few minutes they could also have their sand dome filled and get a supply of coal that was more than enough to cover the remaining 50 miles to Southport.

From time to time, I visited this operating terminal, for it was a little diversion in the evening routine of a small town like Ralston. Listening to and chatting with the engine crew and machinist about their railroading experiences or things taking place on the branch were the most interesting diversions. One warm spring evening, one of my classmates accompanied me to the section-house lounge, where an engineer invited us to ride along on the next shove up the hill. We could ride either in the cab or back on the tender in the doghouse.

When the train that was to be assisted arrived and the lead pusher was taking water at the plug, my buddy and I (he later became an engineman and retired as an engineer) climbed onto the tender of the lead engine, rather than the Ralston pusher, to seat ourselves in the doghouse. In this position we were seated directly in front of the rear I1's smokestack, and soon after we got started we decided it was a drastic mistake. What began as loud exhausts turned into a deafening roar that we had to endure for the next six miles. Reaching Leolyn, and before the train came to a complete halt, we dropped off and went back to the rear Ralston pusher, where we climbed into the doghouse for the return trip down the hill to Ralston. This segment of our trip was the reverse of the slow, noisy grind up the hill. All the engine noise was behind us, and we had an unobstructed grandstand perch and a large, intense headlight on the right side of the tender to illuminate our passage.

Running at a leisurely pace, we had time to view everything the light was projected on: numerous rabbits, deer that didn't pay any attention to this rattling monster's intrusion in their feeding areas, and, backing down the siding from Max, even a skunk waddling between our track and the main. Evidently the skunk wasn't bothered, for it didn't spray any of its perfume on the I1. Our ride ended when we stopped at the water plug. After thanking the engineer for allowing us to have this experience, he surprised us by offering an invitation to ride along again some other time, but the opportunity never came, for less than three months after the Ralston terminal opened, the Company closed it again without notice and moved the I1 pusher back to Williamsport.

No one at the terminal knew the reason for the sudden closing of the Ralston terminal, but after a few days O.P. found out through the grapevine what had prompted the closing of this efficient operation: the accounting division of the payroll department had spotted an irregularity that was traced to a greedy engineer on the second trick. It seems that the payroll people wondered why this particular engineman was drawing earnings every pay period in excess of other engineers on even the highest-paying runs. A check of the time slips revealed that this man, in addition to turning in his regular day's time, was also turning in a hostler's rate every time he moved an engine from the pit track to the coaling ramp, thus sometimes earning two days' pay in one trick. Furthermore, if he was on duty when a fresh I1 out of Williamsport was exchanged, he turned in four hours time for the time he was allowed by rules for changing engines. When officials reviewed what had transpired, they simply removed the Ralston pusher immediately and closed the terminal.

When O.P. told me all this, I asked him why the Company chose to close a terminal that had been needed so badly to ease the heavy flow of traffic on the branch, instead of taking other corrective action. He explained, "According to our work rules, this man was entitled to all the additional time he turned in, and the Company is obliged to honor his time slips. To make matters worse, the other two engineers, now that they know what this engineer was doing, can also turn in their slips and receive additional pay, so the Company was saved this extra expense. The other engineers, who also lived at home in Ralston while working this pusher, wanted no part of this episode. They consider themselves fortunate that they could work at home. At least for a time they didn't have to deal with the rationing board for their supply of gasoline and tires needed to drive to work in Williamsport." (The Company refused to help its employees deal with the rationing board, a war austerity move; instead, it advised them to ride passenger trains.)

I asked another question: "If you were working here, would you have turned in the extra hostling and engine exchange time?"

O.P. answered without hesitation: "No, and I don't condone anything like that, at least under the present circumstances. Actually, this engineer was working against, not for, the war effort. Work rules or not, you can't expect to be paid for everything you do to help the Company. Besides, he was moving an engine in his spare time." Then he added, "If the other men who worked at Ralston could confront this engineer in the right place, they'd probably crucify him. They're really mad about losing this hometown job."

While we were on the subject of pushers, I projected another of my ideas in O.P.'s direction: "Pop, why don't you bid on a pusher job? There's engineers on these crews now that hired out after the 1921 merger of the divisions, and you're always saying these jobs would allow you to be at home after you put in your day. From what I heard while listening to the crews when they worked out of the section house at Ralston, most of the pushers at Williamsport are called out on the eight, and with the I1 pay rate they're now drawing more money each half than they have since hiring out."

"That's exactly right," O.P. replied. "I could have one of these crews, but that is about the last job I'd take. To begin with, running a pusher engine is an extremely dirty job. Not only do you sit on the rear of the train amid all the dust the movement kicks up, you are also subjected to all the coal dust blowing off the hopper cars. Going west out of Williamsport pushing a loaded coal drag, the I1's don't pound you too bad when they are working hard, but running one of them light for sixty-five miles coming back from Sned to Williamsport is enough to shake your gizzard loose, especially if you do it day in and day out. Then, if you get the hill job pushing out of Ralston, at the end of the day you have to run in reverse for thirty-five miles. That isn't a pleasurable trip, either. It's hard to see around the tender and all the dirt on the tender blows back into your face, plus you're on the wrong side to see signals. One of the really nasty things about running backward occurs when it's about twenty degrees below zero and the only protection you have is the canvas drop curtain in back of the cab to keep the cold out. The crews almost freeze from this exposure to the elements."

He also mentioned the story of how the Elmira Division assigned him to pusher service for more than sixty straight hours just to qualify on the segment from Newberry Junction to Ralston. This, of course, happened back in 1910, when he first arrived. "But," he said, "I made a vow to myself to never again run a pusher steady if I can help it. In other words, I learned that these pusher men don't have a picnic, even though they aren't involved in handling trains. They earn every cent of their wages." He concluded by saying: "As far as I'm concerned, the only people that ride on the rear end of trains are conductors, and I'm an engineer, not a conductor."

My train-viewing from a schoolroom window ended on Graduation Day late in May 1943, and it was a transition for me, from an easygoing lifestyle to one of a more serious intent. In fact, I had been accepted at college starting in the fall of 1943. To help with college expenses, I had to get a job, which, during the war years was not difficult. As soon as an application was filled out, companies were ready to hire you. But I wanted a job where I would earn the most money in the short time I would be working. The place that was offering the best wages for inexperienced workers was at the railroad's roundhouse, but before applying I thought it prudent to get O.P.'s approval. When I mentioned this and gave him my reasons, he immediately implied that I should think in another direction, "That's the dirtiest, greasiest job imaginable. Besides, you'll have to tell the foreman you're only going to be working until fall. They'll saddle you with everything the other fellows don't like to perform."

So I took his advice and went to work at a factory that had a defense contract to produce 105 mm cannon projectiles (shells). Fortunately I got the second shift and was therefore able to ride with O.P. Each afternoon, O.P. would drop off at the yard office and I would take the car to the storage garage. After completing my shift I would do the reverse. Many nights O.P. did not get in at 11:35 P.M. as scheduled, but the waiting was no problem. It gave me an opportunity to watch the activities at this busy terminal and allowed me time to become reacquainted with workers I had met in the past. Also, working the same hours gave me a chance to spend time with O.P.

This arrangement came to an end too soon, though. In less than a month the company I worked for changed our work hours to address a personnel shortage. In order to meet production quotas, two ten-hour shifts were adopted. Being one of the newest employees, I was given the second shift, from 8:00 P.M. until 6:30 A.M., six days a week. From then on, I spent very little time with O.P. About the only way I could see him was to leave for work early, ferret him out in the yard, and ride around on the B6 with him for a while, or on Sunday before he left for work, That, I found, was a consequence of steady employment.

When I left for the institution of higher learning in the fall of 1943, I was removed not only from my family but also, to my despair, from all sounds and goings-on associated with railroading, which I had grown up with. The community where the college was located was served by just a small rail line, and about the largest service it rendered was supplying coal to the college's power plant. Trips seemed to be infrequent and unscheduled, because I never was able to witness any movements. To add to my woes, I was unable to have my car with me because of wartime restrictions. At best, it was difficult to find suitable transportation to and from Williamsport from this location. The only possibility was a secondary bus line with an inconvenient schedule. Consequently, I made only a few visits home during my first two semesters.

Returning home after I had completed the spring semester in 1944, I discovered that having both my sister and myself in schools at the same time was creating a financial burden on our parents, so I decided to forgo furthering my education for a year, or until the war ended. This would allow my sister to complete her schooling in the fall, and give me the opportunity to accumulate enough money to ease the stress on the family budget when I returned to complete my own education. Before going back full-time to the defense plant where I had worked in the summer of 1943, I spent a day in Williamsport while the engine of my car, a 1930 Ford Model-A Coupe that, despite its age, nonetheless provided cheap and dependable transportation, was being overhauled.

Later that evening I met an old acquaintance, the third-trick yardmaster. I was telling him about my plans to work for a year or so before continuing my education when he suggested that I hire out as a fireman. Explaining that the Company was having difficulty finding men capable of handling that job, and that my slight physical handicap would not be a deterrent, he offered to give me his personal letter of recommendation. That would almost certainly be insurance in the hiring process.

At home seated at the kitchen table with O.P., I told him about my conversation with the yardmaster. I expected my father to approve of what seemed like an opportunity of a lifetime. From his expression, though, I could see he wasn't happy about the idea. It would be no problem, he admitted, for me to be hired on as a fireman. In fact, his signature on my application would do it. He then added what could be considered a compliment: "I know you'd make a good fireman, but if you choose to do that it would be the end of your schooling, and both your mother and I think it's more to your advantage to continue with your education. I can tell you one thing for certain: you might as well pack your bag if you follow railroading. You'll be shunted from one terminal to the other, from Sodus Point to Southport, Renovo, Altoona,

Northumberland, Enola, even some of the small terminals in between, just to have a job."

The last thing he said on the subject was something I never thought I'd hear from someone who had spent a lifetime railroading, enjoying the work and studying all its intricacies: "This railroad is no good, and it's never going to get any better."

I decided to take his advice and went to work in the defense plant, though at the time I felt I'd allowed a dream-come-true to slip away.

Once again, as a new employee, I was given the 8:00 P.M. to 6:30 A.M. shift, six days a week. And once again the time I spent train-watching and the time I could spend with O.P. was limited. As a result, though, I had some pleasant surprises. One came when the valley's solitude was interrupted by an unfamiliar whistle on a Sunday afternoon. Hurrying down to the area of the water plug, hoping to intercept whatever strange engine was entering town, I found nothing there, but, glancing down the tracks, I saw a westbound movement just coming onto the creek bridge. Going immediately to this spot, I saw an awesome locomotive with huge cylinders extending beyond the boiler front. From my vantage point, I saw that those cylinders were powering four drivers on the left side, and directly behind these wheels I saw a smaller cylinder arrangement powering four more drivers.

The locomotive was progressing onto the bridge at a snail's pace, and on the large deck affair above the front cylinders a special-duty fireman I recognized was riding and relaying forward hand signals to the engineer. Gathering my thoughts, I determined that the engine was a mallet compound and that it might be too heavy for this overhead truss-type of bridge. Closer observation of this huge mallet showed it had the familiar keystone number plate on the smoke-box door and the word "PENNSYLVANIA" was lettered on its odd-looking tender. Another feature similar to that of Pennsylvania engines, but atypical in design, was the monkey house fitted directly behind the tender's coal bunker. But no other features made it an engine of Pennsylvania design.

After this "foreign" engine crossed the bridge, the engineer opened it up, but all it gave out was a muffled blast from the stack and lots of smoke. Its consist was the same as that was found on a diker: mixed freight cars, coal hoppers, a Pennsylvania cabin, and the customary two 11's pushing. After the train passed, I intended to go to the water plug to talk with the engine crews and examine the huge engine better when it came back down the siding for water, but I was unable to do that because officials had the area surrounded when I got there, so I couldn't get close. The only thing I could do was go on home.

That evening I left home early and went to the yards to ask O.P. about what I had observed. I told him I'd seen the big mallet come through Ralston westbound, and filled him in on all the details of the incident, and I was surprised that he was able to give me a lot of information about the movement. The grapevine informers had been watching this trip from the time it left Altoona until it reached its destination at Southport. O.P. first told me the engine was an older Y-3 class locomotive that was one of the several the Company had received from the Norfolk & Western in an attempt to help relieve the existing power shortage. Trying to find a suitable area to use these older mallets, officials had decided that the dikers' 175-mile run would be just the place.

But that turned out to be a fiasco. Evidently no one had bothered to check what clearance a mallet needed. Just after starting up the Elmira Branch out of Newberry Junction, one of the oversized front low-pressure cylinders hit a bridge truss on the first crossing of Lycoming Creek. This bridge was one of sixteen across the creek between Newberry and Ralston, and there were several smaller bridges spanning the tributaries of the Lycoming. So I had been mistaken in my assumption that weight restrictions were the reason for the train's slow speed through the bridge coming into Ralston. The reason had been the extremely close clearance.

As for the engine crew's evaluation of the mallet, at the water stop in Leolyn engineers on the pushers had talked with the head-end man and reported their findings when they returned to the house in Williamsport. It seemed this large locomotive was slow and clumsy; compared with an I1, its only virtue, they believed, was that it rode much better than the 2-10-0's. The crews determined that even if it had been able to clear the bridges on the Elmira Branch, it was too slow and plodding to be of any value on this long haul. This was the only time the mallets made an appearance on the Williamsport Division.

Another innovation that officials in the Motive Power Department inaugurated during this period—the object being to operate trains with higher tonnage ratings up the Elmira Branch—was to use an additional I1. Apparently someone believed that if the additional engine was placed twenty cars back from the head end, the power needed for the maneuver would be evenly distributed.

Coming home from work early one morning, I caught up to what I thought was an ordinary diker a short distance south of Ralston, and it turned out to be this new type of movement. As I ran parallel past the train, I spotted a working I1 buried several cars back of the lead 2-10-0. O.P. later filled me in on why this four-engine power was utilized on a few runs, but the result was not the intended one. From Newberry Junction to Ralston and on up the hill to Leolyn, everything had gone according to expectations, but when it encountered the roller-coaster grades to Sned, the head end had trouble coordinating the extra power, especially when braking. That situation produced pulled drawheads. The crew also found that switching the I1 in and out of the train to take frequent water consumed too much time, though the switching was necessary not only at Newberry and Sned, but also at water stops at Ralston and Leolyn.

By the time I talked with O.P., the Company had abandoned this concept, reasoning that any extra power should be double heading, to allow for better train control with pushers attached. Even though the experiment proved unsuccessful, it was quite a thing to see and hear a train with four 2-10-0's blasting out of Ralston.

On one of my visits with O.P. at work I was greeted by an unusual surprise. Waiting just below the Walnut Street crossing, an engine with a bright rear headlight was coming out of the west end of the freight house. The swallow-tailed shape of the tender led me to surmise that it was a B6 with O.P.'s crew. As it neared, though, I could see that I was wrong. It was the basin crew's A5, but it was being run by O.P.

As I climbed aboard this diminutive engine, one I had seen many times before, O.P. explained that his B6 had developed mechanical problems and had been taken to the house, where they gave him the 1203, which had spent the day receiving needed repairs, to finish out his trick. They had just started to work with it, and he and the fireman reminded me of two boys with a new toy. Everything about the 1203 seemed to tickle them.

As we started shoving the string of cars back to be cut into the freight house, O.P. pointed out that each exhaust it made at slow speeds could be felt. The boiler was actually shifting from side to side, and it bobbed up and down even when attached to a car, and had a tendency to swing abruptly in a lateral motion going into a switch. Coming back out with another string of cars, O.P. called over to the fireman, "This damn thing, for the size of it, certainly has an amazing amount of power, and it really handles easily."

One evening, while I was riding on his B6, O.P. mentioned that his traditional leather gauntlet gloves were almost worn out. As the war dragged on, he, like other railroaders, could not purchase replacements, so he suggested that if, in my travels, I could find gloves like his, or a suitable substitute, I could solve this problem for him. I did try to find them, but all the stores that sold gloves advised me they were unable to find a supplier for leather gloves. The only thing I found even close was a shorter version of gauntlet gloves, made of coarser leather with canvas backs. These gloves were a necessity for workers handling shells in the defense plant where I worked, and there was no restriction on the number of pairs an employee was entitled to. Thinking that these gloves might solve O.P.'s problem, I borrowed two pairs, and the next time I boarded his B6 I presented both him and the fireman with a pair of these wartime specials, explaining that they were the best I could find. Both assured me they were suitable, though a bit coarse. On my next visit, O.P. showed me what the gloves looked like after being subjected to oil and grease on the job: they became nearly as pliable as the ones he was used to wearing. The result was that I made sure O.P. had a sufficient supply at home to last for a long time.

During this busy war period, time seemed to pass rapidly, and changes took place almost as fast, even within the family. In the fall of 1944 my youngest sister finished her nurse's training, and while awaiting the results of her examination for certification as a registered nurse, she stayed on at the hospital to work as a general-duty nurse. But that was only temporary, as she had enlisted in the Army Nurse Corps. When she received her R.N. certification, she was immediately inducted into the armed services. In the middle of January 1945, she left home to begin her basic training as a second lieutenant at Camp Lee, Virginia.

When the war in Europe ended in May 1945, the Army notified the defense plant where I worked that many fewer 105 mm shells would now be required, so my shift was eliminated. This allowed me to transfer to a plant that had just been completed and had begun making rocket projectiles for the Navy. It also gave me the chance to select the 7:00 A.M. to 5:30 P.M. shift.

Working in this brand-new plant, plus being on the day shift, was more to my liking, but it meant that I had even less time to spend with O.P. I used to be able to board his engine in the evening, but now he told me that the officials would probably object to an outsider being around the yard in the late afternoon, because the war in the Pacific was still on. Consequently, I had to give up visiting with him on the B6.

Now that I was working on a daylight shift, I could once again watch movements on the railroad through Ralston, at least during the evening hours. One thing I found was that the coaling and sanding facilities installed in the spring of 1943 were still functioning. O.P. was aware of that, and he related that even though the pusher had been removed from the location many of the dikers coming through from Altoona continued to use this service. The Company determined that these trains, instead of waiting for long periods of time at Linden, could have their coal and sand replaced at Ralston with a minimum loss of time. The contractor originally hired still provided workers to supply the coal on a twenty-four-hour basis, but the engine crews had to hook up their air hose and fill the sand dome themselves. (After the war the facility continued for a time, but eventually it was eliminated.)

Early in the summer of 1945, indications were that the war in the Pacific would also soon be over. With this in mind, and according to my plans to continue my education, I reasoned that it would be the proper time to register for the forthcoming fall semester. Taking a day off, I journeyed back to the college to do that. In August 1945 my sister returned home on leave, now a first lieutenant. She had orders to report for duty in the Mediterranean theater next and was to be stationed at a general hospital in Naples, Italy. While she was on leave, the day everyone was waiting for came about: World War II was over.

Almost immediately after VJ Day, the Navy ordered a cessation of the production of rockets. The new plant where I was working did not even finish the remainder of the week. Most employees received a termination notice in their paychecks. With my paycheck, however, was enclosed a slip offering me the privilege of transferring to the machine shop, or an alternative: anyone who had been employed in a wartime production plant was entitled to draw unemployment insurance for a fifty-two-week period at $20 per week. This came to be known as the "52/20 Club."

Only a short time remained before I was to go back to school, so I elected to take the unemployment benefits. Explaining my decision to O.P. one night after returning home from work, and showing him that I could have transferred to the machine shop as a full-time employee, he approved of my decision to go back to school, but said, "Evidently you must have been doing your work properly or such an offer wouldn't have been made. But unless you really want to be a machinist the rest of your life, I think you made the right decision."

Not too long after the end of the war, the railroad also began reducing operations that had been running at unbelievable capacities for almost four years. The yard crews in Williamsport were cut back to working just six days a week, and that was a welcome relief for O.P., who had worked seven days a week during this entire period, taking only a minimum amount of time off for personal affairs.

In the brief interlude before continuing my education, I had more time to spend with O.P., and in the course of our discussions we got around to the subject of the new steam power that had been developed during the war years. In his opinion, these engines were primarily designed for use on the main lines, where they could take trains of full tonnage according to their rated traction effort and run for more than 100 miles at high speeds with no restrictions. Locomotives like the J1 or Q2 freight classes probably would never be used on the Williamsport Division. That would be a waste of power, because there wasn't enough running room and it would be too expensive to run these engines at less than their capacities. The one engine that had been developed—the T1a passenger class—seemed special to O.P., and he even said that he would like to handle such an engine, that it would be like running two E6's under one boiler. (He was almost correct in assuming that the two freight types would not make it in our area, as only one of the J1 class ever ran on the Williamsport Division. The Q2 didn't either.)

Just a few days before I left for college, O.P. came home unexpectedly one evening much earlier than normal. As soon as he entered the kitchen my mother knew something was wrong: his normally ruddy face was pale. She asked immediately, "Are you sick? I know something happened to you." He sat down and reassured us that nothing was wrong with him, then told us about a harrowing experience that had taken place that evening.

The yard and transfer crew had received orders to start their out-of-the-city chores around 7:00 P.M., two hours ahead of schedule, in order to accommodate a coal dealer who wanted two hopper cars of anthracite coal delivered to his siding in South Williamsport. The coal dealer had checked shipping dates and learned that the cars had left the mines more than two weeks ago, and he was concerned that the time lag was causing him to lose fall coal orders, so the Company wanted to deliver the cars to his coal yard as soon as they arrived in Williamsport.

Since the yard and transfer job began, the crews had switched countless hoppers into and out of this elevated coal-trestle unloading facility, but on the previous delivery to the site O.P. had told the conductor that the structure was no longer safe to support an engine, let alone the cars, and that he wouldn't enter it again unless a Company official made an inspection. This particular evening the conductor came to the engine after the train stopped on the main before entering the siding with the two cars of coal and told O.P. that an inspection had evidently been done. A paper was affixed to one of the uprights certifying it as safe. With this assurance, they entered the siding and began pushing the cars onto the dock, but O.P. didn't notice any improvements; it seemed as deteriorated and rickety as ever.

He had just ascended the ramp and started across the level portion when he felt his side starting to settle. Immediately placing the brakes in emergency, he hollered to the fireman to jump clear and started to follow suit. But his attempt was thwarted—he couldn't get off the seat box. Somehow his overall jacket had snagged on something behind the seat when he made this sudden move. Despite all the force he could apply, he could not free the jacket, so he was forced to stop to unhook it. It seemed like an eternity, and all the while the B6 was causing timbers to snap and crack, tipping even more, almost to the point that O.P. was sure it was going to roll over. By the time he freed himself and climbed up over the coal pile and down the sloping tender, there was no more sound of breaking timbers—but the engine was now resting at a precarious angle.

Once off the overhead trestle, inspection from a safe distance revealed that the middle driver of the 0-6-0 had come to rest on a cross-frame steel I-beam, the only thing supporting the engine weight; otherwise it would have rolled off onto the ground at least 15 feet below. The left side of the B6 was still on the rail, but the right side rail had collapsed, the drivers had crushed the ties, and the engine was down on this side more than 16 inches. With a span of only 4 feet, 8½ inches between the rails, it appeared as though a stiff breeze could blow it over.

O.P. and his fireman were relieved by an extra engine and crew to pick up their train. A taxicab took them back to the yard office to mark off. Concluding the tale of his narrow escape, O.P. repeated something he had told me before, the one thing that worried him about having an accident aboard a steam engine: "The only thing I could think of when the engine started to go down and I couldn't get my jacket loose was that a steam pipe would burst, trapping me in a cab filled with high-pressure, super-heated steam."

By coincidence, a local resident approached me soon after O.P.'s mishap and told me he was one of the workers dispatched to South Williamsport to retrieve the B6. When his crew first heard what they were being sent to do, they thought it was just another rerailing chore. But when they arrived on the scene they changed their minds. "You know," he said, telling me what they had found, "Uncle Oscar must have had someone with divine power riding with him. If that B6 had gone an inch or two either way it would have upset." He went on to say that after they sized up the predicament they determined that the "big hook" wrecking crane could not be used effectively. The main was too far away from the dock, and the boom wasn't long enough to reach above the engine's lofty position. And if the tender was removed to allow the wrecker to get near the B6, it too would have had to work on the trestle. With this additional weight, the whole structure was liable to collapse.

The only reasonable approach was to shore up the structure from underneath and use jacks. First the 0-6-0 had to be securely blocked, for the slightest move would cause it to topple. Even after all the blocking and shoring was completed, they had to build up the left rail. The drivers on that side were still setting on that rail, and it was by no means substantial. If that rail had buckled, their work would have been compounded.

All went well in their efforts, but it was late the following morning before the 0-6-0 was backed off the trestle to solid ground. As the engine backed off the dock, this workman said, "Uncle Oscar really had a close one."

The fall semester at college was different from the previous year because I had more freedom. With the war over, I was allowed to take my car with me. Living conditions did not change, though; armed forces trainees still lived in the dormitories and used the dining halls, and fraternities were crowded with returning servicemen. So, as before, I chose to live in a private home and eat my meals at restaurants, but because I had the car I could go home whatever weekend suited me. And it didn't take long for other students from Williamsport to discover I was traveling in their direction frequently, so every time I made this trip I had passengers.

With the money my riders donated for the privilege of riding along, plus what I saved on meals from Friday evening to Sunday evening, I actually saved money by spending weekends at home. That was not my primary motivation, of course; I liked being with my parents and went home at every opportunity. Those weekend visits also made it possible to keep up with railroading, not only on the Elmira Branch but also in general. O.P. always seemed to have a lot of information.

O.P.'s yard and transfer crew had settled down to the peacetime routine with only occasional diversions, one of which came during a snowstorm sometime in January 1946, not long after marking up for the afternoon trick. They were dispatched to go to the Lycoming Motors plant, along what had been the main line to Elmira, to pick up two loaded boxcars of airplane motors that had a priority shipping schedule. The cars were located down a steep ramp that led to the loading platform, and on the way out after picking them up, the heavy snowfall, coupled with the steepness of the ramp, caused the B6 to begin to slip and finally stall about halfway out.

A workman plowing snow with a large Caterpillar-type bulldozer that had been fitted with rubber instead of the usual steel pads saw what had happened and stopped plowing. He gave O.P. a stop hand-signal, then came over to the engine with an offer to pull it out of the hole. O.P. was about to decline the offer, but the operator seemed especially proud of his machine. Explaining that it was equipped with a powerful winch that could pull anything, he claimed that getting the 0-6-0 out would not even strain it. O.P. gave his consent, and the operator attached his cable, moved the machine more than 100 feet away, and gave a signal that he was ready to start pulling.

The crew assembled in the cab watched as the cable tightened. The B6 did not move, and neither did the bulldozer—not at first. But then the front of the machine began to rise up. The operator, watching intently to the rear, possibly expecting the engine to start moving, failed to notice what was happening. As it reached the point where O.P. thought it was about to topple it over backward, he blew a sharp blast on the whistle, to signal the operator of his predicament. In response, the operator hurried to shut the machine off and O.P. alighted from the engine and motioned the operator to back down. When the cable had been retrieved, he thanked the man for trying to help and explained that he did not doubt the power of the dozer and its winch, but rather that it might be dangerous to keep trying, lest the cable snap and cause serious damage or injuries. After the cable had been unhooked and the machine was out of the way, O.P. backed down the ramp to where it leveled off. Applying sand all the way, he reversed, and under a generous amount of sand and steam he pulled out of the hole without slipping a wheel.

In the early spring of 1946, on one of my weekend visits at home, O.P. told me about a new job being advertised on the bid board. The job was an engine exchange crew whose purpose was to reduce the time lost when the yard crew changed their tricks; instead of every engine crew going to the engine house to get their engine at the beginning of a trick and returning it to the house at the end of the day, the crews would board the locomotive at the yard office. The engine exchange crew would report for duty at 1:30 P.M. and work until all yard crews, except the basin job, had a serviced engine. Each afternoon O.P. and his fireman would start with a freshly serviced B6 from the engine house, take it to the yard, and exchange the serviced engine for a working engine. This engine was then taken to the house to be filled with water, sand, and coal, to have its fire cleaned and the locomotive serviced, and for any needed minor repairs. This process would be repeated until all four yard crews had serviced B6's. Last, the H10 No. 7799, or an available H9, would be delivered to Newberry, and the L1 No. 1975 would be taken back to the house for servicing. When this move was completed, the engine exchange crew could mark off. The Newberry crew would retrieve the serviced L1 after setting off the nightly drag of cars brought into the Williamsport yards.

O.P. reasoned that this new job would be a diversion from the routine of the past nine years, but also that on the recently published roster he was number two. Most all the older engineers had retired at the war's end, and the number-one man had the Susquehannock passenger run. With this in his favor, all he needed to do was put his name on the bid sheet and he would become part of the engine exchange crew. He placed his bid, and, as he'd figured, got the newly established engine exchange crew. He quickly came to like the job. Although the pay was at the yard rate, it wasn't too low; the

L1-class scale boosted it considerably over the normal B6 scale, and the hours were especially to his liking, for he usually was back home between 7:00 and 8:00 in the evening.

The machinist who rode to work with him the entire time O.P. worked the second-trick jobs told me how he managed to arrange these short days. "When he brings a B6 into the house," he said, "O.P. doesn't stand around idly waiting for workers to service the engine. He actually does much of the work himself." Pointing out that it was just an in-and-out procedure, he went on to say that O.P. and his fireman cleaned the fire, filled the tank and sand dome, and made any necessary mechanical adjustments. He then said, laughing, "Oscar would probably coal the engine too, but that is one thing he can't do. He doesn't know how to operate the steam clam-crane."

Aware that he had been pitching in like that, I asked O.P. how he could quit so early every night—just to see what his reaction would be. He gave me a straight answer, telling me he pitched in to get the engines serviced and explaining that he still liked to get off duty before his time was up, getting paid for doing nothing. His hurrying once almost got him in trouble, he told me. On that particular occasion, the last yard service run was to deliver a B6, but a K4 was blocking his approach to the servicing area by a scant three feet. Another unfavorable factor was that the K4 was protected by blue flags attached to the rails, both in front and in back. These warned that workmen were under or on board the locomotive and that it was not to be coupled up or moved.

Aware that this engine wasn't supposed to be moved, O.P. faced the prospect of spending valuable time waiting until this was cleared before he could move. His thought was to move the engine, but in the proper way. According to the rules and regulations, he should first find a hostler to assist him, but that too would be a time-consuming affair. The quickest approach, he decided, was to simply get permission from the machinist or whoever had placed the flags and was working on the K4, and move it the short distance necessary to clear himself. Walking around one side of the K4 and then the other, he couldn't find anyone working on the engine. From just a casual inspection he could see that all the running gear was intact. Climbing into the cab, he found no workmen there, either. So rather than waste any more time, he made an immediate decision to go ahead with the move.

Opening the bell valve, he reached up to release the independent brake, but found it wasn't even set. Then he discovered that the reverse lever was already placed in the forward position. There was nothing else to do but start, so he cracked the throttle just enough to get the engine under motion. After moving the desired distance, he set the independent brake, but to his dismay nothing happened. The K4 just kept rolling. He instinctively reached for the reverse lever to reverse the motion as a means of stopping, but that did not function either—the K4 just rolled along. Finally, after traveling almost two engine lengths, he locked couplers with another parked engine and stopped.

Now he was in an unholy predicament. He had moved an engine without authorization, he had run over a blue flag, and he might also have fouled up whatever servicing was being done on the K4. As far as he could determine, though, the only maintenance taking place was on the air pump, and in his haste he had failed to notice that it was shut off.

He reported to the engine-house foreman what he had done, expecting to be reprimanded for taking matters into his own hands, but he was told that because there were no injuries and no damage to Company property the best thing to do was forget about it. O.P., however, regarded his behavior as inexcusable. "I've spent almost all my life in the cab of an engine," he responded, "and when I found that the brakes on that K4 weren't set, I should have known enough to make an air test, or, above all, I should have checked the air-pressure gauge. It shows how easy it is to make a mistake when you act with too much haste."

There was one element O.P. couldn't circumvent on the exchange job: the lunch period the second-trick engine-house workmen took early each evening. O.P. joined them whenever he could. Seated next to one of the younger workers on one of these breaks, he heard the young man comparing an H6 parked nearby with the larger engines in use. O.P. could tell that he knew little about the subject, but rather than being rude or attempting to offer any educational pointers, he only listened politely. Then, pointing to the small drivers, the young man said confidently that this class of locomotive couldn't run very fast the way it was equipped with small drivers. "In fact," he added, "a fellow riding a bicycle probably could go faster."

That was more than O.P. could take. He felt personally offended. "I felt it was my duty to defend the H6," he told me. "After all, I grew up with those engines on my first job out on the road as an engineer. I proceeded to tell this young jasper that if I had that H6 and about thirty-five or forty cars behind me out on the main, it wouldn't take me long to have your hair standing on end. You'd find out whether those little drivers could go very fast." That ended the conversation.

Rainfall during the last few days of May was heavier than usual. On May 26, as O.P. was doing the regular chores of exchanging engines in the yards, rising waters were slowing road movements and causing people in the Williamsport railroad hierarchy to be alarmed. Engine 7799, coming in with the

Berwick local, was running late due to minor flooding in low-lying areas. It was the power designated for the exchange at Newberry, and the delay forced O.P. to get behind in his hurry-up routine. When the Berwick local did arrive, the H10 had to be serviced before he could deliver it, adding to the time he had already lost.

Around 9:00 P.M., as O.P. was in Newberry making the exchange with the 1975, the EC6 from Enola was pulling in, also running late. (To remove congestion, a wye had been constructed at Linden [Nesbit] to allow the runs to use the south-side freight line to enter the Newberry yards instead of coming through Williamsport.) By the time O.P. got his orders to return to the engine house, the M1 off the EC job was cut off and also coming in to the tower to receive running orders into the city. Although the train crew terminated at Newberry, the engine crews still used the Walnut Street yard office and the engine house in Williamsport. Written orders gave O.P. a clear block to the yards in Williamsport, and he wasted no time starting back on the straight single track with his L1.

Just as he neared the wye intersection leading to the Elmira Branch, a distant signal positioned near the Lycoming Creek bridge suddenly changed from clear to stop. That indication was contradictory to his orders, but he brought the L1 to a halt near the wye call box, surmising that some kind of emergency had come up from the adverse weather conditions. Then he noticed in his headlight's beam that floodwaters were lapping against the rails that approached the bridge. He got off the engine and notified the operator that the bridge signal was indicating stop, suggesting that the rising waters might be causing a short circuit in the system. The operator confirmed that his orders were still in effect, though, that the block was clear and that he had permission to proceed. Satisfied that the operator knew it was a signal malfunction, O.P. got back on board, crossed the bridge, and took the 1975 to the engine house. At the engine house, he learned that the EC3 crew—with the M1, following O.P.—had met with a disastrous accident. The west side of the creek bridge abutment was washed out, and the M1 had plunged into the raging waters. The fireman escaped, but no trace of the engineer was found.

As he was marking off, one of the crew clerks in the yard office informed him the Elmira Branch was out of service; floodwaters were washing out a section of track just north of Ralston, and lines of communication were no longer operating. He then cautioned O.P. about trying to get to Ralston, that portions of the highway up the valley were impassable, and that perhaps it would be wise to spend the night in Williamsport. O.P. didn't follow that advice, though, but instead of attempting to get home via the main roads, he did detour on back roads through the surrounding hills. One point on that route concerned him: a bridge over Lycoming Creek at Bodines, some four miles south of Ralston. When he reached that point, the waters had receded enough for him to continue his journey.

The following morning, O.P. was able to survey the flood damage in the Ralston area, but the only means of finding out what was transpiring in the surrounding regions was radio, for all public and rail telephones were out of commission. The Williamsport area was just beginning to experience the effects of the rising waters, he learned, particularly the western sections. This was attributed primarily to the rampaging Lycoming Creek, which was at levels never before reached at flood stage. This unprecedented flow of water was the result of a cloudburst north of Ralston the previous evening; the runoff was unable to flow into the river, causing extensive flooding.

News reports also related that the city's main highways and rail accesses were flooded, except the route O.P. had followed the previous evening; that hilly back road was still open. With the usual communications unavailable, O.P. was not sure whether the yards were still in operation, and his curiosity about what was going on led him to report to work as usual. Following the hill route, he reached the city with no problems. In the vicinity of the yard office, water was covering the streets, but still not over the curbs to the sidewalks. Parking his car about three blocks away on higher ground, he walked to the yard office. Along the way he noticed that the roundhouse looked like it was in the middle of a lake. Despite that, an exceptionally large number of locomotives in this area were still under steam. As he entered the yard office, he was greeted like a long-lost friend. The crew clerks had been desperately trying to find an engineer but had been unable to locate anyone, not even a fireman, because of the flooding.

The yardmaster told O.P. that a ballast-cleaning train, parked on a siding opposite the Park Hotel passenger station in full view of the Number 9 offices and officials, was in danger of being damaged by floodwaters and had to be moved to a higher track. This was an urgent move because this train was made up of new equipment the Company was leasing on a trial basis. The yardmaster informed O.P. that the H9 used on this train was serviced and waiting at the roundhouse. A brakeman had been called to handle the switching, but the best they could find to handle the firing duties was a fire-tender working at the house. Once the H9 had been coupled to the ballast-cleaning train, O.P. was to take it west to Rose Street, switch to the former Elmira Branch main, and continue on this line past the Lycoming Motors plant to a point where it crossed Lycoming Creek. Then the yardmaster explained that this location had been chosen because the main-line bridge to the Newberry yards, where this train normally would be transferred, had collapsed when the

EC's M1 was crossing it the previous evening. Miraculously both the engineer and the fireman had escaped this tragic mishap.

On his way to the house, O.P. had to wade through about four inches of muddy water. He had prepared for something of this nature by having donned his rubber boots. The makeshift crew was ready when he reached the H9, but the inlet/outlet track to get to the westbound main past the Walnut Street yard office was blocked with stored engines. The only other exit was out the lower end of the house to the main in the vicinity of Hepburn Street. Taking that route, they found the water much deeper at the lower end of the track. The top of the switch target was the only thing marking the intersection. To find the operating lever for the main switch, the brakeman had to wade in water up to his knees, then probe in the muddy waters with the coal pick to find it.

From this point they backed through the yards to the station, coupled to the designated train, and took it to the selected safety tracks. Food was brought out to the crew later in the evening, but that was the last anyone from the Company visited this location. It was just the beginning of a long wait. Even after sixteen hours on duty, no relief came. The only fortunate turn was a restaurant-cafe they found near the manufacturing plant, within easy walking distance of the train.

Around daybreak, after spending a restless night trying to sleep on an engine seat box—a position to which O.P. had never been able to adjust but which, he reasoned, was more comfortable than the seat on the left side, which his companions had to share—they went to the restaurant. There they learned that the river had crested sometime during the night and was now slowly receding. Most of the city was still flooded, especially the downtown area. The heavy damage sustained from the high water almost equaled that of the disastrous 1936 flood. The news of the receding waters was encouraging, but an attempt to reach any of the Company's offices by telephone was unsuccessful; all the lines were still out of service.

Twenty-four hours passed, and they were still on duty with nothing to occupy their time except watching the water level in the boiler and keeping steam up. Around 4:00 P.M. a crew clerk arrived with orders to bring the train back into the yards and mark off. By the time they got the train set off, put the H9 in the house, and reached the yard office, O.P. found that he had spent more than twenty-nine hours on duty. With little sleep during that period, he was apprehensive about driving home, but once under way he didn't even feel drowsy. At least he could again travel the main highway.

Arriving back in Ralston that evening, he found my mother nearly frantic from worry about why he had been gone so long. When he left after lunch the day before, she thought he'd probably gone to work, but when he didn't return by the following morning she began to suspect something unusual was going on, but she was unable to find out what.

On Friday, two days after Central Pennsylvania was ravaged by flooding from the west and north branches of the Susquehanna and its main tributaries, I completed my final examinations at the end of the spring semester. Another student from Williamsport accompanied me on the journey home. Not long after leaving the plateau where our school was located, we entered a valley containing one of the river's tributaries. There we could view the damage caused by the floodwaters. The main highway on which we were traveling had been washed out in some spots, but temporary repairs had been made. Towns all along our route were covered with mud and all kinds of debris.

Arriving in the valley, we could see that the river was still high and swollen. All the low-lying areas resembled muddy lakes. When we tried to enter Williamsport, we found that our access was closed and we had to detour. The West Fourth Street Bridge crossing Lycoming Creek had been damaged enough that it was unsafe for vehicular traffic. But there were no other problems getting to my passenger's home in the north end of town; it was well out of the reach of any floodwaters. After dropping him off, I stopped to visit my oldest sister, who lived in the same neighborhood, and found that she too had not been inconvenienced from the flooding. After this brief interlude, I made my way up the Lycoming Creek valley, where I could see the serious damage along the way, especially to portions of the railroad bed. Fortunately the main highway seemed to have survived this onslaught of water reasonably well, and north of Trout Run, where the road followed the mountainside, no water damage could be seen all the way to Ralston.

The next day, Saturday, O.P., who was enjoying a temporary vacation, and I toured the valley together to survey the damages caused by the flood, concentrating mainly on the railroad. We determined from what we could see that there wasn't a mile of track from Max, just north of Ralston, all the way to Williamsport that had escaped being washed out one place or another. The place that sustained the most damage was at Powys Curve, where the roadbed and tracks were completely gone for almost a quarter of a mile. The creek now ran where they had once been placed.

Our tour took us next to the yard office in Williamsport, where O.P. learned that everything on the railroad remained at a near standstill. Emergency yard crews were conducting some switching of preferential freight, but work trains were about all that was moving. Over-the-road traffic was expected to begin either later that day or on Sunday. Harrisburg, to the south (east on the railroad), reported that water there had receded enough to start movements and that everything west to Renovo had been repaired. As far as could be determined, things should start to run in the normal manner by Monday, but it would be difficult to get in and out of Williamsport going east or west until the bridge in the west end over Lycoming Creek was repaired. The city was restricted to the main over the river bridge in the east end.

The creek bridge was a priority. Big hooks from both Northumberland and Renovo were already there, ready to lift the M1 out of the creek and raise the damaged span. O.P. suggested that we should finish our tour by going to the accident site for a firsthand view of what had happened to the M1. As we traveled up West Third Street, O.P. told me what he knew about that near-tragic event from accounts on the radio, newspaper articles, and what he had heard via the Company grapevine.

On Tuesday evening the raging waters of the creek had undermined the west-end abutment, allowing the span to collapse when the total weight of the M1 was between it and the center pier. The front of the engine was almost on the middle pier, but the back portion, where the cab is located, plunged down onto the creekbed. The tender followed, and the force of the flooding stream swept the engineer from the cab. Somehow, between the force of this water and his trying to swim in heavy work clothing, he managed to reach a radio-transmitting tower more than 500 feet east of the bridge. He was rescued from that framework early the next morning when his shouts for help were heard. The fireman managed to get on the tender—a coast-to-coast version—and crawl up over the coal pile all the way to the monkey house. It didn't take rescuers long to reach him there, for according to the grapevine, he was screaming loudly amid a tangle of downed communication and power lines. Adding to the precarious position he was in, many of the wires were arcing, thus making his rescue more challenging and time-consuming. Other than back injuries the fireman sustained, neither he nor the engineer was seriously injured.

When we reached the West Third Street Bridge, we had a clear view of the accident scene. Half the railroad bridge was still intact, and one of the big hooks was perched on this span. The M1's resting position looked like a partially folded jackknife. A portion of the cab was still submerged in swirling waters on the creekbed, but the pilot was higher than the remaining portion of the bridge deck. The rear of the tender rested on what remained of the washed-away creekbank. A work train was on the west end, on the remaining tracks there. A large crew of workers were preparing temporary tracks to allow wreckers to get near the engine and tender.

As we watched, O.P. began talking almost as if he was thinking aloud: "If that had happened when I was crossing the bridge just minutes before that M1, I probably wouldn't be here. You know I can't swim."

During the first few days of my summer vacation, I tried unsuccessfully to find a job, but most of the firms in and around Williamsport were concentrating on cleaning up from the effects of the flood, and others were in the process of changing from wartime production to peacetime manufacturing. My only alternative was to rejoin the 52/20 Club and collect unemployment between semesters.

O.P. and my mother took advantage of the fact that I wasn't gainfully employed, and rather than see me idle away the entire summer they came up with something to keep me occupied. Our house needed painting, something that had been postponed because of the war, and now many other homes in town needed to be painted too, and all the local painters were booked months ahead. Although I was inexperienced when it came to house painting, my parents knew I could handle it and assured me that they would provide all the necessary equipment; they even allowed me to engage a neighbor boy as a helper.

It did not take me or my helper long to realize that painting a multistory dwelling was a time-consuming venture. The first step was to scrape all the loose paint off, then we had to nail down all loose siding and replace putty on window sashes where needed. After we applied one coat of paint, we found that the paint was absorbed into the siding and a second coat was necessary. Having put two coats of paint on the entire house, we started on the trim, including the many windows, sashes, casings, and window trims, plus the house trim boards. Last came the two porches, which constituted a sizeable area to paint too, particularly the front porch that covered about one-third of the house. This project, taking into account a rash of inclement weather that persisted from time to time, took much longer than first anticipated. We completed the job only a few days before the fall semester was due to start.

A positive feature of spending the entire summer at home was that it gave me the opportunity to keep abreast of railroad activities, mostly in nightly conversations with O.P. His engine transfer job resumed its schedule as the crew clerk had stated, and about a week later the West End Bridge over Lycoming Creek reopened, allowing the yards to conduct normal operations again. It took considerably more time before Elmira Branch rail traffic was moving. Nearly four weeks were required to repair the extensive flood damage.

Just when things were running smoothly, a nationwide strike by the United Mine Workers of America disrupted this pattern. In order to conserve coal supplies as the strike persisted, the railroad began abolishing passenger trains. One of the timetable trains affected was the Williamsport–Harrisburg Susquehannock on the Williamsport Division, the run held by the engineer who was number one on the roster, and as things evolved, he bumped O.P. This proved that although number two was a high position on the sheet, it was not always high enough. But O.P. bumped back on the yard and transfer crew and worked that old standby until the coal strike was over.

Returning to college after my summer vacation, I was in much the same position I'd occupied when I originally enrolled three years earlier: again without transportation. The rear main crankshaft bearing of my Model-A coupe bearing wore out, and rather than have expensive repairs made or replace the motor, I sold the car for considerably more than what it had cost me. Now lacking convenient transportation, I resigned myself to staying at school and making only occasional visits home.

Six weeks passed before I got home again. A student I knew mentioned he was driving to Williamsport for the weekend and invited me to accompany him. I accepted the offer. My first stop when we arrived in the city was to pick up O.P.'s car at the storage garage, then I went to the yard office to check on his whereabouts. As close as the crew clerk could determine, he had just taken a B6 to the house, and that is where I found him.

O.P. told me this was the last yard engine to be exchanged for the day, and that then he had to take the 7799 to Newberry and bring back the L1, which would take about three hours to complete. I could pick him up about that time, he said. This plan gave me an opportunity to visit my married sister. Fortunately it was suppertime, so I was able to enjoy my first home-cooked meal in many weeks.

At home later that evening, O.P. surprised me by suggesting that I purchase another automobile. "Your mother and I enjoyed having you come home on the weekends," he said, "and with both you and your sister away it gets lonely for us. If you got another car you could be home more often. I know you have enough money saved for your school years, and if getting a car causes you to run short, we'll help out." That was fine with me, and the next afternoon, Saturday, I went along with O.P. to find a used vehicle that would be suitable and within my budget. It didn't take us long to find a dark-green 1935 Ford Coupe V8 that at one time had been a deluxe model. Careful examination revealed that it was free of dents and bruises, and a road test showed it was in good mechanical condition. All it needed was two new tires. The following Monday, O.P. handled the transaction with the dealer before going to work. He wrote me at school that I could pick up my car on Friday on my way home, adding he had used a service for fast delivery of the license plates and that he would take them, and two new tires he had purchased for me, to the dealer.

On Friday I hitchhiked to Williamsport to find everything in order, picked up the car, and stopped at the roundhouse to tell O.P. I was on my way to Ralston. Not having any use for Ford products, O.P. for the first time expressed reservations about whether I had made the right purchase, but added that if it suited me it was all right with him. At the Ford garage in Ralston on Saturday morning, I had my car serviced and tuned up by a mechanic who grew up with Fords. He assured me that I had made a decent purchase, and he pointed out a feature I wasn't aware of—my car was equipped with a specially designed differential (rear end) that reduced engine wear, improved gas consumption, and provided more speed. The only fault I eventually detected—an insignificant one—was that in less than 500 miles it had used a quart of oil. Other than that, it proved to be a dependable means of transportation to get me to and from school every weekend.

While at home over the Thanksgiving vacation, I met an attractive blonde nurse who had been in training with my sister. We chatted, and she agreed to have me escort her the following weekend. During that first evening together we enjoyed each other's company, and it became one of many weekends we spent with each other. In fact, our acquaintance expanded to include vacation periods. So, although I had always liked going home, this fine young woman certainly was an added incentive to make my trips as frequent as possible.

At this time, operations on the railroad were nearly back to peacetime operations. When 1947 became the New Year, the engine exchange crew was still functioning as originally intended. For O.P. it had become a routine daily job, but one spring afternoon, shortly after he began changing yard engines, something happened that pleased him enough that he sent me a letter describing what happened. I rarely got letters from home after I began returning to Ralston every weekend. When I came home the following weekend understanding only most of what had transpired, O.P. went over all the details with me and put them in a broader perspective.

On the afternoon in question, he had just returned to the house with a B6 after the first exchange of the day. The foreman rushed over as he was getting off the engine and excitedly related that the K4 on the Buffalo Flyer had developed mechanical problems at the station in Lock Haven and that machinists from the Lock Haven engine house were unable to make repairs. Number 9 called with explicit instructions: a replacement engine was to be dispatched at once, because they did not want the premier passenger train on the division detained for a lengthy period.

The foreman explained he had a K4 that could go out immediately, one that had arrived a short time before on the passenger off the Elmira Branch, but the yard office told him it would take well over an hour to call out an engine crew. Number 9 responded that this was too long to hold the Flyer at Lock Haven and instructed the yard office to take any yard engine crew available in this emergency. The logical selection was the engine exchange crew, and O.P. was instructed to call the dispatcher immediately.

The dispatcher told him to leave with the K4 at once, that everything was lined up and that a clear block would be the order all the way. O.P. explained to the dispatcher that he was no longer qualified, that more than five years had passed since he went any farther out on the road than Linden. To this he received a curt reply: "Right now, Oscar, the officials in the main office down the hall don't care who takes that engine out, just so it gets to Lock Haven and they have the Flyer moving again. In my personal opinion, they'd send a hostler out if they thought they could get away with it."

Making a hurried inspection on the K4, O.P. got under way. All switches were aligned out of the house inlet onto the main. When he approached the tower at Newberry, a clear block was indicated, and as he passed the operator outside with his hoop he received written orders confirming the dispatcher's oral orders. Once by Linden, O.P. opened the K4 up on the double-track main, something he enjoyed doing, especially when he was fortunate enough to run light. Not worrying about the speed he was traveling, he came in under twenty-eight minutes for the 28 miles from Williamsport to Lock Haven, terminal to terminal.

All the switches at Lock Haven were lined up for him. He was reversed from the westbound main to the eastbound track, ran by the train, switched back over, and backed down to make a coupling. The Flyer's crew immediately climbed aboard and started on the rest of their trip to Renovo. The problematic K4 had been backed on the wye track connection to the Bald Eagle Branch. When O.P. got to where it was sitting, the engine-house foreman informed him that a connection between the tender and the engine broke. Activating the injector did not pump water into the boiler, but rather pumped it on the ground. The foreman said a yard engine was coming to drag the K4 back to the house, where they would knock the fire until a replacement fitting could be obtained. Out of curiosity, O.P. asked him whether he could take a look to see what might be causing the problem, and the cocky response was: "My men and I did everything we could to repair the broken fitting. You'll find that the only solution is to install a new one."

Before crawling underneath between the engine and tender, O.P. had his fireman get on board with the instruction to open the injector on the left side when he signaled. It didn't take him long to see that the main fitting was broken enough that water intended for the boiler-feed lines on either side was just being discharged on the ground. Coming back out from under the engine, he hollered for the fireman to shut the injector off but remain in the cab. Then he asked to use one of the machinist's large monkey wrenches and crawled underneath again, this time changing valve position on the piping arrangement. After he made these adjustments he had the fireman activate the left injector, and to the amazement of onlookers, this time, after priming, there wasn't even a drop of water being pumped to the ground. It was all going directly into the boiler, as it should.

O.P. then asked the fireman to fill the water glass and get the steam up. They were ready to take the K4 back to Williamsport. But the Lock Haven engine-house foreman wanted an explanation. Not about to crawl underneath again to show him, or take the time to go into the details, O.P. merely explained that he had found a couple of valves closed and had opened a valve to a bypass line. Then he went to the nearby tower to obtain orders to take the K4 back and a line to the dispatcher, but when he arrived, before he could put in his request, he was told that transportation was being arranged to get O.P. and his fireman back to Williamsport. When O.P. said they didn't need transportation, that the problem had been solved, the dispatcher, when he was contacted, at first didn't believe it was possible for a locomotive the machinists couldn't repair to now be capable of running under its own steam. He then exclaimed, "I don't know what you did, Oscar, but if you say you can bring her in I'll line things up for you to return. Put the operator on again. I'll have him give you written orders to that effect."

His orders again gave him clear blocks, this time the entire way eastbound to Williamsport. He backed the K4 up the wye to the Bald Eagle Branch track and headed east. The switch was set for his entry to the eastbound main, and after a brief stop to fill the tender with water, he started rolling again at speeds exceeding 60 miles an hour.

When he arrived at the engine house in Williamsport, the foreman came over to greet him. "Oscar," he said, "I don't believe this, and neither do the officials up in Number 9. You have everyone in a dither. They're wanting an explanation of how you could bring this engine all the way back when machinists at Lock Haven couldn't repair it for the Flyer's crew."

Without a doubt, O.P. was pleased with what he had managed to accomplish, but he wasn't about to claim too much credit or make it difficult on the men in Lock Haven, so he merely stated truthfully that he had only switched valves. But that explanation didn't satisfy the foreman, who said, "I still can't figure out how you could valve around both main supply lines. Get under the engine and show me exactly what you did manage to do." The two men then both crawled underneath the K4, and O.P. pointed out the valves that had been closed and the one that he'd opened. Back with their feet on the ground, the foreman confessed, "I've repaired all kinds of leaks on engine piping systems, even uncoupling tenders from the engines different times, but I never knew you could bypass the main line to the injectors. Where in hell did you find out that could be done?"

He had discovered this auxiliary line years ago, when he was running the dikers from Ralston to Altoona, O.P. explained. On a westbound trip with an L1, this main fitting had cracked as he was nearing Tyrone, although it was not leaking as badly as the one on this K4, so he was still able to get enough water in the boiler to enable him to get the engine house without making an emergency stop. He expected that he'd have to get another engine to complete the trip, but a veteran machinist inspected the fitting and told him he could continue after adjustments were made in the piping system. This met with O.P.'s approval, and while the machinist was making the adjustments, O.P. accompanied him underneath to see exactly which valves were closed and which were opened. The task completed, the machinist cautioned that only the left injector would function, that O.P. could continue on but that the broken fitting should be noted on his engine report. Altoona would have the parts to make the repair. That was the only time O.P. had ever run into this problem, so when it occurred again this time he discovered that the piping system from the engine to the tender on the K4 was the same as it was on the L1 and was able to make the adjustments himself.

The consternation among the officials was not limited to Number 9. Officials from the main operating offices in Philadelphia were concerned too. O.P. learned of this the next afternoon, when he went to the engine house to begin his daily exchanging routine. The foreman told him that officials had been calling to inquire why the Flyer had been detained due to an engine failure when it was still in operating condition.

"Oscar," the foreman said, "you have no idea what it's like trying to explain what you did over a telephone, especially to someone in authority who doesn't know one pipe on an engine from another. One thing, though. I was instructed to commend the engineer who brought the supposedly disabled locomotive in for his ingenuity and knowledge of a steam engine. That made sense to me."

I had questions for O.P. as he told the story. One thing I wanted to know was how fast he was running on the trip to Lock Haven. More or less evading this line of interrogation, he didn't tell me exactly, but he did say that he might have been traveling between 70 and 80 miles an hour on straight sections of track, maybe even faster, and added that a K4 could really run if you let one out, especially when you were running light. At this he smiled, and summed it up as he often did: "I was going so fast you couldn't see my coattail for dust."

When I asked why he had been running so fast on the return trip to Williamsport, when there wasn't any urgency to get the engine back, he had logical reasons. First, he had a light K4 and a clear block all the way, and second, there wasn't any reason to run at slower speeds. Besides, it wouldn't look good to be in command of such an engine, and just poke along. "It didn't take me long to determine that the Flyer's engine was in better shape than the one I took in exchange," he continued, "so I might as well take advantage of the pleasure on a nice spring afternoon. One thing I forgot before leaving was a pair of goggles, so I had to dodge a lot of cinders trying to see ahead."

I had another question: "If you'd been the engineer on the Flyer and had this engine with just the one injector on the left side, would you have taken the passenger train on to Renovo?" O.P. assured me without hesitation that this engine could have run all the way to Buffalo. Out on the road he had experienced problems with his injectors, he explained, but always continued on, using the one on the left side or, on some locomotive classes, the water pump. To meet federal regulations, these two devices had to be installed on every locomotive and be in working order.

O.P. had recently begun talking about his desire to have a road job if he could be home every day. He always considered himself a road engineer, but waiting for a run to his liking. Not long before the end of the spring semester, O.P. told me he'd recently had the opportunity to run an engine of a class that had eluded him during his entire tenure as an engineman and asked if I could guess what that engine might be. He gave me the answer as part of a story.

To begin with, one of the B6's assigned to the yards had developed a problem the engine-house crew was unable to repair, so it was stripped of its rods to be shipped dead to Renovo for a complete overhaul. Because a replacement was urgently needed but another B6 was not available, a substitute class, an engine destined for the Philadelphia area, was assigned. Under the circumstances, officials detoured this substitute engine, which turned out to be a B8, to the Williamsport yards instead of resorting to a road engine for switching chores. The B8 was an older class of switcher, with slide valves, saturated steam, and a Johnson Bar reverse lever, and it generated less power than the B6 class. When O.P. first spotted this brand-new stranger at the roundhouse, he assumed that it had developed problems as it was being ferried from the shops after an overhaul and was stopping for some adjustments.

He learned that was not the case, though, when it was the first engine to be taken to the yards to exchange for a working B6.

Leaving the house with an engine he had seen in the yards since hiring out in 1904—one of this class was assigned to Ralston for many years—O.P. found it difficult to believe that an engine this old was still in active service. It was equipped as originally built: slide valves, saturated steam, and a Johnson Bar reverse lever to control the inside valve motion. It even brought back memories of his first running job, when he was assigned to the Williamsport yards as the engineer in the lowest position on the roster. When he started on that crew, he fully expected he would be using that class of engine, but instead he got a Class R (H3) freight locomotive. He reasoned that whether he had a B8 or a Class R, the Johnson Bar these engines were equipped with was not the easiest device to use when switching.

He was amused to see the reaction of the engine crew when he delivered the shiny B8 to them to use for the rest of their trick. To say the least, they had a number of disparaging comments. Talking about this old 0-6-0 that had more years of service than he had working for the Company, O.P. began recalling the numerous classes that he had run up to the present, and the order in which they were run.

Looking back nearly forty-three years, he told me about how hard it was to imagine that at the time the Class R was the main freight-hauling engine. On the L&T the Class P was a fairly new passenger engine; many of its sister classes were still hauling limited trains. When he started running from Ralston to Tyrone in 1910, the 2-8-0 H6a with slide valves was leading the parade handling most of the freight chores, followed by the H6b with piston valves, and finally, as they were either constructed or put in for class repairs, H6b's modernized with a superheater. In 1918 he got his first H8s and H9s, 2-8-0's, but the still-larger L1s 2-8-2 bumped them out by 1921. In this period he test ran one of the early I1s models, but it wasn't suited for the long diker hauls, even if it was the largest power the Company had to offer for road service.

Also during this time he made test trips with the non-Pennsylvania 2-10-2's, the N1s and N2sa, and, like the 2-10-0 I1s, they proved to be too slow. Consequently the L1s reigned in this area until 1930. Although the M1-class 4-8-2 made its appearance on the system in 1924, it was not until 1931 that O.P. ran one from Southport to Altoona, and then only with a train of empty hoppers. In 1924, however, when he took a job testing engines fresh out of the shops at Renovo, the opportunity to handle many classes he had missed along the way became available, including assorted D's, the 4-4-0's; E's with a 4-4-2 arrangement, including the E6 class; K2's, 4-6-2's; and even the F3's, or 2-6-0's.

In 1933 on the Altoona to Harrisburg passenger run, he finally had the privilege of handling the Company's best-known engine: the K4 4-6-2. Without a doubt, O.P. said, it proved to be the best locomotive he ever ran. "Just thinking about all these engines, especially the ones I ran regularly during that period, they all did a good job doing what they were designed for—even the I1 after they got around to doctoring it up so it had some speed to go along with its power." The only engines on the roster that did escape his hand were the C1, an 0-8-0 used primarily in the larger yards, and the G5 4-6-0's, designed for commuter passenger runs and thus not in use on the Buffalo, Erie, or Williamsport Divisions.

The employment picture had improved by the time my 1947 summer vacation came about, and as a result I had no problem finding a job. I began working as a laborer for a construction firm that was building a concrete retaining wall on the east side of Lycoming Creek to protect the city's well fields, raising the West Third Street Bridge, and tying these portions into the existing dike along the river with dirt fill. The project was scheduled to last beyond my return to school for the fall semester. A union job, it paid above the scale of an average factory worker, and the hours weren't bad, either: 8:00 A.M. to 4:30 P.M., five days a week, no overtime. My wage was eighty cents per hour.

Another benefit that I didn't expect was the construction taking place near the Pennsylvania's main line to and from Williamsport. It provided an excellent spot from which to watch all the movements entering or leaving the city. I even caught O.P. returning from Newberry one afternoon with the L1, and for some reason unknown to me he was traveling as fast as the passenger trains. I asked him later why and he answered, "When the 1975 is used for switching, cinders accumulate on top of the boiler and on the running boards. If I can run fast enough they all blow off. This makes it better for the engine crew. When you're switching, these cinders are always blowing around, especially when it's windy. Sometimes it becomes almost as bad trying to see as it is when running out on the road."

Cinders from the firebox were a constant threat to the eyes of enginemen. Their only protective recourse was goggles, but these were worn only when the locomotive was in motion. Meanwhile, cinders gathered on every flat surface of the locomotive, and even while the train was standing a sudden gust of wind would dislodge these fine particles, which would sometimes enter the unprotected eye, causing irritation and watering. If not removed, a cinder could damage the eyeball. O.P. collected his share of cinders in his eyes over the years, and his method of dealing with them was common: he turned his eyelid over using a large wooden match, a generous supply of which he carried to light his pipe; made a swab by wrapping his handkerchief around a second match and moistening it with his mouth; looked up, down, left, and right until he had located the invading cinder; and touched the cinder with the moistened swab, thus removing it. As potentially irritating and dangerous as this maneuver, which he had to use frequently, was, he never once had to seek professional treatment for his eyes. And only in his later years did he need glasses, just for reading.

After a few days, I found that the portion of the dike on which I was working was only a small job. The main construction was just getting started on both sides of the river from Maynard Street to the east end of Williamsport. I also learned that truck drivers were being hired to operate ten-wheel dump trucks hauling fill dirt from a borrow pit (the excavation of fill dirt to be used elsewhere) located in the lower portion of South Williamsport (present-day site of the Little League's National Championship playing field). The better feature was that the drivers were paid a wage higher than what I was earning. They were working ten hours a day, six days a week, and making one dollar an hour, the union scale.

This information aroused my interest, enough that I decided to become a truck driver, so I began leaving home two hours early and presenting myself at the hauling contractor's office before 7:00 A.M. That way I still had plenty of time to report for work for my present job if I wasn't hired as a driver. The first morning, I did not get a flat refusal, but the closest I came to getting on as a driver was to fill out an application and hear that no trucks were available. Later that day or tomorrow, more would be coming from the main headquarters, I was told. Receiving the same answer the next morning didn't affect my determination, and on the fourth day I was hired.

The first two trips I made as a truck driver, another employee accompanied me, to show me what I was expected to do, from loading at the pit, through the residential area of South Williamsport, onto Market Street, which was also U.S. Highway 15, across the narrow river bridge to the Williamsport side, down Front Street, and then on to the dumping site. From the very beginning this was quite an experience. I had driven small trucks a few times, but nothing to compare with the size of these ten-wheelers, hauling at least 14 tons of dirt, negotiating through heavy traffic, and crossing the bridge with only enough clearance for two trucks to pass. Despite these unforeseen complexities, my driving was satisfactory and I was put on as a full-time driver.

On this job, train-watching was even better than my previous work site. Not only did the route traveled cross the Pennsylvania freight-line cutoff on the south side, but after crossing the Market Street Bridge to the city it also crossed the Reading's double-track main. The numerous movements on both these lines were a hindrance to the dike trucks, creating traffic jams even if it did allow me to scrutinize what these railroads were hauling.

The power on the Pennsylvania consisted of classes I was familiar with, but viewing the Reading engines was an entirely new experience. From time to time in the past I had seen this foreign line's locomotives, though not up close, and I had not paid any particular attention to them. Now I was in a position to observe them at close range while on the fill portion of the dike or waiting at the crossings.

All the passengers stopped at the Reading station just west of the Market Street crossing. Most were hauled by a 4-6-2 type, but on occasion a 4-4-2 Mother Hubbard (camel-back) was the head-end power. Usually freight trains had a 2-8-2 engine on the heavier movements. On trains with fewer cars, they also used a Mother Hubbard version 2-8-0. To switch the freight house located between Market and Williams Streets, a variety of small freight engines were engaged. The Reading locomotives were interesting to study, and I even tried to compare them with some of the Pennsylvania's classes. But the only similarities were the wheel arrangements and the freight engine's small, shrill-sounding whistles. They were not, however, nearly as shrill as those used on the Pennsylvania freight classes.

When I was telling O.P. about the engines the Reading had working through Williamsport, I found that he must have looked them over to some extent, for he knew all about their oddities. The strange-looking firebox at the rear of the boilers was designed to burn the anthracite (hard) coal that was readily available to this line throughout the hard-coal mining area it traversed. Anthracite produced a sizeable amount of revenue for this relatively short line railroad. The large firebox was the reason many Reading engines had their cabs mounted on the center of the boiler; it was too large to accommodate a cab in the usual position.

Through the years, O.P. had talked with engine crews that handled engines equipped with camel-back cabs, and he could see that they were not favored by Reading crews. Their complaints were logical. The center location of the cab made it uncomfortably hot in the summer and cold in winter, and firemen had little protection in adverse weather. Also, because there was no visual contact between engineer and fireman, communications were limited to a speaking tube, which wasn't very effective when the locomotive was working. In addition, Reading workers were always afraid a rod would break and shear off one side of the cab, resulting in serious injuries or death to the occupants.

O.P. reminded me of a serious wreck the Reading had in the winter of 1936. It involved the Reading passenger train that competed daily for years with the Pennsylvania's Susquehannock after it was inaugurated, operating almost on the same arrival and departure schedule at Philadelphia. On the morning of the accident, the Reading train, powered by a 4-4-2 with a Mother Hubbard cab, for some unknown reason did not slow for a bridge-approach curve below Muncy and the engine and several cars plunged into the river. Both men on the engine, several trainmen, and a number of passengers were killed, and many people were injured.

An intensive investigation was conducted, but officials were never able to prove why the veteran engineer failed to obey the speed limit on this curve. The possible cause of this tragedy was revealed by the engineer's widow. On the previous westbound trip this engineer had made over his division, temperatures were ranging well below zero and his ears became frostbitten. Suffering from the pain of the frostbite, he was unable to sleep the night before he left on the ill-fated trip. The most logical conclusion, then, was that the motion and vibrations of the engine had easily lulled him to sleep.

None of the engines I observed the Reading running in and out of Williamsport matched the size of the M1 or I1. O.P. told me that the Philadelphia & Reading Railroad, as it was originally named, had some larger classes elsewhere on their system, citing a case when the Reading's power could outclass what the Pennsylvania had working. In the Harrisburg area these lines ran near each other, and both to the same destinations, so crews naturally competed to make the best running time when traveling in the same direction at the same time. Until the I1 was introduced to this region, odds were almost equal, but in its original form the Pennsylvania's 2-10-0 could not run fast enough to provide competition, much to the delight of the Reading crews. This all changed after the proper valve adjustments were made on the I1; then the Reading had the problem of keeping up.

O.P. also pointed out that, according to recent literature, the Reading was currently constructing large models of the 4-6-2 wheel arrangement and that these modern locomotives might even outperform the K4. The Reading had also developed a large 4-8-4, the T1 freight engine. Like the 4-6-2, the T1 incorporated modern technological features, which made it rate among the best steam power any road had operating.

These T1 locomotives made an appearance at the end of the steam era on the Pennsylvania's Williamsport Division, assigned to haul the EC fast freights between Newberry and Enola, and even at times in pusher service on the Elmira Branch. The Pennsylvania engine crews found them to be good riding and easy steaming, with lots of power available to start heavy trains. But in comparison to the M1, the T1 did not have the snap to handle trains at speed. A T1 did win acclaim later, when it powered the Freedom Train in the east.

I hadn't been driving on the dike job long when O.P. became interested in the project. He explained that the topic of discussion among the rail-roaders was the amount of money truckers with leases were earning, and he wondered whether there was any truth to that. At the time I thought he merely wanted me to confirm that his co-workers were right, and I assured him of that. A little arithmetic gave him a reasonably close figure for what the private truckers earned. These trucks were paid according to the yards of dirt hauled. Nearly all trucks were hauling the same tonnage due to weight restric-tions on the Market Street Bridge, and all made about the same number of trips to and from the pit to the fill. By figuring just daily earnings, then multi-plying, I came up with weekly or monthly totals that revealed a sizeable gross income. I then made the point that, though it looked good on paper, it was nearly impossible to purchase a truck large enough to meet the requirements. Used trucks that weren't already worn out were just not available for purchase. That was the reason premium haulage rates were in effect.

A short time later O.P. surprised me. He was, it turned out, more than idly interested in the dike project. Somehow he had located an acquaintance in the automotive field who could supply a brand-new dump truck, and the delivery was less than two weeks away. The way he saw it, we were set to go into the trucking business—almost. My mother also heard our conversation, and she promptly vetoed the venture. We couldn't dispute her reasoning, either. It could not be a profitable investment. O.P. was almost ready to retire, so quitting the railroad now just didn't make good sense, and if I was to be the designated driver I would have to forgo my education. That didn't make sense either.

The summer of 1947 was uneventful for the engine exchange crew, except for something O.P. never expected to happen. After forty-three years of service the Company's new work rules gave him a paid vacation. He was eligible for four weeks, to be taken at his discretion. He chose to take two weeks during the summer, one week during small-game hunting season, and one week dur-ing deer-hunting season.

O.P. had often mentioned that if he were to retire at age sixty-five he then only had one more year to work. Evidently he was giving retirement some thought, and somewhere in his mind he harbored the idea that it would look better on his record if he ended his working days on a road crew rather than in the yard. There was still the one obstacle to his going back out on the road: all the jobs running out of Williamsport had layovers where they terminated before they returned, and O.P. still wanted a job that would allow him to go home at the end of each work day. I also knew he wanted to have a fast-freight road run once again, but I suspected he was telling me that just to make himself feel good.

In my last week driving on the dike before returning to school in the fall, O.P. made a surprise statement that fulfilled his promise to himself. The EC3 and EC6 crew from Newberry to Enola was open, and he had placed his name on the bid sheet. He reasoned that the EC job laid over in Enola for only a few hours beyond the mandated eight-hour rest time and that most of his off-duty time would be in Williamsport. Even if it didn't quite meet the criteria he'd held out for since he began yard service in 1937, it did give him the satisfaction that the record would show he had retired as a road engineer. As the number-two man on the roster, he assured me, he would be out on the road again when the job was let, and be running the EC3 and EC6 crew in four days.

Back in my usual routine, I returned home at the end of the first week of the fall term. Now, though, in addition to spending time with my parents and girlfriend, I would spend my Saturdays driving on the dike. According to his schedule, O.P. should have been on the road that weekend, but I found him at home when I arrived. At first I was worried that he was ill and unable to start the fast-freight run as planned, but that was not the case. He had withdrawn the bid on the EC3 and EC6 crew when the job he'd been looking for, one that would return the same day without a layover, suddenly appeared on the bid sheet, and he was going to take that job rather than the EC. Meanwhile, when he was awarded the EC bid he relinquished his engine exchange job and now he was without a job until the other bid on the no-layover crew was awarded.

This job, the RN1 and RN2, was for years between Renovo and Northumberland, but according to an austerity move by the Company a new schedule was to be inaugurated. The run was handled by four crews, and the main terminal was at Northumberland. It was now being changed to just one crew, with Williamsport as the terminal point. The new run was from Williamsport to Renovo, with a turn there and a return to Williamsport on the same time slip.

Listed as a fast freight, it was a seven-day-a-week job with the scheduled calling time set at 1:40 A.M. each day. It also qualified as a mileage run with a total of 108 miles, paying over thirteen hours at a rate determined by the weight of the engine used on its drivers. Everything about this newly established over-the-road crew was considered to be created to O.P.'s specification—except the unholy calling time. But O.P. compromised on that, knowing that he would have no layover time away from home.

EIGHT

THE FINAL FAST-FREIGHT CREW

In late September 1947, O.P. began what was to be the last crew he would handle before retiring, and when he marked up at 1:40 A.M. it became apparent why the odd starting time for the RN1 had been selected. Some time was spent at the roundhouse inspecting the assigned I1 before it was accepted. Then he moved out to the yard and coupled to his train. By the time the brake tests had been made it was after 3:00 A.M. Ready to move the RN to Renovo, he had a clear block on the distant signal board, an indication that the early movements that took place nightly had all cleared and that the single-track main was cleared to the double-track junction at the Linden Tower.

They arrived at Lock Haven after 5:00 A.M., and in keeping with orders pulled into the siding to perform switching that would require more than an hour. Cars, local loads, and empties, destined to go over the Bald Eagle Branch west to Altoona, were set off, and cars headed west for locations in Erie and Buffalo were picked up. Once clear out of Lock Haven, the RN was run over the double tracks to its first termination at Renovo and the train was set off in the yards. Again, this took time, and when O.P. finally took the 2-10-0 to the house for servicing it was nearly 8:00 A.M. With servicing completed, the I1 was turned on the table and sent back out to the yards to pick up its train for the return trip. It was nearing 11:00 A.M.

Running eastbound on the double track under clear blocks, the train did not take long to reach Lock Haven. Once again cars were set off and additional ones picked up. When the switching was finished, the RN2 completed the run to Williamsport, where the train was set off in the yard, the engine was taken to the engine house, and O.P. marked off. It was after 2:00 P.M., giving him an on-duty time of more than twelve hours. The time involved in completing this 108-mile trip wasn't exactly befitting a fast freight; it was more like what would be expected of a local movement.

None of the crew members who made up the RN had ever worked with O.P. before, and although he had seen the men around the railroad from time to time, he wasn't really acquainted with them. The fireman was a total stranger who had hired out before the Depression but almost never worked out of Williamsport, spending most of his time at the Northumberland terminal. He had been furloughed during the 1930s until just before World War II, and after returning he fired for a while again and then, during the latter part of the war, was "set up running." Recently he had been set back to firing status and held a job on one of the RN crews out of Northumberland.

When that run was changed to Williamsport, he decided to stay on the shorter version turnaround scheduled, and consequently bid this job in. From the first trip, O.P. had reservations about this man's ability to fire a steam locomotive. He not only used the blower to get up a full head of steam before starting, but also never shut it off, even when the engine was running at more than the road speeds, and that irritated O.P. On their second trip, after O.P. had the I1 set up and running around 50 miles an hour, he called the fireman over and suggested that the blower be shut off, because it wasn't necessary to keep the engine steaming. To this the fireman gave what O.P. considered a feeble reason for using the blower continually: it enabled him to keep an even fire even when the engine was working. So, not about to cause an argument, or go into detail about how the practice was using coal and water unnecessarily, he merely dropped the subject. This fireman displayed another strange trait: he would place himself on the right seat box, and not occasionally, but every time O.P. was off the engine. One such incident took place on the third trip with the RN. In addition to the nightly switching at Lock Haven, orders included a stop at North Bend, just a short distance east of Renovo, to pick up a car from an industrial siding. Arriving at that location, the train was stopped on the main, and after the car was coupled up to the train, O.P. dropped off the engine to notify the operator on this block that he was ready to proceed into Renovo. After placing the call, he started to leave the call box location. Looking toward the parked I1, he saw the fireman as usual occupying the right seat box. Reasoning that the fireman was in the position to start the train and thereby save some time, he gave a hand signal indicating that forward proceeding should begin.

Just as O.P. was giving the signal, though, he relived for a moment that time years ago when he first started firing and had been in about the same position. On that occasion, for some inexplicable reason, the engineer had started the train without a hand signal and went through the siding switch, which caused the Class R locomotive to upset. O.P. pushed that flashback aside, though. It couldn't happen again—for one thing, this time they were sitting on the main.

Nevertheless, he had an uneasy feeling that something was going to happen, and it did. He heard the fireman open the throttle and heard the expected burst of steam, and then he waited to hear it shut off. But that didn't happen. Instead, the massive 2-10-0 gave a sudden lurch forward. This unorthodox start by a supposedly qualified engineer ended just as O.P. thought it would: the train parted three cars back of the tender with a crack that sounded much like a cannon had been fired. Inspection revealed that the drawhead had broken on the rear of the third car. At least that would allow it to be set off in the siding they had just worked.

Back aboard the engine, O.P. politely told the fireman that he would appreciate it if he stayed over on the left side where he belonged. At that, the fireman began to apologize. "Don't worry about this, Oscar," he said. "I'll take the blame, and the time [five days without pay for pulling a drawhead]. All you have to do is put it in your report that I was handling the engine."

Now O.P. was really ready to explode, and he responded sternly: "If you've been on the railroad as long as you say, you should know better. It doesn't matter who was running the engine. I'm the one the Company authorized to handle the train, I'm the one that's responsible, and I'll be the one getting the time off."

On my first weekend home after this incident, O.P. confided that he was leery of his fireman. Although he found the fast-freight run to his liking, he felt he had to be constantly aware that a member of the crew was either deliberately trying to cause trouble or perhaps was a Company man sent to evaluate O.P.'s ability to handle the job.

I was troubled to learn that he might get five days off for the drawhead incident and asked when that might be determined. He went on then to tell me that it was unlikely to happen, and explained how he had gotten around the rule. Proceeding west from North Bend to Renovo, O.P. kept thinking about how an everyday routine could all of a sudden mar his reputation as an engineer, and about this rule infraction becoming a part of his record even if it wasn't his fault. He knew that someone connected with the car shops would find out the cause of this incident, and he realized that he was a complete stranger to the workers at the terminal and car shops, so no one would be likely to give him the benefit of the doubt. He would simply be regarded as a negligent engineer pulling a drawhead. Running along mulling over his predicament, he recalled a man he had been associated with many years ago when both had been conferred with their Masonic degree. At the time the man was employed in the car shops in Renovo, so at the yard office he inquired whether the man was still employed by the Company. One of the crew clerks told him that indeed he was, as a general foreman. That was gratifying to hear, and O.P. went to the man's office, taking advantage of a privilege the Masonic Order afforded members, one he never thought he'd use. The two men talked, and O.P. told him how the drawhead had been broken. He never asked for any direct interceding on the foreman's part, and no assurances were given, either. The foreman merely said that the outcome would be determined after workers had examined the crippled car. Two trips later, the crew clerk at the yard office handed him an envelope that contained a short note from the car shop foreman. It stated that an inspection revealed the drawhead had a concealed 75 percent metal fracture, causing it to part under normal operating procedures.

Meanwhile, still unable to predict what his fireman was going to do next, O.P. did not find much relief from the tension felt in the cab. He didn't know what this man might do or when. Eastbound out of Lock Haven with orders permitting the RN to run in advance of a passenger movement, O.P. had the 2-10-0 set up to generate its maximum speed. Watching ahead to see the indication displayed on the distant signal controlling the block at McElhattan, the fireman suddenly hollered across the cab to stop. Initially this command startled O.P., but his surprise quickly changed to astonishment when he learned that the fireman had blurted out "Stop!" just because his cap had blown off. And the man insisted that he be allowed to get off to retrieve his head cover. That was one of the most absurd requests O.P. had ever heard. At the speed they were traveling, it would be at least a mile before they could come to a safe stop, and he ended the discussion by pointing out that it would be difficult to convince officials that a passenger train was delayed just to pick up a $2.00 cap.

Another incident took place at the yard office after marking off at the end of a completed trip, and O.P. discovered to his dismay that the fireman's method of keeping an engine steaming was affecting his reputation as an engineer. A number of peers were assembled in the rear locker room when O.P. entered. Exchanging greetings, one of the younger men made a comment loud enough for everyone to hear: "Oscar, we don't even have to look to see if it's the RN approaching. All we do is listen. You're the only blower engineer around."

O.P. felt it would have been better if this man had actually hauled off and struck him, for that remark affected him personally. Not about to reinforce this slur, O.P. controlled his anger, but he intended to clarify his status as engineer to this audience. He had never been ridiculed openly that way, and there was no alternative but to defend himself—not in anger, either, but in a manner that would ensure that these men got his message.

Addressing his accuser with deliberation, he stated: "Young man, I was running a steam engine before you were even thought of. And up to the present, no engine ever appeared that I couldn't keep steam up in when I was working it out on the road. I went as far for coal and water as any engineer on this division, perhaps the whole system could be included, and I'm still capable of doing that." He then pointed to his fireman standing nearby. "On my first trip on the RN, I cautioned this man that using the blower continually wasn't necessary. He didn't take my advice, as you seem to notice. Rather, he told me that was his way of firing, to keep an even fire. I'm sure this unacceptable manner of firing an engine is costing the Company money by blowing a large amount of coal out the stack and producing steam that is not used to haul the train. The important thing is that I have enough steam to get the train over the road. With this in mind, I'm unable to register any complaints. But for your information, I don't approve of this practice."

Shortly after this confrontation, the Company inadvertently came to O.P.'s rescue. His fireman was, according to his own declaration, set back up as an engineer. Where he went after leaving Williamsport, O.P. never found out, as he never saw or heard of him again.

When the fireman's slot was open for bids, O.P. had the opportunity to work with extra men who were all in the group that hired out at the beginning of or during the war years. Some had even fired for him in the yard and at that time left much to be desired. He was thus skeptical about having this younger generation of firemen handling the firing duties on an engine out on the road. But his fears were short-lived. They all proved to be adept at using the stoker.

Before the due date for bids on the fireman's position on the RN crew, O.P. found his protégé from yard service. Knowing that he'd never held a road job other than his trial trips and an occasional extra run, O.P. talked the man into bidding on the fast freight, assuring him that he'd learn what railroading was all about. He did that and was awarded the job. On their first trip together, after coupling to the train with the assigned I1, O.P. began watching his protégé make preparations for the run and learned the man's short stature was a deterrent in handling his chores, especially when setting the lubricator; he had to crawl up and around the boiler backhead much like a small red squirrel. Out of the yard on the first leg of the trip, it was also apparent that the new fireman wasn't very well versed in the principles of firing with a stoker. He did, however, manage to keep steam up until they reached Lock Haven.

After finishing the required work at this point, the run to Renovo began, and orders gave them clear blocks all the way. The faster O.P. got the 2-10-0 running, the more the fireman increased the volume on the stoker. The discharge of solid black smoke out the stack was an indication of what was going to happen, and when the gauge started to show steam pressure was falling, O.P. instructed the fireman to shut off the stoker. Opening the firebox door revealed that the arch was nearly plugged. Most of the firebox was covered with a layer of green, unburned coal. Only a few bright spots existed, prompting the fireman to exclaim, "What the hell do I do now, Oscar? If I don't get some steam up, we're going to have a steam failure."

The best thing he could do, O.P. told him, was get the shaker bar and the long fire rake and start working. He then opened the blower, placed the reverse lever farther forward, and opened the throttle wider to give the I1 more draft. The fireman shook the grates and raked and pounded on the mass in the firebox, and together they kept up enough steam to keep the train under motion. By the time they reached Renovo, the fireman had shed his overall jacket, and another one worn beneath that jacket, and was still perspiring profusely. The firebox, meanwhile, was still a mass of clinkers when they took the engine into the house.

On the return trip, O.P. watched the stack discharging plumes of black smoke, and the fireman giving the stoker more volume as speed was increased. Rather than have the fireman create the same mess he had on the westbound trip, O.P. called him over to the right side and advised him to shut the stoker off. He then explained that the volume of coal fed into the firebox should be decreased as speed was gained. Firing an engine equipped with this device differed from hand-firing in that only a shallow amount of fire was necessary. Actually, what was taking place was an explosion, with the majority of the coal fed into the firebox burning before it hit the grate area, and the residue it produced being discharged out the stack.

He then gave the fireman an analogy to help him have a clearer understanding of what transpired. "A steam engine," he said, "can in many respects be compared to an automobile. When a car is started cold in low gear, the choke is used to give it a richer mixture as gas is injected in a large volume. As more momentum is gained, the choke is fully opened and less of the rich gas mixture is fed to the motor. When running in high gear, the motor needs only a minimal amount of gas, and at various speeds the fuel is shut off when coasting. If more speed is required, fuel is again fed into the motor."

He continued: "On this engine, or any other steam engine, you, as the fireman, control the power available in the form of steam. Starting a train, the engineer places the reverse lever in the forward or reverse position, near the bottom notch on the quadrant, depending on the direction he wants to travel. The throttle is opened wide, and now you are required to furnish a large amount of steam. Then, instead of shifting gears, the engineer starts notching back on the reverse lever and reduces the amount of steam fed to the cylinders with the throttle. Finally, at the speed he chooses to run, the reverse lever will be moved close to the center, and although the throttle is still open, only a small amount of steam enters the cylinders. If you listen to how the engine is working and pay attention to the steam gauge and water glass, regulating your stoker will be easy. Many times it even can be shut off."

O.P. then went over to the left side and showed the fireman which settings on the stoker valve were needed for the speed at which he was traveling. He adjusted the valve to properly distribute the coal evenly in the firebox. With careful observation of how the fireman was performing, and with a bit of coaching from time to time, O.P.'s protégé became one of the better stoker firemen he ever worked with.

From time to time the conductor on the RN crew gave subtle hints relating to the speeds that these trains attained, but O.P. disregarded these comments. He suspected that this conductor did not appreciate riding on the rear at anything above the average speed a freight usually traveled. During one mild confrontation concerning speed, O.P. gave the conductor some insight on how he'd always handled a train from the head end. When he was on the main running with a clear block ahead, he explained, it was his duty to get to the next block as fast as conditions permitted, never deliberately going slow just to put more time on the time card or tying up other movements. "Consequently," O.P. told the conductor, "over the years I've earned a reputation with the train dispatchers and operators of adhering to their orders within their given time limits. As a result, I am likely to be allowed to advance ahead of other movements and not be holed up in a siding wasting time. Another thing: you receive a copy of the same orders that I'm given, so you should know the reason I'm handling the trains as fast as I possibly can." In closing, O.P. pointed out that he wasn't considering changing any of his established practices.

For a while, nothing more was mentioned about traveling too fast, but that did not last long. After marking up one night, O.P. learned that he was getting an M1 locomotive, and at the engine house he found out why this class was to be sent out on the RN: the engine was suffering from internal leaks that were impossible to repair at a regular engine house. The RN was being used to shuttle it to the Renovo shops, which were equipped to make the necessary repairs. O.P.'s customary inspection did not reveal anything actually wrong with the M1 mechanically, nor could he spot where it was leaking. He alerted his fireman that the 4-8-2 had been put on the repair list and stressed he should pay close attention to any abnormal leaking that might occur.

Out in the yard, as they backed down to their made-up train, they were greeted by the conductor, who explained he had a problem. In the process of making up the RN, a yard crew had smashed his steel cabin, causing enough damage to render it useless. This was bad enough, but insult was added to injury when he learned that the only available cabin was the old wooden "Mae West" N6 model used by the yard and transfer crew. The only good news the conductor had was that they had a very light consist, only twelve cars, and there wouldn't be much switching to handle in Lock Haven.

Leaving the yard and all the way to Linden, O.P. observed closely how the M1 was doing. Nothing seemed out of order. It was steaming well, plus it was in very good mechanical condition. Past Linden on the double-track main, O.P. began setting the big 4-8-2 at running speed. After all, he thought, it was equipped to be used as a passenger engine, with cab train control signal, steam heat control, and an original short tender. With only twelve cars plus the cabin, it would be a shame not to use this engine in the manner it was designed to perform.

Running at around the maximum allowable freight speed of 60 miles an hour, or perhaps a little faster, O.P. was startled when he heard the air go into emergency just as he neared the bottom of the Jersey Shore hill. Looking to the rear he was unable to see anything amiss with the train. Rather than continue on in this locked-up condition, which would produce flat spots on the drivers and car wheels, he released the emergency position and made an immediate heavy air application, bringing the train to a stop in a shorter distance than if the wheels were sliding.

He advised the fireman to look out his side to the rear for any signs of trouble, and the reply was negative. Now the only thing that could happen would be to have the conductor decide they were traveling too fast, and the fact that he was riding a wooden cabin probably magnified his fear of speed. Watching to the rear, O.P. saw the glow of a lantern emerge from the cabin and move forward. When the figure carrying this lantern reached the cab, he could see that it was the conductor, who blurted out, "That damn cabin isn't fit to ride in at the speed you're traveling. The windows are sliding back and forth and the doors are swinging open and shut. It's really awful."

But instead of being irritated by this unnecessary emergency stop, O.P. was amused by the conductor's revelations and told the conductor, "It's riding real good up here. Perhaps the best thing for you to do is climb aboard and ride with us."

Not accepting this invitation, the conductor went back to the cabin. O.P. did not slow down, though, and ran at the same speed into Lock Haven and then the remainder of the way into Renovo. Nothing was heard from the rear-end crew, nor did the subject of running too fast come up again. Evidently, though, the conductor still wasn't pleased with the rides he was getting.

A short while later O.P. received an L1 that had just come out of the Renovo shops, completely overhauled and shining, to make the eastbound trip to Williamsport. Between Renovo and Lock Haven this 2-8-2 was put to several tests and proved to be in excellent shape, riding well, running fast, the stoker producing steam freely. At Lock Haven, after conducting their switching chores, orders were issued that permitted them to leave ahead of a passenger movement. Instructions were to take the siding at McElhattan, clearing at this point to allow the passenger to proceed. With only a short time to make this move, O.P. got the L1 set up and was running as fast as he could with a sizeable train. True to form, the conductor again decided they were going too fast and put the train into emergency. This time, after placing the automatic brake in full release, O.P. did not make another application to bring the train to a stop. Instead, he pumped the air pressure back up, and when it held with no variation on the gauge, he opened the L1 up and continued to run at the same fast pace until he reached the designated siding at McElhattan.

Stopping after clearing the main, he expected the conductor to come forward to explain why the train was placed into emergency, but that did not happen. The scheduled meet had passed, and they were again running on the main as if nothing had taken place, so O.P. had reason to believe that the conductor was merely demonstrating that he too could control how fast the train traveled. If he had stopped on the main to investigate, as the conductor intended, the passenger would have been held up, and that would draw a reprimand. The conductor could then easily persuade officials that the emergency stop was necessary by coming up with a number of logical excuses and directing fault to the engineer. Without a doubt the conductor would point out that the train was being handled in a manner contrary to safe operating procedures.

After marking off at the yard office in Williamsport, O.P. called the conductor aside and told him: "I want you to know that this is the last time you're going to pull the air on me just to please yourself. This afternoon when we left Lock Haven you had a copy of our orders, and if you read them thoroughly you should have been aware that we had to move to get to McElhattan ahead of the passenger. Also, you know that if I didn't get there at the specified time, the passenger would be delayed and I would be held responsible for tying it up, probably ending up in a reprimand."

O.P. knew there would be excuses, but not the one he expected. The conductor avowed: "We picked up a bad order car in Lock Haven that had a speed restriction on it. When you began running more than thirty-five miles an hour, I decided that was too fast and pulled the air to slow you down before something happened."

Hearing this reason as an excuse, O.P. almost exploded, but he did manage to control himself. "It was your responsibility," he countered, "to tell me that we had a car with speed restrictions, either directly or through the dispatcher, but you failed to do that. Orders we received would have indicated that. If this actually is the truth, we would have been held, not allowed to advance on the main out of Lock Haven. Furthermore, if you determined that you had a legitimate emergency, you should have left your air valve open, and I wouldn't have been able to proceed to the siding. Also, when we were holed up, you never came forward to notify me of this condition, nor was the dispatcher notified. Instead you permitted me to continue on into Williamsport." O.P. concluded, "I think you'd be better satisfied riding on the rear end of some other crew. You're undoubtedly aware that this isn't the only job on the division." The conductor didn't take this advice. He stayed on the RN, but he never used his air valve again.

Although I spent every weekend at home, the hours O.P. was working did not allow us much time to discuss railroading, and usually no time at all. The 1:40 A.M. call the RN had, usually with twelve hours or more on duty seven days a week, often didn't even allow O.P. enough time to get enough rest. Normally it was 2:00 P.M. or later when he arrived home, at which time he ate the meal my mother had prepared for him, bathed, and promptly went to bed. Around 10:00 P.M. he arose, glanced through the daily newspaper, ate, and was ready to leave for Williamsport around 12:30 A.M.

When I told my mother that was a job more suited to a younger man, she said I'd never convince O.P. of that. "He thinks he's a young man again," she explained.

O.P. did have a regular respite from his rugged schedule. He exceeded his allowable mileage earnings every month, which entitled him to five or more days off to rest. During the Christmas vacation, O.P. was off on his mileage break. That gave us ample time to catch up on what was transpiring, both on the railroad and with him personally.

Still concerned that he might have a run that was too strenuous, I approached him about the long hours he was putting in and asked if they might be detrimental to his health. To this he replied in the negative. Although the job was a seven-day-a-week position and entailed being on duty longer than many other road jobs, much of the time was not spent running. That led to another line of questioning. I observed that he hated wasting time and that he was always trying to find ways to improve on getting either to or from a destination as quickly as possible and without delays, and then I asked: "Why don't you practice this on the RN?" He had tried, he admitted, but found few avenues open to any of his endeavors.

Then I got a comprehensive rundown on the obstacles hindering his effort. Westbound to Renovo was the only leg that offered an opportunity to run as a fast freight was intended to. When they were ready to leave the yards at Williamsport, all the early passenger trains in and out of the city had cleared, and as a scheduled freight the RN was given preference over other movements. Normally O.P. ran clear all the way to Lock Haven with few restrictions, and again ran clear the remaining leg of the trip after switching chores there were taken care of. At Renovo, though, things began to deteriorate, and it was impossible to save any time there. After the train was set off in the yard, the engine was taken to the house and serviced, or an exchange engine would be provided. Whatever the pattern, it was never a quick process. Once that maneuver was accomplished, O.P. would go back out in the yard and couple to the train for the return trip. Then there was another waiting period before receiving permission to occupy the main.

About mid-morning, it seemed that other eastbound movements would be advanced ahead of the RN—all them slow, heavy-tonnage trains. The most prevalent intruder was an iron-ore movement off the Buffalo Division; another was a diker with coal assembled at Renovo and bound for Southport; the third was a foreigner, a New York Central train that originated in Clearfield and ran along the headwaters of the West Branch of the Susquehanna River to the village of Keating, then on Pennsylvania tracks to McElhattan, then back on its own rails to its Avis terminal. Its consist was mainly made up of loaded coal hoppers, with some mixed freight.

If odds put any of these movements ahead of the RN, O.P. found that for most of the run to Lock Haven he could expect restricting signals displayed on the block distance signals. The worst culprit was the Central movement; not only were restricted signals given, but on occasion, due to mechanical failures, even stop signals. The area railroad men had a name for the Central's trains, and O.P. felt that it described them very well. They were referred to as "hookers." The way they handled their trains contradicted statements the Central's engine crews made around him, extolling the superiority of the Central's locomotives to those used by the Pennsylvania. On this river grade from Renovo to McElhattan, an M1 class, a comparable engine, could easily maintain freight speeds with the same tonnage the Central was having trouble moving.

O.P. found it was imperative to clear Lock Haven by at least 11:00 A.M. If he didn't, he could expect to put in a long afternoon. Mixed in with trains advancing ahead of him on the eastbound side of the double-track main, he also had to contend with movements off the Bald Eagle Branch, as well as the scheduled passengers that dominated the rails until mid-afternoon. If he was behind all these trains, the last bottleneck to hinder his progress came about at Linden.

He had to contend not only with eastbounds but also with trains coming westbound out of the city on the single-track main. On this section of track, trains coming off of or heading onto the Elmira Branch at Newberry Junction came into the picture, adding to the congestion. With all the factors presented, O.P. concluded, the RN didn't offer many loopholes for improving the time it took to make this short-distance turnaround day any better. At times he would just barely make it into the yards before he was outlawed.

The only day that gave O.P. any running room to speak of was Sunday, and even though there weren't as many movements on that day, he could still encounter delays. One of these was perhaps the most unusual he had ever dealt with during his entire career, and although it resulted in a loss of time, it turned out to be amusing.

On the first Sunday trip eastbound from Renovo, his orders included a directive to stop at an isolated block station along the east bank of the Susquehanna, about halfway to Lock Haven, pick up an operator, and drop him off at a small town down the river a short distance away, in another remote location. Approaching this block station, there wasn't any chance that he would fail to pick up the passenger. He could see a stop signal displayed on the semaphore. Stopping the I1 directly in front of the tower, his first surprise was to see an older woman emerging from the station. She was almost as broad as she was tall. He and the fireman looked at each other in amazement. Then, as she neared the 2-10-0, her first utterance came in the form of a command: "I can't get up on that damn engine unless one of you fellows gets down here and helps me."

Obligingly the head brakeman dropped off, placed both hands on her posterior and began shoving when she mounted the first step. When she got about halfway up this vertical ladder, the fireman and O.P. reached down and, grasping her arms, literally lifted her up the rest of the way and into the cab. At her destination, the same procedure was performed in reverse to get her back onto the ground. All during these loading and unloading operations, O.P. was secretly wishing someone could be on hand to photograph the bizarre procedure.

O.P. was not a stranger to this segment on the western part of the Williamsport Division. He had fired to Renovo on crews out of Sunbury, and for a short time in 1924 he tested engines out of the Renovo shops, but now there were only a few people he knew at this terminal. The woman operator that he had picked up was one of these people, and in order to satisfy his curiosity about her role on the railroad, he asked some questions when he reached Renovo on the following day.

A crew clerk at the yard office knew this woman's background and gave O.P. a complete rundown of her status as an employee. She was one of the women the Company hired as operators during World War I, and she had remained on the roster, working at block stations in the area from Lock Haven to Renovo. During this lengthy career, she never learned to drive an automobile, relying instead on passenger trains to get to and from the blocks worked. On Sundays, any convenient freight movement provided her with needed transportation. She also raised goats on a small farm: not the common variety, but championship stock. As a result, she had come to be affectionately known as "the goat lady."

During Christmas vacation I learned another function the RN had adopted since it began as a turnaround crew out of Williamsport. The machinist who had accompanied O.P. back and forth to work during the years spent on the yard and transfer crew, a roundhouse employee, related that it did not take the foreman at this facility long to determine that the RN was ideally suited for taking engines that needed shopping to the Renovo facility for repairs.

In a way, they were taking advantage of their long relationship with O.P. and of his general manner and reputation as a congenial engineer. Some of the engines they assigned to the RN were in such bad shape that their fires should have been knocked out and the engine moved to Renovo cold. The machinist cited one example of this method that had been used recently.

An I1 assigned to Williamsport had been in such bad shape when it arrived that it was not to be sent out over the road as head-end power, so it was relegated to pusher service exclusively. The pusher crews were constantly turning in bad order reports on it, and as a result it was a frequent visitor inside the house as attempts were made to keep it in passable running condition.

One afternoon the pusher engineer assigned to the 2-10-0 refused to accept the engine and filled out a rejection report detailing all the major defects. This refusal and rejection convinced the foreman that if he continued to patch up this engine and classify it as suitable for service, not only he but also the men who did the repairs would be held liable if a federal inspector examined it.

It would, without a doubt, receive a Form 5 card from the government man, which would mean it had to be removed from service immediately. Aware of this, the foreman was taking a chance by sending it out on the westbound RN, but it would save the Company money, and he was acting in his position as foreman.

The employees at the roundhouse knew the I1 was not in any shape to be sent out, especially on the head end, and the decision made by the foreman initiated a betting spree among these men. The consensus was that O.P. would never get this derelict 2-10-0 all the way to Renovo under its own power. Others allowed that, if he was lucky, he might make it as far as Lock Haven, and one man was betting that he couldn't get out of the yards with a train. The machinist confessed that he had an advantage over the other men. He had known O.P. from the days he ran out of Ralston, and knew he could get an engine over the road regardless of its condition. He bet O.P. would get the engine and train to Renovo. Consequently he won most of the money that was wagered.

Possessing this expanded view of the RN's purpose, other than freight hauling, I approached O.P. and asked about the condition of the engines used on this run. He gave me a complete evaluation of the motive power used as freight haulers on the Williamsport Division, cautioning that consideration had to be given to the age of these locomotives. Almost all of them had been around for more than twenty-five years, except the M1a class. During the war years they had been used continually without mercy; even when shopped only absolutely necessary repairs were made. Surprisingly, though, he felt most of these engines were in pretty good shape.

There were times, however, when a bad one came around, and they always seemed to be assigned to the RN to be delivered to Renovo for shopping. By this admission it was apparent the personnel at the roundhouse weren't fooling him, as they believed.

That led me to ask why he accepted an engine he knew wasn't suitable for road service, and he explained that it could be regarded as a gesture of accommodation. If it was a long over-the-road run, it would be different, but on a short trip of only 54 miles the engine could be nursed along to cover this distance, as long as he could maintain steam at a decent level. The advantage to accepting these bad order engines was that at Renovo he would get a decent engine for the return trip to Williamsport. At times he even got an engine that had just been released from the shop after having been completely overhauled.

Actually, the refurbished engines emerging from the shops were better than when originally constructed, regardless of their age. New innovations were incorporated internally. Changes were made in the running gear assemblies and the cylinders, valves, and pistons were modified, and, when needed, a new boiler was mounted on the frame. Outwardly these engines appeared to be the same. But while visible changes were difficult to detect, internally many changes were incorporated to increase their operating efficiency.

One change to all engines did alter the appearance of their front end, and it was made in the interest of safety. The headlight was placed on top of the smoke box, the generator was lowered to the top of the smoke-box door, and a wide platform was added at the bottom of the smoke-box door. This new positioning allowed workmen to stand on the platform when they were servicing or repairing the generator. O.P. believed that the platform would have been more practical if it had been installed years ago, when enginemen had to climb up on the smoke-box front to light their oil-burning headlights and marker lamps, and then repeat the exercise to extinguish them. He did concede that the new platform made it easier to clean the headlight reflector and glass lens.

On the I1's, as well as getting the new front-end treatment, the sound quality was improved. Each had the old-style small screecher whistle removed and replaced by the larger passenger-tone version. These whistles were salvaged from passenger-class locomotives that had been retired and were on their way to scrap yards. On one occasion, while O.P.'s 2-10-0 was being serviced at the engine house for its return trip to Williamsport, workmen installed a big whistle as part of their routine, which, of course, pleased him. Another part of upgrading the I1 class engines was that most of them came out of the shops with a coast-to-coast tender, a feature O.P. had advocated for many years. It was something he believed had long been necessary to reduce costly stops for water. Evidently the people in the motive power offices had come to realize this, as well as the fact that it also sped up running time.

Everything during the winter of 1948 ran along without change. The RN was still keeping within the sixteen-hour time limit on a daily basis, and O.P. enjoyed the time off gained each month when he exceeded his allotted mileage. He noted, however, that the weather was always bad when he took this time off, so instead of working during major snowstorms, extremely cold temperatures, or torrential rains, he was always at home.

When the weather started warming in the spring, O.P. discovered an attraction that gave him and the other engine crewmen a pleasant diversion on their daily trips. Entering Lock Haven on a bright sunny morning, a comely young housewife was in her backyard adjacent to the tracks hanging up clothes. In response to O.P.'s friendly wave, she returned the gesture, and he in turn responded with a short, soft salute with the whistle. Their exchange of pleasantries was repeated the following day and became a daily ritual for quite some time, giving the crew something to look forward to.

One day as they were passing through, however, she didn't appear, nor was she there on succeeding days, giving the crew some concern. While conducting the switching chores, the head brakeman inquired about her to one of the local workmen, describing where they usually waved to her and explaining that they had no idea where she had disappeared to all of a sudden.

It did not take long for the grapevine to come up with an answer, one that didn't please the RN's head-end crew. The woman's husband had returned home unexpectedly just as she was offering her daily goodwill gestures to the passing crew, and his reaction to this performance was to go into a jealous rage. He resorted to physical violence, accused her of having an affair with one of the train's crewmen, and threatened then to administer the same kind of treatment if he again found her waving to a train crew.

Happenings out of the ordinary seemed to crop up during the return of pleasant spring weather. While waiting for the clear signal to occupy the main one morning at Renovo, the head brakeman spotted two men believed to be hoboes standing near the tracks just beyond the signal board. Both the brakeman and the fireman were extra men on this day, and while both were trainmen from the younger generation, they had been around the railroad long enough to suspect the 'boes were going to board the RN for a free ride. Discussing the situation, they approached O.P. with a proposition. Each was betting five dollars that he couldn't get the I1 and train moving fast enough to prevent the hoboes from getting aboard.

O.P. had reservations about taking them up on such a bet, but he finally conceded after a bit of cajoling. He informed the fireman that he'd better have his fire in shape to provide plenty of steam if he was going to demonstrate what a 2-10-0 was capable of. When the signal dropped to the clear position, O.P. opened up the I1 and, under a heavy application of sand, blasted out much like the Buffalo Flyer leaving from a station stop without slipping a wheel. By the time he reached the signal board position, he had built up enough speed that he thought the hoboes wouldn't attempt to hop the train.

As the train passed their waiting spot, however, both hoboes ran out about ten cars to the rear of the engine. The fireman and brakeman watched the action from O.P.'s side and gave out a shout of victory when one of the hoboes grabbed the irons and swung up onto the step. Then the second hobo made his charge to the following car, successfully getting a grasp on the grab iron, but unable to get his legs going fast enough to hop on. Still hanging on and running along the tracks, he failed to see the oil-illuminated switch target in his path, so when he came in contact with this device it sent him flying out into the nearby underbrush, and that was the last the crew saw of this hobo.

After witnessing this unfortunate attempt to get aboard the train, the brakeman and fireman decided that because only one of the two managed to get on neither they nor O.P. had won, and the bet was counted as a draw. The RN ran the entire distance to Lock Haven on clear blocks, and the brakeman in the monkey house on the rear of the tender reported that he could see their rider from time to time peering over the top of a boxcar. Arriving in Lock Haven as the train slowed to enter yard limits, the hobo dropped off and disappeared.

The morning after this incident, at the Renovo yard office to get his orders for the return trip to Williamsport, a crew clerk commented that the RN left town in a hurry the day before. Apparently everyone in the entire complex had stopped to listen to the manner in which the I1 was being worked. It had caused quite a commotion, he noted, adding that a section foreman came into the office reporting that someone tried to board the fast-moving RN but had gotten tangled up with a switch target; the switch marker had been hit with such force that it was smashed beyond repair.

When the noise of the 2-10-0 thundering out of the yard aroused their attention, the foreman related that his crew had stopped working to see what was going on. After seeing the man attempt to board the train and get thrown into the brush and not reappear, they went to investigate. Looking around the area near the broken marker, they found him lying unconscious in the brush. Unable to determine how badly the man was injured, they summoned an ambulance, which transported him to the nearest hospital at Lock Haven. As it turned out, the man had multiple cuts and bruises and two broken legs. When the hospital contacted the yardmaster to find out how the injuries occurred and whether he was employed by the Company, the yardmaster stressed this person had been trespassing on railroad property and that no one knew anything else about him. Listening to the crew clerk's recap of this unfortunate event, O.P. didn't add anything, but he deeply regretted that someone had been hurt as a result of his actions.

Nothing more ever evolved from this accident. O.P. surmised that the Company had dismissed the incident as just one more event related to the operations of a railroad.

At the end of the spring semester in 1948, I again became a truck driver on the river dike project, and living at home gave me an opportunity to talk about railroading with O.P. He still seemed well satisfied working the RN crew, so much so, in fact, that instead of taking his retirement this summer at the age of sixty-five, he intended to work another year, which would mean that he had worked for the Company for an even forty-five years. About the only problem he had—and it was a minor one—was that his protégé fireman started marking off. That occasionally left O.P. at the mercy of extra firemen, something he still had reservations about.

At first the fireman would take only a day, and at intervals that were not too alarming. But as time passed, he would mark off for two or three days in a regular pattern. As it turned out, this did not perplex O.P. much, for he was finding the extra men quite capable. In a way, he enjoyed working with the new generation of fireman. One day, after his protégé returned to duty following an interlude, O.P. asked him why he was more or less neglecting his job. The answer he received from this man, whom he regarded as his "regular-extra" fireman, was both a shock, a perspective O.P. found amusing. He said, "You know, Oscar, working seven days a week, and with our mileage, I'm making more money than I ever did before. Now I find that I have to take time off to spend some of it."

Not long after, O.P.'s protégé bid in a yard job and left the RN for this less-demanding kind of service. The loss of this fireman, who was near the top of the fireman's roster, seemed to establish a precedent. O.P. found that he never had a regular fireman very long before the man was bumped. After a time, O.P. figured he had worked with almost all the men hired out in the early 1940s who were established at the Williamsport yard office, plus men who were on the extra board.

As more and more of the I1's that O.P. was receiving to handle the daily RN trip were equipped with coast-to-coast tenders, he began noticing that some of these large models had a trait that could be dangerous at times. The large tenders attached to the M1a's he ran on the EC jobs had never displayed this tendency. Most swayed more than the smaller-size models, but now, for some reason on specific portions of the run, they rolled from side to side when running at around 50 miles an hour. It wasn't noticeable running in either direction between Williamsport and Lock Haven, or when running eastbound from Renovo to Lock Haven, only on the westbound run from Lock Haven to Renovo.

On one trip the head brakeman came forward down over the coal pile shouting, "You've got to slow down, Oscar. That damn tender's rocking back and forth so bad I can barely sit on my seat in the monkey house. The water is splashing around with enough force to pop open the tank lids, and it's flying all over the place." O.P. began watching how the tender was swaying and concluded that this only occurred when negotiating the many gentle curves found in the track as it followed the banks of the river in the narrow valley between Lock Haven and Renovo. The same engine was serviced and turned for the eastbound trip over the section where the tender's swaying forced him to reduce running speed. Nothing more than the ordinary amount of rocking motion was experienced between Renovo and Lock Haven, nor did any unorthodox motion occur on the line between Lock Haven and Williamsport.

A few days later O.P. was assigned the same I1. Again between Lock Haven and Renovo the swaying became so violent he was forced to run at reduced speeds to alleviate this condition. Now he was certain that when the water in the tank was at or near the halfway level, the swaying became dangerous, and when rounding curves this action was further aggravated—and that this was directly attributable to the design of the coast-to-coast tender: a combination of improperly arranged baffle plates in the water tank, and a suspension system that was not rigid enough to stabilize swaying at the half water level.

Still obsessed with this unusual trait of these large tenders, O.P. began discussing the problem with other enginemen. None claimed to have noticed or experienced any abnormalities other than the usual swaying characteristic that all larger tenders have. Finally, though, he was able to verify his findings with an engineer who had handled passenger runs from Renovo to Harrisburg for years. This engineer related that after the M1a class made its appearance, some models were fitted with a train control apparatus and the Company started using them on the crack Buffalo expresses over the entire distance to Buffalo with one engine, instead of changing at Renovo. This arrangement never worked as officials had planned. Excessive swaying developed on certain sections at passenger speeds, forcing slow running. Because of crew complaints and late schedules, the M1a's with coast-to-coast tenders were dropped from use, and the M1's with regular tenders were put back in service.

This man then described another attempt to utilize these large tenders. According to him, a number of K4's were equipped with them around the same time, and these engines were used all the way from Harrisburg to Chicago. Once again the coast-to-coast tenders did not perform as anticipated, and the Company stopped running them from Harrisburg to Pittsburgh. West of Pittsburgh they lasted a little longer. Eventually all these tanks were removed from the K4's. "The Company stated that they added too much weight to the trains," the engineman concluded, "but I still think they never revealed the real reason for discontinuing them." At least O.P.'s findings were confirmed: the coast-to-coast tender could be unstable, particularly at higher speeds, but it was still better in freight use than the small models used for many years.

At this time, a new type of motive power began appearing on some of the crack passenger runs. As time went on this intruder was also seen frequently as the head-end power on through freights. O.P. had mixed emotions. The value of diesel/electric power, when compared with the reliable steam engine, led him to believe that this might be nothing more than an attempt by the Company to reduce operating costs in some areas. He had serious reservations about how this type of locomotive could ever replace the entire steam fleet in use on the system. Nevertheless, he was curious about how one of these locomotives performed. He discussed their virtues with the men who had used them as passenger power and on freight runs from Renovo to Harrisburg's Enola terminal.

All the engineers he talked with claimed the diesels were relatively simple to operate, rode better than a passenger coach, and were real smooth when starting a train. The only complaint the passenger men seemed to have was the difficulty they experienced when trying to make up time if they were running late. Governors (speed control devices) held their speed to just a trifle more than 80 miles an hour. The only thing that bothered the freight engineers was their sluggishness when running at speed. These new locomotives, if slowed, did not have the snap to pick up a train fast. They believed that an M1 was a better-suited all-around engine when it came to handling a train.

One morning, at the end of the westbound trip at Renovo, O.P. spotted a diesel newcomer parked on the ready track near the engine house. While his I1 was being serviced, he took the liberty of climbing aboard. He was surprised at what he discovered in the cab of the diesel. It was roomy, with comfortable seats on both sides for the enginemen, plus a smaller seat between for the head brakeman. Controls and gauges were conveniently arranged, and, combined with the large windshields, visibility was excellent. Although the cab windows were at the same height as a steam engine's, somehow everything seemed much higher. Further examining the interior, he found it was equipped with windshield wipers, defrosters, heaters, a water cooler, and probably the most outstanding feature: a toilet. This device was a necessity, though, as the engine didn't have a handy scoop shovel or coal pile to use when Mother Nature called. But he didn't like the whistle sound, claiming it was a nickel-and-dime foghorn, the same cheap version the Company affixed on the electric locomotives.

In the face of all the luxuries of these new locomotives, O.P. began to feel he had hired out thirty years too soon. He worried he wouldn't have a chance to test one of these newcomers before his planned retirement date.

Later in the summer of 1948, a bus company established service from Williamsport to Ralston, and its scheduled runs were suited to O.P.'s call time for the RN, so he opted to use the bus for his trips to and from home, with the exception of Saturday night, when no buses operated after midnight and on Sunday. He drove on Saturday nights so he would have transportation for Sunday. But it didn't take him long to fill the gap in the bus schedule. While I was at home, he appointed me to provide him with transportation on Sundays. There was no set time for me to be in Williamsport, just as long as I was there by noon. If he got in earlier, he would wait; if he got in after the designated hour, I would wait.

One exceptionally hot and humid Sunday in August when I got to the yard office, a crew clerk obligingly checked on the RN's eastbound progress. It had just cleared Lock Haven, he informed me, and even if it could run clear from that point, including the time it would take O.P. to get his engine in the house and mark off, I would be waiting at least an hour. Rather than wait around the railroad and suffer in the heat, I told the crew clerk to tell O.P. when he arrived that I would be waiting at a small club less than a block away.

A number of railroaders had the same idea. Out of the heat, they could also partake of a cool beverage. In the company of these men, many of whom were old acquaintances, the time passed quickly. I had only been in this establishment for a short time, though, when the flagman off the RN made his appearance and came to the bar to join me, announcing O.P. would be following directly. In the conversation we had, and without any prompting, he stated that the RN job was probably one of the best money-making runs on the division, then added, "We'd make a lot more if your dad would slow down. He runs too damn fast."

Taken aback by this assertion, and not about to become involved with this line of reasoning, I let it pass without comment. The subject was dropped abruptly when O.P. appeared, looking more like a workman who just came out of a coal mine than an engineer. His first words of greeting were that it was the coolest spot he'd been in all day. Wasting no time, he ordered a cold beer, to wash out an abnormal amount of cinders that had collected in his throat, he explained. I interjected that he'd also collected another carload of cinders on his face. The only white showing was around his eyes, I added, making it seem as though his goggles were still in place.

He wasn't offended by my observation. The normal amount of grime associated with riding the cab of an I1 was compounded today, he said, by the heat and smoke that rolled down on his side of the cab all the way from Renovo every time he was drifting after shutting off the throttle. Adding that it was his normal practice to wash up in the bullpen in the yard office, he said that since he was going directly home, all he bothered to wash was his hands. "A bath and a change of clothes is what's needed to clean up properly," he said.

After he quenched his thirst and we were making our way up the highway to Ralston, he mentioned that he had seen the flagman and me talking when he arrived at the club. He could guess what he was telling me, he offered, saying, "Both the men riding on the rear of the train are always complaining to someone about how fast I run the RN."

There was no purpose in denying something O.P. was aware of, but I did add that his fast running had caused the flagman to feel he was earning less as a result of O.P.'s fast running. That came as no surprise to O.P., but he told me that attitude wasn't in the best interests of the Company. Many of the crews seemed to think that all they had to do was report for duty, and even that the Company owed them a living. They do little to protect their jobs but are always ready to draw their pay every half, he added.

"They fail to understand that the Company must make a profit in order to run trains over the rails, and they must satisfy the customers that use the service being offered. If these customers aren't receiving the proper service, they're bound to look for other means of transportation. Consequently the railroad is going to suffer, and if it's not making money, trains will be abolished. This is happening too, and yet fellows like I have riding on the rear of the RN still have this attitude. If I were to slow down for their reason, the RN wouldn't be running very long. Then they'd wake up one day and wonder what happened to their jobs. Not today or tomorrow, maybe, but that will be the eventual outcome."

Still musing, O.P. said he was thankful that he'd soon be retiring instead of staying around to watch the railroad disintegrate.

At the end of the summer I returned to school for the fall semester. I now had something in common to look forward to with O.P. Not that I expected to retire as he did, but rather in January the first phase of my formal education would be completed. Unless there was a catastrophe, my degree would be conferred at graduation. To be sure I completed a required course, however, I had to change the routine I'd followed for a long time. I had a class on Saturday mornings, which eliminated my visits home over the weekend. In a way I welcomed the change.

There were enough activities at college to keep the weeks from dragging too much. Even the football team helped, having a winning season and achieving national ratings. This made it enjoyable to attend the Saturday afternoon contests when played on the home field. When there were no scheduled home games, I did go home for the weekend, and for the Thanksgiving and

Christmas vacations. O.P. was off on both those holidays as usual, due to excess mileage, so that gave us an opportunity to do some railroading together. He didn't have much to offer, though. Everything was running as it should, and there was plenty of business to keep all the crews working steady.

After Christmas and just before New Year's, there was an unusual incident on the Elmira Branch directly related to a rare cold snap. During the day the temperature began falling, and by late afternoon it was below zero, and early that evening when O.P. took a reading it had dropped to 20 degrees below zero. Other than being far below the normal temperature, this low reading wasn't alarming, and the thermometer went unchecked for the remainder of the evening. Early the next morning, when I went to purchase the Sunday newspaper, it was bitter cold out. Still the thermometer went unread. At the establishment that sold the papers, the proprietor greeted me with a question: "I'll bet you had to let your Ford drift down the hill to get it started this morning."

That hadn't been necessary, I told him. Although it was slow turning over, the motor started right away. He replied that I was one of the more fortunate persons around town, that not many cars were starting. He then asked, "Do you know how cold it is?" then directed me to step outside to check the thermometer on the side of the building. What it registered made me feel as though I would freeze before I got back inside. It was 35 degrees below zero.

Immediately I exclaimed that the instrument must be way off, but the proprietor assured me it was correct and claimed that the radio had said it was 40 below in some of the higher elevations nearby. Then he told me that sometime Saturday evening a wreck on the hill between Roaring Branch and Leolyn had tied up the railroad. He said it looked like all the engines out of Williamsport were laying at the water plugs in town. Before heading home I drove by the railroad tracks, where, as the garage man had said, a string of I1's was occupying both the main and the siding. It was too cold to waste any time counting the assembled engines or bothering to get any information about the wreck.

O.P. was waiting for the paper when I returned, and at first he didn't want to believe me when I told him how cold it was. After checking our thermometer's minus-32-degree mark, he still expressed disbelief, stating emphatically that something was wrong. He claimed it had never been this cold in Pennsylvania. Then I told him it was colder downtown, and there were radio reports of even colder readings in the higher elevations. I gave him the news of the wreck on the hill, but this didn't seem to trouble him. He even offered that the temperature would make it foolish to drive to the scene to see what had happened.

It remained well below zero into the afternoon, but I again braved the extreme cold and ventured out, where I learned at a public gathering spot that the wreck was a minor one. A car had derailed, tearing up a section of track.

Driving to the vicinity of the water plugs, I discovered all the I1's were gone. In the early evening a neighbor, who was an engineer too, came by to visit with O.P. and give us the details from last evening and tell us what transpired after the accident. He told us that he, along with other engine crews, was called out as relief for the pusher and head-end enginemen that were detained at Ralston. They had gotten word that the tracks would be cleared soon after they arrived and that they should be prepared to move again. Crews began getting steam up in anticipation of this order when it was discovered that most of the engines could not get water into their boilers. Pipes from the tenders to the feedwater heaters had frozen during the waiting period.

A count was made, and seven of the eleven I1's detained were now disabled. There were two pushers from the wrecked hill train, three off another diker held at Bergen (Marsh Hill), and three from the EC3 that made it as far as Trout Run. Machinists and their helpers were sent from Williamsport, but on the scene they found they did not have the proper tools or equipment to correct this rare condition. This complicated matters further, and orders were given to dump the fires on all the engines. They were to maintain only enough steam for lubrication so the engines could be returned to the Williamsport engine house to be thawed out. After switching out the I1's that hadn't frozen up, two were sent to push the errant train on through, and one was used to drag the seven disabled engines back to Williamsport. The neighbor was the engineer doing the towing, and after getting the dead engines back to the house, he and the other engine crews were ordered to mark off. There wasn't enough motive power available to send them out again.

This bizarre series of events caused O.P. to express profound disdain at an outcome that shouldn't have happened. "If I was the road foreman of engines," he said, "I'd fire the men who let their engines freeze up." He then retracted this harsh form of punishment, saying, "Maybe not going as far as firing them, but I'd give them enough time off without pay to think about how they forgot to do their jobs. There is absolutely no excuse for letting those lines freeze up. All they had to do was reverse the flow from the feedwater heater so it would circulate a small amount of water back into the tank."

The neighbor, also a veteran engineman, agreed with O.P., averring that had he been in such a situation he would have done exactly that with the feedwater heater. He could not explain why the engineers involved didn't do this, supposing either they didn't know how to reverse the water flow or that they were simply neglectful of their duties. O.P. was interested in finding out whether the engine crews were reprimanded for what he had considered gross negligence, but according to the grapevine and as far as he could determine, no such action was taken.

Once into the year 1949, the month of January seemed to pass quickly, and the day I had striven to achieve was soon at hand. Fall semester graduation exercises were to be held on the last day of the month, a Monday, and all pre-liminaries, such as final examinations and removing all my possessions, had been taken care of. The only obligation left now was to be present when degrees were granted.

My parents, my youngest sister, who was back in the service but home on special leave, and my oldest, married sister were anticipating attending the ceremonies. With their promise to be in the audience, I left Ralston early on Sunday evening. On my last journey back to school, weather conditions were ideal—cold, but under the glow from a full moon. It was almost like travel-ing in broad daylight.

Later that evening, my roommate for the past three years, who was also finishing his education, and I, after visiting a few familiar haunts, returned to our room again under the light of the brilliant moon. But when we arose the following morning we found more than 12 inches of snow on the ground, and it was still snowing hard. I had to mount a pair of tire chains and shovel the driveway clear in order to get to the nearby street, but I was fortunate enough to be able to drive into town and onto campus.

Later in the morning my parents called to inform me that they hadn't been as lucky. It was still snowing hard, and advisories being broadcast advised them not to attempt driving until the highways were properly cleaned. The snow didn't stop, though; it continued to fall until shortly before noon, by which time it had accumulated to more than 15 inches. My family was unable to attend the graduation exercises, and even an uncle living only 10 miles away couldn't manage to make it.

Almost as abruptly as it started, the weather changed, and under sunny skies the snow began melting. By the end of the ceremonies, nothing but slop and slush remained on the roads. I was able to travel back to Ralston without difficulty and without tire chains. When I arrived, the family was regretful about missing my graduation, but they were excited to see the sheepskin cre-dentials I had been given.

I elected to spend some time relaxing as I made my decision about what work would be best suited for me, and O.P. and I had opportunities to talk frequently. Once, he invited me to accompany him some night on the RN. It wouldn't be a complete round-trip, he said, because it was too risky to be aboard the engine in the yards at Williamsport, especially when returning in the afternoon. Too many officials were around then. The best location for me to board, then, would be at Lock Haven, so I was to be there at 4:00 A.M. O.P. even had the Renovo end figured out: I could drop off after entering the yards, wait in a nearby restaurant, and reboard as the train was leaving on the eastbound leg.

Although the offer pleased me, I didn't want to commit myself at the time, so I begged off with the promise that I would wait until warmer weather to make that trip. That met with O.P.'s approval, and he told me that any-time I wanted to go along all I had to do was say so. (Realizing I had an open invitation, I kept procrastinating until it was too late, and thus never made the trip in the cab with him on the RN run.)

Nearly a month after graduation I accepted a position with a commercial refrigeration firm in Williamsport as a sales representative, but the job also required layout work and supervising some installations. The job kept me busy and was quite interesting.

Later in the spring I responded to a request from a person who was estab-lishing a tavern and needed assistance in selecting the proper refrigeration equipment. I met with the owner, who, immediately after introductory for-malities, asked, "Are you by any chance related to Oscar Orr?" I replied that I was his son.

At this he told me that before deciding to become a tavern proprietor he had been a fireman on the railroad, and that the last job he held was firing for O.P. on the RN crew. For a time our conversation was centered on and about O.P., the former fireman doing most of the talking. It didn't take him long to conclude that O.P. must have discussed many of his work experiences with me, which elicited another direct question: "Did he ever tell you about the day we had the honor of hauling the superintendent and his private car back from Renovo on the RN?"

He had mentioned the incident, I replied, but didn't seem to think it was anything out of the ordinary. This apparently amused the former fireman, who, laughing, explained that it had turned out all right in the end, but could have been a major disaster.

In a hurry to get the superintendent back to Williamsport, they had been running as fast as O.P. could get the I1 moving, proceeding east on the west-bound tracks. Rounding a curve on his side, he was startled to see a group of section hands desperately trying to scale a sheer cliff along the trackside. He couldn't figure out why these men were trying so frantically to get away. Then the I1 gave a lurch, followed by a series of sharp snaps that were audi-ble above the noise the I1 was generating. The fireman immediately looked across the cab at O.P. sitting on his seat box smoking his pipe as if nothing had happened. When he went over to the right side of the cab, though, he could see that they had just run over a section of track that had been jacked up. The snapping sound was caused by the jacks being smashed to pieces.

They could have been derailed, the excited fireman asserted, and O.P. agreed, but since that wasn't the case O.P. urged him to forget about it; they probably would be hearing soon enough what had happened, he said. Ending his tale, the former fireman said that he'd followed O.P.'s advice and remained quiet. Other than breaking a number of jacks, he knew nothing more about the incident. He did suspect, though, that the near tragedy was quickly squelched by the person or persons responsible for allowing a train to occupy tracks under repair.

Later, when I approached O.P. with this information, he knew immediately who had divulged it, and, smiling, admitted he was surprised that I had heard the story. I asked him why he hadn't mentioned the incident sooner, and he responded somebody would be fired if certain officials knew what had happened. Since nothing was ever actually reported and there was no inquiry at the time, whoever made the mistake must have successfully managed to keep it under wraps.

O.P. then told me what happened that day. He arrived in Renovo as usual, sometime after 7:00 A.M., and when the I1 was taken into the house, a hostler was waiting. He had the first inkling that something out of the ordinary was going on when he was told his engine would be serviced without delay. At the yard office, the yardmaster gave O.P. the reason: the superintendent, the division's head man, had arrived the previous afternoon on the Buffalo Flyer to inspect the Renovo operations and now had to be back in Williamsport no later than 11:00 A.M. to oversee an emergency. The trainmaster had instructed the yard office to call out an extra engine crew and get a K4 ready to make this move.

The yardmaster proceeded accordingly, only to learn from the enginehouse foreman that no K4 was available. Checking his engine list, he found he didn't even have an M1 with the passenger train controls needed for the superintendent's special car. Only freight engines were available. After another round of telephone consultations, the superintendent was informed of their dilemma, and to the relief of all he agreed to use a freight-class engine, noting that his car would be warm enough for him to endure the short trip without steam heat.

Before arrangements for a freight engine were made, however, someone noticed the RN rolling into the yards and suggested that the special car be attached to the RN's eastbound movement. That would eliminate the need for an extra crew and would not tie up the freight power. More calls were made, and the idea was approved. The RN crew would handle it. To further expedite the eastbound run, the trainmaster instructed the yardmaster to remove the cars destined for Lock Haven and to have the yard crew couple the special car at the head end of the train, directly behind the engine. The dispatcher was alerted to the urgency of this move and ordered all blocks to be cleared, allowing the RN to run as a "hotshot," nonstop over the entire distance to Williamsport. These arrangements, especially running nonstop under clear blocks, appealed to O.P., but he was apprehensive about the state of confusion under which the officials were working. He sensed that in their haste too many errors could be made.

Everything went according to plan. O.P. had the I1 out of the house post-haste and was backing to couple to the train at about 8:30 A.M.; written orders gave him an open railroad all the way into Williamsport. Then he noticed something that wasn't in his orders: a heavy-tonnage iron-ore movement was pulling out onto the eastbound main. After coupling up and pulling to the signal board, O.P. found what he expected: a stop signal being displayed.

Just as he stopped, a messenger came running to the engine to announce that somehow communications between the operator and the dispatcher had broken down during the confusion of this hurry-up atmosphere, permitting the extra train to proceed ahead of the RN. O.P.'s orders were canceled, but only temporarily, as it turned out. New orders were issued that permitted the RN to leave the yards on the eastbound main. In a short distance it would be switched to run east on the westbound main to Lock Haven, where it would be switched to continue its trip again on the eastbound main.

This corrected one mistake, but O.P. didn't exactly appreciate these new orders. He never felt safe when he ran in a reverse direction, because signals were positioned to govern the intended direction. In a sense, such a move was more hazardous than running on a single-track main. Throughout his career he ran in the reverse direction many times over short distances, but never for the distance he now faced. But with these new orders he had no alternative but to proceed. Under the circumstances, he wasn't sure he could trust the directions of either the dispatcher or the operator.

Receiving clearance to leave the yards, the RN ran under a proceed-with-caution signal until crossing over to the westbound main. Both the mix-up in orders and having to run under the caution signal cost O.P. valuable time, but on the reverse main he soon had the 2-10-0 set up to run at its maximum speed.

The slower iron-ore movement was soon overtaken, and with steady running it was gradually being passed. Still running alongside this train and in the same direction, O.P. was nearly around a sweeping curve when he suddenly saw that the track and ties on his side were raised above the ballast with absolutely nothing beneath it. The speed at which he was running, and the short distance ahead, gave him no time even to attempt to place the train into emergency. All O.P. could do was think to himself, "Here goes the I1, the superintendent's car, the ore train, and my train. Everything will end up down in the river below."

Hitting the first portion of raised track, the 2-10-0 started to pick up on the right side, but then suddenly slammed down. A succession of loud snapping noises followed. Once this section was passed, everything quickly returned to normal. His train was moving along undisturbed. With this in mind, O.P. just kept on moving at the speed he had set for the I1.

The fireman, visibly shaken, rushed across the deck to the right side, hollering how he had seen the track workers frantically trying to escape before the engine lurched and the loud cracking occurred. "What the hell happened anyhow, Oscar?"

Passing off the seriousness of what might have transpired, O.P. explained that they'd merely run over some jacks under the rails on his side. Although the suddenness of this incident passed, O.P. couldn't stop thinking what the consequences might have been if the tracks had spread or a rail buckled. For once he was thankful he was running the heavy, massive I1. If he had been assigned an M1 or a K4 for this run, with their four-wheel pony trucks and thus lighter weight distribution at this point on the engine, they would have raised more when he hit the elevated tracks and caused a derailment.

For the remainder of the trip the RN ran as ordered, crossing over to the eastbound main at Lock Haven and from there into Williamsport, running on the proper tracks for the direction traveled. O.P. kept the 2-10-0 pounding all the way in, nonstop until he reached the yards ahead of the 11:00 A.M. deadline. At the Park Hotel station, the head brakeman came forward from his monkey house on the tender to do the switching when the superintendent's car was set off. Neither he nor the other trainmen gave any indication that they suspected anything unusual had taken place on the trip. So O.P. opted not to fill out a report about what had transpired. When none of the yard office employees mentioned hearing anything, O.P. cautioned the fireman not to discuss the incident unless officials asked for a report on the eastbound trip.

The following morning, when O.P. arrived at Renovo, he expected someone to inquire about the previous day's happenings, but nothing was said either at the engine house or the yard office. It was now obvious that whoever issued the wrong orders had successfully covered up the mistake. When they were about to depart for the eastbound portion of the trip, a workman approached the standing I1 and without hesitation he introduced himself as the track foreman in charge of the crew repairing the curve elevation east of Renovo the previous morning. He explained that he'd just found out through the grapevine that O.P. was the engineer handling the RN running east on the westbound main that morning, then blurted out, "You know you're really lucky to be back here today," and added, "I guess my men and I are just as lucky."

The foreman went on to give his version of what happened leading up to this incident. His work schedule instructed him to travel to the location of the curve and raise the outside elevation of the westbound track that had settled somewhat over the winter months. He left the yards at 7:00 A.M. with a motor car and a trailer car with supplies and equipment. He was under orders to run on the westbound main to the designated work area. There the cars were set off to the side of the tracks, and after the portable phone was connected the operator was notified that their equipment was clear. While on the line, he also wanted to know how much time would elapse before there would be any westbound movements, and was told that nothing was showing on the operation sheet until 11:00 A.M., when a train was scheduled to leave Lock Haven.

Starting under this premise, the crew began by jacking up the section to be repaired, proceeding to clean and tamp the ballast. Around 8:30 A.M. another call was placed to the operator, who assured the foreman that the line would remain clear until the originally stated time. When the foreman and his men heard the eastbound train approaching, they stopped their work and moved back along the cliff to wait in safety until the movement passed.

"The men were taking advantage of this interruption by relaxing for a few moments," the foreman said, "but someone saw your engine coming around the curve. You were almost upon us, and we had no warning either, due to the noise the passing train was creating. We were well aware that the section of track we were working on wasn't safe to cross, and we were attempting to escape from what seemed to be certain doom. We were trapped by the cliff behind us, although some of the men desperately attempted to climb up to get out of the way. All I heard was the jacks exploding, all six of them, as you thundered by. What kept the whole section from spreading at the speed you were traveling has to be some kind of miracle.

"After you got by safely and the other train cleared, I immediately called the operator, telling him in no uncertain terms he almost killed the entire crew, and very nearly caused a serious accident to boot. All he could say was he was sorry this happened, stating that an unexpected movement had to be made and there wasn't any way to notify us. I didn't believe his answer. He could have given you a slow order between the mileposts where we were working. This would have given both your train and my crew some protection.

I also called my boss, explaining what had taken place and informing him that this hampered my schedule. There wasn't any way to complete the work without jacks. The boss assured me that he'd inquire to find out who was responsible for this uncalled for mistake, and that I should spend the rest of the day cleaning up the mess and get the track in shape so it would be safe for other movements.

"It took all day to realign the tracks around the curve. They had shifted nearly four inches. At the end of my shift at 3:00 p.m., I entered the boss's office ready to fill out requisition forms to procure replacement jacks, and asked if additional forms would be necessary since all I could turn in as evidence of my need was small broken pieces. Normally, to get one replacement it almost takes an Act of Congress, but to get six at once would be next to impossible. To my surprise the boss told me not to worry about filling out any forms, that replacements had been set out for me and I could pick them up at the stores building. He also told me that because no one was injured and there was no damage to the train, there wasn't any cause to be further concerned, and stressed that it would be best if the incident were forgotten."

Hearing this testimony, O.P. was now convinced of what he suspected. Everything had been quickly covered up, but there was no doubt that the person responsible for the error was the operator in the Renovo block station. Normally a track car or track repairs would not be placed on the movement sheet, and during the confusion that developed when they had to get the superintendent's car moving in a hurry, the track repair under way on the westbound was simply forgotten. And that is exactly what O.P. did: he forgot about the entire matter.

The spring of 1949 passed, and O.P.'s sixty-sixth birthday was nearing. I approached him about the date he intended to retire, but he evaded my question. He was quite secretive about this, even refusing to give my mother a firm date. His only mention of the subject came in a terse remark that he would let us know the date after he retired.

He was still working after his July 20 birth date, and it began to appear that maybe he wouldn't retire after all. Not even the members of his crew had any idea that he was about to retire, but when he brought the RN into the yards at Williamsport, cut off, and took his I1 to the roundhouse, only he knew that it was the last time he would ever handle a Pennsylvania engine. At the yard office he marked off as usual, instructing the crew clerk to remove his name from the board. Then he handed in his retirement papers.

Thus ended forty-five years of service on the Pennsylvania Railroad. He had worked from the bottom of the roster to the top position. Remarkably, in this time span, after he was "set up running" as an engineer he was never set back, and his name never appeared on the extra board. He always held a regular crew assignment.

O.P. arrived home with his overalls and other items used in a life working as an engineman. That was the way he let my mother know that he was done with railroading. Now that his career had ended, he explained why he didn't want anyone to know the exact date he intended to retire: there wasn't any fanfare when he hired out, so he didn't want any commotion when he retired.

It didn't take O.P. long to find that being retired wasn't at all hard to take, but after just three weeks his newfound enjoyment was interrupted by a letter from the division superintendent requesting him to be at his office at a specified date and hour. This message aggravated him to no end. There wasn't any logical reason why the boss would want to see him, especially since he was now officially retired.

O.P. appeared in the chambers of Number 9 as punctually as he did when marking up for duty and was promptly ushered into the main office. Inside he was greeted by not only the superintendent but also the road foreman of engines. Both men in turn offered comments, mostly praise relating to his fine and lengthy record as an engineman. Finally the superintendent handed him an elaborately framed certificate that read: "This PERFECT SAFETY AWARD is presented to O.P. Orr, Engineman, by the Pennsylvania Railroad for completing 44 Years and 11 Months Service."

He graciously accepted the award, but he knew it was wrong. It should have read "45 Years Service." Following the presentation, the superintendent added that he considered it an honor to be a part of such a ceremony, adding that very few enginemen on the division would ever be eligible for such an award. "In fact," he said, "not many men on the entire system would match such an achievement." While the superintendent was making this eulogy, O.P. was thinking that this official, indirectly, almost ruined this record about five months ago when his private car was hurriedly attached to the eastbound RN.

Later in the day, O.P. showed me his award and related what had transpired in the main office. With mixed emotions he regarded his visit as an honor, but in no way was he proud of the inscribed 44 years and 11 months on the certificate. After all, he had worked an extra year just to have an even 45 years of service. "It's like a lot of things the Company tries to do," he said. "They get close most of the time, but never seem to get things exactly right."

Epilogue

O.P. was not to enjoy his retirement for long. He made his last run on earth on May 8, 1954, just shy of his seventy-first birthday.

GLOSSARY

The brief definitions here are the author's own. They are the not technical definitions one might find in a textbook about steam technology or railroad procedures, and they were created to help people who are not familiar with steam-railroading terminology understand what the author and Oscar P. Orr are describing. Precise technical definitions may be found in more-technical railroading sources that are readily available.

air-brake system: Brings an engine or train to a halt. Air produced by a compressor on the engine and held in a reservoir on the engine and in cylinders on individual cars is distributed by piping that runs through the train under the cars, coupled by hoses, and is controlled by triple valves. These valves apply the brakes either at the initiation of a crew member or when the distribution system experiences a reduction of pressure in the air cylinders.

air cylinders: Used to hold air in the brake line under pressure when not braking a train.

air test: A reduction in air pressure initiated to test the braking system, followed by a release of the brake to see if air pressure, when pumped up, is maintained at a set pressure.

air valve: Used to control the air application in a braking system.

angle cock: A quarter-inch-diameter rod with a 90° bend at its end, positioned flush to the side of individual rail cars near the air-brake cylinder. When the angle cock is pulled out and turned, air pressure is released and the brakes are set. To recharge the brakes, it is turned and pushed back in.

ash pan: A large finlike device suspended beneath the firebox to collect residue from the burning process.

bark: A description of the sound the locomotive's exhaust makes when it is working.

Belpaire: An almost-level crown sheet firebox, used to heat boiler water to steam and distinctive for its flat appearance atop the boiler. *See also* crown sheet.

bid on: To declare one's intention to fill a posted vacancy. When there is a vacancy on a crew, it is advertised to employees on a *bid sheet*. Interested qualified employees can then state their intention to take the job; in other words, they *bid on* the position in writing on a certain form. The position is awarded to the senior employee, the bidder who has the most time in service among those qualified for the position.

bid sheet: *See* bid on.

blasting out: Making a fast start from a standing stop.

block: The designated distance on the timetable controlling a specific segment of track.

blower: A series of steam jets within the firebox, used to control increases in the draft flowing through the firebox.

board or call board: The listing of qualified trainmen in regular active service and their assignments. Variations include the *extra board* (trainmen not in active service but called to work in an emergency and listed in order of seniority, the most recently hired being the last one to be called).

builder's plate: An oval brass plate affixed on the boiler above cylinders indicating the company that built the engine, the date of manufacture, and the engine class.

bump: When a particular job is abolished and releases a senior employee from his work, the senior employee can *bump* a less-senior employee out of the position to take it for himself. An employee so bumped can in turn bump someone below him on the roster.

cab train control signal: An air-line system on passenger trains for trainmen in the cars to signal the engineer in the locomotive.

cabin: A railroad car intended as quarters for the conductor and flagman, and as a place from which to watch over the train. Usually at the rear of the train. Also known as a *caboose.*

call: A summons to work.

call box: A telephone housing mounted on a telephone pole.

call boy: A railroad employee who is sent to seek out and notify crew members to report for duty at a specified time.

class repairs: A locomotive that undergoes *class repairs* is virtually torn down and rebuilt. This rebuilding involved repairing or replacing the flues; rebuilding the valves and cylinders; turning the driving wheels on a lathe; replacing or repairing the firebox, crank pins and rod bushings, driving boxes on the axles, the superheater if so equipped, the smoke box chamber, the many and varied piping assemblies, the air pumps, and so on, to include every device that made up the locomotive.

clear block: Permission for a train to occupy the main track through to the next designated block.

clear signal: A train movement signal. When green, it means the train is clear to proceed on the main line.

company notch: The reverse lever set in a full forward position.

conductor: The person authorized by the railroad to control train movements.

consist: The rolling stock (cars) making up a train.

coupling pin: *See* coupling rod.

coupling rod: A rod connected by chain to the coupling pin and extending from the coupler to the (out)side of a car or locomotive. When this rod is lifted, the pin then releases the coupler, allowing the cars or locomotive to separate.

crew clerk: A railroad employee who works in a yard office and whose duties are to call crews for extra movements and, in an emergency, to record crew time slips, to keep the call board in order, and to record railroad cars in and out of the yard.

crown sheet: A plate affixed atop the firebox that is covered at all times with water that is used to produce steam. *See also* Belpaire.

cutoff: One of the four events that take place during a single stroke of the slide and piston valves, cutoff is a setting of the amount of steam allowed into the cylinder.

cylinder head: The round steel plates on cylinders, gasketed and held in place by numerous bolts. *Cylinder head packing* is gasket materials surrounding the piston rod where it enters the cylinders.

derailing device: A device attached to one rail of a storage track or siding. When placed across the rail, it will cause a rail car or locomotive to derail should it attempt to enter a main line when the switch is in a closed position.

doghouse: A rear-facing cupola located behind the coal bunker on a tender, housing the head brakeman and making it possible for him to watch over the train to his rear.

double-heading: Two locomotives coupled together at the head end of a train.

drawhead: *See* pulled drawhead.

duplex stoker barrel: Two oblong cylinders, one running up each side of the boiler's backhead and themselves containing auger screws. They lift coal delivered by the stoker screw to the firebox and work in conjunction with each other.

8-A-1 man: An employee removed from road service by the railroad's examining physician due to a disability and assigned permanently to yard or limited service.

engineer: *See* engineman.

engineman: One who operates or runs a locomotive. This designation was used by some railroads, including the Pennsylvania, instead of *engineer*. It often refers to either the engineer or the fireman, both of whom worked in the cab of a steam locomotive.

extra: When referring to a train, a nonscheduled movement; when referring to a person, someone not a regular crew member and thus likely to be called for any movement as needed.

extra board: *See* board.

firebox arch: Formed by fire bricks in front of the firebox, allowing heated gases and smoke to enter the flues of the boiler.

flagman: Second in command of a train crew whose principal duty is to go at least twenty car lengths back from a stopped train on a main track and, using a red flag during daylight and a red lantern during darkness, to warn any approaching train of a stopped train ahead.

foreign sections: A portion of right-of-way not normally used in an established run.

gangway: Covers the gap between the locomotive and its tender.

grate shaker bar: A bar the fireman attaches to the grate rods on the floor on each side of the firebox and rocks back and forth to dump residue from the fire out of the firebox into the ash pan.

head brakeman: A trainman who rides on the locomotive and is responsible for handling switching activity when the train is picking up or setting off cars.

head end: Refers to the locomotive or to the front end of a train.

hostler: A worker who moves locomotives around the engine house and in and out of the roundhouse; turns locomotives; moves locomotives for coal, water, sand, and to the pit track; and takes locomotives from storage to the ready tracks.

independent brake: The air brake that operates only on the locomotive and tender.

injector: A pumping device that lifts water from the tender's tank and puts it in the locomotive's boiler.

inside mounted reversing gear: A Stephenson valve gear used inside the cams on the driving axle to control valve motion.

Johnson Bar: A manually operated lever mounted on a notched quadrant and used to reverse engine motion and control steam passage to the cylinders.

journals: The assembly at the ends of each axle under a rail car that attaches the wheels to the truck frames.

limited passenger train: A train designated as a "limited" has seats that must be reserved in advance and thus "limited" to the number of spaces on the train. Every passenger has accommodations, and once the train is full there is no space for additional passengers. (Commonly, though, if one train is sold out, an additional train, or "section," is added to the scheduled run.) Such trains ran on a fast schedule and frequently charged passengers an extra fare. A *named limited* is a fast passenger train with luxury accommodations and higher fares, such as the Broadway Limited or the Pennsylvania Limited.

lubricator: A mechanical device under pressure that oils cylinders, valves, pistons, air pumps, and valve rods.

mallet compound: A locomotive that uses steam twice, akin to two locomotives under one boiler. The rear set of drivers uses high-pressure steam from the boiler, then passes it off in steam pipes to the front set of drivers, whose cylinders operate on exhaust or lower-pressure steam.

meet: A term for opposing trains meeting at a designated location.

Middle Division: Trackage from the Harrisburg, Pennsylvania, vicinity to Altoona, Pennsylvania.

motive power: Refers to the type or class of any locomotive, steam or diesel, assigned to haul a specific train.

notches: Divisions cut into a quadrant for the reversing lever, with center being neutral and the divisions, or notches, running out to full forward or full reverse.

operator: The individual who controls a specific *block*. The operator gets instructions from the train dispatcher, who is customarily located at division headquarters. The operator, who is housed in an elevated structure (a tower) or at ground level or in a bay window as in passenger stations, passes instructions to train crews via written orders or signals.

outlawed: Refers to a worker who has reached the maximum number of hours one could work without a rest.

out of square: Refers to a valve setting that causes the cylinders to work in opposition to each other.

outside mounted Walscheart reverse gear: A device operated by an off-center rod connected on the outside of the main rod on the main crank pin to control valve settings.

pass: A card issued to a trainman to enable him and his wife to travel free on most trains, except limiteds and excursions. Other immediate family members are issued *trip passes*.

pilot: An engineer who is not familiar with a certain portion of the railroad is accompanied by a pilot to advise about the nature and special characteristics of the unfamiliar line.

piston valve: A round valve, housed in a cylinder, that controls steam flowing to the main cylinder.

pit track: A track at a locomotive service facility that housed a vat, or ash pit, mounted between the rails and filled with water to quench hot residue dropping from the ash pan when released by the fire cleaner at the terminal.

pulled drawhead: The condition that occurs when part of the coupling device holding the train together breaks, separating the train.

Pullman cars: Passenger cars built and operated by the Pullman Company. These include sleeping, lounge, buffet (dining), and parlor cars for which passengers paid an additional fare to book space.

pusher: A locomotive coupled up at or near the rear of a train to assist movement, most commonly when the train is ascending grades.

road foreman of engines: The person who supervised all enginemen on a division.

roster: The seniority list. A person started at the bottom of the list when hired, and as additional men were hired moved up progressively.

running light: Describes a train with either only locomotives or a locomotive and a cabin but no rail cars.

running orders: Permission from the dispatcher or block operator to run on a main line.

saturated steam engine: A locomotive that runs using "live" or "wet" steam. (*Wet steam* is made in the boiler, not heated to remove water particles, as in superheated steam.)

screw reverse mechanism: A valve-setting device used to control forward or reverse motion, operated by a hand wheel in the cab connected to a gear box that controlled the rod to the reverse link.

semaphore: Single or dual rectangular blades mounted on a mast at trackside. The blade setting, controlled by the block operator, tells the train crew whether to proceed with caution, stop, or proceed clear.

side rod: A device that connects driving wheels together on the outside of the wheels and is attached to the main crank pin.

slack: The space that exists between coupled cars in a train. *Pushing in the slack* refers to compressing that space. The locomotive pushes in the slack, and as a train is started this few inches of play actually allows each car to start separately.

slide valve: A flat valve that permits steam to pass through to a cylinder.

snapper: A locomotive connected to the front of a train to assist it on a grade. When the train has topped the grade, the snapper is cut off and runs ahead of the train and into a siding.

special-duty man: A man working in conjunction with the road foreman of engines to monitor conditions and practices of engine crews. Firemen are usually elected for this duty.

spin: When a locomotive's driving wheels lose traction with the rails, allowing wheels to turn without exertion and force. When this happens with the locomotive's throttle fully open, it is a *wide-open spin.*

stall: When a train loses forward or reverse motion and comes to a halt.

steam freely: A condition in which a locomotive's fire is burning at a level that will produce enough steam to move a locomotive and its train with ease.

steam heat control: A device mounted in the locomotive cab to control boiler steam passed through piping to passenger train consists and to the head brakeman's doghouse on the tender.

steam jets: Distribute coal delivered by the stoker by blowing to proper places within the firebox.

stoker: A device used to convey coal from the tender to the firebox by means of an auger screw. A *stoker motor* turns the auger screw(s) in the stoker.

superheater: A tubing device located in front of a locomotive's boiler that heats steam to a higher degree and thus removes moisture to dry the steam before it is passed to the cylinder. Dry steam exerts greater pressure than wet steam.

switch target: An indicating device that rotates as a switch is opened or closed, to allow an engineman to see that the switch is properly set for the intended movement.

symbol freight: Any freight engine with an assigned letter or letters and numbers, such as RA-13 indicating "Ralston-Altoona eastbound." Train orders carry such designations instead of being designated as "extra" trains. A symbol freight also has a set *calling time* (the time the crew is to go on duty).

taken out of service: Having one's name removed from the call board, indicating unavailability for duty.

times out: The number of *times out* indicates the time remaining before a crew would leave the terminal. For instance, when six crews are at the terminal a new crew arriving would be "seven times out." That means six crews have to be called and leave the terminal before you, the seventh, are classified "first out" and ready to depart.

tonnage: A capacity rating, expressed as the total weight of rail cars in tons that a specific class of locomotive can move over a designated section of the railroad.

tower operator: *See* operator.

trackage rights: An agreement giving a foreign railroad the right to operate trains over the owning railroad's track.

tractive force or effort: The amount of power a locomotive could produce, measured in pounds.

trailing truck: An auxiliary set of small wheels placed behind a locomotive's driving wheels and under the firebox, to equalize the weight of the boiler.

trainmaster: The employee who regulates the movement of trains into and out of yards.

trick: The length of a work day in yard service.

vestibule: The enclosed space, separate from seating areas or rooms, found between passenger cars that take on passengers at either end.

waste: Remnants of string, mostly cotton, a residue from the garment industry that come in ball form. This waste was wadded and used instead of cloth for a multitude of chores.

waterglass: The elongated glass tube on the backhead of a boiler that indicates the amount of water in a boiler.

wide-open spin: *See* spin.

wye: A three-sided track arrangement that resembles the letter "Y" with the top closed by the third section of track, used in lieu of a turntable to turn a locomotive or a train. The locomotive or train to be turned proceeds through one side of the arrangement until it clears the far switch; then the switch is thrown and the locomotive or train backs along the second side of the arrangement until it clears the second switch. Next the second switch is thrown, and the locomotive or train pulls forward along the third side of the wye to pass through the third switch and be facing the direction from which it came.

yardmaster: The individual responsible for a variety of details pertaining to the operation of a railroad yard, including the switching movements of rail cars entering the yard; the making-up of cars into trains for correct destinations; assigning, in consultation with the dispatcher, the motive power necessary to move a train; supervising the work of the crew clerks, including the overseeing of crew callings, registrations for duty, and mark-off time; and the like.

FOR FURTHER READING

For more information about railroading during the era this book covers, and about the history, operation, equipment, and culture of the Pennsylvania Railroad, the following will be useful.

Bruce, Alfred W. *The Steam Locomotive in America: Its Development in the Twentieth Century.* New York: W. W. Norton & Company, 1952.

Burgess, George H., and Miles C. Kennedy. *Centennial History of the Pennsylvania Railroad Company, 1846–1946.* Philadelphia: The Pennsylvania Railroad Company, 1949.

Caloroso, Bill. *Pennsylvania Railroad's Elmira Branch.* Andover, N.J.: Andover Junction Publications, 1993.

Cupper, Dan, ed. *The Pennsylvania Railroad: Its Place in History, 1846–1996.* Wayne, Pa.: Philadelphia Chapter, Pennsylvania Railroad Technical & Historical Society, 1996.

Drury, George H., comp. *Guide to North American Steam Locomotives.* Waukesha, Wis.: Kalmbach Books, 1993.

Drury, George H., comp. *The Historical Guide to North American Railroads.* Edited by Bob Hayden. Milwaukee, Wis.: Kalmbach Publishing Company, 1985.

Fundamentals of the Steam Locomotive. Omaha, Neb.: Simmons-Boardman Books, 1949.

Gunnarsson, Robert L. *The Story of the Northern Central Railway.* Sykesville, Md.: Greenberg Publishing Company, 1991.

Henry, Robert Selph. *This Fascinating Railroad Business.* Indianapolis: Bobbs-Merrill Company, 1943.

McGonigal, Robert S. *Heart of the Pennsylvania Railroad: The Main Line, Philadelphia to Pittsburgh.* Waukesha, Wis.: Kalmbach Books, 1996.

Prior, Frederick J. *Modern American Locomotive: Construction and Operation.* Omaha, Neb.: Simmons-Boardman Publishing Corporation, 1925.

Spearman, Frank H. *The Strategy of Great Railroads.* New York: Charles Scribner's Sons, 1904.

Staufer, Alvin F. *Pennsy Power: Steam and Electric Locomotives of the Pennsylvania Railroad, 1900–1957.* Self-published, 1962.

Staufer, Alvin F., with William D. Edson and E. Thomas Harley. *Pennsy Power III: Steam, Electric, MU's, Motor Cars, Diesels, Cars, Buses, Airplanes, Boats, Art.* Privately published, 1993.

Staufer, Alvin F., and Bert Pennypacker. *Pennsy Power II: Steam, Diesel, and Electric Locomotives of the Pennsylvania Railroad.* Privately published, 1968.

Stevers, Martin D. *Steel Trails: The Epic of the Railroads.* New York: Minton, Balch & Company, 1933.

Videotapes

The interested reader will find that videotapes provide valuable background information about the Pennsylvania Railroad in the steam era.

See especially *Working on the Railroad: The Story of Altoona, Pa.* (Pennsylvania Railroad). Penn State Television, 102 Wagner Building, University Park, PA, 16802. Originally produced as part of WPSX-TV's PARADE series. 1989.

The following videotapes, among others, are available from local libraries, libraries specializing in railroad videos, and other video outlets and sources:

Juniata's Jewel (K4 #1361 locomotive, owned by the Altoona Railroaders Memorial Museum). Produced by Berkshire Videography, Inc.

Memories of Pennsy Steam. Produced by Mark I Video.

The Ore Train. Produced by Penn Valley Pictures.

Pennsylvania Collection (four vintage Pennsylvania Railroad documentaries). Produced by Interurban Videos.

The Standard Railroad of the World (Pennsylvania Railroad). Produced by Interurban Videos.

The Susquehanna Division (of the Pennsylvania Railroad). Produced by Penn Valley Pictures.